TRANSITION TO MARKET

Studies in Fiscal Reform

Edited by

VITO TANZI

INTERNATIONAL MONETARY FUND

1993

© 1993 International Monetary Fund

Design and production: IMF Graphics Section

Library of Congress Cataloging-in-Publication Data

Transition to market : studies in fiscal reform / edited by Vito Tanzi.
   p. cm.
   Includes bibliographical references and index.
   ISBN 1-55775-275-3
   1. Fiscal policy—Europe, Eastern. 2. Capitalism—Europe, Eastern. 3. Fiscal policy—Former Soviet republics. 4. Capitalism—Former Soviet republics. 5. Fiscal policy—Developing countries. 6. Capitalism—Developing countries. I. Tanzi, Vito. II. International Monetary Fund.
HJ1023.7.T73   1993
336.3'0947—dc20

                                        93-19120
                                            CIP

Price: US$30.00

Address orders to:
International Monetary Fund, Publication Services
700 19th Street, N.W., Washington, D.C. 20431, U.S.A.
Telephone: (202) 623-7430   Telefax: (202) 623-7201
Cable: Interfund

PREFACE

Over the past couple of years, membership in the International Monetary Fund has increased sharply as many new countries have found it in their interest to join this institution. Most of these new member countries had centrally planned economies. Their interest in becoming members of the IMF reflected their desire to move from central planning to an economic system relying on market forces. Since this transition requires fundamental change, these countries have been in urgent need of assistance and advice from the rest of the world.

The countries in transition have been experiencing the consequences of four gaps: an information gap, a conceptual gap, a skills gap, and a financial gap.

Because of the past isolation of these countries from the market economies, little was known about their institutions. And these countries knew little about the institutions of market economies. Therefore, before assistance could be given to them, those providing the assistance had to fill this information gap. The second gap to be filled could be called the conceptual gap. Economists had no experience of and no literature on countries moving from central planning to market economies; in the past, the movement had generally been in the opposite direction. Thus, those working on these countries, both domestic experts and those coming from the outside, were confronted by difficult problems in institution building, in the sequencing of reforms, in the interaction of different policies, and in the interpretation of variables and statistics. It soon became clear that simply transplanting institutions or even policies from the market economies to these countries, without proper adaptation, could lead to serious difficulties. But, determining what the "proper adaption" would be was not easy. The third important gap could be referred to as the skills gap. This gap is essentially the lack in centrally planned economies of legal, accounting, financial, and other related skills indispensable for the smooth functioning of a market economy. Despite the high level of literacy and general cultural sophistication of the population of these countries, this lack of those technical skills has slowed the transformation to a market economy. In a way, the situation is comparable to that of being trained to play tennis and then being asked to play golf. This skills gap will take time to fill. Finally, many of these countries would need to fill financial gaps since the breakdown of their economies has, in most cases, sharply reduced output and incomes and has made it difficult for them to provide the necessary resources for new investments, new infrastructure, and other requirements. If the necessary savings cannot be generated domestically, the need for foreign assistance will be great.

From the beginning, the IMF has been willing to play a large technical and, in some cases, even a financial role. Technical assistance has been provided both by the many Fund missions that have visited these countries to discuss general economic policy and by more specialized missions sent to assist the reorganization of institutions in the financial and fiscal sectors, as well as in other areas. Starting with very little knowledge, Fund staff participating in these missions have had to accumulate new information at a very fast pace. After several missions, the participants had accumulated a considerable amount of knowledge about the countries that they had visited that was probably not available elsewhere. Much of the information accumulated was contained in technical reports, which for the most part were confidential. In the fiscal area, the staff of the Fiscal Affairs Department of the IMF carried out a good deal of work.

A couple of years ago, I had the idea that it might be useful if this knowledge became more widely available to policymakers and others in universities, research institutions, ministries of finance, central banks, and other places. I then planned to publish two books, both dealing with fiscal issues.

The first would deal with analytical issues in taxation, in public spending, in the creation of safety nets, in budgeting, and so forth, as these issues applied to economies in transition. This volume would constitute a basic guide to those providing technical assistance and would also be useful to officials trying to implement changes in their countries. It would focus on issues and not on countries. This first volume was published in early 1992 as *Fiscal Policies in Economies in Transition*. It proved a useful and popular book. I have been happy to receive many positive comments on the book from officials in the transition countries and to learn that highly placed individuals in these countries often consult it. A Russian language edition of this book will become available in 1993.

The project also contemplated a second volume that would contain case studies in fiscal reform in many of these countries. Even though this book would deal with issues, it would do so within the context of specific countries. This is the subject of the present volume. The information contained in these country studies is difficult to acquire since it is often unpublished or, when published, is available only in languages inaccessible to most people. The IMF is probably the only place where this book could have been assembled.

The book covers 15 countries and contains 19 chapters. It is divided into four main parts. Part I deals with general issues of fiscal reform in five Central and Eastern European countries. Part II deals with specific fiscal issues or experiences in Central and Eastern European countries. The issues discussed in these chapters range over privatization, fiscal federalism, social safety nets, and, even, the net worth of the Soviet Union.

Parts III and IV deal with fiscal reform in Asian and African countries. These sections cover, in Asia, countries such as China, Viet Nam, Mongolia, and Kazakhstan, and, in Africa, Algeria, Angola, and Ghana. The first chapter tries to provide a simple introduction to public finance and financial markets in the transformation process.

As already mentioned, the book contains a wealth of information not available elsewhere. For this reason, it should prove useful to researchers and academics, as well as to those directly involved in the practical side of the transformation process. The authors share two characteristics: they were very busy carrying out their normal heavy duties and they were directly involved with, and thus very knowledgeable about, the countries on which they were writing. A more leisurely pace in the drafting of these chapters would have produced a more refined product, but time has been an extremely valuable and scarce commodity in the IMF during this period, especially for these authors.

All the authors are staff members of the IMF, with the exception of Professor Bös, who wrote the chapter on privatization in east Germany while he was a Visiting Scholar in the Fiscal Affairs Department. It is essential to emphasize that in their writing the authors have expressed their own opinions, which may not necessarily reflect those of the IMF. It is also necessary to add that references to the Soviet Union, Czechoslovakia, Yugoslavia, and east Germany concern those states as they existed before they were replaced by their successor states.

I express heartfelt thanks for the extremely valuable assistance I have received from David Driscoll, who has chased authors to make deadlines, has checked chapters to see that these were presented in a standard format, and has organized contact with the External Relations Department of the IMF to facilitate the production of the book. Without his assistance, it would have taken much longer for this project to be completed. I am grateful to Esha Ray and Leo Demesmaker of the External Relations Department for their editorial comments and for seeing the book through to publication. The authors sacrificed much of the little time they had available to spend with their families to write these chapters. They all did this with enthusiasm: I am happy to record my admiration and gratitude here.

Vito Tanzi
Director
Fiscal Affairs Department

CONTENTS

Part V. Index

The following symbols have been used in this book:

... to indicate that data are not available;

— to indicate that the figure is zero or less than half the final digit shown, or that the item does not exist;

– between years or months (e.g., 1992–93 or January–June) to indicate the years or months covered, including the beginning and ending years or months;

/ between years (e.g., 1992/93) to indicate a crop or fiscal (financial) year.

"Billion" means a thousand million.

Minor discrepancies between constituent figures and totals are due to rounding.

The term "country," as used in this book, does not in all cases refer to a territorial entity that is a state as understood by international law and practice; the term also covers some territorial entities that are not states, but for which statistical data are maintained and provided internationally on a separate and independent basis.

CHAPTER 1

Financial Markets and Public Finance in the Transformation Process

Vito Tanzi

In an interesting and thoughtful essay on "Issues in the Reform of Socialist Economies" Fischer and Gelb (1991) made an assessment of the time that it would take for various reforms to be completed. They estimated that most reforms would take at least a few years, but some would take longer. "Institutional reforms" and "large-scale restructuring and privatization" would require ten years, while "other financial market reforms" would take more than ten years. The reform of the public finances was not included in this assessment, but it is unlikely that it can be completed within a decade.

The fact that different sectors will require different times to be successfully transformed implies that the process, far from being smooth, will be a very bumpy one. The staggered introduction, or better completion, of institutional changes will create uncertainty and will affect decisions. Economic agents will continually face the possibility that each step might not be followed by the next required step. In some cases the option value of waiting will become particularly high.

An important aspect of the transformation process that has not received the attention it deserves is the complementarity or interdependence of institutions and skills in a modern economy.[1] Modern economies are like ecological systems: their various components—institutions, industries, professional skills—support each other. In planned economies, the planners tried to anticipate and cope with this interdependence directly but, as we now know, they often failed badly. In a market economy the required skills and institutions often develop on their own on the basis of competition, with some governmental assistance and, at times, with some governmental hindrance. The market mechanism and the freedom of action of individuals not only ensure that the right amounts of goods and

---

Vito Tanzi is Director of the Fiscal Affairs Department of the IMF. This paper was originally prepared for a conference on "The Economic Consequences of the East," sponsored by the Center for Economic Policy Research and held at the Deutsche Bundesbank in Frankfurt, March 20–21, 1992.

[1]Some aspects of this issue have been discussed by the sequencing literature. See, for example, McKinnon (1991).

services (with well-known exceptions) are produced. They also ensure that, to a large extent, the right amounts of skills and the right kinds of institutions come into existence.[2]

One can theorize that over several decades, advanced Western economies have achieved a sort of social "ecological balance" among their institutions and the available skills. The demand for certain skills (accountants, tax lawyers, economists, managers, engineers) and certain institutions (commercial banks, savings and loans institutions, futures markets, real estate markets, regulatory agencies, investment banks) has brought those skills and institutions into existence so that some kind of institutional and professional equilibrium has been established.

As the centrally planned economies attempt to transform themselves into market economies they will come to require some of these skills. For example, the restructuring of the commercial banks and of the public enterprises, or the introduction of a full-fledged tax on the profits of the enterprises, will require accounting and managerial skills not available in these countries and these cannot become available in sufficient quantities in the short or even the medium run. This deficiency will inevitably slow the transformation process and will increase the chance of derailment. It will also require that, in order to economize on those skills, the institutions that are created, especially at the beginning, must be the simplest possible. Thus, transplanting sophisticated Western institutions to these countries without major adaptations will not do. This particular problem must be kept in mind as we discuss future developments of financial and fiscal institutions.

The staggered introduction of institutional reforms implies also that at any one time the spotlight of reform will be on a particular social group, be this the workers or the managers of particular enterprises or the managers of commercial banks. As is well known, the most difficult reforms to carry out are often those that increase the general welfare at the immediate cost of particular groups. These groups will have a strong interest in organizing themselves politically and in opposing some of the changes. In a democratic environment they have the freedom to articulate and defend their views. It will take strong and enlightened governments and much public explanation of the need for reform to keep the process going. The need for public explanations will be particularly strong in justifying policies aimed at reducing government expenditures.

The subject of this paper is broad and accordingly can be dealt with only in broad strokes and by focusing on a few major issues. The paper will briefly discuss the very limited role played by financial markets and

---

[2]This discussion does not wish to imply that the market achieves this objective smoothly and optimally. It would be easy to think of exceptions (cobweb situations, monopolies, and so on). It also does not imply that all institutions are created by the spontaneous action of the market. Clearly, the government needs to play a significant role in several areas.

public finance institutions under classical central planning; it will also highlight the fragility of the traditional setup and the reasons why it could not survive the transition to a market economy. This is largely a descriptive section that could be skipped by those familiar with the institutions of centrally planned economies. The paper will then discuss the main changes that need to take place in the financial institutions, some of which are already taking place. Next, it will discuss the needed changes in fiscal institutions and call attention to a few selected issues where the limitations in financial institutions may limit the scope for fiscal policy and where the limitations in the fiscal institutions may limit the scope for monetary policy. To my knowledge the issues discussed in this section have not been addressed before, even though they are fundamental to the reform process. Finally, the paper provides a brief conclusion.

Essential Fiscal and Financial Elements of Central Planning

We start with a situation where the typical citizen owns few if any assets besides money holdings. Much of the country's wealth is socially or publicly owned. The citizen is not expected to save and accumulate wealth since the state will take care of him in old age or illness. Unemployment does not exist officially since the state enterprises are required to hire individuals even when they do not need them.[3] These state enterprises account for anywhere between 70 percent and 100 percent of total production.[4] The individual receives a cash income from work that is much smaller than the total compensation. A large proportion of the individual's total income is in the form of subsidized housing, free education, free health services, subsidized transportation, subsidized food, and subsidized vacations. In other words, many consumption decisions for the individual are made by the state (or the public enterprise in which he works).[5]

To a considerable extent the state decides and determines both the *level* and the *pattern* of consumption of the individual. Even the way the individual uses his cash income is greatly influenced by the state because of its influence on the availability of goods and services and on their relative prices. At times, the individual is forced to save because of the unavailability of goods in the shops or because of the long time required

---

[3]This, of course, is one of the reasons for their low productivity.
[4]In Czechoslovakia (1986), the German Democratic Republic (1982), and the U.S.S.R. (1985), the output of state enterprises was about 97 percent of total output. See Thumm (1991), p. 49.
[5]Some of this noncash compensation is provided by the government, some by the state enterprises.

to buy goods (queues).[6] Credit to individuals is rare and, when available, is directed toward particular and socially approved purchases, such as houses. Interest rates on individuals' savings held in banks are low or even negative in real terms. Individuals are, for the most part, prevented from holding any other financial assets, except for the rare occasions when there are government bonds that they can buy.

Individuals, as individuals, have little influence on the allocation of resources, on the overall rate of saving, on the pattern of production, on the level and allocation of investment, on the rate of interest, on relative and absolute prices, or on imports and exports. Even decisions as to where the individuals will live or work are largely made centrally through the allocation of housing or jobs. These decisions greatly constrain the (free) mobility of labor within the economy.

The key instrument for the allocation of resources is the annual plan. The plan is conceived in physical terms and prices play largely an accounting role. The plan determines the shares of the total physical resources of the country that will go into consumption and investment. It determines the level of production of different products and the allocation of investment to different industries and enterprises.[7] It is also through the plan that budgetary decisions are essentially made. Of course, the plan must occasionally cope with unexpected developments such as natural disasters, weather fluctuations, and large changes in import prices. As a consequence it cannot ensure the final outcome. In the 1980s planned outcomes and actual outcomes started to diverge by increasing amounts in all the centrally planned economies. The plan had been more effective in dealing with a simpler economy. Its effectiveness was reduced by the increasing complexity of a modern economy.

Within this classical system the role of financial markets and of public finances, as this role is understood in the West, was very limited. Within its own parameters the system developed by classical central planning was very effective. It is easy to see how some Western economists came to be fascinated by it. There was an attractive aesthetic quality to it. It did not require messy financial and fiscal institutions, and the allocation of resources was achieved simply and effectively.[8] The distribution of income was determined directly through the control of prices and wages, by government-imposed obstacles to saving and wealth accumulation, and by the government-imposed utilization of labor on the part of the state enterprises. Private activities were forbidden or discouraged; when

---

[6]Thus the consumption function of individuals would have to include, as independent variables, time as well as income. For a theory that emphasizes the importance of time in consumption, see Tanzi and Zee (1993).

[7]For example, enterprises have either not been allowed to keep depreciation funds on their capital assets or the depreciation allowed has been too low. The reason was that investment decisions, even for replacement, were made centrally.

[8]See Campbell (1991) especially Chapter 5, pp. 92-118.

allowed, they were taxed at prohibitive rates. Economic fluctuations in output and prices were not supposed to occur; therefore, there was no need to develop policies aimed at stabilizing the economy.

Unfortunately, this simplicity and effectiveness carried a high and increasing price tag. While the resources may have been allocated simply and effectively, they were also allocated very inefficiently. Leontief once remarked that these economies had developed a peculiar input-input system: resources went into the system but nothing came out of it! As time passed, corruption became a national pastime and more and more resources were siphoned off to a growing underground economy.[9] This underground economy became a cancer for the official economy leading to more and more distortions of the official accounts. The loss in output resulting from the inefficient allocation of resources also became progressively larger and the income gap between the centrally planned economies of Eastern Europe and the market economies of Western Europe became very large. This gap would eventually undermine the system.[10]

Let us consider briefly the financial and fiscal sectors within this classical central planning system. Normally, banking and credit operations were monopolized by a state bank (a monobank), with unlimited power to create bank deposits.[11] Credit was allocated directly by this bank or by its branches, which specialized in various activities or regions. Interest rates and the exchange rate played no allocative role and no role in determining the total amount of money in circulation.

The monetary system—consisting broadly of the monobank and its specialized branches—was a tool of the plan. As Sundararajan (1991, p. 251) has put it:

> the physical plan dictates a financial plan, decomposed into a budget, a credit plan, and a cash plan. Monetary policy is exercised through controlling the volume of credit to state enterprises and budget entities and making available the growth of cash in line with the planned gap between monetary receipts and outlays of the household sector. The state bank has little autonomy but is charged with monitoring the observance of the central plan by guaranteeing the enterprises the loans needed to carry out planned transactions and by seeing that these loans, and the enterprises' own deposits, are used for these transactions. Every transaction of any importance, such as enterprise withdrawals of cash for wage purposes, must be effected through the drawing of a check on the state bank.

The state bank combined the role of commercial bank and central bank and was also the treasurer for the government's public finances. The

---

[9]See Grossman (1982) and Gábor (1989).

[10]For a discussion of the misallocation of savings and resources in Eastern Europe, see Easterly (1991), Thumm (1991), and Tanzi (1991a). Over the past decade the incremental capital output ratios for these countries became extremely large. See Thumm (1991), p. 48.

[11]For details see Sundararajan (1991), especially pp. 250-52.

accounting system for public finances facilitated immediate and automatic access to monetary financing of fiscal deficits. Risk considerations did not affect lending decisions to state enterprises since the borrowers were public entities and presumably could not or would not be allowed to go broke. When the monobank lent money to the state enterprises it was as if the public sector were lending to itself. In any case, the losses of some enterprises were expected to be covered by the gains of others. It should be emphasized that when the monobank lent money to losing enterprises which would be unlikely to pay back, it was performing not just a banking function but essentially a fiscal function. The state enterprises themselves, by providing several social benefits to the workers, were performing important fiscal functions. Therefore, it was difficult to separate fiscal from monetary or even industrial policy. This issue is addressed again below.

The state bank with its branches also played another important fiscal function besides that of treasurer and cross-subsidizer of the activities of the state enterprises, namely, it facilitated the collection of taxes. Given that producer and consumer prices were both controlled, turnover tax rates reflected essentially the difference between these two sets of prices, a difference that, for some products, could be negative.[12] Since producers and retailers both had accounts with the state banks[13] and since production quotas indicated the level of production of the state enterprises, especially assigned fiscal agents could monitor the sales by the enterprises and, on the basis of the fixed prices, they could easily determine the required tax payment. Thus, the account of the producer was adjusted downward by the size of the tax payment.

Taxes on wages were also collected directly from the enterprises, often by simply adjusting the cash transfers made to them to pay the wage bill.[14] Profits taxes were not based on any clear and objective definition of income but were largely negotiated amounts that did not require precise measurement of the enterprise's profits.[15] All this means that these countries did not have, and did not need, Western-style tax administrations and the skills needed by those administrations except for the administration of local taxes on the few private activities. These activities were mostly levied with some kind of presumptive taxes so that detailed accounting was not required.

This was an almost idyllic situation from a tax administration perspective. The confrontational situation that exists in the West between tax-

---

[12]There were hundreds or even thousands of these implicit tax rates. These rates were not legislated and could be changed at the discretion of the planners.
[13]Each enterprise was constrained to have an account in only one branch and to make all payments, except wages which were paid in cash, by checks drawn on that branch.
[14]All wages were paid in cash.
[15]For a more detailed description of these taxes see Tanzi (1991c) or the various relevant chapters in Tanzi (1992).

payers and tax administrators was largely absent. As the director of taxation of one of these countries recently put it, somewhat nostalgically: "the life of a tax administrator was easy. He often had to deal with just one enterprise. Much revenue came from an occasional telephone call. Now you have to work for every cent."[16] This highly effective mechanism was able to generate levels of taxation that exceeded those of most industrial countries.[17] It was, however, a mechanism that could not survive the change to a market economy. That change would bring about (1) price and wage liberalization; (2) the growth of private sector activities; (3) the lack of controls on the output of enterprises; and (4) the liberalization of the methods of payment. These changes would sharply reduce the information available to the tax inspectors and would increase the confrontational nature of tax collection as well as tax evasion.[18] These changes would require the development of a totally new statutory tax system and the creation, almost from scratch, of a new tax administration. Of course, both of these changes would need skills (accounting, legal, managerial) which are in scarce supply in these countries. It is a change that will require many years to complete.

The experience of countries that have started the journey toward a market economy indicates that the level of taxation achieved under central planning could not be maintained. A realistic expectation is that tax revenue as a share of GDP will fall dramatically over the years.[19] It is thus important to accompany this fall by reductions in public spending especially since, for a long time, these countries will not be able to finance large fiscal deficits in noninflationary ways.[20] Efficient reduction of public spending will require, inter alia, the establishment of a competent budget office able to scrutinize the various budgetary requests, relate them to expected tax revenue, and attempt to maximize the benefits that the countries will get from the use of tax money.

Reform of Financial Institutions

The economic transformation of the Eastern European countries will be complete when:

- a large proportion of the total wealth of these countries is owned by individuals and not by public sector entities;

---

[16]Oral communication to the author.

[17]The fact that the state enterprises were very large and relatively few in number facilitated the task of tax collection.

[18]Since tax evasion did not exist, or was not supposed to exist, in centrally planned economies, there were no laws against tax evasion.

[19]The fall in the tax level in China, Hungary, and Poland in recent years gives empirical support to the statement. It should be added that reducing the level of government revenues and expenditures has also been an important structural goal for the governments in order to reduce the influence of the state in resource allocation.

[20]See, on this point, Cheasty (1992).

- most prices, including wages, interest rates, and exchange rates are free to reflect the opportunity cost of using resources and thus to influence decisions;
- within limits imposed by legitimate regulations, individuals are free to start and carry out any economic activity they wish;
- individuals are free to buy and sell any asset (tangible or intangible);
- savers can choose from a range of financial assets (reflecting different risks and maturity structures) to invest their savings;
- individuals are free to make the basic decisions on how to allocate their earnings;
- individuals are confronted by a legally based and objective tax system which can only be changed by a legitimate legislative process.

The role of the financial market in this transformation process is very important. As stated by the President of the Federal Reserve Bank of New York, "a particularly important function of a banking and financial system in a market economy is to help mobilize a society's savings and to channel those savings rigorously and impartially into the most efficient and effective uses and investments" (Corrigan (1990), p. 2).

The fundamental functions of a financial system are, first, to mobilize savings and, second, to allocate them to the most efficient uses. It is not clear the extent to which centrally planned economies succeeded in mobilizing household savings.[21] It is very clear, however, that they were very inefficient in allocating them.[22] The transformation process must ensure that both of these objectives are achieved. To create institutions that replace the plan in mobilizing savings while letting them go down the drain would be the worst possible folly. In recent discussions on the process of transformation, too much emphasis has been placed on the mobilization of savings and not enough on the efficiency of their utilization.[23] Because of the imbalances in the "social ecologies" of these countries, there is the possibility that the institutions and the conditions that make possible a greater mobilization of savings in the reformed economies come to be developed before those that make possible a better allocation of those savings. This point is discussed later.

In spite of the constraints on spending by households, owing to scarcity of goods in the shops and long lines, the saving ratios of households in the Eastern European countries have been relatively low in recent years (Table 1). Whether the propensity of households to save will increase or not during the transition will depend on various developments such as (1) the availability of goods in the shops; (2) the availability of relatively

---

[21]Given the extremely high investment ratios in these countries, one could argue that they were successful in mobilizing total savings, although "mobilizing" may be the wrong word for the process that took place.

[22]As indicated by the very low growth rates that accompanied the high investment rates.

[23]For a discussion of this point, see Tanzi (1991b).

Table 1. Savings Ratio of Households[1]

(In percent)

	1987	1988	1989	1990
Bulgaria	4.2	6.1	2.9	. . .
Czechoslovakia	3.8	3.0	2.5	. . .
German Democratic Republic	6.1	6.0	4.8	3.0[2]
Hungary	–1.3	1.5	–0.3	4.7
Poland	7.9	7.8	9.9	. . .
Romania	. . .	. . .	3.7	8.3
U.S.S.R.[3]	5.3	6.0	7.4	6.6

Source: Economic Commission for Europe (1991), p. 54.
[1] Ratio of increment in savings deposits to money incomes of the population.
[2] Savings as percentage of disposable income.
[3] Data for 1989 and 1990 for the U.S.S.R. are somewhat lower than those reported by other sources.

safe and liquid financial instruments paying positive real rates of return to store the savings; and (3) the extent to which there is a pent-up demand for consumption goods. To the extent that the development of financial markets provides a menu of financial instruments with varying risks and maturities, this should be an important factor toward mobilizing savings and perhaps even toward raising the rate of saving of households.[24]

The transformation of the Eastern European economies will require that the power to allocate resources shifts largely from the government to the private sector.[25] If this shift is not accompanied by the establishment of private monopolies, and is not hindered by excessive government regulations, it should improve the allocation of resources. To be completed, this transformation would require the establishment of a financial and equity market, a market for labor, a market for the exchange of real property (houses, apartments, land), a market for foreign exchange, and many other more specialized markets (private pensions, insurance). To the extent that citizens come to recognize that there is a relationship between the taxes they pay and the public services they receive from the government, an implicit political market would also have been established for

[24] Actually, if at the same time that individuals have greater access to financial instruments to place their savings they also have greater access to credit to finance their current spending, the net result may not be an increase in the rate of saving. It must be understood that eventually saving by household and private enterprises will need to replace saving by the state.

[25] This does not imply that the government will not play any role in resource allocation. However, that role must be limited to the existence of public goods, externalities, and other conditions that justify government intervention in market economies.

government services. This market would, of course, use votes as a form of currency. Under central planning the connections between taxes paid by individuals and the services received by them were neither emphasized nor obvious. Thus a public campaign may be required to sensitize the population to this connection in order to raise tax compliance.

Many obstacles will need to be removed before this transformation is complete. For example, the establishment of a market for real property and a genuine market for labor will very much depend on the privatization of land and especially of houses and apartments. As long as land and houses are publicly owned, or property rights over them are unclear, they will not be traded and many workers will continue to be immobilized by their places of residence and by the difficulty they would face to find lodging close to potential new jobs. The scarcity of housing has created enormous constraints on the mobility of labor in these countries. Restructuring would be facilitated if these constraints were reduced.

In a society where incomes have been relatively even and where access to credit is very limited, the number of individuals who would be able to purchase a house or a piece of land will be limited.[26] It will be much more difficult to find domestic buyers for large state enterprises even assuming that these enterprises were viable or could be restructured to make them viable.[27] Thus, privatization would be facilitated by the existence of a capital market. If such a market existed, it could at least be able to finance the purchase of small properties and the setting up of small new activities.

A priority in the development of a capital market should be the reform of commercial banks and the creation of an interbank money market, even if only a rudimentary one. A less immediate objective could be the establishment of an equity market. Commercial banks can to a large extent perform some of the functions of a stock market, whereas the latter cannot perform the functions of the commercial banks. It has been pointed out that, historically, the commercial banking system has been far more important in allocating resources to enterprises than the stock market in the majority of industrial countries.[28]

An important first step toward the reform of the banking and financial systems of the economies in transition has already been taken by most of these countries with the creation of two-tier banking systems. This transition occurred in 1987 in Hungary, in 1988 in the U.S.S.R., in 1989 in Poland, and in 1990 in Czechoslovakia and Romania. The two-tier banking system involves the splitting of the monobank into a national bank and a group of (public) commercial banks. The national bank has assumed

---

[26]Information on the distribution of earnings in Eastern European countries is provided in Atkinson and Micklewright (1991).

[27]In some of these countries consideration is being given to the distribution to the population of vouchers that would allow them to purchase houses and shares in enterprises. There is still no experience of how well such schemes work.

[28]See Corbett and Mayer (1991).

some of the traditional functions of a central bank, namely the conduct of monetary policy (that is, regulating overall credit and interest rates), the broad oversight of the financial system (the regulatory function), and the direct participation in selective aspects of the operation of a payments system.[29] The commercial banks have taken over the responsibility of deposit and loan transactions with households and enterprises.

Many legal and organizational problems need to be solved before this separation parallels closely that of Western countries. The establishment of a clear delineation of the respective functions of these institutions and a clear separation of commercial and central banking functions has taken longer than initially envisaged in many countries. The national banks have not yet assumed the full range of the activities expected from a mature central bank and they continue to perform activities of a commercial and fiscal nature. They are still groping for a well-defined role and the degree of independence from the government is still a major issue, although some attempts have been made in some of these countries to provide independence to these new institutions. As long as they are not independent, they will provide the government and even the commercial banks with a kind of "soft budget."[30] It is important for these banks to reduce their fiscal functions and to concentrate on their basic monetary roles.

For the commercial banks to be able to perform well the functions of mobilizing savings and allocating them to the most efficient uses, several conditions must obtain, of which the most important are the following:

(1) Their decisions vis-à-vis lenders and borrowers must be guided by arm's-length principles. Special relationships carried over from the past or developed currently should not influence their borrowing and especially their lending decisions.

(2) They must have good information as to the risks they are taking when they lend to particular customers and must know how to use this information.

(3) Each lending decision should be relatively independent of past ones; in other words, the existence of past loans must not be a key factor in providing new loans.

(4) They should be able to push customers into bankruptcy if customers default on servicing their loans.[31]

(5) They must be guided by bottom-line considerations: that is, they must see themselves as profit-making operations and should worry about their own solvency.

The reform that brought the two-tier banking structure into existence was potentially important. However, at least for the time being it has not

---

[29]See Corrigan (1990).

[30]One strong indication is the payment of reserve requirements with government paper.

[31]For this reason bankruptcy laws are essential.

created a banking system that would be able to mobilize savings and efficiently channel those savings toward the most productive uses. The problem is that the reform did not solve many of the existing problems. The new commercial banks were born with particular handicaps.[32]

First of all, these commercial banks are, in most cases, very large and public. Both of these characteristics imply that competition may be limited. Second, they continue to depend on the central bank for subsidized funds even though the central banks have tried to raise the cost of borrowing. Third, their clients continue to be, for the most part, state enterprises, many of which are not profitable. Fourth, the banks are under pressure to continue lending to these state enterprises because of long-established relationships.[33] Fifth, they are often still run by the same individuals who had run them before the banking reform and are constrained by lack of specialized skills and well-defined statutes. Sixth, and most important, many of the assets that the commercial banks inherited from the monobank were low-interest loans to the state enterprises. Many of these loans are nonperforming. To a large extent the banks have continued to lend to the state enterprises in order to be able to continue showing as assets the loans on their books. When interest comes due, or loans mature, the banks often extend new loans to the enterprises to allow them to pay or service the old loans so that these "assets" can be carried on their books. It is a pity that there is no secondary market to assess the real value of these assets as happens with the loans of commercial banks to developing countries. If such a market existed, the market value of these loans would be far less than their book value.

The effects of this behavior are fourfold. First, by continuing to lend to inefficient enterprises, the banks are contributing to a major misallocation of savings. As Brainard (1991, p. 15) has put it: "the existing banking structure . . . is acting as a fiscal 'black hole,' misallocating capital to cover the losses of the state-owned enterprises." Technically these loans are *fiscal* subsidies that, if justified, should be made through, and financed by, the budget. By being made through the banking system, they do not swell the fiscal deficit and thus distort the fiscal accounts, giving an inaccurate view of the tightness of the country's fiscal policy.[34]

Second, the accumulation of bad loans implies that it is difficult to assess the real value of the banks' capital assets. Therefore, the profitability of the banking system and its basic soundness is an open question. The situation and behavior of the commercial banks imply the existence of large and increasing contingent liabilities for the government and

---

[32]See, especially, Brainard (1991) and Sundararajan (1991).

[33]Thus, to some extent, state enterprises continue to face soft budget constraints.

[34]This explains how, at times, the fiscal accounts of some countries have been in surplus while they were experiencing high rates of inflation. This has been Yugoslavia's experience and, to a more limited extent, Poland's. For a discussion of the experience of Yugoslavia, see Liviatan (1993).

raise concerns about future fiscal outcomes. In the absence of clear and believable protection schemes for depositors, this situation discourages them from putting their savings in these institutions and (because of the fiscal implications) may discourage private investors from investing in these countries.[35]

The poor quality of the loans reduces the profits (or increases the losses) of the banks. This leads either to increases in the subsidies the commercial banks receive from the central bank (or in some cases from the government), or to a lowering of the compensation paid to depositors, thus discouraging financial saving further, or to the raising of interest rates on performing loans. Finally, to the extent that the lending to the public enterprises absorbs much of the funds available, new private enterprises face greater difficulties and higher costs in getting needed funds. Therefore, this process creates an obstacle to the development of the private sector.[36]

Progress from a two-tier banking structure to a three-tier one in which the third tier would be made up of additional and—one would hope—private banks has been uneven.[37] But, provided that the private banks could be closely supervised so that the savings of depositors could be protected, they could play a very important role in mobilizing savings and in channeling them to the booming but small and credit-hungry new private activities. Over the longer run it is the success of these new activities that will determine the success of the transformation. Unfortunately, given the high rates of inflation prevailing in many of these countries, banking is a very difficult and precarious activity that can only be supervised with great difficulty.[38]

The discussion above has shown the close links that exist among policies. Until state enterprises are privatized, successfully restructured, or, at least, are allowed to go bankrupt, they will continue misallocating resources on a large scale. They will also impair the banking system and progressively reduce its solvency, thus preventing it from playing a major role in financing new private enterprises. Under these conditions, mobilization of savings may not be as desirable an objective as one would wish. It might be better to leave the resources in the hands of potential

---

[35]Like large public debts, these contingent liabilities may require higher tax payments in the future.

[36]This also raises questions about the effects of credit restrictions on the economy. To the extent that these restrictions crowd out private sector borrowers *before* they crowd out state enterprises, they may slow down the process of restructuring and reduce the efficiency of the economy.

[37]In Hungary, Poland, and Russia, new banks have been licensed. While Poland and Russia have pursued liberal licensing policies leading to the creation of many small banks, Hungary has pursued a more cautious licensing policy.

[38]The lack of proper supervision of these new private banks has led to questionable practices on the part of some of them. Unfortunately, the skills needed for proper supervision are still in very scarce supply.

savers. In such case an informal market for credit would come into existence and perform more efficiently than the official market.[39] The political choice may come to be that between, on one hand, continuing to subsidize the state enterprises and, on the other hand, subsidizing for a while the workers who become unemployed when the enterprises close through training and unemployment compensation. If unemployment benefits are not high, are limited in time, and are restricted to those who genuinely lost their jobs, this second alternative would be clearly preferable on efficiency grounds.

The cleaning of bad debts from the books of the commercial banks is a necessary though not a sufficient condition for their restructuring. It is not sufficient to ensure that they will not refill them with future bad debts. Only the enforcement of arm's-length relationships, competence, and good judgment on the part of the banks' management can ensure this. This would require adequate prudential supervision designed to contain various banking risks, and well-conceived licensing policies to ensure good management. It is not clear whether such progress is possible as long as the managers of these banks and the managers of the state enterprises come from the same background and respond to the same signals as in the past. The umbilical cord between these two groups must be cut. Recent financial and banking scandals reported for some of these countries have shown how important it is to cut that cord. Abuses may be particularly serious during the process of privatization when valuable assets of state enterprises may be bought by insiders using highly subsidized credit from the banks.

If banks were assured a solid capital base and became oriented to profit, they could play a major role in the restructuring of public enterprises, a role similar to that played by Japanese and German banks.[40] In any case, their restructuring would put them in a position to assist the booming but credit-hungry private sector. With the growth of the private sector and the shrinkage of the state enterprises, the latter would become progressively less important in any case.

In principle, the commercial banks could raise the lending rate while increasing the spread between what they pay to the depositors and what they pay to the borrowers. However, this might crowd out new businesses while allowing the state enterprises to continue borrowing. One solution that has been suggested by some writers is the one adopted by Chile in the mid-1980s and by some other countries. In Chile, the Central

---

[39]The informal market that I have in mind is similar to the "curb market" that was so important in Korea. The kind of informal market for credit that has been established among state enterprises in the economies in transition (which have been lending to each other) is contributing to distortions and is reducing the effectiveness of credit policy. It is also allowing some of these enterprises to remain in existence.

[40]See Corbett and Mayer (1991) for a discussion of this point. However, the question of whether banks would have the competence to perform this important function remains.

Bank bought the bad loans of the commercial banks with long-term bonds carrying negotiated and positive real interest rates. In this way, the commercial banks were assured a secure stream of income to facilitate recapitalization. However, the fiscal position of the public sector obviously deteriorated.[41] In a way this solution shifts the problem from the financial to the fiscal sector and highlights the importance of a fiscal reform.[42] Buyout operations of bad debts similar to that of Chile seem to be "in the pipeline" in the former Czechoslovakia and Bulgaria.[43] Romania took a different approach; in 1990, as part of introducing the two-tier banking system, fairly large amounts of bad debts of state enterprises were written off against unusually large government deposits with the new commercial banks.

In conclusion, the reform of the financial sector must create conditions and institutions that make it possible for individuals to channel their savings toward financial assets which are relatively safe and which pay a reasonable real rate of return. In order to satisfy these conditions, the financial institutions and particularly the commercial banks must be able and free to allocate those savings toward investments which generate rates of return high enough to compensate the lenders and to cover the costs of intermediation. Under present circumstances, the financial institutions are not able to perform both of these functions in a satisfactory way. As long as they continue to accommodate the financial needs of unprofitable state enterprises, they can pay reasonable compensation to savers only if they receive implicit fiscal subsidies from the central banks or explicit fiscal subsidies from the government. In either case this becomes a fiscal problem.

Reform of the Public Finances

Many of the current reforms in the Eastern European countries essentially deal with accommodating the existing institutional setup to the changing role of the government and defining its scope. In the pre-reform situation, when much of the economy was public, it was difficult to separate an area that could properly be called "public finance." In a way, all finances were "public" and many social objectives were pursued directly by the public enterprises rather than by the spending ministries. The transition must focus on what should remain public and what should

---

[41] Because of the interest that it had to pay on the bonds, the Central Bank ran large quasi-fiscal deficits. A very conservative fiscal policy by the Government was required to compensate for this fiscal deterioration.

[42] A convinced Ricardian might argue that the increase in public sector debt would be accompanied by an increase in private saving with no effect on the economy. However, given the institutional setup of these countries, even convinced Ricardians might have doubts on the realism of that outcome.

[43] In the former Czechoslovakia, there is a plan to use the proceeds from privatization to buy out some of the bad debts on the books of the banks.

become private and should draw a sharp distinction between these two areas.[44] In this context, a discussion of the proper role of the state would be highly appropriate. This role is also likely to diverge in the short run from what it would be in the long run when the process of transition is complete. At least for a while there will be many gray areas but these areas should progressively be reduced. The final role of the government in taxing citizens and in supporting social activities should become explicit and well focused. This role would determine the objectives to be achieved in terms of, say, level of taxation and public spending in the economy.

Many of the existing public subsidies are implicit rather than explicit. They are given through subsidized interest rates, through overvalued exchange rates for qualifying imports, through the provision of free or inexpensive lands for some activities, through the provision of cheap energy and housing, and so forth. These subsidies do not show up in fiscal statistics. The same is true for some implicit forms of taxation. For example, many banking regulations such as under-remunerated reserve requirements, and liquid asset ratios requiring captive holding of government securities, serve as implicit taxes on the banking system.

Most Western economists generally agree that in a well-working private economy, subsidies and taxes should be explicit. In other words, they should be given through the budget since only in this way can they be subjected annually to a full political scrutiny.[45] However, explicit subsidies and taxes are more demanding in terms of institutional requirements than implicit subsidies and taxes. In other words, they require good institutions such as tax systems, good budgetary systems, and various other institutions through which government programs are carried out (social security, welfare institutions, and so on). Until the proper institutions are in place, the government may have the choice between abandoning the pursuit of particular objectives or continuing to depend, to some extent, on implicit subsidies and taxes to achieve some goals considered socially desirable.[46] Since the pursuit of these objectives through implicit means is inefficient, the need to speed up the process of reform is obvious.

These countries have been raising levels of tax revenues that have exceeded those of most industrial countries.[47] It is unlikely that they will be able to maintain these levels over the longer run. The fragility of the

---

[44]This is not going to be an easy task since there are great differences between, say, the American view and the European continental view. The economies in transition must at some point choose between these two views of the role of the state.

[45]Of course, some subsidies may be explicit but given outside the budget. Most economists would be against extrabudgetary activities.

[46]For example, it is generally better to give cash to families rather than subsidies through what they buy. But cash transfers may require higher tax revenue and institutions that may not be available in the short run. Implicit transfers can be achieved simply but less efficiently through, say, the overvaluation of the exchange rate or the subsidization of the price of energy.

[47]See Tanzi (1991c).

revenue system undergoing changes in the economy was emphasized above. This fragility makes imperative a substantial rapid reduction in the level of public spending accompanied by the restructuring of the tax system. To achieve these objectives, many legislative and institutional changes must be made. These changes will be made difficult by the fact that many of the policies that these countries need to pursue over the next several years will have important linkages among them and will have major implications for the public finances.

A couple of examples will help highlight this point. Whether some state enterprises will be able to pay taxes may depend on whether they continue to receive credit from the banks and on whether the government can force them to pay. In Poland, many state enterprises are reported to be in arrears in making tax payments. Sometimes arrears toward state enterprises by other state enterprises may bring about tax arrears by the former toward the government as well as arrears in servicing bank loans. Therefore, the netting out of debt among state enterprises and the securitization of such debt would be useful steps. The revenue contribution of some forms of commodity taxes will depend on the price liberalization policy. As long as prices remain controlled, it might seem pointless to introduce a modern value-added tax (VAT).[48] However, price liberalization is progressing rapidly in many of these countries.

Large price changes will have major impacts on real wages, on employment, and on income levels of different social groups. If the standard of living of some groups, for example, pensioners, is reduced too sharply, there will be a need for compensating them. An increase in subsidies will, to some extent, reduce the positive impact on the budget coming from price liberalization. In some cases, prices may change so drastically that it will become very difficult to estimate the measures needed to reduce the impact of those changes on vulnerable groups. In these cases, measures taken to alleviate these effects may end up being either too generous or too austere. If they are too generous, they will create a precedent for the future and will reduce the ability of the government to improve its fiscal accounts. If they are too austere, they will create a political backlash that will in some cases force a reversal of the policies. All this implies that many difficult decisions will have to be made by policymakers who have had no training to deal with these questions and who may have little information on which to base their policies.[49]

---

[48] All the Eastern European countries have plans to introduce a VAT by 1993 at the latest. Hungary was the first to do so after a long preparation. Russia and most of the other states of the former U.S.S.R. introduced a VAT on January 1, 1992, with very little preparation. Bulgaria, the former Czechoslovakia, and Romania planned to introduce a VAT on January 1, 1993. For a full treatment of VATs in these countries, see Tait (1992), pp. 188–208.

[49] For example, nobody knows the impact on various income groups that would result from the bringing of the energy price in Russia to the world level. In fact, in the absence of an equilibrium rate of exchange, it is even difficult to determine what the world price would be in rubles.

There are five major building blocks for the reform of public finances: (1) the setting up, almost from scratch, of a tax administration; (2) the reform of the tax system; (3) the setting up of budgetary institutions; (4) the reform of the public expenditures; and (5) the reform of social security systems.[50] A few observations on each of these follow.

Setting Up a Tax Administration

The need to set up a modern tax administration is overwhelming.[51] This objective should receive the immediate and full attention of the policymakers in all countries.[52] The tax revenues that these countries collected in the past are no indication of what they will be able to collect in the future. These revenues were essentially transfers from some part of the public sector, mainly state enterprises with surpluses, to other parts of the public sector, such as state enterprises with losses, and spending ministries. The number of taxpayers (that is, the state enterprises) was only in the thousands, and they could be easily controlled. The transformation of these economies (1) will increase the number of taxpayers from the thousands to the millions; (2) by liberalizing prices and removing production quotas will reduce sharply the information available to the tax administration; and (3) by stimulating services and small public sector activities will increase the proportion of total income originating in the part of the economy that is most difficult to tax.

It will be important to preserve some good administrative features of the former system, namely the payment of taxes through the banks and the widespread withholding at the source. These two features would be an important asset in the new tax administration and would release staff resources to pursue more important activities such as audits, taxpayer identification, taxpayer assistance, and so forth. The need to preserve withholding at the source and to limit the number of taxpayers who need to file returns will or should influence the kind of tax systems that are brought into existence.

Reform of the Tax System

The tax system that comes to be established should be simple and easy to administer.[53] Anything that requires complex administrative procedures or a large number of filing taxpayers will not work. It is thus important that foreign experts do not try to experiment with their pet

---

[50]All these areas have been discussed at length in various papers included in Tanzi (1992).

[51]For a full treatment of issues of tax administration, see Casanegra de Jantscher, Silvani, and Vehorn (1992), pp. 120–41.

[52]In Hungary, the setting up of a modern tax administration is well advanced since that country started earlier. In other countries only limited progress has been made so far.

[53]For details on various aspects of tax reform, see Chapters 5–11 in Tanzi (1992).

ideas and do not try to simply transplant the tax systems with which they are familiar. For example, the attempt to introduce a global income tax, a pet idea of many Western economists, would almost surely lead to disappointment. A global income tax would require large-scale filing and complex administrative procedures for which these countries are not prepared. Such a tax does not easily lend itself to widespread withholding at the source, especially when it is accompanied by highly progressive rates. Therefore, income taxes with relatively low rates that minimize filing and thus rely on withholding at the source for wages, interest, and perhaps dividend incomes, would be desirable. Similar considerations could be made vis-à-vis VATs with multiple rates and zero rating of some commodities. For these taxes, the close link that exists between the exemption threshold and administrative simplicity must be recognized. The lower the threshold, the greater the number of taxpayers, and the greater will be the administrative complications. The interest that many of these countries have to become part of Europe implies that they will attempt to develop tax systems that are compatible with those of the Western European countries. While this is a worthwhile objective, compatibility may be achieved by a simplified system rather than by the cloning of the European tax systems.

Reforming countries should resist the temptation to continue discriminating among groups and activities. The point of going to a market economy is to let the market make the choices. This mistake was originally made by the first reforming country, Hungary, when it introduced a Western tax system. It was forced to levy high tax rates because of preferential treatment accorded to many groups or industries, and, recently, has been trying to correct these mistakes. These countries should resist the temptation to pursue too many social objectives through the tax system and they should try to minimize policy mistakes at the beginning. Some of these mistakes (as, for example, the provision of widespread deductions and exemptions), once made, are difficult to correct, especially at a time when parliaments are trying to make their presence felt.

Social Security Reform

One area deserving special attention is social security.[54] Many of these countries are experiencing serious crises in their social security systems. In many of them, for example, in Hungary, the former Czechoslovakia, and the states of the former U.S.S.R., the level of social security taxation is so high as to be unsustainable over the longer run; in spite of this, these systems are in many cases experiencing large losses.[55] A market economy

---

[54]See Kopits (1992), pp. 291–311.

[55]The demographic situation in some Eastern European countries is an important continuing factor to the unsustainability of the current social security scheme.

with social security taxes on employers as high as those existing in some of these countries will give strong incentives to underground economic activities to avoid paying them.[56] Furthermore, such high taxes on labor will inevitably hurt the competitiveness of these countries. There is a strong need for a major reform of the social security system, that is, increasing the retirement age, scrutinizing potential pensioners more closely, especially for disabilities, and, of course, reducing the number of beneficiaries and the level and the coverage of benefits to what the country will be able to afford in future years, considering the many claims on the reduced government revenues.

Setting Up a Modern Budgetary System

Under central planning, there was no budget office in the sense understood in market economies.[57] Allocation for some social expenditures by the relevant ministries was made by the planning office with limited input from the spending ministries. The state enterprises themselves played an important role in providing social services to their workers and their families. In a market economy, the enterprises will no longer play this role so that the importance and the financial needs of the spending ministries will increase. Budgetary decisions must be made keeping in mind (1) resource availability and (2) efficiency considerations. The budget office must establish close links between total budgetary appropriations for the budget year and expected government revenue, which are in turn influenced by developments in the economy. The budget office must develop good forecasting techniques to assess the impact of the economy on revenue and expenditures. It must also closely scrutinize the results of public spending in order to maximize its welfare impact and to keep costs under control. A unified budget format that encompasses all programs would enhance the usefulness of the budget as a policy tool. In sum, a modern budget office must be established. Given the complexity of this task, it will take several years before it is completed.

Reform of Public Expenditures

The level of public spending will need to fall substantially over the next few years and the current structure of public spending will need to change drastically in order to reduce the importance of subsidies. The newly created budget office will have to play an important role in making the basic decisions on public spending. These decisions will be politically difficult because of resistance on the part of those who will find their

---

[56]For the connection between high social security taxes and the underground economy, see Del Boca and Forte (1982) and Contini (1982).

[57]For details, see Premchand and Garamfalvi (1992).

benefits reduced, and technically difficult because of uncertainties over the development of the economy and because of problems in quantifying the effects of certain policies on certain groups. In any case, substantial savings should come from the elimination or reduction of subsidies to enterprises and consumers and, in several of these countries, from lower military expenditures. The rationalization of the system of social insurance should also reduce spending. On the other hand, there will be strong pressures in particular areas. For example, the need to generate new skills may have significant impact on educational spending. The health sector has been somewhat ignored in recent years. In fact, life expectancy in some of these countries has been going down. Thus, health expenditure will need to increase.[58] The growing number of unemployed will create strong pressures to assist them. And, of course, the restructuring of the state enterprises will require some spending. In any case, the more competent the technical staff involved in these decisions, the more likely it is that the final outcome will be more efficient.

Fiscal-Monetary Links

A total and clear separation between fiscal and monetary policy is next to impossible in any economy. There are always areas where they overlap. However, well-managed market economies attempt to keep these two policies separate and try to use each policy toward the objectives for which it is comparatively more efficient. Normally, price stability and the mobilization and efficient allocation of savings are promoted through the use of monetary policy, while short-term demand management, the provision of public goods, and the redistribution of income are pursued through fiscal policy.[59]

In the Eastern European countries, these two policies are greatly intertwined and a clear separation between them may be difficult to achieve for a long time.[60] At the moment the two policies intersect in many areas; fiscal goals are pursued through monetary policy and, to some extent, monetary goals through fiscal policy. In these countries, an explicit goal of economic policy should be the reduction in the scope of these overlapping areas. Some of these areas have already been mentioned earlier.

---

[58]Whether health expenditure will remain a responsibility of the public sector or is shifted to the private sector is one of the many important decisions to be made regarding the role of the state.

[59]Whether monetary policy should also be used for stabilization remains a controversial issue. The recent recession in industrial countries seems to have promoted once again such a role for monetary policy.

[60]In general, these two policies are less clearly separated in developing countries than in industrial countries. For example, in Latin America, the central banks have, in several cases, financed activities that have caused them to experience large quasi-fiscal deficits. The reason is the one mentioned earlier—the less developed the institutions, the more difficult is the separation of policies.

However, a listing of some of them may help attract attention to an important but relatively unknown problem.

First, the banking system has financed and continues to finance many economic activities through highly subsidized credit. If these activities deserve to be financed, in principle, this should be done through the budget. If this were the case, the fiscal deficit would reflect more precisely the current imbalance between public revenue and public expenditure and would give a clearer indication of the required fiscal adjustment. As reported earlier, in some countries, balanced budgets, or even budgetary surpluses, have at times coexisted with high rates of inflation. In these situations the budgetary outcome (the fiscal deficit) clearly sends wrong signals that may confuse policymakers and other observers on needed policy changes.[61] The policy implication of this is that either these subsidies should be eliminated, or they should be shifted from the monetary to the fiscal area. However, if the tax system is not well developed, the second is not a realistic alternative. If the government insists on subsidizing the activities, or if the political process forces it to do so, it may have no choice but continue using monetary instruments to pursue fiscal objectives.

Second, in some of these countries, the internal public debt has reached very high shares of GDP. In the former Soviet Union, for example, that share reached more than 60 percent of GDP. In this situation the level of the real interest rate at which public debts are serviced will have a large impact on the measured fiscal deficit. There has been a tendency to keep real interest rates low, or even negative, so as to facilitate the financing of the deficit and to reduce its measured size. This action once again shifts the burden of adjustment from fiscal policy to monetary policy and implies that no real adjustment takes place.[62] Once again this sends wrong signals and distorts the objectives of policy. This danger is particularly acute during high inflation. If the holders of the debt are the commercial banks, their earnings will be reduced. On the other hand, they will gain from the seigniorage they receive from unremunerated or under-remunerated deposits. Of course, if the holders of the debt are enterprises, their profits will be reduced.

Third, recent writing by M. Boskin, W. Buiter, and others has emphasized the importance of the net worth of the public sector. As the public sector acquires better-defined boundaries, so that it is more clearly distinguishable from the private sector, attention comes to be paid to its net worth. Recently there have been pressures to push the governments of

---

[61]When fiscal objectives are being pursued through monetary instruments, the fiscal deficit as commonly measured is not as significant a variable as often assumed. In this case, balancing the budget may not necessarily be a worthwhile policy goal.

[62]When the measured fiscal deficit is given great prominence in the negotiation of adjustment programs, there is the danger that countries may be induced to keep the deficit low by perpetuating the recourse to policies that artificially keep the deficit down.

these countries to pursue policies that tend to nationalize debts while shifting valuable assets in private hands.[63] As Mark Allen (1992, pp. 67–79) has pointed out, the public sectors of these countries were supposed to own much of the economy's wealth since most assets were publicly owned; therefore, their *net* wealth could be reduced mainly by foreign indebtedness. However, as time passes, because of the nationalization of debt and the privatization of assets, their net wealth appears smaller and smaller, raising concerns about the long-run fiscal solvency of these countries. The possibility that the government or the central bank may have to inject large, but still undetermined, capital in the commercial banks implies that the public sector's net worth will fall and that its long-run fiscal stance will be weakened.[64]

Fourth, and closely related to the previous point, several economists have recently called attention to the importance of the public sector's contingent liabilities in assessing a country's fiscal stance. The bad loans of the commercial banks, the foreign debts of the national banks or the governments, which with large devaluations can grow enormously in domestic currency and can, thus, sharply increase the measured fiscal deficit, and the many other implicit or explicit future commitments, including those provided through social security institutions, imply that the present value of future public sector liabilities may be very large. This again highlights the underlying weakness of the public finances and the need for a major fiscal adjustment.

Fifth, at the moment, public spending not financed by ordinary government revenue is financed either through implicit subsidies (such as through the overvaluation of the exchange rate or bank credit to state enterprises provided at concessional rates) or through monetary expansion. The development of a financial market, with the introduction of securities with different characteristics and maturities, can introduce a channel through which the government could mobilize financial savings to finance fiscal deficits in ways other than those mentioned above. The example of Italy indicates that, if the government stimulates a fast rate of innovation in the financial market, the financing of substantial fiscal deficits is facilitated, especially if the saving rate of the household sector is high (see Caranza (1991)). This development would help preserve the

---

[63]Some observers are urging the governments in these countries to assume the debts of the enterprises before privatizing them.

[64]Given the weakness of current fiscal institutions, this may not be the right time to inject this capital in the commercial banks. But waiting will only increase the size of these liabilities. The Chilean solution, which required the Central Bank to assume debt equivalent to about 25 percent of GDP, was introduced when the Government was making great and successful efforts to improve the public finances. There must be a firm cut-off date when a Chilean-type solution is contemplated. All debt and financial problems prior to the cut-off date may be alleviated, as long as it is understood that, after the cut-off date, banks face hard budget constraints and are on their own.

separation between monetary and fiscal policy.[65] It would also reduce the possibility that, by using different financing sources, governments can intentionally manipulate the measures of their fiscal stance. However, the government must not have the power to force banks, enterprises, or even individuals, to buy government securities.

When a government can force banks to buy securities to finance the deficit, or when enterprises can pay "profit taxes," which are not based on real profits, only by borrowing from the banking system, a balanced budget or an apparently noninflationary deficit might hide the fact that it is the fiscal policy that is out of control and not the monetary policy. In this case inflationary finance may be masked as tax revenue.

Lastly, as governments bail out banks and other financial institutions, fiscal deficits are likely to widen. At the same time, if privatization is ongoing and is generating significant revenue, there will be a temptation to use privatization receipts to finance current expenditure rather than to reduce public debt. This will contribute to the precariousness of the fiscal situation because, while privatization revenue is transitory, increases in current expenditure tend to become permanent. Under these circumstances, one way of containing fiscal deficits might be to recapitalize financial institutions using equity in state enterprises rather than by transfers from the public sector. If the financial institutions became major shareholders in enterprises and could influence their business decisions— much along the lines of the German and Japanese models of corporate control—there could be a significant improvement in efficiency and profitability. This would benefit enterprise managers, workers, and shareholders—who therefore would have an incentive to seek such an improvement—and the economy as a whole. There would also be additional tax revenue for the budget, which would allow some increase in productive spending without threatening fiscal instability.[66] Of course, the quality of the banks' management and the existence of hard budget constraints for the banks would be very important in determining whether this option is a realistic one.

Concluding Remarks

This paper has surveyed the role of financial markets and fiscal institutions in the transformation process that is going on in Eastern and Central Europe. It has highlighted many areas: (1) the need to create some sort of "social ecological balance" necessary for the working of a modern market economy; (2) the need to develop financial institutions that mobilize savings; (3) the need to solve some fundamental problems faced by the

---

[65]However, by facilitating the financing of the deficit, it might also delay the required adjustment, as has happened in Italy.

[66]See Hemming (1992) for a discussion of this point.

commercial banks so that the savings that are mobilized by them can be efficiently allocated; and (4) the need to reform the public finances including the setting up of modern tax administrations and budgetary institutions, the enactment of tax laws, the solution to urgent problems faced by social security institutions, and the need to reduce and restructure public spending.

The paper has called attention to the extent to which monetary and fiscal policies overlap in these countries and the extent to which fiscal objectives are often pursued through nonfiscal instruments. It is thus important to create institutions that allow a separation of these policies. But the creation of these institutions will take time. Until the right fiscal institutions are created, certain social objectives can only be pursued through less efficient means. Therefore, the policymakers can only choose between abandoning those objectives or pursuing them inefficiently. To a large extent the success or failure of the transformation process will depend on how quickly modern fiscal institutions can be created.

References

Allen, Mark, "Government Debt Management," in *Fiscal Policies in Economies in Transition*, ed. by Vito Tanzi (Washington: International Monetary Fund, 1992).

Atkinson, Anthony B., and Renato Brunetta, eds., *Economics for the New Europe* (London: Macmillan, 1991).

Atkinson, Anthony B., and John Micklewright, "Economic Transformation in Eastern Europe and the Distribution of Income," in *Economics for the New Europe*, ed. by Anthony B. Atkinson and Renato Brunetta (London: Macmillan, 1991).

Atkinson, Paul E., and William E. Alexander, *Financial Sector Reform: Its Role in Growth and Development* (Washington: Institute of International Finance, 1990).

Blommestein, Hans, and Michael Marrese, eds., *Transformation of Planned Economies: Property Rights Reform and Macroeconomic Stability* (Paris: Organization for Economic Cooperation and Development, 1991).

Brainard, Lawrence J., "Reform in Eastern Europe: Creating a Capital Market," in *Finance and the International Economy: 4*, ed. by Richard O'Brien and Sarah Hewin (Oxford: Oxford University Press for the AMEX Bank Review, 1991).

Calvo, Guillermo A., "Financial Aspects of Socialist Economies: From Inflation to Reform," in *Reforming Central and Eastern European Economies: Initial Results and Challenges*, ed. by Vittorio Corbo, Fabrizio Coricelli, and Jan Bossak (Washington: World Bank, 1991).

Campbell, Robert W., *The Socialist Economies in Transition: A Primer on Semi-Reformed Systems* (Bloomington: Indiana University Press, 1991).

Caranza, Cesare, "Government Financing, Domestic Debt Management, and Monetary Policy: Some Lessons from the Italian Experience," in *The Evolving Role of Central Banks*, ed. by Patrick Downes and Reza Vaez-Zadeh (Washington: International Monetary Fund, 1991).

Casanegra de Jantscher, Milka, Carlos Silvani, and Charles L. Vehorn, "Modernizing Tax Administration," in *Fiscal Policies in Economies in Transition*, ed. by Vito Tanzi (Washington: International Monetary Fund, 1992).

Cheasty, Adrienne, "Financing Fiscal Deficits," in *Fiscal Policies in Economies in Transition*, ed. by Vito Tanzi (Washington: International Monetary Fund, 1992).

Commission of the European Communities, *European Economy: The Path of Reform in Central and Eastern Europe*, Special Edition No. 2 (Luxembourg, 1991).

Contini, Bruno, "The Second Economy of Italy," in *The Underground Economy in the United States and Abroad*, ed. by Vito Tanzi (Lexington, Massachusetts: D.C. Heath and Company, 1982).

Corbo, Vittorio, Fabrizio Coricelli, and Jan Bossak, eds., *Reforming Central and Eastern European Economies: Initial Results and Challenges* (Washington: World Bank, 1991).

Corbett, Jenny, and Colin Mayer, "Financial Reform in Eastern Europe: Progress with the Wrong Model," *Oxford Review of Economic Policy*, Vol. 7, No. 4 (Winter 1991), pp. 57-75.

Corrigan, E. Gerald, "The Role of Central Banks and the Financial System in Emerging Market Economies," *Quarterly Review*, Federal Reserve Bank of New York, Vol. 15 (Summer 1990), pp. 1-7.

Del Boca, Daniela, and Francesco Forte, "Recent Empirical Surveys and Theoretical Interpretations of the Parallel Economy in Italy," in *The Underground Economy in the United States and Abroad*, ed. by Vito Tanzi (Lexington, Massachusetts: D.C. Heath and Company, 1982).

Downes, Patrick, and Reza Vaez-Zadeh, eds., *The Evolving Role of Central Banks* (Washington: International Monetary Fund, 1991).

Easterly, William, "Distortionary Policies and Growth in Socialist Economies," in *Reforming Central and Eastern European Economies: Initial Results and Challenges*, ed. by Vittorio Corbo, Fabrizio Coricelli, and Jan Bossak (Washington: World Bank, 1991).

Economic Commission for Europe, *Economic Survey of Europe in 1990-1991* (New York: United Nations, 1991).

Feige, Edgar L., ed., *The Underground Economies: Tax Evasion and Information Distortion* (Cambridge, England: Cambridge University Press, 1989).

Fischer, Stanley, and Alan Gelb, "Issues in the Reform of Socialist Economies," in *Reforming Central and Eastern European Economies: Initial Results and Challenges*, ed. by Vittorio Corbo, Fabrizio Coricelli, and Jan Bossak (Washington: World Bank, 1991).

Gábor, Istvan R., "Second Economy and Socialism: The Hungarian Experience," in *The Underground Economies: Tax Evasion and Information Distortion*, ed. by Edgar L. Feige (Cambridge, England: Cambridge University Press, 1989).

Grossman, Gregory, "The Second Economy of the U.S.S.R.," in *The Underground Economy in the United States and Abroad*, ed. by Vito Tanzi (Lexington, Massachusetts: D.C. Heath and Company, 1982).

Hemming, Richard, "Privatization of State Enterprises," in *Fiscal Policies in Economies in Transition*, ed. by Vito Tanzi (Washington: International Monetary Fund, 1992).

Kessides, Christine, Timothy King, Mario Nuti, and Catherine Sokil, *Financial Reform in Socialist Economies* (Washington: World Bank, 1989).

Kopits, George, "Social Security," in *Fiscal Policies in Economies in Transition*, ed. by Vito Tanzi (Washington: International Monetary Fund, 1992).

Liviatan, Oded, "Impact of Public Financial Institutions on Fiscal Stance," in *How to Measure the Fiscal Deficit: Analytical and Methodological Issues*, ed. by Mario I. Blejer and Adrienne Cheasty (Washington: International Monetary Fund, 1993).

Marer, Paul, and Salvatore Zecchini, eds., *The Transition to a Market Economy* (Paris: Organization for Economic Cooperation and Development, 1991).

McKinnon, Ronald I., *The Order of Economic Liberalization: Financial Control in the Transition to a Market Economy* (Baltimore: Johns Hopkins University Press, 1991).

Newbery, David M., "Sequencing the Transition," CEPR Discussion Paper Series, No. 575 (London: Center for Economic Policy Research, August 1991).

Premchand, A., and L. Garamfalvi, "Government Budget and Accounting Systems," in *Fiscal Policies in Economies in Transition*, ed. by Vito Tanzi (Washington: International Monetary Fund, 1992).

Sundararajan, V., "Financial Sector Reform and Central Banking in Centrally Planned Economies," in *The Evolving Role of Central Banks*, ed. by Patrick Downes and Reza Vaez-Zadeh (Washington: International Monetary Fund, 1991).

Tait, Alan, "Introducing Value-Added Taxes," in *Fiscal Policies in Economies in Transition*, ed. by Vito Tanzi (Washington: International Monetary Fund, 1992).

Tanzi, Vito (1991a), "Fiscal Issues in Economies in Transition," in *Reforming Central and Eastern European Economies: Initial Results and Challenges*, ed. by Vittorio Corbo, Fabrizio Coricelli, and Jan Bossak (Washington: World Bank, 1991).

——— (1991b), "Mobilisation of Savings in Eastern European Countries: The Role of the State," in *Economics for the New Europe*, ed. by Anthony B. Atkinson and Renato Brunetta (London: Macmillan, 1991).

——— (1991c), "Tax Reform and the Move to a Market Economy: Overview of the Issues," in *The Role of Tax Reform in Central and Eastern European Economies* (Paris: Organization for Economic Cooperation and Development, 1991).

———, ed., *The Underground Economy in the United States and Abroad* (Lexington, Massachusetts: D.C. Heath and Company, 1982).

————, ed., *Fiscal Policies in Economies in Transition* (Washington: International Monetary Fund, 1992).

————, and Howell H. Zee, "Time Constraints in Consumption and Savings Behavior," *Journal of Public Economics*, Vol. 50 (February 1993), pp. 253-59.

Thumm, Ulrich R.W., "World Bank Adjustment Lending in Central and Eastern Europe," in *Reforming Central and Eastern European Economies: Initial Results and Challenges*, ed. by Vittorio Corbo, Fabrizio Coricelli, and Jan Bossak (Washington: World Bank, 1991).

PART I

Central and Eastern Europe: General Issues

CHAPTER 2

Bulgaria's Transition to a Market Economy: Fiscal Aspects

Sheetal K. Chand and Henri R. Lorie

The primary objective of modern economic systems is to promote orderly growth. After four decades of central planning under communism in Bulgaria, it became abundantly clear that a fundamental change in the economic system was required if a satisfactory rate of growth was to be restored. Accordingly, the Bulgarian authorities decided to move to a market-oriented system. The successful implementation of such a move requires at the outset the introduction of appropriate market infrastructure such as commercial laws, the right to private property, and accounting conventions. The reforms needed will have to go beyond liberalizing prices and promoting market clearance to include revamping many of the institutions on which central planning relied. In particular, the Government's all-pervasive role in the economy will have to be reduced in favor of decentralized public and private decision making, and new instruments for indirect control will have to be established.

The reform of the public finances is at the core of the institutional adjustments required to operate successfully a market economy. Beginning in mid-1990, and especially in 1991, Bulgaria has initiated important steps in this direction. This paper describes these reforms in the light of what is needed under Bulgarian conditions to operate a satisfactory market economy.[1] The paper begins with a brief macroeconomic overview of the situation in Bulgaria. This is followed by a review of the organization of the public finances prior to the reform. The next section examines the general nature of the fiscal reforms needed. The remaining sections consider the achievements to date and the unfinished tasks.

Macroeconomic Context

In the 1960s and 1970s, Bulgaria achieved fairly high rates of economic growth through rapid industrialization, particularly in heavy industries

---

Sheetal K. Chand is Chief of the Fiscal Analysis Division of the Fiscal Affairs Department, and Henri R. Lorie is Advisor in European II Department.

[1]For an account of some of the requirements for a successful fiscal policy in economies in transition, see Sheetal K. Chand and Henri R. Lorie, "Fiscal Policy," in *Fiscal Policies in Economies in Transition*, ed. by Vito Tanzi (Washington: International Monetary Fund, 1992).

(such as machinery, metalwork, and chemicals), and increased trade integration within the area of the former Council for Mutual Economic Assistance (CMEA), in particular, the former Soviet Union on which it depended for cheap raw materials. Those results were obtained under a tightly controlled system of central planning that redirected resources toward large state-owned industrial enterprises and away from the agricultural sector. The latter was itself largely converted into inefficient agroindustrial enterprises.

The limits of this strategy were reached progressively in the 1980s, despite some attempt at upgrading industrial investments by the state (mainly in electronics, chemicals, and the energy sector). In particular, the high dependency on imported equipment and inputs both dampened domestic growth and placed increasing pressure on the balance of payments with the convertible area. A number of exogenous factors also contributed to the deterioration of Bulgaria's macroeconomic situation from 1985. These included years of drought, which reduced agricultural output, and the declining purchasing power of oil producing countries in the Middle East, as well as the end of the war between Iraq and the Islamic Republic of Iran, which depressed Bulgaria's substantial exports to the countries in that region. The poor quality of much of these exports has prevented their redirection toward Western markets.

Increasingly since the mid-1980s, domestic economic activity, investment, and consumption were sustained by expansionary fiscal policies backed by growing recourse to external borrowing in favor of enterprises. In the process, broad money grew systematically faster than nominal GDP, which resulted in a slow but steady buildup of a monetary overhang.

Both the external and the domestic situation became increasingly unsustainable during 1989–90. As a result, Bulgaria was cut off from new external borrowing (and from March 1990 ceased to meet most external payments). Further, imbalances between goods demanded and supplied were heightened. Growing popular discontent, the demonstration effect of events in other East European countries, and the tacit agreement of the Soviet Union led to a change of political regime in December 1989 and the decision to move to a market-oriented economy. However, initial steps in that direction during 1990 were largely uncoordinated. In particular, a move toward external liberalization, including reliance on market forces to determine the exchange rate, was not immediately reflected in domestic prices. It encouraged diversion to exports and speculative buildup of inventories. Since budgetary and monetary policies were loosened rather than tightened, shortages worsened. On the supply side, the constraint on foreign exchange and imported inputs forced enterprises to cut back their activities.

Perhaps more than any other East European country, Bulgaria formulated and initiated a comprehensive reform program in early 1991 under especially difficult external circumstances; namely, the war in the Middle East and the dissolution of trade arrangements under the CMEA. Even the long-anticipated impact of the move to international prices from January 1991 for trade transactions with the former CMEA partners (including for oil and other raw materials from the former Soviet Union), which was projected to result in a 30 percent deterioration in terms of trade, did not fully anticipate the extent of the collapse of trade with the Soviet Union. The problem was compounded by the withdrawal of virtually every kind of trade financing and the delay in promised disbursements of foreign assistance.

Not only has the environment for reform not been propitious, but the adverse exogenous developments caused the fiscal situation to deteriorate. This, of course, makes it more difficult to employ fiscal policy, badly needed as it is, to stabilize the economy. The scope for employing fiscal policies to undertake the vital tasks of reconstructing the economy is further limited by the prior requirement to restructure the public finances in conformity with market conditions, so as to forge a usable instrument for indirect control.

Structure of Public Finances Inherited from Central Planning

Organization of Budget and Extrabudgetary Funds

The unified and all-encompassing state budget reflected the key role of public finances under central planning for meeting government requirements for managing the economy and promoting distributional objectives. The Bulgarian state budget has five constituent elements, of which the principal part is the so-called republican budget.[2] It implemented undertakings of nationwide significance, including key redistributive and regulatory functions. In particular, it received or paid funds related to foreign trade equalization operations and managed subsidy payments during the 1980s; the latter consistently amounted to about 25 percent of budget expenditure, equivalent to about 15 percent of GDP (Table 1). Within the state budget, the social security budget, which derives its receipts mainly from social security contributions paid by employers in the form of a payroll tax, finances a comprehensive system of social benefits. These amounted to almost 20 percent of budget expenditure, equivalent to some 10 percent of GDP. The social security system has tended to operate fairly independently, but sizable surpluses in the early 1980s were systematically transferred to the republican budget; these

---

[2]The other elements are (1) the budgets of the ministries; (2) the budgets of the regional people's councils; (3) the budgets of the municipal people's councils; and (4) the social security budget.

Table 1. Bulgaria: General Government Operations
(In percent of GDP)

	1988	1989	1990 Budget	1990 Actual	1991 Budget	1991 Projected
Total revenue	58.0	60.1	60.5	53.1	41.4	39.3
Tax revenue	47.4	49.5	51.3	42.2	39.5	36.4
Nontax revenue	10.7	10.7	9.2	10.8	1.9	2.9
Total expenditure	63.7	61.6	63.2	65.7	44.9	54.2
Current	53.0	53.1	57.4	60.2	43.3	52.3
Capital	10.7	8.4	5.8	5.3	1.6	1.9
Budget	5.4	5.5	3.7	3.1	1.7	1.9
SICF[1]	5.3	3.0	2.1	2.3	-0.1	—
Overall deficit (–)	-5.6	-1.4	-2.7	-12.6	-3.5	-14.9
Of which:						
Bank financing	6.3	2.8	4.2	6.3	-0.5	6.1
Cash deficit (–)[2]	-5.6	-1.4	-2.7	-8.5	0.1	-3.7
Primary deficit (–)[3]	-3.6	1.6	2.6	-3.2	4.6	2.6
Domestic deficit (–)[4]	-3.6	1.6	2.6	-3.9	1.8	-3.3
Memorandum item:						
GDP (in billions of leva)	38.3	39.5	40.0	45.6	146.5	138.4

Source: Ministry of Finance.
[1] State Investment Credit Fund.
[2] Includes only external interest paid.
[3] Excludes all interest payments.
[4] Excludes all external interest payments.

surpluses have dwindled in recent years, and a deficit emerged in 1990, which necessitated support from the republican budget.

Public policy objectives are also implemented through the operation of certain extrabudgetary funds. The largest of these funds is the State Investment Credit Fund (SICF). It was created in 1987 to finance high-priority large-scale investments (in sectors such as coal and electricity, metallurgy, and heavy and chemical industries) at extremely low interest rates to stimulate growth. In effect, this fund has allowed the removal of some government investments from the regular budget. Another extrabudgetary fund that is gaining greater importance under the reform process is the Professional Training and Retraining Fund; it is responsible for unemployment benefits, the training and retraining of dismissed and redundant workers, and labor market information. Because of the public policy character of these extrabudgetary funds, they have been included in the coverage of general government operations presented in Table 1.

Overall Deficit Trends

During most of the 1980s, the state budget (excluding the SICF and other extrabudgetary funds) was close to balance; and even the largest state budget deficit (in 1986) did not exceed 3 percent of GDP. However, the contribution of the state budget to direct money supply creation increased in the second half of the decade, reaching some 2 percent of GDP in 1988-89, a development that largely coincided with a falloff in foreign financing of the budget.

Nevertheless, the relatively small size of the overall fiscal deficits during the 1980s underestimates growing state budget difficulties and the expansionary stance adopted. Indeed, budgetary expenditure alone increased in the 1980s by almost 10 percentage points to nearly 60 percent of GDP. It largely reflected a rising trend in subsidies, social security payments, and (until 1987) in capital expenditure. In addition, during 1987-89 the SICF invested heavily in the energy sector and in heavy industries, averaging about 5 percent of GDP, and mostly financed by bank credit. Hence, the *general* government's overall deficit increased markedly in 1987-88, to more than 5 percent of GDP, before falling back to about 1.5 percent of GDP in 1989, as a consequence in large part of higher profits taxes and cuts in capital outlays. The general government's deficits are clearly better indicators of the more expansionary fiscal policy stance adopted during most of the second half of the 1980s.

Structure of Expenditure

The most striking feature of general government outlays, representing more than 60 percent of GDP at the outset of the reform program, was the importance of subsidies. As indicated earlier, these amounted to about 15 percent of GDP, compared with an average of 3 percent of GDP among member countries of the European Community. With the weakening of central planning, an increasing share of subsidies took the form of transfers to cover operating losses of certain unprofitable industrial sectors and, in 1990, of consumer subsidies, as higher factory purchase prices were not accompanied by increases in retail prices. Without clearcut reference to international prices, the distinction between producer and consumer subsidies can be blurred, but the allocation of subsidies among commodity groups clearly reflected the social objective to provide for the entire population basic foodstuffs (such as dairy products and meat) and consumer items (in particular, children's clothing) at very low prices, as well as the objective to sustain industrial growth. To some extent the application of subsidies was in lieu of wage increases, given the policy of keeping wages frozen at an artificially low level.

Typically, maintenance and operating expenditure tended to be high under central planning, at about 14 percent of GDP or nearly one fourth of total outlays. This indicated the important role of the state not only in the health and education sectors, with little attempt at cost recovery even from those most able to pay, but also in cultural and leisure activities, representation, and urban development. Indeed, visitors to Bulgaria cannot but be impressed by the relative opulence of the state and municipal facilities compared with the very modest standards of living of the population.

One feature of central planning has been a comprehensive system of social benefits reflecting the commitment by the state—often in return for relatively low nominal wages—to provide for old age, sickness, disability, and child care. However, the question of unemployment and poverty alleviation assistance did not typically arise, because of the artificially maintained full employment policies and the distributional policies. Nevertheless, social outlays typically reached more than 10 percent of GDP, mostly related to pensions for about one fourth of the population and to child allowances.

Revenue System

The Government relied heavily for the financing of these large outlays on its take in the state enterprises' so-called profits, which at times was so excessive as to contribute to the growing recourse by the enterprises to bank financing for their operations, and the resulting large increase in their level of indebtedness. By 1989, 67 percent of profits was taxed. In Western terms this level of taxation is even higher since the system of accounting did not provide for items of deductions, such as interest payments, that are normally allowed as a cost of doing business. However, by the same token the state would bear many costs of enterprises that are more properly borne by those enterprises.

Another mainstay of the revenue system was the turnover tax, which earlier comprised more than 2,000 rates, varying by commodity, but was reduced at the beginning of 1988 to some 40 rates. This tax essentially functioned as a wedge between the retail and wholesale prices of the good, both of which were fixed and only infrequently adjusted. Excise duties were also levied on a variety of goods, including those considered dangerous to health, such as alcoholic beverages and tobacco products, with the rates set as percentages of retail prices, except for petroleum products for which specific taxes applied. Under central planning, which relied on comprehensive quotas on imports and exports and therefore had little need for tariffs, domestic and border prices at the overvalued exchange rate were reconciled through a complex system of trade-related revenues and subsidies in the form of price differentials. Substantial revenues were derived but large subsidies were also paid out.

Since wages were directly determined, there was little need for a personal income tax. The use of this tax was essentially to apply highly discriminatory rates to those few with privately earned incomes in an attempt to equalize their incomes with the relatively low wages in the public sector. The former could be subject to a top marginal rate of 85 percent, compared with a top marginal rate of 14 percent on wages. In contrast to the personal income tax, social security contributions paid by employers have been sizable, amounting to some 30 percent of total remuneration since the early 1980s.

Administrative Structures

With private sector activities virtually curtailed and the state enterprise the dominant mode of organization, some 98 percent of taxes was (and still is) collected through the state enterprises as the primary collection points. Broadly, this amounted to one part of government collecting tax from another, with the amounts to be collected determined as an outcome of the central planning exercise. The administrative requirements were therefore simple. Because the number of monolithic state enterprises was relatively small, periodic field audits of all enterprises easily ensured compliance. There was no functional organization of the revenue collecting department, which was instead organized on sectoral lines, with tax officers specializing in the activities of their assigned sectors and being responsible for all aspects of revenue collection and payments of subsidies. Revenue control was reinforced by giving the monolithic banking system the power to transfer periodically revenues from enterprises to the budget by adjusting their bank accounts.

In practice, there was no sharp distinction between taxes and subsidies. The payment of the latter was undertaken by the same department entrusted with revenue collection and could in fact be viewed as a negative tax. This department—the State Financial and Tax Department—was also responsible for auditing government accounts. Some devolution of authority to the municipalities was provided, whereby they received the profit and turnover taxes collected from the municipal state enterprises and all of the taxes levied on physical (private) persons.

Initial Reform Steps

Budgetary Difficulties of 1990

The decision to move toward a market-oriented economy from early 1990 was accompanied by a sharp deterioration in the budgetary situation. The original state budget approved by parliament in March envisaged only a small deterioration of the overall deficit of the general government to 2.7 percent of GDP, largely on account of higher interest payments as a result of a devaluation of the exchange rate, while the primary surplus was expected to improve to 2.6 percent of GDP (despite higher social security outlays in connection with a hike in minimum pensions). Revenue was to play a critical role in achieving this objective and was projected to rise to about 61 percent of GDP.

In the event, the revenue target proved overly ambitious, and tax revenue fell short of the budget target by 8 percentage points of GDP, largely on account of deteriorating profit taxes. This reflected the impact of a sharp decline in economic activity (by an estimated 12 percent), and excessive growth in real wages.

Expenditures were subjected to upward pressures, partly because of the adverse consequences of piecemeal liberalization, which had the effect of making explicit previously implicit subsidies, particularly with respect to the overvalued exchange rate and the low fixed nominal interest rate. Accordingly, total expenditure reached 66 percent of GDP, or some 3 percentage points higher than the budget target. Expenditure overruns in social security payments arose from a de facto indexation and an agreement by the Government to reduce further the effective retirement age for certain occupations, which increased pensions. An overrun occurred in subsidies, which reached 15 percent of GDP, on account of unprofitable production as output prices were not adjusted in line with factor costs. The composition of subsidies also shifted, from agricultural producers to consumers of food products as agricultural purchase prices were raised without similar adjustments in retail prices. Most important, interest obligations reached 9 percent of GDP on a due basis, compared with the original budget estimate of 5 percent as a consequence of the depreciation of the market exchange rate used to value (and effect part of) these obligations.

As a result, the overall deficit of the general government reached 12.6 percent of GDP in 1990 instead of the budgetary target of 2.7 percent. A part of the financing needs was met by the moratorium on most external debt payments, but domestic financing still amounted to 10 percent of GDP. In an attempt to contain monetary expansion, the Government floated securities to the nonbank public in late 1990, essentially state enterprises with surplus liquidity, carrying an effective interest rate of almost 45 percent. As a consequence, bank financing was reduced to about 6 percent of GDP, and was entirely responsible for the 7 percent (in terms of leva) broad money growth during the year (higher than nominal GDP growth).

Developments in 1991

Fiscal Program

Early in 1991, a coalition Government launched a comprehensive reform program aimed at rapidly transforming the Bulgarian economy along market lines. The key immediate elements of the program were comprehensive price liberalization, unification of the exchange rate—

which would be determined on an interbank market—and sharp increases of domestic interest rates in line with market conditions. A few prices were to remain administratively determined but only for a transitional period. These prices were mainly in the energy sector, and were increased by threefold to as much as tenfold in some cases. Incomes policy was to be tightened substantially to generate a decline in measured real wages of about 30 percent, in part to offset a similar decline in terms of trade. (However, the actual decline in real wages would be less, because the widespread shortages in 1990 at the official retail prices, now removed, overstated real wage levels.) These measures had significant effects on the 1991 budget.

Fiscal policy was intended to be supportive of the stabilization and restructuring program. Both to contain inflationary expectations that were bound to accompany the large once-and-for-all increase in the retail price index (projected to be nearly 300 percent) and to channel new foreign financing expected from the Group of Twenty-Four and the World Bank directly to the enterprise sector—especially the emerging private business sector—the 1991 general government budget aimed at a balance on a cash basis (after external rescheduling). This was to be consistent with a domestic surplus of 1.8 percent of GDP,[3] compared with a deficit of 3.9 percent of GDP reached in 1990, while the overall deficit (on a due basis as regards external interest payment) would be limited to 3.5 percent of GDP.

Price reforms were expected to affect both the revenue and expenditure sides of the budget. First, the elimination of receipts from price and exchange rate differentials and other ad hoc transfers from enterprises was projected to reduce nontax revenue by almost 10 percentage points of GDP. Second, tax revenue was expected to decline by 6 percentage points of GDP,[4] largely on account of (1) a tight wages and incomes policy and higher unemployment that would shrink the base for the income tax and social security contributions; and (2) the specific nature of excises on petroleum, which were not increased with inflation, essentially because of already large increases in the wholesale prices since mid-1990. In addition, a reform of the income tax toward greater equality of treatment for all sources of income was expected to lower revenue. However, despite a lowering of the effective overall profit tax rate on state enterprises from 67 percent to 52 percent as part of the ongoing reform of the tax system, profit tax receipts were expected to remain stable in terms of GDP at about their reduced level of 1990. This was to result entirely from the projected decline in real wages, which was expected to favor profits, and from measures taken to limit depreciation allowances and interest

[3]On excluding external interest due, which is a better indicator of fiscal policy stance as it is more directly correlated with domestic aggregate demand.
[4]Based on an earlier estimate of 1990 GDP.

deductibility. The latter were viewed as critical to maintaining the base of the profit tax under transitional high levels of inflation.[5]

Turnover tax receipts were projected to rise as a result of streamlining tax rates and broadening of the base. As indicated earlier, the turnover tax was to be applied first at the ex factory level, and subsequently on the trade margins at the wholesale and retail levels.

More than half of the budgeted 25 percentage points of GDP reduction in general government expenditure was to reflect the sharp reduction in subsidies made possible by the price reform and liberalization, from 16 percent to 3 percent of GDP. The remaining subsidies would include small amounts for heating and electricity, and transfers to certain enterprises in agriculture and industry to cover operating losses. The budget also provided for most other expenditure categories to decline, especially maintenance and operating outlays in nonessential areas.

In formulating fiscal policy, account was taken of the need to redirect social benefits, noting the implications for self-sufficiency of higher income differentials, and to provide for unemployment and welfare benefits for those (temporarily or permanently) affected by the transition to a market economy. Social outlays were expected to show a significant increase, owing to rising unemployment, the specific welfare problems associated with changes in relative prices, and the impact of the removal of consumer subsidies on the purchasing power of pensions. However, it was not thought possible to change rapidly the "universal" feature of many social benefits in the short run; this is of course necessary for realizing the expenditure savings that should accompany better targeting. Hence, in 1991, social security outlays were projected to be above 13 percent of GDP.

Outcome

The macroeconomic program pursued from early 1991 had two immediate and noteworthy effects. First, massive "once-and-for-all" price increases were effected without creating underlying inflationary pressure (indeed, the retail price index hardly increased at all during April–May). Second, the interbank exchange rate stabilized rapidly, although at a much more depreciated exchange rate than initially targeted (which necessitated a second round of price increases in June–July), with some

---

[5]Projections on profit tax receipts took into account the expected negative impact on the base of both the deterioration in the terms of the trade and of systemic changes related to the move to a market-oriented economy. The latter included (1) replacing consumer subsidies by higher prices that would not affect enterprises' receipts (but increase GDP at market prices), and eliminating subsidies on inputs that would reduce accounting profits; and (2) the fact that real labor costs faced by the enterprises could decrease by less than the real wages of population because of the need to compensate for the removal of consumer subsidies by higher nominal wages. Higher interest rates were also expected to increase sharply profit tax receipts from banks.

partial reversal of the overshooting thereafter. Both these occurrences point to a successful early stabilization phase with regard to abating monetary pressures on price increases. However, inflation still averaged some 4 percent a month for the remainder of the year. Domestic demand—in particular household consumption—declined much more than anticipated and was not offset by the projected higher exports, which collapsed with the dismantling of the CMEA arrangements, while encountering difficulties in penetrating markets in the hard currency area. As a result, economic activity as measured by the GDP declined by an estimated 23 percent for 1991 as a whole, or substantially more than anticipated. However, unemployment rose by considerably less, to some 10 percent of the labor force or about 400,000 workers by year's end, indicating substantial labor hoarding and declines in productivity. Most of the deterioration occurred in the first half of 1991.

The larger-than-projected decline in household consumption in early 1991 resulted from (1) wage increases by enterprises that were well within the ceilings set under the program's incomes policy, leading to a decline in real wages of some 50 percent; and (2) an overshooting of prices that were freed, owing to the exercise of monopoly power by firms at the outset of the price reform, which further lowered real wages and depressed demand (the jump in the retail price index in the first three months of 1991 was substantially larger than expected—280 percent instead of 240 percent (at the end of the period)). Surprisingly, there was hardly any spending response from households to the large increase in their interest incomes. Indeed, despite mortgage interest rates being lower than deposit interest rates, households to a significant extent repaid loans, further reducing real monetary assets on hand and depressing consumption demand. Nominal wage increases exceeded inflation in the fourth quarter of 1991 and contributed to a recovery of real wages, which by the end of the year reached about 70 percent of their level of 1990. It appears, however, that this recovery was largely at the cost of rekindling inflation.

Broadly, the high interest rate policy appears to have had a much stronger contractionary effect than anticipated. The demand for new credit—to come from state enterprises restructuring and from new private sector businesses—was depressed, while other highly indebted state enterprises in difficulty attempted to capitalize the much higher interest due on their old debt. At the same time, they found the squeeze on liquidity made it difficult to secure new credits as long as they were not servicing their old loans. Such reluctance of banks—supported by regulatory and prudential measures imposed by the central bank—may have been quite rational since the restructuring of prices—in particular, of energy and other imported inputs—is likely to have made a large part of existing industries nonviable.

The macroeconomic developments in the first half of 1991 dramatically reduced government revenue. The bases of the two key revenue sources, the turnover tax and the profit tax, essentially collapsed, the first because of a decline in retail turnover by an estimated 70 percent, and the second because of the negative impact of demand-induced lower capacity utilization, in addition to terms of trade deterioration and higher costs of non-labor inputs. Furthermore, the general liquidity squeeze and the uncertainty surrounding the massive realignment of prices and their effect on taxable profits made tax assessment and collection that much more difficult in an environment used to centrally planned tax liabilities and limited scope and incentives for noncompliance. Developments regarding the wage bill also contributed to shortfalls in social security contributions, while commitments on entitlements had to be met. In comparison with the original budget's target, the revenue shortfall in the first half of 1991 reached about 30 percent in real terms. However, the situation improved in the second half, which allowed the partial unwinding of noninterest budgetary arrears.

Two other institutional reforms have contributed additional pressures and uncertainty on the Government's ability to collect revenue. The first is the introduction on April 1, 1991 of the new accounting system, which, as noted earlier, lowers the profit base while giving greater freedom to enterprises in determining depreciation expenses. To contain the immediate erosion in revenue, authorities have responded with the transitional measure of limiting interest deductibility for state-owned firms. In addition, because of its emphasis on prudential rules, the accounting law treats asymmetrically unrealized short-term capital losses and gains, with the latter not being treated as current revenue and thus not taxable.

The second change affecting revenue collection is the breaking up of the monolithic banking system and highly integrated system of firms into independent commercial banks and enterprises. This process affects in particular the tax payment system. While essential for developing the financial sector and the economy, it has loosened the control of the tax administration, as a growing number of state enterprises have different accounts in a growing number of banks. In any event, it is likely that profit-motivated banks will increasingly demand remuneration for operating tax-withholding services on behalf of the Government.

The breaking up of firms into many enterprises, and in particular the multiplication of wholesale and retail outfits as distinct from factory outlets, together with price liberalization, have led to a massive increase in the burden on tax administration. It is virtually impossible for the limited tax administration capabilities that were inherited to collect the turnover tax on trade margins at the wholesale and retail level, as was intended by the new turnover tax law. This has contributed to the revenue shortfall and points to the nature of the tax administration improvements that will have to be realized before the value-added tax (VAT) can be successfully introduced. The authorities, who plan to introduce the VAT in 1993, are in the process of strengthening their tax administration personnel, through both recruiting and training on a crash basis.

For reasons mentioned earlier, systemic changes in Bulgaria are bound to reduce considerably receipts from the profits tax on state enterprises. While there are signs of an emerging private business sector, this has been largely autonomous and the sector has escaped the tax net. Progress in privatization has been very slow so that state enterprises will remain the principal sector for taxation for some time to come. The authorities are fully aware that in addition to broad-based taxation of consumption, taxation of incomes of physical and juridical private persons will need to gain importance. Indeed, it is from this source that incremental revenues are most likely to be obtained through broadening of the base even if rates are cut.[6] But as noted above, the required administrative capabilities remain to be developed.

The authorities reacted to the revenue shortfall in the first half of 1991 by cuts in expenditure, other than entitlements, and by delaying payments. This meant further declines in real terms for maintenance and operating outlays, defense and security, and capital expenditure. However, on an accrual basis, subsidies were somewhat above targets, largely because of the needs of the electricity and petroleum sectors, whose domestic prices reflected until May a less depreciated exchange rate than that prevailing early in the year. Social security outlays—including unemployment compensation—were protected and remained at the fairly high level of 13 percent of GDP. The resulting shift to a more expansionary fiscal policy stance appeared justified in view of recessionary tendencies that had developed in the economy. However, the authorities managed to keep the growth of expenditures below that of revenues in the second half of 1991, which enabled the domestic deficit to be contained to 3.3 percent of GDP, compared with the original target of a surplus of 1.8 percent of GDP.

The growing imbalance between maintaining the universality of social benefits as currently provided and the capacity to mobilize revenue to finance them has become a major structural problem on the expenditure side of the budget. It is a factor crowding out outlays on government economic services needed for the restructuring of state enterprises and for effecting the privatization program, and no allocations have so far been made for these purposes in the budget.

Another dramatic budgetary implication of the reform program in Bulgaria relates to the move to market-oriented interest and exchange rates. This has resulted in an official depreciation of the lev from 3 leva per U.S. dollar to about 20 leva per U.S. dollar, and a tenfold increase in domestic interest rates to some 50 percent in 1991, which has put considerable pressure on budget outlays.

---

[6]Income tax receipts represent less than 4 percent of GDP in Bulgaria, compared with about twice that level on average in the European Community (EC).

Under central planning, it was not customary to tie servicing of debt liabilities to the end borrower, in part because the state owned both the enterprises and the banks. This was particularly evident in the case of external financing, for which the entire, sizable, external debt of Bulgaria (about US$11 billion) was contracted by the Foreign Trade Bank on behalf of the state, but which remained on the books of that bank. Only limited amounts were actually on-lent to the state budget (to pay for some capital expenditure), the borrowing being largely used to finance enterprise imports of material and equipment. Most enterprises paid cash for the foreign exchange, or borrowed leva at a low interest rate with no foreign exchange risk. In consequence, the Foreign Trade Bank found itself with large net foreign liabilities on which it paid international interest rates, while it earned very little on domestic assets, thereby progressively going into debt. This situation forced the state budget to take over the interest payments falling due. The recent large devaluations of the lev made it more difficult for the enterprises to service their debt and further weakened the balance sheet of the Foreign Trade Bank. As a result, the full amount of the quasi-fiscal deficit had to be transferred to the state budget. The latter encountered a huge increase in its external interest payments (in leva), from the equivalent of 3 percent of GDP in 1989 to an estimated 18 percent of GDP in 1991. Bulgaria's declaration of a moratorium on its external debt servicing does not alter the fact that devaluation has made more transparent the eventual resource needs of the budget if inflationary financing is to be avoided.

Higher domestic interest rates have sharply increased the domestic interest payments of the budget. They have also dramatically increased the cost of house financing for the population and of circulating and investment capital for the enterprises. Given the extremely high level of indebtedness of enterprises, market-oriented interest rates have resulted in massive losses, creating severe liquidity problems, while showing how nonprofitable many past activities were. As a result, the loan portfolio of banks has become increasingly nonperforming and resources will have to be found to prevent the inflationary financing of resulting losses and to recapitalize the banks. The pressure of these various demands on the budget will be felt, especially when the planned substitution of government bonds for nonperforming loans takes place, which will have significant net costs for the budget.

Legislative Goals in Taxation

A noteworthy feature of the fiscal reform was the work initiated in mid-1990 to rewrite the tax laws. This formed part of broader legislative initiatives, which included a new accounting law and a privatization law, to meet the requirements of a market-oriented economy.

Regarding direct taxation, the draft new law proposed:

(1) A lower corporate, flat rate, profits tax of 40 percent in lieu of the variable rates amounting to an average effective rate of 67 percent in 1990 and earlier. The new profits tax would apply to all juridical persons, whether state owned or private; multiple past exemptions and special privileges are to be eliminated, although lower rates will apply to agriculture and joint ventures. The base for taxable profits would also be determined under the new accounting law, modeled after Western European standards. A main difference with the socialist accounting practices applied earlier was that certain payments made out of after-tax "balance sheet" profits under the old rules would become expenses before profits under the new rules, in particular interest payments, overhaul and repairs expenditure, management salaries and workers' bonuses, insurances, and a number of research and social outlays.[7]

(2) Uniformity in the taxation of individual incomes, whether resulting from labor, professionals' and artists' activities, or business activities of physical persons. The proposed taxation eliminates the punitive taxation of nonlabor incomes, for which marginal rates quickly reached 85 percent. Interestingly, taxation of interest and dividend incomes would be introduced (the proposal is for final withholding of 20 percent), which under the existing regime are tax exempt, a feature that was earlier justified by the extraordinarily low (and administratively set) remuneration of capital and savings. The draft individual income tax law envisages marginal tax rates starting at 20 percent for incomes above the minimum wage, rising to a maximum marginal tax rate of 40 percent.

By the beginning of 1992, the above draft laws had still not been approved by parliament. However, a series of amendments to existing laws were passed as a transitional measure that largely affected the main provisions of the draft profits and income tax laws; in addition, the new accounting law became effective from April 1, 1991. Indicative of the confusion that can surround the move to a market economy, these amendments also introduced a number of tax incentives for private physical persons, such as full deductibility of investment expenses and loan amortizations, in addition to the deductibility of interest, a combination that has probably never been seen in most capitalist countries. While such excesses are to be repealed under the proposed law, they may have encouraged purely speculative activities.

In the area of indirect taxation, the Bulgarian authorities indicated from the outset their intention to replace the turnover tax with a modern VAT system similar to that in EC countries, but with strong preference for a single-rated VAT. During the transition, the turnover tax has been rapidly revamped, particularly to take account of price liberalization, since the turnover tax could no longer be defined as the difference

---

[7]It is estimated that the effect of the new accounting rules, had they been applied in 1990, would have been to reduce taxable profits by some 30-40 percent.

between administratively set retail and wholesale prices, and the emphasis on the turnover tax as a main instrument to mobilize revenue under price and trade liberalization rather than to regulate demand and supply as under central planning. The turnover tax law was amended at the beginning of 1991, also to pave the way for the introduction of the VAT in 1993. Under the new turnover tax, rates of 0, 10, and 22 percent apply on final consumption goods and services, with the lower rates applicable to necessities. In theory, the base of the turnover tax was the retail prices (inclusive of the tax), although the law provides for it to be levied at different stages: first at the ex factory level, and second at the wholesale and retail levels, where it would be based on the trade margins. This provision seems to have anticipated difficulties in effectively administering the tax at the trade level in the context of newly liberalized price and trading practices, with a tax administration still only geared to taxing a few integrated large-scale state enterprises.

Interestingly, trade taxation has received only limited attention, although most quantitative restrictions have been removed and certain revenues have been eliminated from import price differences following price and trade liberalization. Most import duties have remained low (between 0 percent and 30 percent) on imports from industrial countries, while higher tariffs apply to certain luxury items such as imported alcoholic beverages and tobacco. Imports from former CMEA trading partners have continued to enjoy de facto duty-free status.

A draft law on tax administration has been prepared that will permit a revamping of the tax administration and provide it with the powers needed to enforce effectively a market-based tax system. The draft law proposes a much-needed centralization of the tax administration, whose functions were formerly distributed among several different agencies. Specific responsibilities and obligations are set up for taxpayers and the tax administration. These include powers that were formerly not needed, such as those allowing the tax administration to inspect business premises and books of account, as well as to ask for tax returns and, if necessary, to require taxpayers to come to the tax administration office with needed documentary evidence. Without such enabling legislation, the assessment of tax and its collection would remain a matter of voluntary compliance.

Conclusion

Bulgaria has initiated several important steps to bring about the profound transformation to a market-based economic system. A major beginning has been made in revising the laws to give legal expression to key market institutions, such as property ownership rights and the rendering of accounts in a manner that facilitates market transactions. A beginning has also been made in changing the institutions so as to give proper vent to these laws. Such actions are essential for price liberalization and market orientation to work well so as to secure the benefits of greater economic efficiency that are now being sought, which requires decentralization in decision making, preferably in the context of widespread private ownership and competitive modes of organization, in place of centralized command and control.

A corresponding sea change is needed in the public finances. Instead of providing the bulk of the needs of the population, the role of the government will have to be greatly reduced and the extent of state ownership of assets curtailed, so that government confines itself more to functions that are supportive of the private sector rather than discharging these functions itself. The resources to finance these limited activities will have to be raised with the consent of the population and in a manner that does least damage to economic efficiency, while the reduced outlays are more carefully related to their purposes, which will also have to be acceptable to the taxpayers. Many reforms are required of the various public finance components to bring about the needed overhaul, and some initial steps have been taken. The tax system is to be changed in the direction of a nondiscriminatory set of rules so as to provide a level playing field, dependent on lower marginal rates of tax that apply to a reasonably broad base. However, much of the proposed legislation has still not been enacted and in the meantime transitional rules are being applied, some of which are discriminatory and not consistent with the objective of raising revenue. An overhaul of the tax administration is needed urgently to ensure that state-owned enterprises pay their share to the budget, despite full decentralization of their activities, and that the newly emergent private sector is taxed effectively. The present state of confusion over tax laws in the minds of taxpayers, together with a highly deficient tax administration, can only lead to erosion in the revenue base.

On the administrative side, several comprehensive institutional restructurings are necessary, with the appropriate enabling legislation. Freeing private enterprise and promoting privatization will result in an explosion of private entities registering. It will no longer be practicable to audit each entity frequently and comprehensively; instead, a system of self-assessment will have to be encouraged. The size of the tax administration will have to be increased sharply, and officers with a different set of skills will have to be trained. Further, new procedures and functional specializations will have to be developed, while certain functions, such as disbursing subsidies and audit activities, will have to be assigned to other agencies set up for these purposes.

Price liberalization with full pass-through is eliminating one source of subsidies but it is making explicit those that were hidden because of below-market interest rates or foreign exchange rates. The macroeconomic reforms are also exposing the nonviability of several lines of activity, causing increased unemployment, which is unfortunately being further affected by the general contraction in demand aggravated by the collapse in demand from traditional export channels and a severe deterioration in the terms of trade. This is exerting pressure for increases in social welfare outlays. At the same time, greater outlays are also needed for infrastructural reforms to facilitate a more vibrant private sector.

The public sector compensation policy has to be reformed to internalize into the wage structure many of the benefits that were provided through generalized subsidies. But this will erode some of the savings from price liberalization. Above all, ensuring the efficient functioning of the new administrative structures will require adequate attention to incentives and the conditions of service of their staff. This will need to be combined with the elimination of overmanning so as to contain costs.

More effective systems of budgeting and targeting outlays are needed, with much greater reliance on contracts to ensure performance, than the past practice of direct orders. However, the appropriate budgeting procedures remain to be developed. A critical requirement is to have an accurate overview of the evolving budget, which will now be affected by variables such as interest rates and the exchange rate that are free to move and are beyond the direct control of the authorities. A flexible framework for estimating the changes in the budget and responding in time is needed that would be operated by a properly constituted macroeconomic policy and analysis unit in the Ministry of Finance.

As the account in this chapter demonstrates, a great deal remains to be done before the budget can become a satisfactory instrument of policy in a market context. The budgetary reforms required are difficult even in the best of circumstances, but in Bulgaria have to be undertaken while the budget itself is adversely affected by the macroeconomic reforms and the exogenous shocks. This greatly limits the tasks that the budget can accomplish in the short term. For the immediate future, the emphasis will have to be on stabilizing the economy, while meeting social safety net requirements that are urgently needed to maintain the consensus behind the reforms.

CHAPTER 3

The Czech and Slovak Federal Republic: Government Finances in a Period of Transition

Jim Prust

This chapter discusses the ongoing transformation of public finances in the Czech and Slovak Federal Republic. It starts with a survey of the constitutional crisis created by pressures for secession from the federal state for the country's constituent Czech and Slovak Republics. This is followed by a brief overview of the state of the Czechoslovak economy in the late 1980s and of developments since the "Velvet Revolution" of December 1989, then by a summary description of the structure of the public finances, and finally by a discussion of some of the main issues now facing fiscal policymakers. These issues include macroeconomic stabilization, tax reform, subsidy reduction, and price reform, as well as concerns raised by the ongoing, and related, processes of privatization and restructuring of bank balance sheets.

Constitutional Issues

When the communist regime was overthrown in December 1989, the preservation of the federal state encompassing the Czech and Slovak Republics did not appear to be seriously in question. Although demands for greater autonomy for the republics, and especially for the Slovak Republic, were openly voiced from the outset of the reform process, it was generally assumed that the two republics would both continue to adhere to the federal state.

Apart from historical and cultural factors, the appeal for autonomy (and later for secession) in the Slovak Republic was nurtured by distinctive features in the structure of its economy and in its performance during the reform period from 1990. Heavy industry, including an important arms

This paper was mainly written in the first half of 1992 and takes no account of developments since that time and, in particular, of the dissolution of the Czech and Slovak Federal Republic on December 31, 1992 into the Czech Republic and the Slovak Republic. At the time of writing, Jim Prust was an Advisor in the Fiscal Affairs Department. The author gratefully acknowledges the helpful suggestions and factual corrections provided by Tessa van der Willigen, who, however, is not responsible for any errors that may remain.

producing sector, has been dominant, relying mainly on intra-CMEA[1] trade for its markets and for the supply of relatively cheap raw materials. Consequently, it was hard hit by the collapse of the CMEA and a decline in the arms trade. The period of economic reform thus coincided with a steeper decline in activity and rise in unemployment in the Slovak Republic than in the Czech Republic. These factors have underpinned a widespread attachment in the Slovak Republic to preservation—or at most very cautious reform—of the state-owned industrial sector. In the Czech Republic, by contrast, support for rapid reform of the state sector is stronger, as evidenced by the results of the election in June 1992.

It is conceivable that independence for the two republics would, in the first instance, accelerate the pace of reform in the Czech Republic, while having the opposite effect in the Slovak Republic. However, the outlook is highly uncertain. Any attempt to anticipate future events can only be speculative. Thus, vital though they are to the country's future, constitutional issues and their implications are not discussed further below.

The Czechoslovak Economy in the Late 1980s

The intensity of macroeconomic imbalances with which post-communist policymakers in the Czech and Slovak Federal Republic have had to contend has been considerably less than elsewhere in Central and Eastern Europe. During the years of communist rule, the extent to which macroeconomic imbalances—as evidenced, for instance, by external debt-servicing difficulties and by open or repressed inflation—were allowed to emerge was considerably less than in many other economies in the region. Against this background, the post-communist governments have been able to proceed rather fast with the liberalization of prices and external trade and with the concomitant changes in the tax and subsidy regimes, while avoiding excessive inflation or balance of payments problems.

Prior to World War II, Czechoslovakia was an advanced industrial country with income levels comparable to those then prevailing in Western Europe. Although this favorable heritage eroded over time, it was not completely obliterated during the years of communist rule. Partly as a result of prewar traditions, as well as because of disenchantment with the quality of manufactured imports from other CMEA countries, Czechoslovakia produced an extremely wide range of manufactures. On the eve of the dramatic changes of 1989, its economic situation compared favorably with that of other Eastern European economies. Based on current commercial exchange rates, per capita income in 1988 was estimated at the equivalent of US$3,300, high by Eastern European standards; estimates based on purchasing power comparisons are substantially higher.

---

[1]The former Council for Mutual Economic Assistance. Its members included, among others, the former Soviet Union and the planned economies of Central and Eastern Europe.

Czechoslovakia weathered the problems of the 1980s relatively well. External debt was low to start with, and the authorities pursued a cautious policy with respect to foreign borrowing; the debt-to-export ratio in convertible currencies, which reached a peak at just under 120 percent in 1980, was far lower than in neighboring Hungary and Poland. Modest external financing pressures in the early 1980s necessitated a temporary curtailment of domestic expenditure. Thereafter, however, moderate growth in output and consumption was resumed during the remainder of the decade. Officially recorded prices were virtually stable, and there were no external financing problems.

Although monetary aggregates increased faster than nominal output, most commentators, supported by anecdotal evidence, are of the view that problems of repressed inflation and shortage were far less acute in Czechoslovakia than in many other countries of the region. The general perception—although hard to corroborate unequivocally—is that this relatively fortunate state of affairs was partly attributable to the greater importance attached to financial developments by the central planners in Czechoslovakia than in most other planned economies.

In sum, the change of regime in Czechoslovakia in 1989 was not preceded by any dramatic economic crisis. The weakness in economic performance was primarily a secular one, which the—in some ways—favorable performance of the economy in the 1980s had done little to address. In fact, the upward trend in consumption that had been maintained during the decade had only been possible at the cost of a falling share of resources being devoted to investment. Gross investment in real terms in 1989 was only slightly higher than in 1980. Meanwhile, net investment was lower by almost one half because of rising provisions for capital depreciation. The result was a growing obsolescence of the country's capital stock and an increasingly poor performance of manufactured exports in world markets.

The communist regime recognized, albeit belatedly and only after the adoption of perestroika in the U.S.S.R., that the country's economic strength was eroding progressively. In December 1987, the Communist Party adopted a reform plan to be introduced in stages. A number of the envisaged measures were implemented in 1988–89. These included a simplification of the administrative hierarchy overseeing industry and agriculture and the breakup of a number of large enterprises into smaller units; a considerable reduction in the degree of detail incorporated in plan directives; increased scope for activity by cooperatives; a weakening of the state monopoly on foreign trade; adoption of a new joint venture law allowing foreign majority participation and profit repatriation; and preparations for the establishment of a two-tier banking system to replace the existing monobank system. A foreign exchange retention scheme for exporters and a foreign exchange auction were introduced, although the latter operated only on a very small scale. As a first step in price reform, wholesale prices were restructured to reflect the requirement of a uniform rate of return on capital, and a reduction in the incidence of price controls was planned.

The initiatives of the post-communist government had thus, in some respects, been anticipated. The program of economic reform and the associated legislation adopted in 1990 were, however, qualitatively different from their immediate antecedents. "Reform within the system" was abandoned as an objective and the new point of departure was the desirability of a massive reduction in the role of the state in economic life and of a correspondingly drastic increase in the importance of private activity.

As in Poland and Hungary, the architects of the current economic reform in the Czech and Slovak Federal Republic had earlier relevant experience on which to draw, notably from the "Prague Spring" period of 1968 and the buildup to it. At that time, considerable thought was given, and some concrete progress achieved, in decentralizing economic structures. In fact, the reform plans formulated in the late 1980s had many similarities to what had been attempted twenty years earlier. Although the reformists' experimentation was stopped in its tracks by the Soviet invasion of August 1968, the experience gained at that time is likely to have left some intellectual legacy in the form of a relatively high level of awareness on the part of policymakers and officials of the issues to be faced. However, as noted above, the boldness of the reform plans adopted in 1990 had no parallel in earlier experience.

In the first six months after the installation of the post-communist government, the authorities were largely preoccupied with the preparation and passage of a large body of reform legislation. Its essential aim was to remove restrictions on private economic activity, to encourage foreign investment and foreign trade, and to pave the way for the denationalization of state enterprises.

Although certain basic objectives were generally supported, views diverged on the appropriate pace of change and on the details of particular measures. These were discussed within the Government in the first half of 1990. In May, a resolution dealing comprehensively with a range of economic reform issues was adopted by the interim Government and subsequently endorsed by the Government that assumed office after elections in June. The resolution called for, inter alia, the rapid liberalization of prices and external trade and major changes in the exchange system and depreciation of the exchange rate as parts of the macroeconomic context in which the transformation to a market economy was to take place. The potential inflationary impact of these measures was to be contained by restrictive monetary and fiscal policies.

In their broad thrust, policies have subsequently remained faithful to these early guidelines. Fiscal policy, which has been supported by a tight monetary policy, has so far successfully prevented the emergence of large budget deficits and, consistent with the objective of reducing the economic role of the state, both revenues and expenditures have fallen in real terms. In particular, price subsidies have been sharply reduced, which has led to a drop in real incomes. The authorities aim to prevent the emergence of a major imbalance in the fiscal position. A continuing curtailment of expenditure will be needed to achieve this objective until the declining trend in output, and thus in the tax base, is reversed.

Fiscal System

As in other planned economies, general government revenues and expenditures have been relatively large. Both expanded in the second half of the 1980s, and in 1989 accounted for about 70 percent of GDP.

Relations Between Levels of Government

The main components of general government are Central Government, which includes the budgets of the Federal Government and of the Czech and Slovak Republics, and local authorities operating at the regional, district, and local levels. In 1989, the last full year before the revolution, the Central Government accounted for 60 percent of general government outlays and the local authorities for just over one fourth. Central Government's share in general government revenues was higher (more than 70 percent) and that of local authorities lower (about 18 percent). Operations by the small number of extrabudgetary funds have been minimal. Of greater importance until their virtual elimination in 1990 were the so-called Funds of the Ministries, controlled by certain ministries and largely used for cross-subsidization of enterprises.

Excluding intragovernmental transfers, in 1989 the Federal Government and the Czech Republic accounted for 45 percent and 34 percent of central government budget expenditure, respectively, while the direct expenditures of the Slovak Republic accounted for just over 20 percent of the total. The pattern of revenue collection was markedly different. The Federal Government accounted for two thirds of central government receipts, while the Czech Republic contributed 21 percent of the total and the Slovak Republic the remaining 10 percent. These disparate shares of different components of government in revenue and expenditure, respectively, were made possible by substantial transfers of funds from the Federal Government to the republics. In 1989, such transfers were equivalent to two thirds of the total direct expenditure of the Czech Republic and over three fourths of that of the Slovak Republic. In addition to their direct expenditures, the republics were responsible for transfers to various local government units in their territories, and to the extrabudgetary funds.

Arrangements for the allocation of revenue and expenditure responsibilities have been modified over time. Prior to 1986, each level of government received the income taxes paid by the enterprises and labor force under its jurisdiction. The Federal Government was responsible for "strategic" industries, such as energy, metallurgy, railroads, and communications. The republics managed other industries, while services and small businesses reported to local authorities. The proceeds of the turnover tax and foreign trade levies accrued to the Federal Government. Some changes to these arrangements were made in 1986. Wage tax revenues previously accruing to the republics were diverted to local authorities, with transfers to the latter being reduced by an equivalent amount. Further major changes took place in 1990-92 to eliminate the need for transfers to the republics from the Federal Government; some transfers were, however, reinstated in 1992 as part of an overall agreement on revenue sharing. At the time of writing, revenue from the profits tax and the turnover tax—the two main taxes—is divided among the Federal Government, which receives 35 percent of the total, and the Czech and Slovak Republics, which receive 41.5 percent and 23.5 percent of the total, respectively. At the same time, the republics have taken over some of the expenditure responsibilities hitherto assigned to the federation as well as some others from the local authorities.

Structure of Government Expenditure

Most general government expenditure (approaching 90 percent) was on current items in the late 1980s. Capital expenditure consisted mainly of transfers to enterprises. Subsidies, whose share in expenditure fell sharply in 1990 and 1991, and social transfers together constituted well over one half of total current expenditure; most of the remainder consisted of wages and salaries and expenditure on goods and services. The social security system provides benefits to retired and disabled persons and widows, child allowances, and maternity, sickness, and (since 1990) unemployment benefits. The Government's domestic debt—to the banking system—has been insignificant and interest payments correspondingly small; external debt has been carried on the books of the banks.

Revenue System

About three fourths of general government revenues have derived from taxes; in the late 1980s, enterprise profits tax and turnover tax both contributed about 25 percent of the total. The payroll tax, conceived as the employer's contribution to social security, accounted for about 10 percent of general government revenue and the wages tax for a similar share of the total. The payroll tax is paid by enterprises and the wages tax is withheld by them. The vast majority of tax receipts have thus been collected directly from the enterprises. Taxes collected from individuals and private businesses have been minimal.

The profits tax is currently collected under three different laws applying to different types of enterprise. The general rate of tax is 55 percent, compared with rates of 75–85 percent before revisions started to be made to the relevant laws in 1989. There are, however, certain exceptions to these general rules. Lower rates apply to joint ventures with at least 30 percent foreign participation (40 percent) and to agriculture and the food industry (50 percent); a special progressive rate structure applies to hotels and restaurants. The definition of profit for tax purposes is restrictive: various items, including advertising, are treated as a discretionary use of profit rather than a cost. In addition, depreciation schedules are typically very long.

Individual incomes are liable to various taxes depending on their type. The most important is the wages tax, which is a withholding tax on wages, salaries, and any other employment compensation. Exempt incomes include sickness benefits and social security payments. The tax is imposed on a monthly basis without annual adjustment and is remitted by the employer. There is no aggregation of the income of different family members; credit for dependents may only be claimed by one taxpayer with one employer. Rates are adjusted depending on taxpayers' family circumstances. For taxpayers with two dependents, a sliding scale of tax rates from 5 percent to 20 percent applies on monthly income of up to Kčs 10,000 and a flat rate applies to incomes above this level. In 1992, the latter rate was set at 33 percent and, at the same time, tax rates, at all income levels, were doubled for those receiving both a pension and a wage. These changes were made to increase the progressivity of the tax system and the targeting of (after tax) social benefits.

Two other taxes apply to individual incomes. The so-called citizens' income tax was introduced in 1990 and applies, among others, to income from trade, crafts, private agriculture, the liberal professions, and investment income from real and financial assets (but excluding interest on bank deposits). There is a progressive rate structure from 15 percent to 45 percent on net income up to just over Kčs 1 million; a 55 percent rate applies on income above that level. Another tax on income from literary and artistic activities has a rate schedule ranging from 3 percent to 33 percent on a progressive scale on income up to Kčs 50,000 annually. Thereafter, a rate of 33 percent applies.

In addition to the above, a payroll tax, which notionally finances the social security system, is applied to all wages at a rate of 50 percent (20 percent prior to 1989) for most sectors but at lower rates for some, including the expanding services sector.

The main indirect tax is the turnover tax. It is levied principally on final consumption goods; exports are exempt. Until 1991, the tax was typically levied as a proportion of the difference between the relevant wholesale and retail prices net of allowed trading margins. This has now been replaced by a system of ad valorem rates.

Property is also subject to taxation, although, partly as a result of numerous exemptions, revenues from this source have been small. An agricultural land tax is levied as varying amounts per hectare depending on terrain, soil, and climatic conditions. There is also a tax on buildings, but it does not apply to those under socialist ownership.

Current Fiscal Issues

Overall Objectives of Fiscal Policy

The salient features of Czechoslovakia's macroeconomic position on the eve of its post-communist transformation were that foreign debt was low, the balance of payments relatively strong, open inflation minimal, and repressed inflation less of a problem than in other formerly planned economies. In the late 1980s, the fiscal balance weakened somewhat. Transfers and budget-financed social consumption were on an unsustainable rising trend; the immediate effect of price restructuring was a jump in subsidies, particularly on food; and the sluggish output affected revenue. As a result, the general government's financial position was in deficit throughout the second half of the 1980s; abstracting from some once-for-all transfers, the deficit was equivalent to about 2.7 percent of GDP in 1989. Nevertheless, this situation constituted a relatively propitious point of departure compared with that of many other reforming economies. Correspondingly, the need for fiscal adjustment as measured by changes in the Government's net financial balance has been relatively small, particularly given the tight credit policies that the monetary authorities have been following.

In 1990, the authorities planned for a small central government budget surplus. Abstracting from the effects of transfers to the banking system to cover devaluation losses on net liabilities in foreign currencies and the takeover of export credits from the State Bank, this target was achieved, largely because virtually all categories of expenditure were restrained.

In 1991, the authorities planned a further surplus of just under 1 percent of GDP. Consistent with the objective of systematically reducing the role of government in the economy, budget plans called for substantial cuts in the real value of both revenues and expenditures. In the event and excluding some exceptional items, the share of general government revenues in GDP fell by almost 10 percentage points to less than 53 percent, mainly owing to reductions in the rates of profits tax and certain turnover taxes and the abolition of foreign trade levies. In addition, revenues were adversely affected by the permitted lags in the collection of citizen's income tax on private sector employees and, more generally, by the increase of the share of the less easily taxed private sector in the tax base.

There was also a cut—of about 8 percentage points to around 55 percent—in the share of general government expenditure in GDP, again excluding some items related to once-for-all stock adjustments. Subsidies were cut mo; t drastically. Even after completion of the takeover of responsibility by the budget for subsidies on low-interest loans for housing and to newly married couples, budgetary subsidies were reduced from 13 percent to 7 percent of GDP. The remaining retail subsidies were abolished in May 1991 and subsidies to agricultural producers were cut by one third. Real government consumption is estimated to have fallen by about one quarter, reflecting in part lags and restraint in adjusting government wages. Real capital expenditure and transfers fell by almost 40 percent. Social security outlays were also considerably eroded in real terms, since pensions were not fully adjusted for price rises and then only with a lag, and family benefits were not adjusted at all.

The budget balance was very strong in the first half of 1991 with the general government surplus equivalent at an annual rate to about 5 percentage points of GDP. Partly because of the initial effects of price liberalization on profits and the value of inventories, revenues were buoyant and, in addition, expenditures were particularly tightly controlled. With GDP falling, however, this situation unwound rapidly in the second half, and a general government deficit equivalent to approximately 2 percent of GDP was recorded for the year as a whole.

Containment of the fiscal deficit in 1992 and beyond will not be easy, especially as the scope for further expenditure cuts diminishes. The Czech and Slovak Federal Republic faces many of the same problems as other reforming economies in this connection. These include a falling revenue base in the contracting portions of the state enterprise sector, partly induced by the abrupt decline in trade with the former Soviet Union; administrative difficulties in immediately extending the tax net to the nascent private sector; and growing demands for certain types of expenditure, including unemployment benefits, during the period of transition. Clearly, the earlier that structural reforms lead to a reversal of the current declining trend in output, the easier will policy choices become.

As described above, the authorities have already substantially reduced the size of government revenues and expenditures in relation to that of the economy as a whole. The old system of economic management involved—to a much greater extent than in typical market economies— the provision by the state sector (including enterprises) of goods and services that were either free or heavily subsidized, such as housing, education, health care, transportation, and various cultural and recreational amenities. These items were, in effect, largely paid for by heavy taxes and other levies on the financial surplus of the enterprise sector. The corollary of these levies was that wages paid directly to the work force had to be relatively low. (Indeed, the disparity with, say, Western Europe in average wages per capita was greater than that in GDP per capita.) The advent of a market economy will require substantial modifications to these arrangements. Essentially, reduced provision of goods and services by the state through nonmarket channels will, other things being equal, permit a reduction in the relative size of government revenues. In addition, a shift of the total tax burden away from the enterprise sector to indirect taxes and personal income taxes will be needed if corporate tax rates are to be brought closer to levels typically prevailing in market economies—an important objective if foreign investment is to be attracted and domestic investors placed on a comparable basis to their foreign competitors.

Tax Reform

The authorities' ultimate aim is a full-fledged reform of the system of taxation of incomes and expenditure. In essence, a system dominated by discretionary levies by the central authorities on enterprises' financial surplus is to be replaced by one in which an arms-length relationship, governed by predetermined and legally binding rules, exists between taxpayers and the tax authorities. The introduction of such a system will, of course, require major changes in the philosophy and practice of tax administration with regard, for example, to the registration of taxpayers, the filing of returns, collection of payments, and audit procedures.

On January 1, 1993, the authorities plan, according to the provisions of legislation that have already been passed, to introduce a value-added tax (VAT), a new regime for the taxation of corporate profits corresponding in its essential features to arrangements typically applied in market economies, and a "global" income tax applying to all personal sector incomes. Also in 1993, the authorities plan to create separate social security funds; these are to be financed by wage-based contributions from both employers and employees that will replace the existing payroll tax. The implementation of these reforms will, of course, be affected by the way in which the powers of the governments of the republics evolve.

Pending implementation of a full-fledged tax reform, the authorities have been quick to recognize the need for interim changes in the tax system. This need stems both from the necessity to safeguard revenues as well as to support the liberalization of the pricing and exchange and trade systems that has already been undertaken.

The most obvious candidate for immediate modification was the turnover tax system. As described above, turnover tax rates had previously, in effect, been determined as the difference between wholesale and retail prices. Small changes in the relationship between the two prices could thus have large, and unintended, effects on tax receipts—a phenomenon that was clearly inconsistent with a regime of flexible prices. The authorities made several important changes to address these problems in late 1990. Turnover tax rates were expressed in ad valorem form, and four rates were established (0, 12, 22, and 32 percent); these rates were reduced in mid-1991 to 0, 11, 20, and 29 percent. A consumer tax (in effect an excise tax) applies at higher implicit rates—the tax is generally specific—to selected items such as alcoholic beverages, tobacco, petroleum products, and passenger cars.

Reform of the pricing and foreign trade system has also necessitated changes in the taxation (and subsidization) of foreign trade. Previously, levies (or subsidies) applied on the difference between import prices and domestic wholesale prices for selected items, including energy products, steel, and other raw materials. This system, which had already been modified in 1989, represented the remnant of an earlier system in which taxes and subsidies had been deliberately and comprehensively applied to remove the difference between domestic and international prices. The rationale of this system lay in the major differences in relative prices between Czechoslovakia (and CMEA countries generally) and the rest of the world. However, with the collapse of the CMEA system and the authorities' desire to link domestic and world prices, this rationale collapsed. The remaining taxes on international trade thus consist only of customs duties and a surcharge, imposed in 1991, of 20 percent (later reduced in two stages to 10 percent) on imports of consumer goods.

Regarding taxes on income and profits, the authorities have also inherited a regime many of whose features—in addition to the high level of tax rates—are inconsistent with their market-oriented policies. One main problem concerns the treatment of capital depreciation, which is markedly different from practices in market economies. Prior to the recently introduced changes described below, depreciation schedules—of which there were over 140—were typically much longer than in market economies. There was a simpler regime for firms with less than 100 employees for which annual rates of depreciation of 2 percent and 12 percent applied to fixed and movable assets, respectively. This provision is thus available to recently established small businesses. In a further effort to allow new businesses to avail themselves of depreciation provisions more similar to those in effect in market economies, a number of changes were introduced in 1991. Accelerated depreciation was made available to cooperatives, joint ventures with over 30 percent foreign participation, and for physical persons taxable under the profits tax law. Fifty percent of the value of movable assets may be depreciated in the first three years of their life.

Another important issue is the lack of provision for loss carryforward in existing arrangements for corporate taxation. Tax holidays are being used as a substitute. Tax holidays are granted at the discretion of the level of government (federal or republic) having jurisdiction over the relevant enterprise. Governments are empowered to grant tax holidays to newly established enterprises—whether domestic or joint ventures— for up to a maximum of two years on condition, inter alia, that savings from nonpayment of taxes be applied to investment. Of the total of

1,600 joint ventures founded in 1990, about 150 received tax holidays. Almost all applications were granted.

In addition to tax holidays granted ex ante, the authorities have considerable discretion in easing tax liabilities ex post. Again, the authority lies with the level of government having jurisdiction over the enterprise in question. In practice, though, this provision has been little used and a further similar provision in the profits tax law to allow a reduced rate of profits tax for joint ventures has not been used at all.

Subsidies and Price Reforms

Budgetary subsidies in Czechoslovakia were relatively less important than in many other planned economies and were concentrated on a narrow range of items. While prices for energy and most primary materials were low, this to a large extent arose from the peculiarities of the pricing arrangements that applied in intra-CMEA trade. Domestically generated price distortions were, by contrast, fairly limited. In fact, the structure of prices was typically revised at the beginning of each five-year plan period to take into account changes in costs. Subsidies tended to rise in the course of each quinquennium but, in connection with the next major revision of prices, would be reduced again.

In 1989, budgetary subsidies were equivalent to 16 percent of GDP (25 percent if cross subsidization through the Funds of Ministries is included), compared with 12–13 percent for several years previously; the increase resulted from the fact that cost changes were not permitted to be reflected in the prices of foodstuffs and other agricultural items. Thus, in 1989, subsidies to agricultural producers and retail subsidies on foodstuffs together accounted for about 60 percent of total budgetary subsidies. Producer subsidies were conferred through various channels, the most important of which was the subsidy to high-cost producers.[2] Consumer subsidies were mostly conferred in the form of negative turnover tax to cover the excess of wholesale prices over retail prices. In 1989, it was estimated that the negative turnover tax on foodstuffs was equivalent to almost a quarter of the value of retail sales of such items.

After food and agriculture, the next most important subsidies were for housing and construction. The most important component was subsidies on state-owned housing, rents for which did not cover costs let alone any return on the state's investment. (In 1988, the average monthly rent on state-owned apartments was equivalent to less than 5 percent of average monthly earnings in the state and cooperative sectors, and presum-

---

[2]Agricultural land was divided into 42 districts according to soil and geography. Prices for agricultural output were determined according to production costs in the 20 most productive districts. The remaining districts received a subsidy per unit of output whose rate was inversely related to productivity and which, for the highest cost producers, came close to 100 percent.

ably to an even smaller proportion of average family income.) In addition, heating for apartment buildings was subsidized and quasi-fiscal subsidies were provided through low-interest housing loans to individuals and co-operatives. Finally, relatively small subsidies were provided for transportation and, at the consumer level, on gas and coal. Electricity generation operated without budgetary subsidies, since profitable gas and nuclear power plants cross-subsidized loss-making coal-fired plants.

The first major step in reducing subsidies was made in July 1990 when retail subsidies on food were eliminated. As a result, food prices rose by about 25 percent and retail prices overall by about 7 percent. The authorities provided direct and universal income support (at a rate of Kčs 140 a person a month or the equivalent of about 5 percent of the monthly wage at that time) to the population in compensation for these price increases. (In principle, there could have been simultaneous and equal reductions in subsidies and in the taxes that financed them. In practice, things are not so simple, partly because of the—possibly major—distributional effects of rapid changes in the prices of essential items. Another consideration is that, to the extent that tax reductions benefited the enterprise sector, the authorities would have had little control over the extent to which the benefits would be passed on to the households to which they would primarily have been targeted.) In order to improve the targeting of government-supplied benefits, the general income support for the economically active population was abolished in January 1992; it was retained for children and pensioners.

Further steps to reduce subsidies were taken in 1991. Negative turnover tax on industrial and most energy products was abolished; no special compensation was given for industrial products, and the revenue effects were balanced by cuts in turnover tax rates on other items. However, for the subsidy reductions on energy items that took effect in May 1991, a modified version of the income support scheme applied in 1990 was used, with income compensation for pensioners and children only. As a result of these measures, budgetary subsidies in 1991 fell to the equivalent of about 7 percent of GDP. Of this total, the major components, each accounting for about one third, were subsidies to agricultural and foodstuff producers and subsidies for housing (including low-interest loans) and residential heating.

Privatization and Bad Debts

The restructuring of assets and liabilities in the Czechoslovak economy taking place as part of the reform process could have an important impact on the public finances. At issue are principally the effects of, first, the privatization of enterprises and, second, the restructuring of banks' and enterprises' balance sheets to deal with the problem of "bad debts." It is too early to assess accurately the likely impact of these factors.

The authorities have developed a range of methods for the privatization of enterprises. (The privatization of land is to be effected largely through restitution to original owners or their heirs, while plans for the privatization of housing have yet to be worked out.) Essentially, different schemes will apply to the privatization of small- and large-scale enterprises, respectively. In devising these arrangements, the authorities have sought to strike a balance among various considerations; these include equity—to achieve widespread share ownership; efficiency—to achieve a sufficient concentration of ownership for effective enterprise management; fiscal impact—to ensure that enterprise sales yield satisfactory amounts of revenue; and the desirability of attracting foreign investment, and associated know-how and market access, to privatized businesses. Privatization of property confiscated after 1948 will be by restitution except that, where the assets in question have been substantially modified, compensation will be paid in lieu of a return of the assets to the original owners or their heirs. Those to whom property is restituted are responsible for defending their claim, if need be in the courts, against any other claims that may be made to the same assets by other parties.

Privatization of "small" enterprises is proceeding by competitive auction. Units are sold without their liabilities, which are being taken over by the National Property Funds. These funds are also the recipients of privatization proceeds. Only citizens may participate in the first round of auctions; units that fail to sell in the first round even at 50 percent of the starting price are reoffered in a second round at which foreigners may participate. By early 1992, about 25,000 small enterprises had been sold—mostly in the first round and for prices on average about 50 percent above the starting price. Sales proceeds were about Kčs 25 billion. The number of units that have been restituted is thought to be several times higher than those privatized by auction.

The privatization of large enterprises on a significant scale started in 1992. Privatization plans were submitted by individual enterprises and other interested parties for review and final decision by the privatization ministries of the respective republics. Privatization may take place through a mixture of direct sale—to either residents or nonresidents— and of "voucher" transactions. Further, not all of a given enterprise's equity need necessarily be disposed of in the same way and some part may be retained in state ownership. Vouchers have been issued to citizens over the age of 18 against payment of a relatively small fee. Voucher holders may invest their vouchers in Investment Privatization Funds. These funds will hold a range of equities in privatized enterprises, depending on the investment strategy of the particular fund, and are being established primarily to make it possible for individuals to acquire a diversified portfolio of assets relatively easily, as well as to facilitate sufficient concentration of ownership for efficient corporate governance. Vouchers may also be used by their holders to acquire equity directly in enterprises undergoing privatization. Sales against vouchers are taking place in a series of rounds, which began in June 1992. Starting prices are based on book value and, in the first round, vouchers purchased equal amounts of book value. Assets not privatized in the first round (either because of heavy excess demand or deficient demand) will be reoffered in subsequent rounds (up to a total of five) with asking prices adjusted to reflect market response in the previous round. Not all large enterprises will be covered in the first wave of privatization and some, particularly in the heavy engineering and metallurgical sectors, will remain under full state ownership, at least for the immediate future. Of the total book value of enterprises to be covered in the first round (of about Kčs 500 billion), about 60 percent will be privatized through the voucher scheme.

Privatization operations are being kept completely separate from the budget. Clearly, though, they will have important implications for the macroeconomy and for the Government's financial position in particular, which will depend on the mix of privatization operations taking place against cash and vouchers, respectively, and on the prices realized for equity in enterprises that are sold for cash.

The authorities also need to reappraise the value of the banking system's claims on enterprises. The level of bank debt carried by an enterprise may be an accident of financial arrangements in effect during the period of central planning. As such, it may have no relation to the enterprise's current, or future, profitability—a fact that could conceivably lead, in the extreme case, to the liquidation of potentially viable units. Bad loans also pose problems for banks themselves and their ability to fulfill efficiently their role as financial intermediaries; to cover the costs of nonperforming loans, banks may be obliged to operate with higher spreads between deposit and lending rates than would otherwise be desirable.

Banks and the Government, especially the ministries of privatization, have started the process of identifying "bad loans" with a view to their being written off or restructured. (Obviously, the treatment of such loans has a vital bearing on the value of enterprises undergoing privatization.) The Government has—on an avowedly once-for-all basis—provided an injection of funds (totaling about Kčs 50 billion) to the banking system to enable it to write off loans. This transaction took the form of a take-up by the banks of bonds issued by the National Property Funds to which the proceeds of privatization will accrue; most of the bonds replaced bad loans in the portfolios of the banks.

The Government does not anticipate any further injections of funds to facilitate debt write-offs and is anxious to avoid the moral hazard problems that could arise if the state were perceived to be the de facto guarantor of all loans to enterprises. Whether the operations already undertaken will prove adequate will depend to a large extent on the scale of assets that banks are in the end obliged to write off and on the possibilities for covering the resultant losses from other sources, including current earnings.

CHAPTER 4

Hungary: A Case of Gradual Fiscal Reform

George Kopits

Among former centrally planned economies, Hungary has been at the forefront in initiating market-oriented reforms in general and overhauling fiscal institutions in particular. The reform effort began in 1968 with partial and often contradictory measures that came virtually to a halt after the first oil crisis. The effort was resumed in the late 1970s, but a comprehensive transition to a market economy was launched only at the end of the 1980s. This protracted process, spanning more than two decades, contrasts sharply with the attempt at abrupt transformation elsewhere in Central and Eastern Europe and more recently in the states of the former Soviet Union.[1] Unlike in Hungary, where both economic and political liberalization was gradual, in these countries the sudden shift from rigid adherence to central planning to commitment to establishing market-based institutions was, for the most part, accompanied by radical political change.

These developments raise a fundamental question—to which the experience of Hungary may provide insights—about the minimum conditions and maximum possible speed for creating market-based fiscal institutions. Although it may be premature to answer this question, certain factors that should facilitate the transition, including in the structure of public finances, can be readily identified. These factors include an opportunity to unify with a Western counterpart (such as the exceptional case of the former German Democratic Republic); historical experience with market-based institutions (such as prior to World War II in Central European countries, in contrast to much of the former Soviet Union); and perhaps most relevant, prolonged experimentation with reform measures (Hungary and Poland).[2]

George Kopits is Division Chief in the Fiscal Affairs Department. This chapter benefited from useful comments by László Garamfalvi, István Keményfy, János Kornai, Álmos Kovács, Mark Lutz, and Paul Marer.

[1]For a comparative assessment of fiscal reform in European economies in transition, see Kopits (1991).

[2]Nevertheless, an implication of the analysis of past economic reform movements in Kovács (1990) is that the pre-1990 experience of these two countries can offer limited lessons for the current largely unconstrained transformation attempted in Central and Eastern Europe. For earlier assessments of the reform process in Hungary, see Antal (1985) and Kornai (1986). For a recent discussion, see Boote and Somogyi (1991).

In Hungary, the reform of fiscal institutions, viewed—as it must be—in the context of overall institutional change, can be divided broadly into four periods. The first period, from the introduction of the so-called new economic mechanism in 1968 until the late 1970s, was characterized by a temporary relaxation of economic planning, followed by restoration of some degree of central allocation and control during the second half of the period—in the wake of the oil crisis and deterioration in the terms of trade. The new economic mechanism represents the first deviation from rigid central planning and the beginning of the end of subordination of fiscal policy to the plan. The concomitant partial price liberalization and limited financial self-management in state-owned enterprises (SOEs) had fiscal implications, in particular for the establishment of nominally parametric tax rates on commodities, enterprise income, assets, and wage payments. These taxes were used largely as micro-intervention tools ("regulators") for stabilization purposes.[3] Meanwhile, fiscal policy continued to play a secondary role to the plan in sectoral resource allocation, and to the controls over prices and wages in income distribution. On the whole, the virtual lack of a postwar tradition in fiscal analysis constituted—as it does at present in other economies in transition—a major handicap for embarking on a sustained and consistent market-oriented reform in this area.

The second reform period began in 1978-79 with a reorientation of economic policy from the pursuit of domestic growth to containment of the external imbalance. This strategy included resumption of price liberalization, especially through a closer alignment of domestic producer prices with world market prices and through increased SOE autonomy. In turn, the tax and subsidy systems were simplified. By 1981, the exchange rate was unified and new forms of private sector activities (notably in the form of economic associations or partnerships, operating independently or attached to SOEs) emerged. However, the further loosening of central directives, despite the continued overall supremacy of the plan,[4] was compensated by a renewed proliferation of regulatory and discretionary

---

[3]According to an authoritative interpretation of the fiscal aspects of new economic mechanism, in Bácskai (1971, pp. 107-108): "With the aid of financial (fiscal) and monetary regulators determined by the state we intend to bring about harmony between plan and market, as well as between the national economy (macro-economic) and enterprise (microeconomic) interests. Enterprise taxation—in the broad sense, including custom tariffs—is playing an outstanding part within the system of regulators. We call our system of enterprise taxation the *system of income-withdrawal*" from enterprises. Further, the two parts of income (one collected by the state and the other left with the enterprise) "may vary in their proportions by industry, and also from time to time. *The extent and the forms of income-withdrawal or income decentralisation depend on deliberations of both economic policy and economic organization.*"

[4]As late as 1982, in the foreword to the official series *Public Finance in Hungary*, the Minister of Finance observed that in Hungary "as an important tool of a planned economy, [public] finances contribute to a balanced growth of the economy, to a permanent increase of production, turnover, consumption and capital formation as well as to a gradual modernization of the economic structure." Ministry of Finance (1982a, p. 5).

fiscal intervention. On the one hand, to contain mounting demand pressures from increasingly independent enterprises operating under a soft budget constraint, regulatory tax instruments (on wages and investment) were tightened and retained earnings of profitable enterprises were made subject to confiscation. On the other hand, to promote supply, to meet trade commitments under the Council for Mutual Economic Assistance (CMEA), or simply to maintain full employment, SOEs (especially loss-making ones) were provided with selective budgetary transfers, central bank credits, and tax preferences on a highly discretionary basis.

The third period, commencing in 1985, in many respects evidenced a more consistent move toward a market economy, including the introduction of transparent, neutral, and indirect fiscal instruments—even when such an intent of specific institutional changes was not always followed in practice. The authorities sought to substitute more subtle forms of microeconomic control—in the form of voluntaristic "price clubs" and "wage clubs" for SOEs that behaved "responsibly"—for formal controls, while allowing occasional adjustments in relative prices and wages. Enactment of a two-tier banking system, a bankruptcy law, a law on enterprises, and a more open trading system, as well as increased scope for private activity (as the limit on the payroll of private enterprises was raised to 30 employees in the mid-1980s and to 500 employees at the beginning of 1989) were aimed at creating market conditions in the economy. Within this context, in 1988, Hungary was the first among former socialist countries to engage in a major tax reform, establishing a value-added tax—officially called the general turnover tax (GTT)—the personal income tax (PIT), and the enterprise profit tax (EPT). In addition, attempts were made at limiting, and accounting more transparently for, subsidies. This process was accompanied by pressures to decentralize fiscal resources and responsibilities both within and outside the state budget—including central budgetary institutions, local government budgets, and extrabudgetary funds. In 1988, market-based government financial obligations were issued for the first time and preparations began to reform the budget process.

By the end of 1989, the stage was set for the fourth (present) period, encompassing a genuine and full-fledged overhaul of the social, political, and economic framework, including fiscal institutions.[5] Unlike the reform initiatives under the former party-state regime undertaken in an institutional context that was in essence alien to markets, the transition begun by the first freely elected postwar government in mid-1990 included abolition of the monopoly state ownership of capital and full recognition of

[5]It is worth comparing, for example, the goals stated in the proposals for public sector reform submitted to parliament, of creating a "socialist market economy," in Ministry of Finance (1988, p. 3), with those of establishing "democracy and market economy," in Ministry of Finance (1989, p. 4).

the need to deal explicitly with poverty and unemployment. Under the new regime, as part of their commitment to create an open market economy, the authorities decided to press for the dismantling of the CMEA and to seek membership in the European Community (EC) as early as possible. In line with these goals, the Government outlined a comprehensive draft reform program for taxation, subsidies, social security, the budget process, and local finances. The program envisages measures to level the playing field for all major taxes and to enhance the cost effectiveness of government expenditures. Some progress has been made toward enacting such measures.

Hungary's long and roundabout reform process leads to four major lessons. Whereas some of these lessons are not likely to be relevant for most other countries in transition, others are already being experienced by a number of countries. The first lesson points to the efficiency of fiscal reform that is unconstrained in creating market-based institutions, as is the case now in many post-socialist economies. This contrasts with the former piecemeal and experimental approach subject to shifting and inconsistent goals—such as those prevailing under market socialism—formerly followed in Hungary. The second is that a gradual reform process confers benefits above all by conditioning the attitudes of policymakers and economic agents to the requirements of a market-oriented economy. Although it might be hasty to assess the relative merits of an extended, albeit uneven, track record as against a consistent and clearly aimed reform program introduced at a break-neck speed, arguably the former is likely to provide a more robust setting for the newly created institutions.

The third lesson is that during the transition the authorities may feel compelled to resort to discretionary micro-intervention and sacrifice the efficiency goal of fiscal reform, in response to macroeconomic imbalances. This policy response was illustrated on several occasions in Hungary in the past, especially when policymakers were confronted by inflationary pressures and external current account deficits. However, this seems to be a far more likely occurrence in other economies which, following a big-bang transition, experience a contraction in output, a shift in income or wealth distribution, and a rise in unemployment.[6]

The fourth, and perhaps more debatable, lesson to be drawn from Hungary's current reform experience highlights a short-run trade-off between a fledgling multiparty parliamentary system of government and the speed of fiscal reform. In Hungary, as well as in neighboring countries,[7] it has become increasingly difficult to enact reform proposals as scheduled,

---

[6]See the discussion of this issue in Kopits (1992b).

[7]Unlike in Hungary, where since May 1989 there has been a full lineup of political parties represented in parliament, most other post-socialist countries elected former opposition blocs or movements to the legislatures—in some cases, as in Poland, under certain restrictions as to the number of seats reserved for the previous official party—and are only beginning, or have yet to begin, to experience the formation of genuine political parties.

without amendments diluting the program on key issues. Clearly, action on so many basic draft laws is bound to be slowed down considerably by the congestion and magnitude of the agenda and by the inexperience of the legislature. At the same time, powerful interest groups strive to prevent a relatively weak legislative body from enacting reform measures aimed at closing loopholes in taxation and social entitlements, at eliminating budget-related rent-seeking activities, and at removing inequities and entrenched complexities from intergovernmental fiscal relations. This tentative lesson, of course, in no way diminishes the overall superiority of the present democratic system of government.

Tax System

Taxation of Goods and Services

The earliest steps in the reform of Hungary's public finances involved an attempt at replacing the Soviet-type revenue system with parametric taxation of goods and services. The heart of that system consists of countless turnover tax rates in the form of variable product-specific wedges between controlled retail prices and producer costs, incorporated at various stages of the production or distribution process. As part of the 1968 price reform, turnover tax rates were to be levied on a fixed ad valorem basis only at consumption—to eliminate cascading. The number of tax rates was substantially reduced from more than 2,500 variable implicit rates to about 1,000 fixed explicit rates. However, during the 1970s, turnover tax rates were frequently cut and consumer subsidies were increased in order to cushion the impact of increasing production costs on consumer prices.

Starting in 1980, again in the context of a new round of relative price adjustments, which included consumer price increases, turnover tax rates were simplified further. In particular, tax rates on clothing products were no longer differentiated by inputs or processing, and a single rate was adopted for a broad range of miscellaneous industrial goods. Although over 100 rates still remained, by 1985 the turnover tax was in principle narrowed down to four basic rates: zero percent for construction materials, children's clothing, and processed or unprocessed food; 11 percent on most manufactured goods; 22 percent on adult clothing; and 30 percent on some luxury goods. At the same time, a set of luxury excises (called consumption taxes) was levied at specific rates on top of the turnover tax.[8]

---

[8]For a detailed description, see Ministry of Finance (1985c).

Following a two-year preparation period[9] and accompanied by further price liberalization, Hungary replaced the existing turnover tax with the GTT, effective January 1988, while continuing to rely heavily on excises. Contrary to outside advice, the GTT base was rather narrowly defined, excluding (besides exports) most services, construction materials, personal imports, and other items, while most foodstuffs were zero rated, all of which totaled nearly one half of private consumption. For revenue reasons, the rates were set relatively high by international standards: a 25 percent standard rate and a 15 percent reduced rate, in addition to the zero rate. For revenue reasons and to contain investment demand by SOEs, the deduction for capital goods was to be phased in gradually over five years. Personal imports, including motor vehicles, were exempt until January 1990. At the time of its introduction, the authorities permitted virtually a full pass-through of the GTT, which not only resulted in an 8 percent increase in the consumer price level but also fueled inflationary expectations, accommodated by an expansionary macroeconomic policy stance.

Much like the former domestic turnover tax, imports were subject to price equalization tax rates (later also called producer differential turnover tax rates), that is, wedges between domestic and foreign prices at the official exchange rate—modified by the so-called foreign trade multiplier, intended to equalize domestic average cost of nonruble foreign exchange earnings, effective until 1976. This system of foreign trade taxation was replaced in 1968 with a three-column import duty structure with respect to convertible currency trade, primarily as a bargaining tool to secure trade concessions from Western trading partner countries.[10] But the import duty structure was retained through early 1991 for trade in nonconvertible currencies, to equalize the profitability of enterprises engaged in CMEA trade with those exposed to world market prices. Imports from the convertible currency area were also subject to nontariff barriers. However, import duties acquired increasing importance with the beginning of trade liberalization and the unification of the exchange rate in 1981, and with widespread availability of trading rights since 1986. The present import duty structure is characterized by a wide dispersion of mostly ad valorem rates averaging about 13 percent on a weighted basis.

Personal Income Taxation

Personal income taxation was not placed on the reform agenda until the 1980s. Previously, income from employment and from savings de-

---

[9]The preparation included IMF technical assistance in December 1985—the first such assistance by an international organization to a European socialist country in the fiscal area.

[10]See Bácskai (1971). Nonpreferential customs duty rates on imports were set at 1 percent for raw materials, from 10 percent to 40 percent for semifinished goods, and between 80 percent and 100 percent for machinery and other finished goods. In addition, various statistical fees were applied.

posits (the only available financial assets) were taxed implicitly through rigid controls over virtually undifferentiated wage levels and interest rates, respectively. In the early 1980s, with the emergence of a second economy, various taxes were imposed on personal income from different sources: highly progressive statutory marginal rates of up to 75 percent on general self-employment income; rates of up to 65 percent on certain income from intellectual and cultural activities; and specific taxes on land and livestock, with a presumptive tax on supplementary income of up to 10 percent on agricultural sales (except cattle and milk).[11]

By 1986, this patchwork tax system was expanded as follows: small craftsmen and retailers were subject to self-assessment or to a presumptive tax on gross receipts; private economic associations were liable to a statutory tax between 3 percent and 40 percent, depending on the type of activity and nature of the association; and SOEs, economic associations, and cooperatives were required to withhold a 10 percent tax on employee compensation, with the employees receiving only a net income. Numerous exemptions were granted (for example, interest income and capital gains), along with considerable latitude for the determination of taxable income from private sector activities.

In January 1988, the variegated structure of individual income taxes was replaced with a broader-based PIT. In its original form, the tax applied in principle, above a personal exemption, to all income from employment or self-employment (defined on an individual rather than a household or family basis) over 11 brackets at progressive marginal rates ranging from 20 percent to 60 percent. Preferential treatment consisted of additional deductions from, or outright exemption of, income from agricultural, cultural, and intellectual activities, social security pensions, fringe benefits, and bonuses. In 1989–90, marginal tax rates were cut in two steps to 56 percent and to 50 percent, while brackets were lengthened and their number halved; also, the tax base was narrowed, allowing for, among others, the deduction of purchases of financial assets amounting up to 30 percent of taxable income. As of 1992, the PIT was further streamlined by cutting the top marginal rate to 40 percent, simplifying the structure to three brackets (in addition to the zero bracket), and narrowing the financial investment deduction to the purchase of newly issued securities only.

As regards capital income taxation, since 1988 a separate 20 percent final withholding tax was imposed on interest and dividend income, with exemption for interest on savings for housing investment. The tax was limited to capital income from financial assets denominated in domestic currency; interest income on foreign currency deposits, which have become very popular since their liberalization in September 1989, remains exempt. In 1992, the withholding tax on dividends was reduced to 10 percent to induce privatization and new ventures.

---

[11]For details, see Ministry of Finance (1983).

Undoubtedly, the introduction of the PIT was the most controversial fiscal reform measure in Hungary. The new tax was greeted with considerable criticism by academicians, leaders of political opposition groups, and taxpayers at large—in the waning days of the one-party regime. Criticisms were leveled at the inadequate one-time gross-up of wages for the PIT to leave after-tax incomes unaltered, supply-side disincentives created by high marginal rates, anti-family bias owing to the definition of the individual rather than the household as the taxable unit,[12] and invasion of privacy associated with the administration of self-declared income tax liability.[13] This last argument was largely based on historical sensitivities developed during the Habsburg occupation[14] and revived under the postwar Soviet occupation.

Taxation of Enterprises

Albeit less controversial, enterprise tax reform has followed a tortuous route—zigzagging between heavy-handed discretionary intervention and the development of objective and stable tax rules—largely because it is closely intertwined with the behavior of SOEs, which have dominated economic activity in Hungary until the present. A major concern shaping enterprise taxation, since the initial allowance for some autonomy under the new economic mechanism, was the macroeconomic implications of the expansionary drive of SOEs operating under a soft budget constraint—that is, easy access to central bank credit and budget subsidies.[15] Along with the direct tutelage by industrial branch ministries and the obligation to abide broadly by the plan, from the end of the 1960s these enterprises were subject to a complicated system of nominally parametric taxes[16] and special-purpose enterprise funds.

Each enterprise was obliged to earmark profits into its reserve fund, profit-sharing fund, and development fund, according to an elaborate set of formulas.[17] Profits allocated to the profit-sharing fund were taxed at

---

[12]This widely held view—given the country's net negative population growth rate—was eloquently argued by some interest groups.

[13]See, for example, Kornai (1990). For a more comprehensive critique of the PIT on these grounds as well as the effects of inflation, loss of competitiveness, and the difficulty of taxing illegal income, see Gergely (1987). For a defense of the PIT, see Kupa (1987).

[14]See Gergely (1987).

[15]See the seminal work of Kornai (1980).

[16]For a discussion of enterprise taxation and its rationale in the early years of the new economic mechanism, see Bácskai (1971).

[17]The allocation of profits between the profit-sharing fund (for distribution to managers and employees) and the development fund (for retention and investment) was defined by the proportion of the wage bill (modified by a multiplier ranging from about two to four, depending on the factor intensity of the industry) to the value of assets. Further, an amount equivalent to 10 percent of after-tax profits allocated to the profit-sharing and development funds was earmarked to the reserve fund (for contingency purposes), until it reached the sum of 8 percent of the annual wage bill and 1.5 percent of the gross value of fixed and financial assets. Allocations into such funds as the housing construction fund, the cultural and welfare fund, and the fund for technological improvement (set up in the 1970s) were deductible from profits.

progressive rates from zero to 70 percent depending on the ratio between profits thus allocated and the wage bill, while profits deposited in the development fund bore a general 60 percent tax rate (varying between 45 percent and 70 percent across industries). The tax base was determined by revenue less operating costs, interest payments, wages, and depreciation calculated according to a large number of conservative straight-line rates, highly differentiated by asset type. Other taxes levied before profits comprised: payroll taxes totaling 25 percent, which included a 17 percent social security contribution rate; a 5 percent tax on the gross value of assets, including debt-financed inventories and financial assets; a production tax designed to soak up advantages deemed exogenous to the enterprise (for example, conferred by the price system); and a 40 percent tax on depreciation allowances, the rest of such allowances being allocated to the development fund.[18] In fact, the taxation of enterprises—more than the rest of the revenue system—was neither parametric, nor transparent, nor neutral across activities. Tax liabilities were open to intensive bargaining between the authorities and the taxpayers; tax preferences were provided both by statute and on a case-by-case basis.

During the 1970s, profit taxation was simplified with the introduction of a basic 40 percent rate, with reduced progressivity and differentiation, supplemented by a 6 percent municipal tax that was later raised to 10 percent. Some tax preferences were granted to foreign investors in joint ventures.[19] Payroll taxes were increased to a combined 35 percent statutory rate, but the effective rate of the tax on assets fell as the base was redefined from gross to net value. Moreover, through a tax-based incomes policy the authorities sought to control generous wage awards by enterprises exposed to insufficient financial discipline, while inducing productivity increases and more efficient management of the work force.[20] Enterprises were subject to highly progressive taxation of average wage increases above certain thresholds, with marginal rates of up to 400 percent. The combination of this regulatory tax and the highly discretionary character of the rest of enterprise taxation may have contributed to restraining enterprise investment demand and wage growth; however, it also encouraged the hiring of redundant workers (to depress average wage increases) and dampened productivity. All along, the regulatory role and supply-side aspects dominated the debate over the appropriate form of enterprise taxation.[21]

---

[18]Among these levies, the taxes on wages and gross assets had been introduced in 1959 and 1964, respectively, to deter enterprises from hoarding labor and capital.

[19]For a comparison of taxation of foreign investors in CMEA member countries, see Jonas (1978).

[20]See Kónya (1971).

[21]See, for example, Rácz and Vissi (1973).

In 1980, there was a renewed attempt at sensitizing SOEs to market forces in part through various tax changes, followed shortly by the abolition of branch ministries and adoption of a more open selection of enterprise managers. Specific tax measures included repeal of the tax on assets, some tightening of tax preferences, and shifts in reliance from payroll taxation (lowering rates to 24 percent) to profit taxation (raising the general profit tax rate to 45 percent and the local contribution tax rate to 15 percent). To correct for supply-restraining and employment-inducing effects, the base of the tax on excess wage increase was redefined in terms of the increment in the wage bill, in excess of a given proportion of the increase in the enterprise's value added. However, in 1982–84, again fearful of the expansionary consequences of increased enterprise autonomy, the authorities confiscated the after-tax earnings accumulated in enterprise development and reserve funds. Meanwhile, enterprises were still liable to a 40 percent tax (with lower rates applied in heavy industries) on depreciation allowances. The effort to contain aggregate demand included stepped-up taxation of excess average wage increases at progressive rates of up to 500 percent, though mitigated in proportion to the enterprise's profitability—measured by the ratio of profits to real assets plus the wage bill.[22]

In a major step toward transparency, in 1985 after-tax earnings were no longer subject to earmarking for special purpose funds, to ad hoc confiscation, or to the tax on depreciation. Upon abolition of these practices, enterprises faced a tax liability consisting of 50 percent combined profit tax and municipal levy, 18 percent tax on investment, 3 percent tax on net worth, and 10 percent wage tax, payable from after-tax profits. But reduced rates and tax reliefs continued to apply for certain activities; in particular, the investment tax rate varied from year to year and across industries. In addition, the tax-based regulations on the level as well as excessive increment of the average wage were enforced at progressive rates of up to 450 percent depending on the applicable regulation.[23]

A milestone in the reform of enterprise taxation, in January 1989, was the substitution of the EPT for the above taxes as well as the taxes on most private enterprise income. The introduction of the tax coincided with the enactment of the law on economic associations, encompassing joint-stock companies,[24] partnerships, and joint ventures, which were opened up a year later to unconstrained private ownership and with no limits in the size of the work force. The general EPT statutory rate was

---

[22]For a detailed description of the formula introduced in 1983, see Ministry of Finance (1982c).

[23]See Ministry of Finance (1985a).

[24]Curiously, the new law replaced the still valid statutes dating back to the Austro-Hungarian monarchy that had been suspended by decree authorizing the Council of Ministers to approve the establishment of other than wholly state-owned enterprises. This authority in effect had not been exercised since its inception in the early 1950s.

initially set at 50 percent (with a temporary 4 percent surcharge) and lowered to 40 percent in 1990. To favor the start-up of corporate activity and enterprises with relatively low profits, a reduced 40 percent rate (35 percent since 1990) was levied on the first Ft 3 million in taxable profit; this reduced rate was repealed in 1991.

While the incorporation of the various taxes into a single EPT represents an important measure toward a market-based tax system, the definition of the tax base remained retrograde. Indeed, the retention of a multiplicity of conservative historical-cost depreciation allowances in a period of accelerating inflation and the adoption of a mere two-year carryforward of losses[25] resulted in a very high marginal effective tax rate by international standards.[26] The reluctance to modernize the tax base and to maintain a relatively high statutory rate was based in part on revenue considerations and on continued concern with enterprise demand pressures. Also, for the latter reason, increases in the wage bill in excess of the growth in value added were not deductible from the EPT base of socialized enterprises—replacing the former progressive tax on excess wage increases. Moreover, the reduction in the general EPT rate in 1990 was accompanied by the imposition of a compulsory 18 percent obligatory dividend payout (raised to 25 percent at midyear) on after-tax earnings of SOEs. Because of its simplicity and predictability, the dividend requirement was an, albeit imperfect, effective attempt to place these enterprises on a comparable footing with private enterprises which are expected by their owners to generate a market yield on equity.

To compensate for the high effective tax rate and in an attempt to target incentives to selected activities, a wide range of tax preferences was granted, mostly in the form of reduced rates, especially for agriculture, food processing, and various services and cultural activities. However, the most generous tax preferences were awarded to foreign investors. For enterprises with a foreign equity participation of at least 20 percent, the tax liability was reduced by 20 percent. In certain activities, deemed as priority activities, a five-year tax holiday (extended to ten years or longer for large-scale investors, on a case-by-case basis) was provided. In any event, reinvested profits of nonresident shareholders were tax exempt. This discriminatory treatment favoring nonresident taxpayers—unusual in host countries to foreign investment—provided a potential vehicle for tax evasion by residents investing in Hungary through channels abroad. All told, the ETP suffered from a combination of relatively high statutory rates, unrealistic measurement of the base, and excessive tax preferences.

[25]The granting of the two-year loss carryover provision is noted in Kupa (1989). An argument by the authorities raised against a longer formal loss carryover provision was that enterprises were permitted, instead, to manipulate the declaration of revenue or certain operating costs—as a form of income averaging—so as to minimize the tax liability across periods.
[26]See the international comparison in Andersson (1990).

A number of the existing distortions were corrected in 1992, especially by redefining the EPT base in line with the adoption of Western accounting standards. In particular, depreciation allowances were significantly liberalized and simplified, bad debt reserves became deductible, the loss carryover was extended to five years, and several tax preferences were tightened.

Subsidies and Social Security

Subsidies

As in other centrally planned economies, Hungary provided a wide variety of consumer subsidies through the price system. Calculated mechanically as a negative turnover tax, negative wedges obtained between controlled retail prices and producer costs. These product-specific subsidies were implicitly embodied in the retail prices of a range of basic foodstuffs (dairy products, meat, bread), energy and fuel for home use (coal, briquettes, firewood), pharmaceuticals, children's clothing, and basic services (public heating, electricity, water). The rationalization of consumer price subsidies paralleled that of turnover taxation. In several rounds (the first commencing in 1968 and the second in 1980), the subsidies were initially fixed at specific rates and then their differentiation by product was reduced.

Besides consumer price subsidies, households also benefited from housing subsidies through controlled rents and long-term mortgages. The National Savings Bank extended mortgages with a 35-year maturity at a subsidized fixed nominal interest rate of up to 3 percent even when inflation accelerated to two-digit rates. All households were in principle eligible for housing subsidies regardless of need.

On the production side, socialized enterprises engaged in CMEA trade had access to price equalization subsidies, which operated as a negative product-differential turnover tax between the external price, converted at the exchange rate with the transferable ruble, and the domestic producer price. In 1980, a notional rebate was provided—initially at a 10 percent general rate, albeit differentiated by industry—as a border tax adjustment to all exporters for the differential tax on energy and raw material imports. Exporters also received ad hoc subsidies to meet commitments under bilateral trade agreements. Next to ruble exports, agriculture was the largest recipient of regular subsidy payments. Moreover, loss-making enterprises had access to discretionary transfers from the budget during most of the period under review. More formally, transfers were made to enterprises in certain depressed industries (such as mining and metallurgy) through the State Lending Fund and the Intervention Fund in the first half of the 1980s, in part from the confiscated retained earnings of profitable enterprises. Transfers from the Rehabilitation Fund were in principle provided to enterprises under restructuring arrangements.

The final round of dismantling of subsidies began in 1985 with a significant simplification and curtailment of consumer price subsidies—especially on foodstuffs—and the termination of transfers to enterprises from earmarked funds. These steps coincided with the simplification of turnover tax rates and the end of confiscation of enterprise earnings, respectively. Following the introduction of the GTT, the export rebate was phased out from a 7 percent rate between 1988 and 1990. However, it was not until 1989 that the authorities decided to launch a program for removing the bulk (nearly two thirds in real terms) of the subsidies over a four-year period.[27]

The subsidy reduction program was accelerated under the new regime. For one thing, price liberalization climaxed with the abolition of the Price Office in January 1991, limiting the scope of consumer price subsidies to household energy, water supply and sewage, transport, and one grade of milk. For another, the Government began to trim substantially producer subsidies to coal mining and heavy industries and subsidies for ruble exports, as trade with CMEA partner countries started to contract sharply—one year before the switch to convertible currency payments. Among all producer subsidies, those to agriculture proved to be the most difficult to discontinue.

The phaseout of the mortgage interest subsidy has been a particularly sensitive issue. In 1988, as part of the banking reform, the National Savings Bank was relieved of the cost of the subsidy which since then has been financed, through the newly created Housing Fund, from general budget revenue and from the sale of special purpose bonds carrying a market interest yield. More recently, access to new low-interest mortgages has been limited mainly to households with several dependents and subject to a means test. Attempts by the Government to induce prepayment of outstanding subsidized mortgages through generous discounts from the principal and to tax the subsidy element—which increases with the rise in nominal market interest rates—on such mortgages met with mixed success.[28] In 1991, holders of pre-1989 mortgages were given a choice between either writing off one half of the outstanding loan and paying the market interest rate on the balance, or paying a 15 percent rate on the entire outstanding amount, both options being subject to a nominal ceiling (Ft 1,500) on the monthly installment in the first year.

---

[27]For an analysis, see Abel (1990).
[28]In March 1990, a tax levied since the beginning of the year on previously subsidized mortgages was overruled by the Constitutional Court.

Social Security[29]

In Hungary, as in other socialist countries, citizens have had the right to work and to free health care and education guaranteed by the constitution and codified under the Health Act of 1975. Further, as provided by the Social Insurance Act of 1975, employees had access through the workplace to retirement pensions, family benefits, sick pay, and to a host of enterprise-specific benefits (vacations at enterprise-owned resorts, housing allowances, acquisition of certain consumer durables at a discount, and so on). Apart from the cost of the latter, borne by enterprises, health-care benefits were financed with general revenue from the state budget and all other benefits with earmarked social security contributions. These contributions consist of payroll taxes imposed primarily on employers. In the early 1980s, employers paid a contribution rate varying from 10 percent for budgetary institutions to 27 percent (up from 17 percent a decade earlier) for enterprises, while employees were liable to a progressive rate ranging from 3 percent to 10 percent.[30]

The easing of eligibility requirements, steady increase in effective replacement rates (that is, the ratio of benefits to the wage level), and adverse demographic trends over the last two decades have been largely responsible for the rise in contribution rates, imposing an uneven burden across sectors. To correct sectoral distortions and to raise revenue, effective 1989, contribution rates were unified at a 43 percent rate for employers, in addition to the flat 10 percent rate (in lieu of the previous progressive rate structure) for employees adopted a year earlier, so that the payroll tax rate totaled 53 percent.

Also in 1989, social security operations were removed from the state budget and placed in a separate Social Insurance Fund (SIF) under the administrative control of the National Social Insurance Directorate. The autonomy of the SIF was initially conceived as involving primarily its oversight by beneficiaries and contributors, and possibly its financial integrity on a funded basis.[31] Further, in an attempt to group insurance-type schemes (as distinct from assistance-type schemes) under the SIF, financed solely from payroll taxation, in April 1990 spending responsibility for family allowances was shifted from the SIF to the state budget, while health-care expenditures were incorporated in the SIF, along with retirement, sick pay, maternity, and child benefits.

In 1992, the SIF was split into two self-governing bodies, the Pension Fund (PF) and the Health Insurance Fund (HIF). Currently each has a

---

[29]For an analysis of the initial phase of social security reform in Hungary, see Kopits and others (1990).

[30]For a description of the social security system as of 1982, see Ministry of Finance (1982b).

[31]Contrary to official intentions, the funding principle was de facto violated when almost the entire SIF surplus for 1989 was utilized to purchase Housing Fund bonds—tantamount to an indirect transfer to finance the budget deficit.

supervisory committee, but from 1993 these committees are expected to be replaced by elected bodies, including a general assembly. In principle, each fund has administrative and financial autonomy. The annual budget of each fund, operating essentially on a pay-as-you-go basis, requires separate legislative action. Still under debate, however, is how far to move toward an insurance basis. In this respect, potentially, the most far-reaching change has been the replacement of the universal right to free health care with eligibility based on actual or deemed contributions to the HIF.

Until the late 1980s, there was neither ideological nor institutional scope for dealing openly with poverty and unemployment. Indeed, these ailments were masked by redundancies in the SOEs' work force and by old-age and disability pensions and sick pay. Social assistance for the needy was left to the competence and resources of local councils that exercised full discretion over the determination of needs and benefits—leaving large poverty pockets untouched. As a temporary measure to avoid open unemployment, effective September 1986, laid-off workers could be eligible for a job-search subsidy on a rather limited scale. Poverty and other social and health-related problems were explicitly acknowledged by the authorities only in 1988.[32] But it was not until 1989 that a formal unemployment compensation scheme was adopted—the first of its kind in former socialist countries, with the exception of Yugoslavia—to replace the job-search subsidy. In 1990, the maximum duration of compensation payments was extended from one to two years of unemployment, but the following year it was again reduced to one and a half years.

The new government aimed at creating a comprehensive social safety net, consisting of targeted income maintenance, to offset in part the removal of consumer price subsidies and to support industrial restructuring. The 1991 budget provides a significant adjustment in retirement benefits and family allowances for anticipated wage inflation. In addition, active labor market programs financed from the budget through the Employment Fund were expanded (to include, for example, a wage subsidy scheme), and under the newly created Solidarity Fund, the financing of unemployment compensation shifted from complete reliance on general revenue to include an earmarked payroll tax (on top of the contribution to the SIF) initially set at 2 percent, payable for the most part by the employer.

In 1992, the employer contribution rate was set at 44 percent, of which 24.5 percentage points were allocated to the PF and 19.5 percentage

---

[32]The change in the name of the Ministry of Health to Ministry of Social Affairs and Health, as well as the establishment of a Commission for Long-Term Social Policy Development, can be viewed as a policy reorientation in this area. The Commission's findings were reported in Ministry of Social Affairs and Health (1989).

points to the HIF, while the employee contribution was divided in 6 percentage points for the PF and 4 percentage points for the HIF. The contribution to the Solidarity Fund was increased to 6 percent. In sum, the total payroll tax rate reached 60 percent—apparently the highest in the world.

Budgetary Framework and Financing

Budget Process, Extrabudgetary Funds, and Local Government Finances

The budget process has been probably the least susceptible to reform in the fiscal area during the new economic mechanism. In fact, it is difficult to identify significant institutional changes in this area until 1989—with the possible exception of the decline in discretionary confiscation of earnings from, and transfers to, SOEs from the mid-1980s onward. Notwithstanding various efforts to clarify the budget process and the functions of the Minister of Finance in 1979 and 1985,[33] the formulation, execution, and control of government expenditures remained essentially a closed process, subject to considerable behind-the-scenes bargaining involving the official Hungarian Socialist Workers' Party (HSWP), the enterprises, the government ministries, and to a lesser extent, the local councils. The budget was prepared formally by the Ministry of Finance, in close collaboration with the National Planning Office and following directives from the Economic Department of the HSWP Central Committee. The actual budget document was treated practically as a state secret and parliament approved it in a highly aggregated version, following a perfunctory debate.[34] No single entity or institution was, however, effectively in control of budget preparation and implementation.

Reflecting to an extent an intended reorientation of the budget process toward principles of transparency, equity, and predictability, enunciated in the Government's 1988–89 budget reform proposals,[35] the 1990 budget was prepared with greater openness and technical know-how and was exposed to more active legislative participation and accountability. Although without formal enactment of the budget reform proposals, the 1991 state budget represented the first detailed public document of gov-

---

[33] See Ministry of Finance (1985b, 1985d).

[34] As an example of the information released publicly and the statements contributed to the legislative debate on the 1987 state budget, see Ministry of Finance (1987). As recently as 1988, parliament was in session no more than 14 days in total. Probably the single most important policymaker in economic matters, including budget decisions, was the Economic Secretary of the HSWP Central Committee. The Minister of Finance and the Deputy Prime Minister for Economic Affairs were entrusted largely with day-to-day administrative decisions (for example, approval of import licenses and tax exemptions).

[35] See Ministry of Finance (1988, 1989).

ernment spending decisions, debated, amended and approved by parliament. Separately, the parliament also acted on the SIF budget.[36] However, both the 1991 and 1992 budgetary exercises point to a number of remaining weaknesses, especially as regards the insufficient time provided for parliamentary discussion.

The transparency of the budget process has been enhanced by passage of the Accounting Act and the Government Finances Act in 1991 and 1992, respectively. The Accounting Act, which applies to all private and public sector entities, lays down fundamental principles of accounting and financial reporting to ensure preparation of true and reliable financial statements. The Government Finances Act includes a requirement that the budget must show in detail the revenue and expenditure of each budgetary institution. Also, the Government is required to present to parliament annual accounts audited by the State Audit Office, showing actual receipts and payments, and end-year cash balances. Further transparency is expected from the requirement that all budgetary institutions produce for legislative approval a founding charter setting out the nature and objectives of their functions.

The institutional structure of government entities and their interrelationships have undergone some changes since the beginning of the 1980s. Most notably, a distinct trend toward fiscal decentralization is identifiable at various levels, largely as a reaction to the former highly centralized and discretionary budgetary decision making. This trend has been reflected in the proliferation of extrabudgetary funds created to finance, from either general or earmarked revenue, specific programs or projects (for example, the Intervention Fund, the State Lending Fund, and the Housing Fund). By 1988, there were altogether 35 funds—excluding social security operations—still consolidated in the state budget. Within the state budget itself, there was also a centrifugal process under way involving specialized central budgetary institutions engaged in various economic activities, including research and development. These institutions have been operating within or under the central or local government administration, with increasing independence and often in the pursuit of profits—shared by the given institution's management and staff.[37]

At another level, local governments—formally consolidated in the state budget—had become increasingly independent from central government control. Without necessarily assuming additional spending responsibilities, local councils secured additional resources through bond financing of local projects and institutions and through taxation; in 1988, most revenue from the newly established PIT was assigned to the councils with less than commensurate cutback in central government transfers. Under

---

[36]See Ministry of Finance (1991b).

[37]For a description of the official status and operations of budgetary institutions, see Ministry of Finance (1986).

the new regime, the move toward regional autonomy gained considerable political momentum, and reform legislation on local self-governments (replacing Soviet-type local councils) was enacted in October 1990.[38] Under this legislation, self-governments carry out their spending responsibilities—broadly defined in the areas of infrastructure, health care, and social assistance—from their own resources (local taxes and property incomes), one half of PIT revenue lagged by two years, central government transfers, SIF transfers (earmarked for health care), and bond issues. Further, the transfers from the central budget consist of normative lump-sum grants defined either per jurisdiction, or per capita recipient of the specific service or expenditure, or on a matching basis,[39] and of targeted transfers (that is, earmarked for a particular project or program). These intergovernmental transfers, comprising one half of total local self-government resources, represent some improvement over the previous system of automatic annual increments subject to bargaining between various levels of government, as well as among party officials. However, many shortcomings remain, especially as regards the lack of transparency and simplicity in the rules affecting the financial relations between the central and local governments.[40]

Management of Government Assets and Liabilities

In the course of 1989, under the former regime, the authorities permitted the ad hoc privatization of a number of socialized enterprises that had been converted into wholly state-owned joint-stock companies in accordance with the Transformation Act passed that year. Typically, privatizations were initiated by the management of the enterprise (often on the basis of insider information) in a deal with a foreign-based partner, in part to take advantage of tax holidays and other preferences. Such cases of spontaneous privatization yielded practically no revenue to the government either at the time of sale or during the subsequent operation of the enterprise. Following a number of such cases, in 1990 the State Property Agency was established to serve as a referee and technical advisor for the speedy and transparent privatization of socialized enterprises. Applications for privatization, accompanied by the necessary documentation to be reviewed by the agency could, in principle, be submitted either by the enterprise to be sold or by the purchaser. Apart from this main institutional conduit, the Hungarian approach is rather pragmatic and accommo-

---

[38]For a discussion of the law on local self-governments and the enabling law on local taxes, see Ministry of Finance (1991a).

[39]In many cases, the attribute of the recipient is defined in excessive detail (for example, Ft 450 monthly per spectator in a provincial theater). For 1991, altogether 22 grant categories are listed, the purpose of which in fact may be disregarded by the recipient self-government.

[40]For an analysis and proposals in this area, see Bird and Wallich (1992).

dates a variety of alternative approaches (including direct issue of equity shares in the stock market, and eventual sales in exchange for restitution bonds).[41]

On the liability side, external and internal government debt has accumulated rapidly over the last decade or so. Whereas the external debt was largely contracted and managed by the National Bank of Hungary, the internal debt was entirely monetized though borrowing from the National Bank. As a first step toward developing market-based instruments, in 1988 the Government began to issue negotiable short-term securities yielding near-market interest rates, for weekly auctioning by the National Bank. Both Housing Fund bonds and short-term treasury bills were placed with commercial banks, financial institutions, or the SIF, and in modest amounts with the nonbank public.

Reform Tasks Ahead

Since 1989, Hungary has been engaged in an economy-wide structural transformation which at the beginning of 1991 was recast into a formal medium-term program. Although the program covers the period 1991–94, the bulk of the structural measures was scheduled for implementation in the first two years; an impressive set of legislative proposals has been submitted to parliament in the course of 1991–92. In the public finances, legislation has been enacted or is pending in the areas of taxation, the budget process, extrabudgetary funds, local government finances, social insurance, social assistance, health care, housing, state property, and privatization.[42] In general, the program was aimed at the creation of market-based institutions—in many instances, comparable to those found in the EC. To provide a greater scope for market forces in the economy, the program called for a substantial reduction of the share of government expenditures in GDP, which still exceeds by a wide margin their share in most Western economies (Table 1).

The recent tax reform, which represents a further step toward broadening the income tax base and lowering statutory rates, requires a similar effort as regards the GTT. Indeed, there is a clear need for extending the commodity coverage of the GTT and for aligning its rates closer to those prevailing in the EC.[43] Tax policy changes have to be underpinned by a determined campaign to strengthen tax administration at a time when revenue from taxes payable or withheld by SOEs is bound to dwindle owing to shrinking output, profitability, and employment, and hardening of their budget constraint. Under the circumstances, greater recourse to voluntary compliance and presumptive taxation—especially of private

---

[41]For a discussion, see Bokros (1991) and Ministry of Finance (1991c).

[42]An informative matrix of the legislative agenda and an overview of goals and major proposals are contained in Government of the Republic of Hungary (1991).

[43]See Kopits (1992a) on tax harmonization in the EC.

Table 1. Hungary: Operations of the General Government

(In percent of GDP)

	1981	1982	1983	1984	1985	1986	1987	1988	1989	1990	1991 Estimate
Total revenue	61.0	59.2	60.9	60.8	60.0	61.5	59.1	63.4	58.9	57.4	56.8
Enterprise income taxes	13.8	12.1	13.1	12.6	9.6	11.1	11.9	8.4	6.9	7.3	5.7
Profits tax	13.8	12.1	13.1	12.6	9.6	11.1	11.9	8.4	5.4	4.5	3.4
Dividend requirement	—	—	—	—	—	—	—	—	—	1.3	0.8
Individual income taxes	0.5	0.5	0.9	0.9	0.9	0.8	0.8	4.7	5.4	6.5	8.0
Social security contributions	8.2	8.8	9.4	12.0	13.0	13.0	12.1	13.4	14.1	13.7	13.9
Domestic taxes on goods and services	20.6	21.3	21.1	17.9	16.7	16.7	16.9	22.6	17.4	16.7	14.4
Taxes on consumption[1]	8.3	8.6	9.3	9.0	9.1	9.7	10.4	15.0	13.3	12.7	12.9
Of which:											
Excises	—	—	—	—	2.4	3.8	5.2	6.0	5.5	5.2	6.0
Value-added tax	—	—	—	—	—	—	—	8.7	7.8	7.1	6.5
Producer differential turnover tax	11.1	11.1	10.6	7.4	7.1	5.3	4.9	6.7	3.8	3.8	1.4
Other	1.4	1.7	1.6	1.8	0.6	1.7	1.6	0.9	0.2	0.2	0.1
Revenue from international trade	3.6	3.4	3.8	3.4	3.1	3.5	2.8	3.0	4.0	3.1	2.9
Taxes on property	2.9	2.7	3.4	4.0	2.7	2.1	2.1	0.5	0.4	0.1	—
Other tax and nontax revenue[2]	11.5	10.5	9.2	9.9	13.9	14.3	12.6	10.7	10.7	10.1	11.9
Current expenditure	53.5	51.9	53.5	51.5	53.2	56.6	54.6	55.6	53.7	52.3	57.3
Wages and salaries	7.5	7.5	7.3	7.2	7.8	8.1	7.6	8.7	8.2	7.6	9.7
Other goods and services	11.6	11.7	10.6	10.5	10.9	11.4	12.0	12.7	12.1	11.2	10.8
Interest payments	1.2	1.1	0.2	0.6	0.4	1.3	2.6	1.6	2.4	3.0	4.1
Social security benefits	11.6	11.6	12.0	12.3	12.7	13.1	12.6	15.3	15.6	19.7	23.5
Consumer subsidies[3]	8.5	8.1	8.2	6.2	5.6	6.3	6.2	5.0	6.6	5.5	4.6
Subsidies and transfers to enterprises	12.3	11.1	14.5	14.0	14.3	15.8	13.3	11.5	8.4	5.1	4.0
Other	0.8	0.8	0.8	0.7	1.6	0.7	0.6	0.7	0.5	0.2	0.5

Capital expenditure	10.5	9.3	8.3	7.9	8.0	7.9	8.0	7.7	6.4	4.6	4.1[4]
Investment	7.1	6.0	7.7	7.3	6.9	6.5	6.0	6.3	5.8	3.6	3.9
Transfers	3.4	3.3	0.7	0.7	1.0	1.5	2.1	1.4	0.6	1.0	0.2[4]
Net lending	0.3	—	—	—	-0.1	0.1	—	0.1	0.1	—	...
Overall balance (+ surplus/ – deficit)	-2.9	-2.1	-1.0	1.4	-1.2	-3.0	-3.5	0.1	-1.2	0.5	-4.6
Financing, net	2.9	2.1	1.0	-1.4	1.2	3.0	3.5	-0.1	1.2	-0.5	4.6
External financing, net	2.1	0.3	0.5	0.1	-0.1	-0.3	-0.6	-0.6	-0.6	-0.5	-0.1
Domestic financing, net	1.1	1.7	0.6	-1.5	1.2	3.4	4.2	0.6	1.9	0.1	4.7
Bank financing	...	...	0.5	-1.1	0.3	5.4	4.1	0.5	3.2	...	...
Nonbank financing	...	...	0.1	-0.4	1.0	-2.0	0.1	—	-1.3	...	...

Sources: Ministry of Finance; International Monetary Fund (1991); and IMF staff estimates.
[1] Including consumer turnover tax through 1988.
[2] Including capital revenue.
[3] Including interest rate subsidies.
[4] Including net lending.

small-scale enterprises and professionals—will be inevitable. Implementation of proper accounting practices, pursuant to the Accounting Act, is an essential ingredient for improved tax administration. Ensuring that the expected flow of tax revenue is actually obtained represents a major and urgent challenge for the Hungarian authorities. In early 1992, tax revenue declined to well below the projected level, and the anticipated budget deficit for the year increased dramatically. Tax forecasting procedures must be improved, and tax enforcement needs to be strengthened.

The Government is committed to a systematic dismantling of remaining product-specific subsidies over the program period, with few exceptions such as those involving services (for example, mass transport) that confer external economies. This effort must be accompanied by a further development of targeted subsidies to households—subject to a means test—experiencing a drop in incomes below the physical subsistence level; such schemes need to be calibrated appropriately as to amounts and duration in order to avoid an assistance-induced poverty trap. More generally, social security reform must be geared to enhance the cost-effectiveness of existing schemes, by tightening legal eligibility requirements for, and control over, benefits so that only deserving recipients—on the basis of either past contributions or genuine need—have access to the appropriate scheme. These measures are indispensable for reducing the excessively high social security contribution rates, including those to the Solidarity Fund.

While implementing the insurance approach in the provision of health-care services, there is need to extend the application of co-payments and to introduce proper accounting practices for such services. For greater transparency and proper accountability, there is a good case for reallocating the existing social security schemes between the PF and HIF on the one hand and the state budget on the other, so that the PF, HIF, and Solidarity Fund encompass mainly insurance-type benefits while the budget finances assistance-type benefits. To this end, it has been proposed that maternity and child-care allowances, as well as the assistance component of old-age pensions and health-care benefits, be moved to the state budget.

Reform of budget practices and structure is another complex task for the near future. Consistent with the 1989 reform proposals, it is necessary to rid the state budget of commercially oriented central budgetary institutions; these institutions should operate in the private sector at arm's length from the budget, with possible access to government grants or contracts through bidding in the open market. All remaining budgetary institutions need to be brought under the effective control of the Ministry of Finance. To exercise influence over the preparation and execution of their budgets, the Ministry must have adequate data on these institutions, thereby ensuring that the allocation of fiscal resources is consistent with the government objectives in each expenditure category. In addition, extrabudgetary funds should for the most part be amalgamated into the budget and thus compete for resources on an equal footing with other budgetary appropriations. The separate status of such funds is justified only on exceptional grounds—notably when they finance contingent government liabilities out of earmarked revenue or when they provide well-defined benefits for user fees.

As regards intergovernmental fiscal relations, the reform agenda includes a clarification of local fiscal responsibilities, overhaul of land taxation, and assignment of certain state property to local jurisdictions. In addition, there is ample scope for simplifying the present mechanism of intergovernmental transfers on the basis of clearly defined criteria of regional equity and additionality. Accordingly, the present normative transfers to local self-governments would need to be replaced with an aggregate transfer related inversely with an index (such as regional or local GDP per capita, possibly in combination with various socioeconomic indicators) that best reflects the revenue capacity and resource need of a given local self-government. Such transfers, of course, would be provided in addition to project-specific matching grants and assistance through nationwide schemes (for example, the Employment Fund and the Solidarity Fund).

Further institution building involves the management and disposition of state property, including compensation for confiscated assets. In this regard, it is necessary to determine the appropriate involvement of financial intermediaries (that is, private insurance funds, pension funds, commercial banks), foreign owners, and own enterprise employees, in the privatization process. Moreover, the allocation of state-owned assets among various levels of government or extrabudgetary funds (for example, to the Pension Fund) and the disposition of proceeds from privatization have direct fiscal implications. The authorities correctly intend to use such windfall revenue primarily to retire government debt. Overall, a number of institutional steps are necessary to strengthen the market-based management of public debt. In particular, the establishment of a treasury to conduct both cash and debt management would be an important complement to the reform of the budget process. By the same token, the issuance of a broad variety of financial instruments—with different maturity, yield, and liquidity characteristics—should contribute to the demonetization of the budget deficit, and to more effective monetary control.

These reform tasks constitute a tall order by any standard. They require far more time than the period allotted for their completion and are not likely to materialize in the initially conceived form. Indeed, within both the executive and legislative branches, fiscal reform issues are competing with many other economic and noneconomic policy issues for the attention of decision makers who may have relatively little relevant experience, resulting in a protracted and inefficient process. But even more crucial is the vulnerability of a technically and politically weak legislature in its first session, facing powerful interest groups determined to dilute key reform measures. These groups are engaged in active lobbying for the retention of subsidies and tax preferences (for example, those benefiting the agricultural sector and foreign investors), easy eligibility for early retirement, disability pensions, sick pay, and other social security benefits (advocated mainly by redundant employees), central budgetary institutions (defended by the management and staff of these institutions), and regional distribution of fiscal resources without responsibilities (favored by some local self-governments), just to mention the most important ones. The demonstration effect from such opposition to reform may in turn weaken the necessary consensus behind the reform effort as a whole. Therefore, the Government bears a heavy responsibility in explaining the reform measures to the public and in stressing the need to view such measures as components of a coherent and indispensable package, whose unraveling could endanger the entire reform effort—as some parts may obviate the others because of second-best arguments and practical reasons. More generally, it is necessary to tackle these tasks in the context of a comprehensive and continuing reassessment of the role of the state in the economy.[44]

References

Abel, I., "Subsidy Reduction in the Hungarian Economy," *European Economy: Economic Transformation in Hungary and Poland*, No. 43 (March 1990), pp. 21–34.

Andersson, Krister, "Taxation and the Cost of Capital in Hungary and Poland: A Comparison with Selected European Countries," IMF Working Paper No. 90/123 (Washington: International Monetary Fund, December 1990).

Antal, L., *Gazdaságirányítási és pénzügyi rendszerünk a reform utján* [*Our economic and financial system on the road to reform*] (Budapest: KJK, 1985).

Bácskai, T., "New Developments in State Enterprise Taxation in Hungary," *Acta Oeconomica*, Vol. 6, No. 1–2 (1971), pp. 107–21.

Bird, Richard, and Christine Wallich, *Financing Local Government in Hungary*, World Bank Policy Research Working Paper No. WPS 869 (Washington: World Bank, March 1992).

Bokros, L., "Privatization in Hungary," in *Privatization in Eastern Europe*, ed. by A. Böhm and V.G. Kreačič (Ljubljana, Yugoslavia: International Center for Public Enterprises in Developing Countries, 1991).

---

[44]For a discussion of this overarching issue, see Kornai (1992).

Boote, Anthony R., and Janos Somogyi, *Economic Reform in Hungary Since 1968*, IMF Occasional Paper No. 83 (Washington: International Monetary Fund, 1991).

Gergely, I., "Személyi jövedelemadó, de hogyan?" ["Personal income tax—but how?"], *Közgazdasági Szemle*, Vol. 34 (June 1987), pp. 711-20.

Government of the Republic of Hungary, "A Program of Conversion and Development for the Hungarian Economy" (Budapest, March 1991).

International Monetary Fund, *Government Finance Statistics Yearbook, 1991* (Washington, 1991).

Jonas, Paul, *Taxation of Multinationals in Communist Countries* (New York: Praeger, 1978).

Kónya, L., "Further Improvement of the System of Enterprise Income and Wage Regulation," *Acta Oeconomica*, Vol. 7, No. 1 (1971), pp. 3-23.

Kopits, George, "Fiscal Reform in European Economies in Transition," in *The Transformation to a Market Economy*, Vol. II, ed. by Paul Marer and Salvatore Zecchini (Paris: Organization for Economic Cooperation and Development, 1991).

―――― (1992a), ed., *Tax Harmonization in the European Community: Policy Issues and Analysis*, IMF Occasional Paper No. 94 (Washington: International Monetary Fund, 1992).

―――― (1992b), "Fiscal and Monetary Policies During Transition: Some Reflections," paper prepared for the Conference on Democratic Governments and the Transition from Plan to Market, University of Twente, Enschede, August 13-15, 1992.

――――, R. Holzmann, G. Schieber, and E. Sidgwick, "Social Security Reform in Hungary," (unpublished; Washington: Fiscal Affairs Department, International Monetary Fund, October 12, 1990).

Kornai, János, *Economics of Shortage* (Amsterdam: North-Holland, 1980).

――――, "The Hungarian Reform Process: Visions, Hopes, and Reality," *Journal of Economic Literature*, Vol. 24 (December 1986), pp. 1687-1737.

――――, *The Road to a Free Economy—Shifting from a Socialist System: The Case of Hungary* (New York: W.W. Norton, 1990).

――――, "The Postsocialist Transition and the State: Reflections in the Light of Hungarian Fiscal Problems," *American Economic Review, Papers and Proceedings*, Vol. 82 (May 1992), pp. 1-21.

Kovács, János Mátyás, "Reform Economics: The Classification Gap," *Daedalus: Journal of the American Academy of Arts and Sciences*, Vol. 119, No. 1 (Winter 1990), pp. 215-48.

Kupa, Mihály, "Személyi jövedelemadó: elvek és viták" ["Personal income tax: concepts and debate"], *Közgazdasági Szemle*, Vol. 37 (June 1987), pp. 721-31.

――――, "Hungary: Tax Reform, 1988-89," *European Taxation*, Vol. 29 (January 1989), pp. 3-6.

Ministry of Finance (1982a), *Public Finance in Hungary: Act on Public Finance*, No. 1 (Budapest, 1982).

———— (1982b), *Public Finance in Hungary: The Social Insurance System*, No. 5 (Budapest, 1982).

———— (1982c), *Public Finance in Hungary: Income Regulation of Hungarian Enterprises*, No. 7 (Budapest, 1982).

————, *Public Finance in Hungary: Fiscal Policy Affecting the Private Sector and the Population*, No. 9 (Budapest, 1983).

———— (1985a), *Public Finance in Hungary: Income Regulation System of Hungarian Enterprises from 1985 on*, No. 22 (Budapest, 1985).

———— (1985b), *Public Finance in Hungary: Act on Public Finances (Unified Text on the Amended Text)*, No. 23 (Budapest, 1985).

———— (1985c), *Public Finance in Hungary: Turnover Tax System in Hungary*, No. 24 (Budapest, 1985).

———— (1985d), *Public Finance in Hungary: Scope of Authority and Duties of the Minister of Finance*, No. 25 (Budapest, 1985).

————, *Public Finance in Hungary: Management of Public Budgetary Institutions*, No. 31 (Budapest, 1986).

————, *Public Finance in Hungary: State Budget, 1987*, No. 36 (Budapest, 1987).

————, "Brief for Members of Parliament on the Budget Reform" (unpublished; Budapest, September 1988).

————, "Public Sector Reform: Proposition to the Parliament" (unpublished; Budapest, May 1989).

———— (1991a), *Public Finance in Hungary: Finances of Local Self-Governments; Local Taxes*, No. 77 (Budapest, 1991).

———— (1991b), *Public Finance in Hungary: State Budget, 1991*, No. 79 (Budapest, 1991).

———— (1991c), *Public Finance in Hungary: Privatization Process in Hungary*, No. 81 (Budapest, 1991).

Ministry of Social Affairs and Health, *Utkeresés és szociális biztonság* [*In search of a path for social security*] (Budapest, 1989).

Rácz, L., and F. Vissi, "Az eröforrások lineáris adoztatása vagy korszerü ár- és jövedelemszabályozás?" ["Linear taxation of resources or price and income regulation?"], *Közgazdasági Szemle*, Vol. 20 (September 1973), pp. 1060-74.

CHAPTER 5

Fundamental Fiscal Reform in Poland: Issues of Design and Implementation

Ved P. Gandhi

Poland was one of the first among centrally planned countries to have committed itself, as early as mid-1989, to the adoption of market-oriented economic reforms. The authorities viewed a fundamental reform of the country's fiscal structure as a major prerequisite for the transition to the new economic system. This chapter highlights the main characteristics of the country's fiscal structure prior to 1989. It then outlines what the author considers to be the major elements of a fundamental reform of the country's fiscal system that would fully support the market orientation of the economy. The paper then reports on progress made on fiscal reform to date and identifies the issues that still need to be addressed.

Pre-1989 Fiscal Structure

Fiscal Indicators

Between the state budget and extrabudgetary funds, the Polish Government appropriated almost 50 percent of GDP during most of the 1980s and, as Table 1 shows, there was little change in this proportion all through this period, despite the partial reform efforts of the Government.

Selected fiscal indicators, calculated from data relating to the state budget, are given in Table 2. Several characteristics of the country's fiscal structure prior to 1989 are noteworthy.

On the revenue side, three trends are predominant. First, the ratio of tax revenue to GDP declined between 1982 and 1988. This was more the result of erosion owing to high inflation than of any large reduction of tax rates or excessive tax reliefs to taxpayers. Second, direct taxes contributed almost 60 percent of total tax revenue, with enterprises accounting

Ved P. Gandhi is Assistant Director in the Fiscal Affairs Department. This paper draws heavily on the unpublished work he carried out jointly with László Garamfalvi, Robert Holzman, and George Kopits in late 1989. Richard Hemming, Gerd Schwartz, and Charles Vehorn have also provided significant help. The author gratefully acknowledges their contributions; however, none of them is responsible for any errors and omissions that may remain.

Table 1. Poland: Major Budgetary Aggregates
(In percent of GDP)

	1982	1983	1984	1985	1986	1987	1988	1989	1990
State budget									
Revenue	43.4	39.1	39.7	40.4	39.9	34.2	35.6	30.8	33.3
Expenditure	46.3	41.2	41.9	41.6	41.0	37.7	37.0	37.0	32.6
Surplus/deficit (–)	-2.9	-2.0	-2.2	-1.2	-1.1	-3.5	-1.4	-6.1	0.7
Extrabudgetary funds									
Revenue	10.0	11.8	12.6	13.0	13.8	16.8	16.6	17.4	18.3
Of which: transfers from state budget	2.6	2.3	2.4	2.6	3.1	3.0	3.2	5.0	6.0
Expenditure	9.5	10.6	10.9	11.7	13.0	14.1	15.2	18.7	16.2
Of which: transfers to state budget	0.2	0.7	0.7	1.3	—	—	—	—	—
Surplus/deficit (–)	0.5	1.2	1.7	1.2	0.8	2.7	1.4	-1.3	2.1
On transactions with state budget	2.4	1.6	1.7	1.3	3.1	3.0	3.2	5.0	6.0
On other transactions	1.9	0.4	0.0	0.1	2.3	0.3	1.8	-0.3	-3.9
General government									
Revenue	49.8	46.8	47.9	48.3	49.4	46.9	48.0	41.5	43.0
Expenditure	52.2	47.6	48.4	48.2	49.7	47.7	48.0	48.9	39.8
Surplus/deficit (–)	-2.4	-0.8	-0.5	0.1	-0.3	-0.8	—	-7.4	3.1
Memorandum item:									
GDP (in billions of zlotys)	5,546	6,924	8,576	10,445	12,953	16,940	29,629	96,549	591,518

Sources: Various publications.

for most of this revenue. Third, between the profits tax and the turnover tax, enterprises contributed almost 26 percent of GDP and 80 percent of total tax revenue. The profits tax and the turnover tax were therefore the most important sources of government revenue. The average burden of the enterprise profits tax was between 45 percent and 50 percent of profits before taxes of socialized enterprises, while the average burden of the turnover tax was about 23 percent of total private consumption.

On the government expenditure side, once again, three facts are apparent. First, subsidies to consumers and producers accounted for almost 45 percent of total expenditure (and were an even higher percentage in earlier years), with subsidies for food, housing, and exports being the most important. Second, wages and salaries of public sector employees absorbed unusually small proportions of total expenditure, and their share in GDP remained almost constant over time. Third, the Government's direct capital expenditure was never a significant proportion of GDP, primarily because socialized enterprises undertook most of the public sector investment.

Investment by the socialized enterprises accounted for almost 20 percent of GDP, over 80 percent of total investment, and almost 90 percent of industrial output in the economy. Based on available data, profits before taxes of the socialized enterprise sector were quite impressive (almost 28 percent of GDP in 1988). Even after paying the enterprise profits tax and dividends to the Government and various benefits to workers, in 1987 and 1988 enterprises retained 70 percent or more of their profits after taxes.

Different Roles of the State and Their Fiscal Implications

The foregoing indicators of the fiscal structure were the by-product of the very active role of the state in the Polish economy. Similar to other centrally planned economies, the state had many responsibilities, each of which had important implications for the country's fiscal structure prior to 1989.

First, in Poland the state played a dominant role as an investor and producer through socialized enterprises. This had major implications for the tax system, public expenditure policies, and the workings of the parastatal enterprises. The tax system came to be dominated by taxes on enterprises, which were frequently negotiated between the Government and each enterprise. The enterprise profits tax system therefore became more of an ex post profit-sharing system, with the Government deciding on the amount of final (tax) payments to be made by each enterprise, based on its final profits, the state-established "norms" for paying bonuses to its workers, and the investment needs of the enterprise for plant modernization and capacity expansion as determined under the plan.

Table 2. Poland: Fiscal Indicators

(In percent)

	1982	1983	1984	1985	1986	1987	1988	1989	1990
Revenue									
Total revenue/GDP	43.4	39.1	39.7	40.4	39.9	34.2	35.6	30.8	33.3
Tax revenue/GDP	39.0	36.3	36.5	37.0	37.5	31.5	33.4	25.2	28.2
Taxes on income and property/GDP	24.2	20.0	20.3	21.9	23.1	18.4	20.5	16.2	21.0
Individuals	4.1	4.4	4.4	4.4	4.5	4.3	4.3	2.7	3.0
Enterprises	19.5	14.9	14.7	16.4	17.7	13.4	15.5	13.6	18.0
Taxes on goods and services/GDP	14.8	16.3	16.2	15.2	14.4	13.0	12.8	8.9	7.2
Domestic	11.5	13.8	13.6	12.3	11.6	10.6	10.8	8.9	6.6
Foreign	3.3	2.6	2.5	2.9	2.8	2.4	2.0	—	0.6
Taxes on goods and services/private consumption	...	...	25.5	24.6	23.6	21.8	23.5	17.1	...
Foreign trade taxes/value of imports	...	...	16.1	16.9	16.6	12.9	10.1	...	...
Socialized enterprise income tax/profits before taxes of socialized enterprises	61.1	46.9	45.7	50.9	49.5	45.6	47.2	31.8	37.7
Direct taxes/tax revenue	62.1	55.1	55.7	59.1	61.5	58.6	61.5	64.7	73.7
Expenditure									
Total expenditure/GDP	46.3	41.2	41.9	41.6	41.0	37.7	37.0	37.0	32.6
Current expenditure/GDP	41.4	35.6	36.7	35.9	35.2	32.2	31.6	33.6	29.9
Wages and salaries/GDP	4.1	4.4	4.5	4.6	4.4	4.2	4.0	5.1	4.1
Purchases/GDP	4.0	3.8	3.7	3.7	3.8	3.6	3.3	2.5	3.6

Subsidies/GDP	20.6	16.5	17.3	16.5	16.3	15.9	16.0	12.9	7.3
Consumer	9.1	7.3	7.5	7.3	7.9	8.8	9.0	8.4	3.9
Food	3.8	3.4	2.8	3.0	3.1	3.4	4.9	3.7	0.2
Coal	0.7	0.5	0.5	0.5	0.7	0.8	0.4	0.2	0.1
Housing	3.0	2.5	3.2	2.8	3.1	3.6	2.5	2.4	2.8
Transportation	1.5	0.8	0.9	0.9	0.9	0.8	0.8	0.9	0.4
Other	11.5	9.1	9.8	9.2	8.3	7.1	7.0	4.5	3.4
Export	2.9	3.1	3.5	3.6	3.1	2.5	2.2		
Coal	1.5	1.4	1.8	1.9	2.3	1.0	1.1	3.3	1.6
Agriculture	1.6	1.5	2.0	1.8	1.8	1.8	1.4	1.0	0.1
Transfers/GDP	8.2	6.8	6.5	6.5	4.2	4.0	4.2	6.3	7.7
Capital expenditure/GDP	4.8	5.5	5.3	5.7	5.9	5.6	5.3	3.3	2.8
Consumer subsidies/private consumption	⋯	⋯	11.8	11.8	13.0	14.7	16.5	9.2	⋯
Socialized enterprises									
Investment/GDP	16.1	15.0	16.1	16.8	17.8	18.5	18.6	10.1	—
Investment/investment in the economy	84.6	78.6	80.5	81.9	83.3	83.9	84.8	58.3	—
Gross operating surplus/GDP	24.4	23.7	23.8	23.8	23.0	27.1	27.3	49.4	29.9
Turnover taxes/GDP	11.7	14.3	14.0	12.6	11.2	10.0	13.9	13.2	7.1
Subsidies/GDP	12.1	10.6	10.9	10.5	10.8	9.1	14.5	13.5	5.7
Profits before taxes/GDP	25.0	19.8	20.8	21.7	22.5	26.2	27.8	55.3	28.3
Income tax and dividends/GDP	15.3	9.3	9.5	11.0	11.2	11.9	13.1	35.8	45.3
Income tax and dividends/profits before taxes	61.1	46.9	45.7	50.9	49.5	45.6	47.2	35.8	47.0
Profits after taxes/GDP	9.7	10.5	11.3	10.7	11.4	14.3	14.7	35.4	16.4
Workers' benefits/profits after taxes	34.4	34.4	37.1	37.9	31.6	22.7	31.3	17.6	—
Retentions/profits after taxes	65.6	65.6	62.9	62.1	68.4	77.3	68.7	82.3	86.6
Development and reserve funds/investment	36.9	44.1	39.0	31.1	33.9	44.2	43.9	—	—

Sources: Various publications.

As regards public expenditures, a number of economic and social functions of the Government were assigned to parastatal entities; as a result, numerous extrabudgetary funds, supported by special levies on enterprises, were established to finance the activities of these entities. This resulted in a large and complex extrabudgetary economy with serious implications for budget monitoring and expenditure control.

Many socialized enterprises grew into inefficient monopolies and enterprises that had to be supported through a variety of open subsidies (such as export subsidies) or hidden subsidies (such as credit subsidies and tax reliefs), and these subsidies came to dominate government expenditure. Moreover, as socialized enterprises had little autonomy in making their investment and financing decisions, or had little control over their depreciation or dividend policies, their finances and indebtedness became closely intertwined with the finances and indebtedness of the state budget.

Second, the state controlled the prices of most inputs and outputs. Among other things, this required the authorities to constantly monitor and in fact frequently increase or decrease the turnover tax rates applicable to individual commodities, with a view to clearing commodity markets, as well as financially supporting unprofitable sectors unable to pay legislated turnover tax rates. On the expenditure side of the budget, it called for massive outlays on consumer subsidies and subsidies to industrial and agricultural inputs.

Third, the state played an active role in incomes policy, particularly in determining wages in the socialized sector and incomes arising in the nonsocialized sector. This, too, had important implications for the fiscal structure. On the revenue side of the budget, individual income taxation played a negligible role in the government revenue structure as, for the most part, wages in the economy were tax exempt. Highly progressive and schedular income taxes were applied on incomes arising from the nonsocialized sector to discourage the development of the private sector and to reduce incomes earned in the nonsocialized sector to the levels prevailing in the socialized sector. On the expenditure side of the budget, with wages nominally fixed at low levels by the state, wages and salaries comprised a smaller proportion of expenditure, while a large proportion of the budget was devoted to price support subsidies and to financing the social welfare system.

Finally, the lack of market orientation of the economy affected macrofiscal policymaking and budgeting. For example, there was little appreciation of the effects of fiscal policies on aggregate demand, output, prices, and balance of payments. As a result, fiscal deficits, arising from the implementation of various nonfiscal government policies, were not of much concern to policymakers. These deficits were frequently monetized with little or no attention paid to external and domestic debt manageent. To cite another example, budgeting was used more as a tool of planning than of fiscal analysis and policymaking. Thus, little or no effort was made to institute appropriate budgetary controls or to develop an adequate cash management capacity in the Ministry of Finance.

Strategy of Fundamental Fiscal Reform

A major transformation from a centrally planned economy to a market-oriented economy therefore required a fundamental reform of the country's fiscal structure. This was essential, particularly because the state was about to shed its role as a major investor and producer in the economy and because most existing socialized enterprises were to be privatized and the inefficient ones among them were to be allowed to go bankrupt. In addition, most price controls were to be eliminated and wages and other factor incomes were to be determined by the market, which also implied fundamental fiscal reform. Finally, once market forces were to start determining resource allocation in the economy, macrofiscal policymaking and budgeting were going to assume their usual important roles. The need for wide-ranging structural fiscal reform thus was both immediate and urgent.

Objectives of Fiscal Reforms

Fiscal reform had three main objectives: (1) to create the conditions under which the market mechanism would exert its allocative superiority; this required a change from the Government as an active player that determined all the key economic variables to one that encouraged the appropriate economic environment and provided an adequate social safety net; (2) to disengage the Government, over time, from the responsibilities of ownership of economic means of production; and (3) to secure fiscal adjustment in the transitional period.

To support the first objective, an entirely different fiscal system had to replace the existing system. This new system was to help curtail the direct involvement of the state in the economy as a producer, a price controller, and an incomes' regulator. Instead, it was to foster private initiative and allow market forces to allocate resources. Public expenditure policies were to be reoriented, for example, from direct investment in, or subsidization of, production and distribution to providing a social and economic infrastructure to facilitate private production and distribution. A new tax system was needed that would not thwart private initiative and enterprise, produce adequate revenue, and also be easy to administer. Further, totally different budgetary procedures and perspectives on fiscal policymaking and fiscal deficits were desirable.

In support of the second objective of fiscal reform, namely, to facilitate disengagement of the state from the socialized enterprise sector and to create healthy competitive conditions, many obvious changes had to be set in motion. Among other things, serious efforts had to be made to privatize and to institute fiscal as well as nonfiscal reforms to help make the remaining socialized enterprises economically efficient.

The final, and equally important, objective of fiscal reform was to facilitate fiscal adjustment during the transitional period. Because of institutional rigidities, the authorities had to reckon that this transition could easily last for several years. During this period, the tax system had to be made productive enough to allow the state to meet the fiscal costs of the economic and social upheaval caused by restructuring the economy.

Main Elements of Fiscal Reform Program

It was clear from the outset that a fiscal reform program for Poland entailing the development of a new fiscal system would have to be comprehensive and consist of at least five elements.

First, it would cover macrofiscal policymaking. Among other things, this would mean redefining the appropriate role of government in the future economy of Poland and instituting a fiscal strategy for domestic and external debt management.

Second, the previous tax system would have to be reformed while ensuring the adoption of taxes to raise needed budgetary revenues in as fair and nondistortionary a fashion as possible and to create an "appropriate" balance between taxation of enterprises and taxation of individuals, as well as between taxation of incomes and taxation of consumption.

Third, fiscal reform would include the reform of the income support system, reducing or eliminating consumer subsidies and reforming the social security system, including the creation of a strong social safety net.

Fourth, the entire budgetary system would need to be reformed. This would entail redefining the role of the extrabudgetary economy and rationalizing the budget organization, as well as strengthening the budgetary procedures and controls.

Finally, the reform of the socialized enterprise sector had to be a major element of the overall fiscal reform. Along with other economic policies, fiscal instruments and institutions had to be used to facilitate the restructuring of their ownership. Their investment decisions and financial behavior also needed to be urgently reformed.

These five categories of fiscal reform are described in some detail below, followed by a possible sequence in which the reforms needed to be carried out.

Reform of Macrofiscal Policies

Given the important linkages among the fiscal deficit and aggregate demand, savings-investment balance, prices, and balance of payments, policymakers needed, even in the short run, to be conscious of the macroeconomic damage that higher fiscal deficits can cause. They had to recognize that many market-oriented reforms of the economy, such as price liberalization, exchange rate adjustment, interest rate reform, and reform of wage policies, were likely to result in significant increases, as well as decreases, in government revenue or expenditure, with major uncertainties as to the "net" fiscal outcome. Policymakers, therefore, needed to be ready with contingency revenue and expenditure measures that could be put into effect to reduce large fiscal deficits.

Over the medium term, at least three fiscal issues will require the attention of policymakers:

First, the exact role of the Government in the future economy of Poland will have to be defined. The future scope and functions of the public sector will have to be carefully delineated to facilitate the reorientation of the economy. Certain functions of the Government (for example, subsidies to consumers and producers) will have to be scaled down substantially. On the other hand, various other functions (for example, investment in the social and economic infrastructure) obviously will have to be strengthened to facilitate private sector growth, while still other functions (for example, unemployment compensation and targeted social transfers) will have to be greatly extended, at least during the restructuring of the economy.

Second, the reorientation of the economy, and the changed manner in which economic resources will be allocated in the future, will have important effects on the composition of production, the use of economic resources, and the distribution of factor incomes. As a consequence, there could be major effects on budgetary aggregates and possibly on levels of fiscal deficits. In order to conduct macrofiscal policy in an orderly fashion, the tax system and expenditure policies will have to be restructured so as to take advantage of the marked shifts in the way national income in the future is likely to be produced, distributed, and used.

Third, debt management will also require closer attention from policymakers. Notwithstanding the sizable reduction in external debt, Poland might be able to negotiate debt restructuring with its external creditors, and new external borrowing should be contracted only where it can be used efficiently; besides, government guarantees will have to be strictly limited. As to the domestic indebtedness of the public sector, it will change its character and entail a direct financial cost, as the Government increasingly finances its fiscal deficits through the sale of treasury bills and bonds to nonbanking institutions and investors instead of monetizing them. A carefully considered policy of domestic debt management, therefore, will need to be established and implemented, taking into account a number of relevant factors.

Reform of Tax System

As mentioned above, the earlier tax system was out of tune with the needs of a reoriented economy. This demanded an urgent reform of the previous enterprise profits tax, personal income taxes, and the turnover tax. In reforming the tax system, the criteria of revenue productivity and elasticity, economic neutrality, equity, and ease of tax administration were most important.

Obviously, to the extent possible, the personal income tax had to be a universal and global tax with a level of exemption and a rate schedule consistent with the equity and administrative criteria. This meant that all incomes had to be aggregated and taxed equally. This also meant that the exclusion of agricultural incomes from income tax, which had been the case so far, and subjecting interest and dividends to a separate flat final tax, which was the preferred solution on incentive and administrative grounds, could run counter to the universality as well as progressivity of income taxation.

The enterprise profits tax had to be broad-based and nondistortionary. This implied that all tax preferences, both systemic and discretionary, granted to selected activities and sectors had to be eliminated. Tax holidays to future foreign investors and foreign-owned enterprises also had to be eliminated in favor of a lower tax rate generally. All interest payments had to be tax deductible. The basis for calculating depreciation allowances had to be liberalized by permitting the use of the declining-balance method, and the number of depreciation rates had to be reduced drastically. Carryforward of losses had to be permitted into the future for a given period, say, up to three years, and subject to a maximum amount, say, up to the value of the assets.

The turnover tax had to be replaced with a broad-based and more uniform-rate VAT. This tax had to be supported by selective excises on sumptuary goods and a few selected luxury products.

In designing the new tax system, thought had also to be given to the reform of customs duties and the fiscal and economic roles they should play in the short run and in the long run. To the extent possible, customs duties should play a limited fiscal role, if any, in the longer-term tax structure of the country but, in the short run, they could be retained while all possibilities for further liberalizing imports and rationalizing tariffs are being explored.

Reform of Social Programs

In order to be socially effective and fiscally efficient, social support programs, which had in the past taken the form of consumer subsidies and monetary transfers, had to be reformed. As restructuring the economy would create large unemployment and price reform would reduce the real incomes of certain households, an appropriate social safety net had to be established for the needy. Consumer subsidies, including housing subsidies, ultimately would need to be replaced with needs- and means-tested monetary transfers.

Reform of Budgetary System

In order to improve overall budgeting and to allow better fiscal analysis, the role of the extrabudgetary economy in Poland needed to be redefined. The Budget Department of the Ministry of Finance had to be reorganized along more functional lines to make it an effective fiscal institution and a new budget nomenclature had to be instituted that was based on an administrative classification of expenditures but from which economic and functional classifications could be easily derived without a lengthy process of reclassification. An administrative unit, within the Ministry of Finance, in charge of cash management of the operations of the general government had to be created in order to facilitate effective fiscal monitoring. The extrabudgetary funds had to be limited to only those few that were fiscally viable and economically justified, while all others that could not function without budgetary transfers had to be abolished.

Reform of the Socialized Enterprise Sector

In the past, socialized enterprises were in many ways indistinguishable from the general government in Poland. Therefore, enterprise reform could not be limited purely to financial flows between enterprises and the state budget but also had to encompass certain nonfiscal aspects, specifically, reform of ownership and market structure, reform of financing and investment decision making, and the elimination of most enterprise subsidies.

The divestiture of socialized enterprises and the widest possible public participation were needed. In addition, an effective antimonopoly law had to be enacted to encourage the systematic and speedy breakup of enterprises.

Politically motivated rescue operations of socialized enterprises, which were faced with hard budget constraints and market prices, had to be avoided as far as possible. Where loss-making enterprises could be rehabilitated through restructuring, this task had to include carefully crafted contractual agreements between enterprise management, workers' councils, creditors, and others, with objective indicators of performance as well as mechanisms of periodic reviews specified in each case.

New structures had to be established so that all future decisions on the public infrastructure would be made according to criteria based on the social rate of return. Further, all government transfers to socialized enterprises, including indirect subsidies through preferential bank credits or exchange rates, would be recorded as expenditures in the state budget. These measures were essential for creating greater transparency in fiscal policy.

As is obvious from the above, a large number of time-consuming fiscal reforms had to be carried out to transform the Polish economy. However, not all of the reforms were equally important, or needed to be undertaken right away. If necessary, the reforms could be carried out in two stages, with their sequencing guided by economic necessity, institutional preparedness, and timing of their likely economic effects.

In the first stage, fiscal reforms of immediate importance that supported the adjustment effort had to be carried out. In this connection, the top priorities were securing government revenue (by broadening the bases of existing taxes, particularly consumption taxes, and capturing the emerging private sector in the tax base), protecting the unemployed and the poor (by instituting a cost-effective social safety net), and containing the fiscal deficit (by, among other things, establishing early on a cash management unit in the Ministry of Finance). The size of the extrabudgetary economy also had to be reduced significantly. Finally, the socialized enterprise sector had to be reformed, by identifying the enterprises to be privatized, initiating appropriate procedures for the privatization, closing down or starting bankruptcy proceedings against unsalvageable enterprises, and designing rehabilitation measures for the remaining (mostly loss-making) enterprises while forcing them to face market forces and to take efficient economic decisions.

In the second stage, fiscal reform aimed at putting a full-fledged new fiscal system in place and building new fiscal institutions needed to be given top priority. So as to provide a level playing field for all economic agents and to secure revenues in the most nondistortionary way, all elements of tax reform would need to be legislated and a thorough review of the tax administration capacity and procedures undertaken for instituting measures to implement new taxes. This stage should also see work initiated on tariff reform consistent with rules under the General Agreement on Tariffs and Trade and the tariff structure of the European Community, including a review of the customs administration and procedures. In order to reduce public intermediation of resources and to prevent price distortions, consumer and producer subsidies would need to be eliminated and the future scope of the functions of government would need to be defined more precisely. To make the best use of public resources, comprehensive budget reform would have to be initiated. This should include the reorganization of the Budget Department in the Ministry of Finance and the rationalization of budget classification and budgetary procedures, the establishment of a debt management unit in the Ministry of Finance, and the development of debt management policies.

Implementation of Fiscal Reform

At the end of 1989, the Polish Government faced an economic crisis. Domestic and external imbalances were widening at an alarming pace, and hyperinflation loomed. The Government, therefore, launched an economic reform program in early 1990 that focused on stabilization. After an initial devaluation of the zloty, a fixed exchange rate, together with a strict incomes policy, became nominal anchors aimed at breaking the inflation spiral. The anchors were supported by tight monetary and fiscal policies, which were remarkably successful. Inflation dropped sharply during the year, while both the fiscal and external accounts swung into surplus. But output fell by over 10 percent and has declined ever since. Efforts to stimulate a recovery have set back the stabilization effort somewhat. The early experience of Poland has shown that the mix of stabilization and structural policies has to be appropriately balanced and that systemic reform has to be accelerated to speed the transition to a market economy.

During 1990, genuine progress was made with price and trade liberalization. But, in most other areas, measures proved to be more difficult to implement, and preparation time was longer than initially envisaged. This section describes the progress that has been made with respect to the individual elements of fiscal reform to date and the problems the authorities have encountered.

Tax Reform

With the exception of adjustments to the structure and level of turnover taxes (carried out continuously since 1989) and steps toward limiting reliefs—and making their application less discretionary—under the enterprise profits tax (mainly in 1990), the tax reform effort to date has consisted of the introduction of a personal income tax (PIT), with effect from January 1, 1992, and of an enterprise income tax (EIT), since February 15, 1992, as well as preparations for the introduction of a new value-added tax (VAT).

The PIT law, passed on July 26, 1991, legislates a progressive tax on earned income, covering wages and salaries, fringe benefits, pensions, and rental incomes. There are three tax rates (20, 30, and 40 percent) applicable to high income brackets which, in future, will be indexed to wage growth. There is a sufficiently high income exemption to keep low-income earners outside the income tax net, and wage and salary earners enjoy a standard deduction equivalent to 3 percent of that income. Incomes from certain types of interest payments and dividends are subject to a final tax of 20 percent withheld at source. While capital gains from the sale of stocks and bonds are exempt from tax for tax years 1992 and 1993, capital gains realized from the sale of real estate are to be taxed at a reduced tax rate of 10 percent. Agricultural incomes and personal interest receipts remain exempt from tax, as are about 35 other categories of receipts. The new PIT operates as a pay-as-you-earn (PAYE) tax that is withheld at source, and the law allows joint filing of tax returns by husband and wife. Since the law is based on the French quotient system, there are some fears that it will result in a flood of income tax returns and present serious problems of income tax administration.

An EIT has also been enacted. Under this tax, a flat rate of 40 percent is to be imposed on enterprise profits. However, the tax contains numerous tax preferences, not the least of which is the complete exemption of agricultural activities. The law also permits accelerated depreciation allowances, generous reserves for bad debts, and a three-year carryforward of losses.

The VAT (called the "goods and services tax") has been debated in parliament for a long time now. When enacted, it will be a broad-based consumption tax, with a wider coverage than the existing turnover tax. Excise duties on alcohol, tobacco, petroleum products, and 12 other items will also be levied. Three rates of VAT are expected—0, 7, and 22 percent. Unprocessed foods, financial services, and a few other services will be the notable exemptions. Exports, medicines, and some agricultural inputs will be zero rated (the last two items until the end of 1995); processed foods, building materials, and a few other items (as well as medicines and agricultural imports after the end of 1995) will be taxed at 7 percent; and all other goods and services, not specifically exempted, will be taxed at 22 percent.

While the proposed structures of the PIT, EIT, and the VAT seem broadly appropriate and in line with the strategy described above, the key to their successful implementation is administrative preparedness. In particular, the detailed design of the VAT, which will be an entirely new tax, would certainly need to be tailored to administrative capacity and adequate preparations for its implementation will need to be made.

Unfortunately, at the time of writing, the approval of the VAT law by parliament and the president has been delayed. As a result, the design of many administrative procedures necessary to implement a VAT cannot begin. Coordination among the various agencies involved in administering the VAT also has been cumbersome. Decisions on data processing remain unfinished, largely because of uncertainties surrounding computer funding and strategy, and reorganization of local tax offices too has been delayed.

Public Expenditure Policy

The principal thrust of expenditure policy so far has been a sharp reduction in subsidies, both to households and enterprises. These stood at about 16 percent of GDP in 1988, but were reduced to 13 percent of GDP in 1989, 7 percent of GDP in 1990, and less than 5 percent of GDP in 1991.

For the most part, these reductions reflect far-reaching price liberalization (only 12 percent of industrial producer prices and 17 percent of consumer prices are said to be subject to price controls in mid-1992). Subsidies on agricultural inputs and food, together with exports, have been virtually eliminated since early 1992; coal subsidy has been abolished. Housing continues to be subsidized, mostly by way of subsidies for housing construction and interest on housing loans, the latter through the banking system.

Capital expenditure has also been curtailed since 1988. It fell by 0.5 percentage point of GDP between 1988 and 1990 (see Table 2). Public investment in infrastructure development needs to be expanded, and the Government is undertaking a major review of public investment.

Much of the reduction in subsidies and capital expenditure has meant a lowering of total expenditure, but there has been some additional spending on the social safety net.

Social Programs

Between 1988 and 1991, expenditure on pensions, family benefits, and unemployment compensation and social assistance increased by about 8 percent of GDP; budget support of these programs rose by 3 percent of GDP. During 1989, the rapid increase in inflation strained the state pension system and eroded significantly the real value of pensions. Since early 1990, in principle, pensions are supposed to be revalued at the end of each quarter in line with the increase in average wages in the previous quarter; in practice, this has not been the case and the real value of pensions has been allowed to erode through inadequate indexation for inflation. Also, in order to ensure a minimum benefit level, the lowest pension is set at 35 percent of the average wage.

Unemployment has risen sharply, a result of stabilization and restructuring, and the introduction of unemployment benefits has been a significant social safety reform. In March 1992, duration limits (of 12 months) and flat rate benefits (equivalent to 35 percent of wage) were established. Nevertheless, unemployment benefits continue to absorb a large part of the Labor Fund's resources. The Labor Fund also finances labor market measures, such as training and retraining benefits, intervention jobs, and credit for the creation of new jobs and activities.

Between 1990 and 1992, social assistance schemes were enlarged to provide some shelter to the most needy from the immediate effects of the macroeconomic stabilization program. Social assistance currently consists of the following: permanent cash benefits targeted to the elderly and the disabled with no pension rights; temporary cash benefits granted under special circumstances, for instance to the unemployed with no benefit rights; special credits for the disabled and for families in temporary financial difficulties; the maintenance of nursing homes; special programs for single mothers bringing up disabled children; and "quick reaction" government programs. Local authorities are responsible for all these social assistance schemes.

Budgetary System

General government in Poland consists of 49 regional governments (*voivodships*) and more than 2,400 communes and cities (local authorities). Previously, the *voivodships* and local authorities were no more than administrative subdivisions of the Central Government. While they had separate budgets, these were jointly enacted in the context of a consolidated state budget.

The structure of the state budget was changed markedly in 1991. In line with the increased autonomy being granted to local authorities, their revenue and expenditures were separated out of the state budget, with only the transfer from the budget to the local authorities recorded as an expenditure item. Local authorities have in the past been required to balance their budgets. Deficits are now permissible, although there are restrictions on access to credit and the ability to issue securities. There are, however, concerns that the financial management of local authorities will become more of a problem than in the past. Establishing mechanisms for monitoring and controlling their expenditure is therefore of high priority.

Imposing such mechanisms, of course, will be part of a wider effort to improve expenditure monitoring and control. While the integration of most of the extrabudgetary funds into the state budget—only the two social insurance funds, the Labor Fund, and a few others are still outside the budget—has provided a measure of additional influence over the expenditure of these funds, existing procedures seem to be somewhat arbitrary. Since 1990, reliance has been placed mainly on assigned cash limits on ministries' spending. With the planned reorganization of the Ministry of Finance, budget procedures may be overhauled soon. Also, it is possible that the budget nomenclature will be changed, reporting procedures will be improved, modern systems of budgetary planning and cash management will be put in place, and attention will be given to strengthening the Government's domestic and external debt management capacity.

Privatization of Socialized Enterprises

Enterprise privatization continues to lag in Poland, partly for the lack of a clear-cut approach regarding property rights. Privatization began in earnest during 1991. However, while the privatization of small-scale shops, the wholesale trade, trucking, and other services has been rapid, the privatization of larger enterprises appears to have proceeded somewhat slowly. It is estimated that there have been only about 100 buyouts by mid-1992, primarily through the transfer and leasing of the assets of the enterprise to the workers or management. The stipulation that share purchases by foreigners must be approved by the Foreign Investment Agency if the par value of the shares exceeds 10 percent of the share capital has caused many foreign investors to take a fairly cautious approach until now.

Concluding Observations

Although Poland has made substantial progress on fundamental fiscal reform, the process has been somewhat slow and uneven. Of course, this is not totally unexpected. Drafting new tax laws, in the face of a vocal and multiparty parliament, and strengthening tax administrative capacity, in the face of shortages of trained manpower, have taken time. It was perhaps easy to reduce consumer and producer subsidies, in order to contain public expenditures, but to design an appropriate social safety net or to formulate an infrastructure development plan consistent with available budgetary resources was not that easy. Shifting expenditure responsibilities on to local authorities, including many social assistance schemes, was also simple, but ensuring their financial viability has taken a lot of time and effort. Instituting a sound budget management system too has lagged, and the Government has had to make do with the imposition of "temporary" cash limits on ministry expenditures. Finally, the privatization of socialized enterprises is proving far more difficult than envisaged earlier.

To sum up, it is not for lack of willpower and effort that the Polish authorities have not—until now—succeeded in instituting the wide-ranging and fundamental fiscal reform described in this paper; carrying out fiscal reform in economies in transition, and doing it right, is simply a laborious and time-consuming process.

CHAPTER 6

Romania: Assessment of Turnover and Income Taxes

Ved P. Gandhi and Leif Mutén

Two major taxes in Romania's tax system have been the turnover tax and wage fund tax. The turnover tax accounted for about 26 percent of general government revenue (over 9 percent of GDP) in 1991, while the wage fund tax, including small taxes on nonwage incomes, contributed less than 25 percent of general government revenue (about 8 percent of GDP) in the same year.[1] Profit remittances, though not labeled as enterprise profit tax until mid-1990, contributed about 15 percent of total government revenue, while social insurance fund contributions accounted for over 26 percent of total government revenue (Table 1).

This chapter makes an appraisal of Romania's turnover tax and income taxes on individuals and enterprises. It also highlights issues in, and the scope of, reform of these two taxes.

Turnover Taxation

Prior to November 1, 1990, as in other centrally planned economies, the turnover tax in Romania was simply calculated as the difference between the producer price and the retail price (net of the trading margins, if any). Since both prices were set by the Government, the turnover tax was nothing but a price differential, intended to transfer funds from a particular sector to the Ministry of Finance. The rate of turnover tax on each product was therefore specified as a fixed sum per unit and, in effect, there were as many tax rates as product categories or items. No turnover tax was payable when an item was sold by one manufacturing or service enterprise to another, all enterprises being owned by the state

---

Ved P. Gandhi is Assistant Director in the Fiscal Affairs Department. At the time the chapter was written, Leif Mutén was Senior Advisor in the same department. Mr. Gandhi is the author of the first part of this chapter, and Mr. Mutén is the author of the second part.

[1] The terms "turnover tax" and "wage fund tax" should be interpreted with some caution. These are not really comparable to taxes in a market economy. In an environment in which both quantities of inputs and outputs and their prices were under government control, they had more the character of transfers to the government.

Table 1. Romania: General Government Revenue

(In billions of lei, unless otherwise noted)

	1985	1986	1987	1988	1989	1990	1991
Turnover tax	161.6	178.2	160.0	148.9	150.6	101.2	182.1
(In percent of total revenue)	40.5	42.7	37.7	39.7	37.0	31.1	26.0
Wage fund	46.0	46.6	47.0	48.2	51.0	58.0	172.0
(In percent of total revenue)	11.5	11.2	11.0	12.5	12.5	17.8	24.6
Profit remittances	72.3	77.7	98.9	79.9	88.7	62.2	105.7
(In percent of total revenue)	18.1	18.7	23.2	20.8	21.7	19.1	15.1
Other							
Social insurance fund contributions	46.1	47.8	49.5	50.7	53.9	63.0	185.0
(In percent of total revenue)	11.5	11.5	11.6	13.2	13.2	19.3	26.4
Miscellaneous[1]	73.4	66.3	70.0	56.9	63.8	41.5	54.8
(In percent of total revenue)	18.4	15.9	16.5	14.8	15.6	12.7	7.8
Total revenue	399.4	416.6	425.4	384.6	408.0	325.9	699.6

Sources: Budget documents, various issues.
[1] Includes various user fees, fees for medical care, rental income from state housing, post office revenue, fines, and penalties.

anyway. This meant that all intermediate and capital goods were exempt from turnover tax and only goods sold to consumers bore the tax. Sales to the Government and exports were tax exempt. Most services sold to consumers were also tax exempt.

With effect from November 1, 1990, with price liberalization, the old turnover tax based on controlled prices obviously became obsolete and the authorities introduced a new tax. Executive Order No. 1109, which describes the new tax, was enacted on October 18, 1990. For the first time, ad valorem tax rates were applied to the sale of domestically produced goods and selected services, based on manufacturing or selling prices, and to imports of goods, based on customs values.

Assessment of the New Turnover Tax

In assessing the new turnover tax, the following features need to be noted. Some of these are positive, while others can be considered negative.

Positive Features

It appears that three structural features of the new tax would facilitate the introduction of a value-added tax (VAT) in due course, and hence can be considered positive.

First, the coverage of the tax has been broadened. All goods are covered, except unprocessed food, salt, agricultural raw materials, mining products (other than crude oil and natural gas), electricity, and thermal power. The list of services subject to tax has also been expanded to cover certain forms of construction and transportation, hotels and restaurants, casinos and night clubs, car repairs, laundry and dry cleaning services, barbers and hairdressers, and a few others.

Second, the rates of tax, which previously used to be specific (they represented the difference between the state-established wholesale prices and the producer prices), have now become ad valorem. The new rates are to be applied to the production (ex factory or manufacturer's) price in the case of domestic products, and the sale price in the case of services.

Third, the number of turnover tax rates has been reduced drastically. Executive Order No. 1109 initially contained 20 rates. Most raw materials, intermediate goods, and capital goods, as well as services, are taxed at rates ranging between 2 percent and 5 percent, while most consumer goods are taxed at rates between 5 percent (salt, milk, edible oils, meat, and fish, and their preparations) and 20 percent (clothes and footwear). As illustrations, furniture and other household articles are taxed at 7 percent, cosmetics, selected fruits, and nuts at 10 percent, sugar products and soft drinks at 15 percent, and cars at 17 percent. Luxury products, such as crystal, leather clothes, furs, and jewelry are subject to higher rates of 45 percent or 50 percent. Typical excisable items are also subject to high rates. These include plum brandy (35 percent), spirits (40 percent), cigarettes and coffee (50 percent), wines, champagne, and beer (60 percent), and crude oil (65 percent). Imported products sold in foreign currency are subject to half of the normal rates.

Beginning in 1992, the number of turnover tax rates has been reduced to five, and what could be termed as high-rate excises were imposed on alcoholic beverages, tobacco products, and gasoline.

Negative Features

However, the new turnover tax seems to have certain structural defects, particularly when compared with a VAT.

First, the goods subject to taxation include raw materials, intermediate goods, and capital goods. Taxes on these goods, even though low, contribute to some cascading in the pricing structure and distort producer choices.

Second, under any multistage turnover tax that has no system of input tax credits, the country's exports can be unduly placed at a disadvantage in world markets.[2] This occurs because the exports are still taxed as a result of the built-in cascading of the tax on inputs at earlier stages of production. No scheme seems to exist in Romania for the refund or drawback of turnover taxes on inputs that have entered into the cost of exported items.

Third, the new turnover tax, which is applied at the manufacturing stage, can distort consumer choices beyond what is the result of tax cascading. Since wholesale and retail margins are excluded from taxable value, and since these margins differ markedly among commodities, the share of the turnover tax in retail prices differs significantly from one commodity to another.

Fourth, on imported goods, the tax is levied on the cost plus insurance and freight (c.i.f.) value of goods, without including customs duties. Thus, the new turnover tax fails to recognize the protective role of customs duties in influencing the level and structure of domestic production. On the contrary, higher taxation of imported goods (say, cosmetics, at 30 percent) than their domestically produced counterpart (cosmetics are taxed at 10 percent) gives the turnover tax a protective role that should actually be fulfilled by the customs tariff.

Fifth, the coverage of the new turnover tax, though fairly wide, is far from complete. Purchases by the Government for defense purposes and stockpiling, for example, are exempt, as are many important services, such as water supply, electricity, telephone and telecommunications, and the construction of new houses.

Sixth, the new law contains no provision for exempting even the smallest of small businesses. This means that all businesses in Romania, irrespective of the size of their turnover, will be subject to tax. As the number of taxpayers subject to the new turnover tax will increase considerably, the difficulties of administering the tax will also grow.

Finally, there is at present no tradition of voluntary compliance with any tax in Romania, and all taxpayers other than state enterprises are audited every year by tax officials. As a result, large numbers of staff are required to administer the tax. In other countries, with reliance on voluntary compliance, modern management, processing and audit techniques, and proper computer support, sales taxes tend to be effectively administered with far fewer staff.

Case for Value-Added Tax

In their Reform Program of August–September 1990, the authorities announced that they will gradually phase out the turnover tax and replace

---

[2]Initially, exports of domestically produced items that were in short supply were to be subject to turnover tax rates ranging between 1 percent and 10 percent. These included construction materials (woods, glasses, tiles, bathroom fittings), natural woods and fibers, matches, and school supplies. The authorities have now exempted all exports from turnover tax.

it by a VAT used in the European Community (EC), and the current plan is to introduce a VAT in January 1993. This is to be welcomed because a properly designed VAT offers many advantages.

First, a VAT, especially if it is a uniform rate VAT, does not distort producers' choices and resource allocation in the economy; it is also neutral between various forms of economic organization, technologies of production, and the number of stages of production and distribution before an item finally reaches the consumer. Second, with an inbuilt system of input tax credits and zero rating of exports, it enables exports to leave the country free of tax. Third, by taxing, equally and on the same footing, domestic production and imported supplies of goods and services consumed in the economy it becomes a major and stable source of government revenue. Finally, a VAT based on a system of sales invoices, showing the amount of taxes actually paid, and allowing input tax credits on the basis of verifiable sale invoices, facilitates tax administration; it also automatically sorts out the end use of a product (that is, whether it is a production input or a consumer good), converts traders into tax collectors, and creates an audit trail.

The Romanian economy will obviously enjoy the advantages of a VAT once a suitably designed VAT has been legislated and a well-functioning VAT administration is in place as and when that occurs. Price liberalization as well as privatization (or, at least, a great deal of enterprise autonomy) will obviously be the two most crucial prerequisites for ensuring that the full efficiency effects of the VAT are realized.

Strategy of Transition from Turnover Tax to VAT

A strategy of replacing the turnover tax by a VAT can consist of: (1) converting the present turnover tax into a tax resembling VAT and (2) instituting an adequate system of excise duties.

On the policy front, this will call for aligning the coverage, base, and rate structure of the present turnover tax to that of a VAT, as well as identifying the items to be subject to excise duties and determining the tax rates to be imposed on them. These policy changes will perhaps need to be carried out in such a way that, at each step, the revenue losses from the adopted measures are, as far as possible, offset by revenue gains from other measures undertaken simultaneously. In this way, the Government's budgetary needs in the period of transition from a centrally planned to a market economy will continue to be met as the turnover tax system is restructured and the efforts directed at macroeconomic stability will not be thwarted.[3]

---

[3] The administrative front will also require changes, that is, the Tax Department will need to develop the appropriate organizational structure and procedures necessary to implement the reform process.

As noted above, the present turnover tax has a number of flaws. Some will be eliminated only when the tax is replaced by an appropriate VAT; for these there are no easy solutions in the transition period. Two flaws of the present turnover tax that fit this description are the tax cascading created by the taxation of intermediate goods and capital goods, instead of consumer goods only, and the levy of the tax at the manufacturer-importer level, instead of the retail level. Complete removal of tax cascading will require a full-fledged system of tax credits, while the inclusion of wholesale and retail margins will require the levy of tax at the retail level. None of these actions is administratively easy in the rapidly changing price and business conditions of the type that exists in Romania.

First Step

Three flaws of the present turnover tax, however, can be readily removed, and the authorities can do this as a first step. First, the coverage of the turnover tax can be expanded to include additional services that would be taxable under the future VAT. The services that can be brought into the tax base are construction of new residential houses, water supply, electricity, telephone and telecommunications, car rentals, leasing and letting of movable properties, and entertainment services (this will require adjusting or removing the separate entertainment tax that exists at present). The coverage of the present turnover tax can also be expanded to include all government purchases, including those for stockpiling by the state and purchases for military purposes, as they will be fully taxable under the VAT, as and when that is adopted.

Second, while the levy of turnover tax on exports has recently been eliminated, ways will still have to be found to reduce, if not completely eliminate, the element of tax that can be attributed to intermediate and capital goods used in exported products. One way to do this in the transition period would be to estimate the share of taxed inputs in exports from the latest input-output table, apply an "average" input tax rate, and give tax refunds to exporters based on these calculations. This is obviously not a perfect solution (VAT alone offers such a solution), but it is administratively feasible since exporters in Romania are likely to be large, although few in number, at this stage of the reform process.

Third, an appropriate small business exemption can be established. This should facilitate the administration of the present turnover tax without much loss of revenue and pave the way for the VAT.

None of the three measures of the reform of turnover tax described above has yet been implemented. The first measure will be greatly revenue enhancing, especially as the service sector becomes dynamic. The last two measures, on the other hand, will be somewhat revenue losing.

Second Step

Further alignment of the present turnover tax to a system of VAT and the adoption of excises can be carried out next, as follows. First, the number of turnover tax rates on all taxable consumer goods and services can be reduced to one or two, at say, about 15 percent, whereas selected consumer items, such as alcoholic beverages, tobacco products, petroleum products, cars, sugar, and soft drinks can additionally be taxed under separate excise duties. Designing the rates of excise duties on these items can take into account their present tax rate, the rates prevailing in neighboring countries, and the revenue needs of the Government. Second, the turnover tax can be applied to the c.i.f. value of imported goods plus customs duties and excise duties, if any, on such goods and at the border instead of at the first point of domestic sales. This can be done because this will be the base on which VAT will be levied on imports in due course.

The first measure recommended above would be revenue neutral, or even somewhat revenue losing, if a few tax rates higher than 15 percent are reduced. However, the second measure would certainly be revenue enhancing and by a substantial amount.

The transitional two-step strategy can help transform Romania's turnover tax structure into a modern system of VAT and excises.

Transitional Issues

A major transitional policy issue that will arise as the present turnover tax is converted into a VAT needs to be noted. It relates to the deductibility from future VAT liabilities of the turnover tax that may have been paid on the inventories of finished goods held by enterprises.

At the date of changeover from the turnover tax to the VAT, some traders will obviously hold tax-paid stocks of finished goods. When those finished goods are subsequently sold, the VAT may also be chargeable, but there would be no automatic deduction for prior turnover tax payments. This can lead to three possible problems:

- An equity issue, as there would be double taxation of the available stocks of finished goods, which may vary from one enterprise to another.
- A pricing difficulty, as traders may adjust prices on the introduction of VAT, on the basis of the old tax-inclusive cost; thus, permanently overstating the price.
- Reduced production, if businesses attempt to reduce inventories in anticipation of the VAT, in order to reduce their overall tax liability.

A few countries adopting VAT in recent years have permitted traders to claim a full or partial deduction of the amount of the replaced tax in their first (or early) VAT returns while other countries have chosen not to allow any such deduction.

The most relevant points in considering whether a similar deduction need be permitted in Romania are whether:

- The turnover tax liability can be regarded as being broadly equivalent to the VAT liability.
- The trader can easily calculate and substantiate the claim for deduction and, thus, whether the VAT office can enforce compliance.
- Significant amounts of turnover tax are involved.

On the first point, the present turnover taxes effectively incorporate what, in a more traditional tax system, would be excise duties. This has been achieved by applying the tax at high rates on selected consumer goods. The excise component is normally not creditable, but then, there is no way in which it could be separately identified.

Regarding the second point, the method of calculation of the turnover tax prior to and even after November 1, 1990 has been such that the tax content of the purchase price has rarely been shown as an "explicit" part of the cost. Therefore, it will be difficult to calculate the deduction in relation to stock acquired under the old tax regime which is still held. Besides, recording systems are unlikely to be able to identify which stock was purchased under which tax regime; therefore, there would be no way in practice to calculate a credit.

On the third point, the introduction of an export drawback scheme for intermediate and capital goods entering into exports would mean that the issue arises only in relation to domestically held retail stocks, which, at this stage, are very low. Unless this changes significantly, the element of double taxation, through the nonallowance of any credit, will be very minor.

Thus, no deduction need be allowed against the VAT for any turnover tax.

Concluding Remarks

Reform of the present turnover tax, to orient it toward a VAT, is a matter of some urgency in Romania. Multiple rates of taxation, tax cascading, and taxation of selected exports are perhaps its three worst features. Removal of these features, accompanied by a further expansion of the tax base, is necessary to ensure the revenue productivity of the present tax while it is being transformed into a full-fledged VAT. However, all this cannot be done without making preparations for implementing the new tax which must include drafting legislation and regulations, designing tax returns and related instructions, training tax staff, registering and educating taxpayers, preparing appropriate procedures for tax filing, payments, refunds, and computerizing return processing and audits, as Romania does not yet have a formal organizational structure to administer the turnover tax which can handle all these quickly. The authorities should pay adequate attention to these aspects of tax reform.

Income Taxation[4]

After the Romanian revolution in December 1989, the new Government inherited an income tax system that was fairly typical of those in the East European countries. This section briefly describes this system, and then discusses the progress that has been made in income tax reform over the last two years and the issues facing the Romanian authorities.

Pre-Reform System of Income Taxation

Taxation of Individuals

Wages and salaries were subject to taxation through a payroll tax on the total wage fund of the enterprise. Social security contributions were made through a separate payroll tax.

Other categories of income earners were subject to progressive schedular taxes, depending on the source of the income. On literary, artistic, and scientific incomes, the rate schedule was open ended, the marginal rate moving from 7 percent to 24 percent at yearly incomes of lei 2,400 and lei 120,000, respectively, and increasing by 1 percent for each additional lei 30,000. On handicraft and trade activities, the rates were stiffer, from 10 percent on the first lei 1,200 to 42 percent for income above lei 50,000, and then growing by 2 percent for each additional lei 15,000, up to an average rate of 45 percent for individuals and 60 percent for legal entities.

Income taxes levied on individuals contributed remarkably little to total revenue. This was, of course, a reflection of the almost total absence of a private sector in the Romanian economy. It is particularly interesting that the largest share of taxes paid by individuals until 1989 was the "bachelor tax," or the tax levied on all individuals above 25 years of age who were not parents.

Taxation of Business Profits

Prior to 1990, the profit remittances, which can be seen as the counterpart of taxation of business profits, were a direct transfer and had two forms: transfer of planned profits and transfer of profits in excess of the plan.

In addition, a host of miscellaneous transfers from enterprises are informative about the accounting practices used in Romania. Each enterprise had an investment fund and was required to allocate money to this from

---

[4]Erik Offerdal has made many useful comments on this part of the chapter.

several sources. One source was "surplus depreciation" that arose as each real asset was depreciated by a straight-line method and a given lifetime. If the asset was still in use after having been written down, the enterprise was required to continue to depreciate it at the same rate as before, but now could apply this amount as a credit toward the investment fund. If the enterprise did not use all of these credits for investment purposes in a given year, it had to transfer the surplus depreciation to the state budget. The effect of these provisions was that taxation cut into the substance of most enterprises.

In a similar fashion, each enterprise had certain plan targets for inventories, bonuses to workers, and "balance in regulation funds" for stimulating exports. If the actual amounts of any of these accounts did not conform to the plan targets (for example, if the actual inventories were higher, paid bonuses were lower, or the balance in regulation fund was higher), the excess had to be transferred to the state budget.

Other Incomes

For agricultural income, the existing law was not widely applied. Rental income, however, was subject to tax at marginal rates, from 11 percent to 91 percent at lei 300 and lei 70,000, respectively, with a ceiling of 75 percent for the average tax. Very restrictive rules applied to cost deductions.

Issues of Income Tax Reform

The Government firmly intends to introduce a global income tax as soon as is feasible. It is certainly an established assumption that such a system best fulfills its purpose of taxing on the basis of ability to pay. Furthermore, a global income tax, combined with a VAT, clearly constitutes the tax system that best will facilitate Romania's ambition of a closer economic integration with countries in Western Europe.

During the transition to this new tax system, the Government has wisely followed a gradual approach, focusing its tax policy efforts on the wage and salary tax and the profits tax, while taking the first steps toward establishing a modern tax administration.

Administration

The change to a market economy will imply that a new tax administration will have to be built up almost from scratch. The tax administration that now exists is primarily charged with enforcement and collection activities related to small, individual taxpayers. Collection of wage and profits taxes is done entirely through the banking system, with only minimal enforcement by the tax administration. Several considerations are therefore important.

One is the need to economize scarce administrative resources. A global income tax will increase the number of taxpayers from the thousands to the millions, and the emergence of a private sector will open avenues for tax avoidance and tax evasion that simply have not existed before. Several steps should therefore be taken to keep administrative procedures as simple as possible. The number of files and the amount of paperwork have to be kept at a minimum. This can be done by keeping the tax on wages and salaries final for the majority of taxpayers, by establishing reasonable threshold amounts for minor taxes on income, and by avoiding excessive reporting from taxpayers subject to the obligation of filing returns. The administrative resources can be expanded by moving staff from those offices previously dealing with the major government enterprises to the tax administration. Also, redundant staff previously engaged in price control could, with limited retraining, be used in the tax administration.

Second, computerization of the operation will, in the longer run, be crucial for efficient control of taxpayer filing status, return processing, audit selection, development of management statistics, and so forth. In the short run, the status of the telephone system is not conducive to any advanced system of on-line connections across the country. There will, however, be room for less ambitious computer systems in local use, which can gradually be networked as the infrastructure improves.

Third, the administrative system about to be built in Romania should be conceived with long-term objectives in mind. For instance, even if taxpayer returns and the number of taxpayer files are held down, long-term planning, say, for taxpayer identification numbers, should be done with the perspective of a later system including a larger number of taxpayer files.

Taxation of Wages and Salaries

The tax reform in 1990 included, as a first step, a withholding tax on wages and salaries of the simple type, establishing a final monthly payment. The "bachelor tax" was replaced with a tax credit of 20 percent for all individuals who have children. The rate schedule was quite progressive; 13 brackets with tax rates ranging from 6 percent to 45 percent. Owing to the inflationary conditions in Romania in 1991, this rate schedule was changed three times that year, effectively indexing the brackets.

For the time being, there is good reason to keep a modified version of this system. The combination of tax credits and cash benefits for children should be removed, and the principle of separate taxation of husbands and wives should be maintained. Moreover, given the difficult situation of the tax administration, the principle of final withholding at source should be kept.

A drastic increase of the social security contributions, from 14 percent to 20 percent, was necessary to make up for part of the loss of the wage fund tax.

Business Profits

In 1990, the system of profit transfers was replaced with a more regular tax on profits, which still, by Western standards, brought in a surprisingly high share of government revenue (19.1 percent). This was achieved partly because the tax base was substantially wider than international accounting practices would allow. The statutory tax rate ranged between 54 percent and 58 percent and was applied to the rate of profitability, defined as the relation between the taxable profit and the total production and distribution expenses. The taxable profit in turn represented the difference between the receipts from the total activities and the expenses referring to them. A further deduction could be made from the receipts for the amounts that were paid directly from the financial result. The effective marginal rate could reach 100 percent when gross profits exceeded 10.5 percent of production and distribution expenses.

This profit tax law was provisional and was superseded by the new law on profit tax adopted by parliament in December 1990. The new law covers not only state-owned corporations, but virtually all other legal entities. It is levied according to an extremely detailed and highly progressive rate schedule, going all the way from 0 percent to 77 percent on the margin. The tax was imposed on the net profit determined as the difference between the collected revenues and the expenses listed in an annex to the law. However, this legislation was rather incomplete, as it contains no references to depreciation allowances, stock valuation, loss carryover provisions, or other factors.

This system was drastically simplified from the beginning of 1992, when the detailed rate schedule was replaced by a two-rate structure of 35 percent and 45 percent. Also, new and more liberal depreciation allowances were introduced, allowing enterprises to choose between a new declining-balance scheme and the old straight-line scheme.

The rules for foreign-owned enterprises and joint ventures have, in general, been superseded by the new profit tax law for foreign enterprises established after January 1, 1990. However, the 30 percent tax rate and the special tax incentives stipulated in Decree-Law No. 96 of March 14, 1990 were maintained for foreign enterprises established before 1990. A new foreign investment code was enacted on April 10, 1991.

While these are important steps toward improving taxation of business profits in Romania, a number of important issues remain to be addressed before a global income tax can be introduced.

The first objective must be to establish a coherent system of taxation of different types of enterprises. The present distinction between "juridical" and "physical" persons based on the number of employees outside the owner's family is incompatible with the market economy. Enterprises should not feel prevented from expanding just because the legal form they have chosen is connected with such a limitation.

Second, a decision has to be made whether Romania, in the long run, should adhere to the idea of a unified business profits tax, that is, a "fence system," making the tax system the same for corporations, partnerships, and proprietary firms, as long as the profit is kept in the business, and imposing a tax (with credit for all or part of the business tax already paid) on profits taken out of the business and given to the owner. It seems as if Romania is not choosing this road, but rather intends to apply a standard European system of company law, with separate tax systems for different legal forms of enterprises. This should be a reasonable policy to follow, not least given the fact that Romania wants to open up to foreign investment and has a natural interest in being assimilated into tax systems prevailing in countries from which prospective investments will emanate.

Third, some issues outside the tax area are crucial to effective enforcement of a business profits tax. Modern business accounting principles will have to be introduced to allow a more realistic measurement of taxable profits. Furthermore, existing bankruptcy legislation should be used effectively to instill financial discipline and accountability in enterprises.

Agricultural Income

Few countries succeed in effectively taxing agricultural income, particularly the income of smallholders. The current draft law on taxation of agricultural income in Romania, which follows a presumptive model, but provides for a detailed calculation of income based on such factors as crops and numbers of cattle, seems overambitious. A far more reasonable approach would be to tax agricultural income in an indirect fashion, based on relatively rough assumptions of the productive value of the land. For the time being, the most important task for the administration should be to establish a properly functioning profit tax system for the major agricultural enterprises.

Rental Income

It is urgent to establish a less-than-confiscatory tax on rental income by making the deductions from gross income realistic, and by reducing the top rate. As a next step, measures could be taken to assimilate the taxation of landlords with those of businesses, and in the long run, taxation of rental income would form part of a global income tax system. Some countries have successfully established withholding tax systems for rental income, but it is unlikely that the situation in Romania would improve very much by adding the number of persons liable to tax in this way.

Income from Capital

At the present time, there are far-reaching reliefs from tax on interest income. In the longer run, interest income should be part of the total income taxable under a global system. This might well have to take some time, given the inflation experience. There is little point in a schedular system for taxing interest income that in real terms is no income at all. Once real interest rates are consistently positive, however, fairness requires some taxation, albeit for technical reasons initially only in the form of final withholding tax.

On the question whether dividends should be taxed in full, it would seem desirable not to get out of line with the European development. A partial integration might be a long-term objective. For the sake of simplicity, however, a low final withholding tax on dividends should be the immediate solution, and this is the system presently chosen.

With respect to capital gains, the principle that they should be taxed is no longer contentious. The problem is the definition of basis, the indexation, and the control of assessments. In these respects, the Romanian situation is not favorable for the immediate implementation of a taxation of private capital gains. What would be realistic is a simpler approach. One element would be a clear definition of business profits to include all profits realized on business assets at the time of their sale, the withdrawal of them from the business, or their removal outside the Romanian tax jurisdiction. Another would be a registration duty for real estate transactions.

In the long run, it might be possible to establish either a cost basis for owners of capital assets, or a "D-Day" valuation, offering a new basis for the taxation of future capital gains. Experience shows that capital gains taxation is never an important revenue raiser. The reason for capital gains taxation is fairness. If capital gains taxation cannot be implemented in a fair and equitable manner, it should rather be omitted.

Part II

Central and Eastern Europe:
Specific Issues

CHAPTER 7

The Realized Net Present Value of the Soviet Union

Adrienne Cheasty

On December 25, 1991, the Soviet Union was dissolved. A cornerstone assumption of much public finance theory was undermined: the life of the government was not infinite. Following the demise of the Soviet Union, its executors were faced with closing the final balance sheet and valuing and distributing the estate—the assets and liabilities of the U.S.S.R. To those of us economists who have attempted to construct public sector balance sheets, it seemed an impossible task.[1] This is how it was done.

Scope of the Task

The compass of public sector wealth is clearly laid out in Willem Buiter's ideal balance sheet of government (Table 1).[2] Its asset side comprises: social overhead capital (nonmarketable); equity in public enterprises (partly potentially marketable); land and mineral assets (marketable); the present value of the future tax and social security contribution program; net foreign exchange reserves; and the imputed net present value of government's cash monopoly. Liabilities of government are: net debt denominated in domestic currency; net debt denominated in foreign currency; the stock of high-powered money; the present value of entitlement programs; and public sector net worth. These assets and liabilities were the legacy of the Soviet Union to its successor states: the challenge was to identify and distribute them.

Making the Task Manageable: Precept of Territoriality

In the event, the newly independent republics drastically curtailed the need to value, and negotiate the disposal of, Soviet assets and liabilities by

---

Adrienne Cheasty is a Senior Economist in the European II Department. She is indebted to Vito Tanzi and Wilhelm Nahr, without whom this paper would not have been written, and to Willem Buiter for valuable insights.

[1]For the definitive statement on the impossibility of valuing a government, see Blejer and Cheasty (1991), especially pp. 1669-75.

[2]Buiter (1993).

Table 1. Stylized Public Sector Balance Sheet

Assets		Liabilities	
(A1)	Social overhead capital	(L1)	Net domestic-currency-denominated debt
(A2)	Equity in public enterprises	(L2)	Net foreign-currency-denominated debt
(A3)	Land and mineral assets	(L3)	Stock of high-powered money
(A4)	Present value of future tax and social security contributions	(L4)	Public sector net worth program, including social security contributions
(A5)	Net foreign exchange reserves		
(A6)	Imputed net value of government cash monopoly		

adopting a de facto principle of territoriality. According to this principle, assets and liabilities that could be identified as pertaining to, or emanating from, a particular state were in almost all cases assigned to that state.[3]

The main consequence of the espousal of territoriality was that little debate over the ownership or valuation of nonfinancial Soviet assets took place. Natural resources, strategic communications facilities, space program infrastructure, and other bodies that had been subordinate to the union reverted to supervision by republic-level or (perhaps more usually) local governments.[4] Thus, practically all potential allocation and valuation difficulties concerning social overhead capital, equity in public enterprises, and land and mineral assets were sidestepped. Moreover, republican governments became the successor governments to the U.S.S.R. authorities, on their territory. The succession bore with it the implied responsibility of the new governments for the entitlements promised by the old, and the implied right of the new governments to collect the taxes exacted by the old. Hence, in Buiter's framework, the negotiable assets of the U.S.S.R. were reduced to net foreign exchange reserves and the imputed net value of the government's cash monopoly.

---

[3]There were probably two reasons underlying the recourse to territoriality: on the part of Russia, the desire to minimize disruption and the scope for conflict among the states; and on the part of some other states, a feeling of incapacity to change the de facto apportionment. However, since all agreements on the subject of sharing assets and liabilities remain in draft (other than that on external debt), some exceptions to allocation by territory may eventually emerge.

[4]In the U.S.S.R., there were three classes of organizations (a concept covering both administrative bodies and enterprises): union-subordinate, covering activities deemed of strategic importance to the whole U.S.S.R. (such as fuel and energy, steel, the space program, and most defense); republic-subordinate, covering the major nonunion enterprises and governmental functions in each republic; and local-subordinate, covering mainly services (such as distribution) and social welfare functions.

Closing Balance of the Soviet Union

The centralization of functions under planning permitted what was left of the U.S.S.R., after application of the territoriality rule, to be conveniently summarized in the balance sheets of three banks. The three banks, between them, had performed the fiscal and monetary functions of the Soviet authorities and managed Soviet financial assets and liabilities. Three committees of the successor states are at present supervising their orderly liquidation.

(1) The State Bank of the U.S.S.R. (Gosbank) had as its main asset the domestic state debt of the U.S.S.R. and, as its main liabilities, ruble issue and the deposits of the U.S.S.R. Savings Bank (Sberbank).

(2) U.S.S.R. Sberbank had acted as the conduit of household savings to finance the Soviet fiscal deficit. Practically its only asset was on-lending to Gosbank of all of the small savings it attracted. Practically its only liabilities were these savings deposits.

(3) The U.S.S.R. Bank for Foreign Economic Activity (Vneshekonombank) held the foreign exchange reserves of the U.S.S.R., and was the official obligor for U.S.S.R. external debt. It on-lent Soviet official borrowing to government and the enterprise sector in approximately equal shares.

Table 2 presents a stylized combined balance sheet for the three banks that now embody the Soviet Union.[5] In a completely consolidated format, the Savings Bank would drop out of the table. What remains is the debt, domestic- and foreign-currency denominated, of the Soviet Union, and its backing. The rest of this paper, first, explains how these financial residues of the U.S.S.R. were valued, and are being disposed of; second, looks at the implications of their valuation for the solvency of the U.S.S.R. at the time it was dissolved; and third, identifies possible problems in their distribution that may delay a conclusive winding up of the Soviet Union.

Domestic Currency Debt

The ruble-denominated debt of the U.S.S.R. amounted to rub 887 billion when the union was dissolved. Prior to 1991, all fiscal deficits had been incurred only at the level of the union: potential deficits of local or republican governments had been foreclosed by transfers from the union budget before the end of the plan year. Hence, the only part of the Soviet debt that could be attributed to identifiable states was that debt that was incurred during 1991, when republican governments were allowed to

---

[5]In order to preserve the confidentiality of unfinished business, only those figures that have been published are shown here. However, the presentation of a more detailed balance sheet would not change the analysis of the paper or the orders of magnitude being discussed.

Table 2. U.S.S.R.: Financial Assets and Liabilities

(In billions of rubles)

Assets		Liabilities	
Gosbank			
Domestic debt		Sberbank deposits	504
of U.S.S.R.	887	Ruble issue	276
Union	781	Bonds and settlement	
States	106	balances	107
Sberbank			
Loans to Gosbank	504	Savings deposits	504
Vneshekonombank[1]			
Foreign currency		Loans from banks, net	103
debt of U.S.S.R.	103	Other net obligations	8.8
Foreign exchange	8.9	Financial net worth	0.1
Total assets	**1,502.9**	**Total liabilities**	**1,502.9**

[1]Convertible currency assets and liabilities are valued at rub 1.673 per U.S. dollar.

indulge in deficit financing. During that time, Russia ran up rub 74 billion in debt, and the other republics combined, rub 32 billion. Rub 781 billion remained to be divided.

The approach taken by the liquidators of Gosbank in allocating responsibility for the Soviet internal debt was to examine its backing. As shown in Table 2, the debt was financed largely by the use of the household sector's surplus (savings deposits of rub 504 billion) and by currency issue (rub 276 billion). Other sources of financing, bonds and unpaid bills, were comparatively insignificant—and (with the possible exception of commodity bonds) rendered more so by inflation in the months following the demise of the union.[6]

The virtue of approaching the distribution of the debt from the point of view of its ultimate creditors was that it permitted the principle of territoriality to be further extended: creditors could be identified by the state in which they lived. Though U.S.S.R. Sberbank had pooled the savings deposits of households across the union, full records remained of the savers. It was argued that each state should (and would, in its own interest) take responsibility for covering its own savings deposits. Likewise, since rubles had been issued to republics free of charge,[7] it was argued that the original destination of the currency issue outstanding on Decem-

---

[6]It happened that the U.S.S.R. banking system was left with net deposits (unsettled balances or "unpaid bills") in the settlement system when the Gosbank balance sheet was closed. Because of the automatic and consolidated nature of the settlement system under planning, the obligees of these balances may never be identified.

[7]All seigniorage went to states, because Gosbank shipped currency upon proof of need, without recovering even transport costs.

ber 25, 1991 provided an appropriate benchmark for identifying obligors for that part of the union debt that had been financed by printing money.[8]

Convertible Currency Debt and Reserves

The debt of the U.S.S.R. denominated in convertible currencies amounted to US$61.4 billion on December 4, 1991, of which US$53.7 billion had been contracted or guaranteed by Vneshekonombank (and was hence defined as official Soviet debt).[9] Western creditors encouraged states to service the debt as an integral unit, rather than dividing responsibilities for parts of it. Hence, a sequence of several agreements led to a commitment by eight states (other than the Baltic states, Azerbaijan, Moldova, Turkmenistan, and Uzbekistan) to be "jointly and severally" responsible for Soviet debt.[10] Each state (including nonsignatories) was allotted a quota for debt service, based on a formula defined on population, national income, and convertible currency trade in 1986–90. Should a state fail to meet its commitments, the others would become liable in its stead.[11] In practice, Russia alone paid debt service in 1992.

The foreign exchange assets (reserves) of the U.S.S.R. amounted to US$5.3 billion at the end of October 1991 (equivalent to one month of convertible currency imports). Other less liquid foreign claims (such as clearing balances with members of the former Council for Mutual Economic Assistance) were more than offset by Soviet obligations: net debt on clearing accounts amounted to rub 8.8 billion.[12]

Solvency of the Soviet Union

The financial collapse of the Soviet Union can be seen in Table 3. Table 3 replicates Table 2, with the single difference that external assets and liabilities are valued at an approximation of their economic cost to the U.S.S.R. at the time of its dissolution (rub 100 per U.S. dollar). The depreciated rate contrasts with the insulated ruble accounting exchange rate of rub 1.673, that had been used by the managers of the Soviet

---

[8]To put this in the context of Buiter's balance sheet: at the time the Soviet Union was liquidated, the value of the Government's cash monopoly was equal to the existing stock of high-powered money.

[9]Nonguaranteed debt is also treated as a Soviet, rather than a state-level, liability.

[10]For a chronology of these agreements, see International Monetary Fund (1992), Annex 2, pp. 91–92.

[11]The largest shares were those of Russia (61 percent) and Ukraine (16 percent).

[12]The value of this figure depends crucially on the exchange rate used. In principle, the fact that the U.S.S.R. has been dissolved means that the prevailing exchange rate at the time it ceased to exist is the correct rate for valuing external assets and liabilities. That rate was rub 1.673 per U.S. dollar—though the claims were recorded, where appropriate, at a rate of rub 5.884 per U.S. dollar. In practice, debates with partners about the valuation of these claims (particularly in transferable rubles) continue.

economy in recording the transfer of resources to and from the rest of the world.[13] The main effect of the revaluation is to multiply the ruble value of external debt by 60, so that it dwarfs all other items on the Soviet financial balance sheet.

The counterpart of Vneshekonombank's debt on its balance sheet was the loans it had made to finance the convertible currency operations of government, foreign trade organizations, and other state enterprises. However, since there was no mechanism for allocating exchange risk (and, for instance, collecting the ruble equivalent of the debt service from the nonfinancial sector), the offset to the valuation change in the debt (net of reserves) was, effectively, an equivalent reduction in the financial net worth of the U.S.S.R.[14] According to this very stylized representation, the financial net worth of the Soviet state at the time of its dissolution was rub –6 trillion.

Obviously, this depressing figure must be interpreted liberally. Specifically, it would probably be more correct to describe Table 3 as showing the effect of the liquidity crisis that hastened the demise of the U.S.S.R. than as a depiction of the fundamental insolvency of Soviet territories.

For one thing, the individual states of the former U.S.S.R. are far richer than was the U.S.S.R. state in its final days. The retreat to territoriality was in itself one of the main reasons for the breakup of the U.S.S.R. The sequestering by republics, in 1991, of the income from their nonfinancial assets (of which convertible currency earners such as oil and gas exports and gold were a big portion) and of their net taxes stripped the Soviet balance sheet of its mainstay sovereign resources, leaving a bankrupt state with the negative net worth calculated above.[15] Had the complete balance sheet described in Table 1 remained intact, and liquid, the fall in financial net worth would not have seemed terminal, placed in context of the vast real wealth of Soviet territories.

Moreover (and related to the intrinsic wealth of the former U.S.S.R.), the exchange rate used to value the foreign debt is not likely to be a purchasing power parity rate. Had the U.S.S.R. not been dismantled, thereby requiring a final balance sheet, many economists would have considered it a needless reflection of temporary volatility to revalue the Soviet balance sheet using the extreme current exchange rate. In one

---

[13]Even the accounting rate of rub 1.673 per U.S. dollar represented a near threefold devaluation compared with the official rate of rub 0.6 per U.S. dollar used by Vneshekonombank.

[14]One interpretation would be to consider it the cumulative net cost of subsidizing the ruble exchange rate at an unsustainable level for several decades.

[15]Bean and Buiter (1987), p. 32, put the point well: "While . . . there is nothing especially virtuous about maintaining net worth intact, it is certainly of interest to trace the evolution of net worth over time, since this will determine the future fiscal elbow room of the authorities." The major manifestation of the Soviet financial crisis was the inability of the Government to continue to balance its budget while insulating the domestic economy from the rest of the world via extensive depletion of real wealth, as it had always done in the past.

Table 3. U.S.S.R.: Financial Assets and Liabilities, Revalued

(In billions of rubles)

Assets		Liabilities	
Gosbank			
Domestic debt of U.S.S.R.	887	Sberbank deposits	504
Union	781	Ruble issue	276
States	106	Bonds and settlement balances	107
Sberbank			
Loans to Gosbank	504	Savings deposits	504
Vneshekonombank[1]			
Foreign currency debt		Loans from banks, net	6,139
of U.S.S.R.	103	Other net obligations	528
Foreign exchange	532	Financial net worth	−6,032
Total assets	**2,026**	**Total liabilities**	**2,026**

[1]Convertible currency assets and liabilities are valued at rub 100 per U.S. dollar.

sense, the extreme exchange rate of the Soviet ruble represented the assessment of the market that the Soviet Government no longer had the authority to furnish real assets in order to meet its financial obligations.

Contentious Issues

The discussion so far gives the impression that the distribution of the assets and liabilities of the Soviet Union has been orderly and is now final. It has indeed been orderly and subdued, but possibly because the states have been too busy with short-term emergencies to pay attention to the process. Since few formal agreements have been signed, the possibility remains, on several fronts, that states will reopen contentious issues. The main identifiable contentious issues are the following.

(1) The offset of savings deposits against the union debt. This is the issue most likely to become inflammatory in the short run. Two objections are at present being raised to the principle that the states should take over responsibility for covering their own populations' savings deposits as a way of distributing the burden of union domestic debt.

First, states with higher historic savings rates argue that it is unfair that they should be left with a disproportionately higher debt burden.

Second, many states want their savings deposits back now, while desiring to postpone discussion of the debt burden until the future. They claim their need has become urgent because increased migration and the combination of high inflation and repressed interest rates have led to runs on deposits that local savings banks have not been able to meet. The Russian authorities have, to date, resisted these demands, on the grounds that the repayment of savings deposits under present circumstances would imply the effective monetization of the entire stock of union debt.

(2) The offset of ruble issue against the union debt. The use of states' shares of currency issue to allot to them shares of union debt has also raised at least two objections.

First, states had differing rates of currency migration, depending on the structure of their trade and the relative sophistication of their financial systems. Some states argue that, in net terms, the stock of rubles outstanding on their territory is far less than measured by the original issue, and hence, that they should be allocated a correspondingly lower share of debt.

Second, the treatment of the ruble stock in circulation at the time of the dissolution of the union has been enormously complicated by the announced intention of several states to secede from the ruble area. States that desire to maintain a common currency area argue that, unless states introducing their own currencies return all rubles to the ruble-area central bank, these rubles will become a claim on the resources of ruble-area countries—that is, a foreign asset of seceding states. In order to remove the incentives for seceding states to keep their rubles, ruble-area states would prefer to record the ruble stock as a claim (as well as a liability) of the ruble-area central bank on the states in which the rubles were issued.[16] However, if that treatment were accepted, the representation of the ruble stock as the backing for union debt would imply unequal treatment for seceding and remaining states: the former would acquire the debt but not the currency.

(3) The distribution of union gold. At the dissolution of the union, gold stocks were much lower than estimated by Western sources.[17] What stocks there were were distributed among producer states, on the argument that the gold was an inalienable part of their physical assets.[18] Other states (particularly the Baltic states), whose stocks had been centralized in Moscow, have not ratified this distribution.

(4) The distribution of external assets. Since the joint and several accord on states' liability for external debt has not resulted in debt service by any state other than Russia, tentative proposals have been made that Soviet external assets be transferred to Russia in return for Russia's adopting full responsibility for Soviet debt. (The main identifiable such assets are embassies and holdings in Vneshekonombank subsidiaries.) Some states have been reluctant to pursue this, in the belief that external assets

---

[16]To use Buiter's terminology, they see the seceding states' rubles as an intrinsic part of the government's cash monopoly.

[17]It was argued that gold had been used over several years to finance implicit fiscal deficits and thereby postpone an announcement of the unsustainability of the Soviet state's financial position.

[18]This is a generous interpretation of the de facto outcome of a politically difficult process.

(which have never been comprehensively audited) are large.[19] The distribution of external assets—obviously not subject to resolution by recourse to territoriality—is most likely to require the application of the difficult and contentious valuation techniques the executors of the Soviet Union have avoided so far.

(5) The shortcomings of territoriality. Some states have objected that the Soviet budget, including revenue from all parts of the U.S.S.R., was the main investor in the physical assets of Soviet territories. Hence, they argue that the application of territoriality could lead to significant injustices, particularly when "lucky" states take possession of large indivisible assets, such as space centers and steel mills that were paid for in part by other states.[20]

Objections to territoriality are intensified by application of the traditional Marxist critique that the center exploits the periphery. Some states contend that, as a general rule, investment was concentrated in certain metropolitan areas. More fundamentally, they posit that the static production and trade patterns imposed by planning were immiserizing for peripheral states. If the periphery was a net loser from the Soviet Union, then, they argue, those who gained (the metropolitan areas—principally Russia) should take full responsibility for all Soviet debt.[21]

Conclusion

Despite the many outstanding issues, it is to the credit of all of the states of the former Soviet Union that the distribution of Soviet assets and liabilities has been handled so far with temperance, and with the pragmatism that generated the minimalist approach of territoriality.

Time, and inflation, are the most likely disposers of what remains.

References

Blejer, Mario I., and Adrienne Cheasty, "The Measurement of Fiscal Deficits: Analytical and Methodological Issues," *Journal of Economic Literature*, Vol. 29 (December 1991), pp. 1644-78.

Bean, Charles R., and Willem H. Buiter, *The Plain Man's Guide to Fiscal and Financial Policy* (London: Employment Institute, 1987).

---

[19] Tables 2 and 3 include Vneshekonombank subsidiaries, as valued in the Sovier accounts.

[20] If capital goods' prices in the U.S.S.R. had been close to world prices, records of state budgets and transfers among states could conceivably be disentangled to assess the extent of "imbalances" in investment. However, the erratic undervaluation of Soviet capital makes this impossible.

[21] This particular debate transcends the question of Soviet assets and liabilities. Peripheral states argue that Russia has an obligation to finance in full its structural trade surplus with other states, since the structure of trade was set by Moscow planners.

Buiter, Willem, H. "Measurement of the Public Sector Deficit and Its Implications for Policy Evaluation and Design," *Staff Papers*, International Monetary Fund, Vol. 30 (June 1983), pp. 304-49; reprinted in *How to Measure the Fiscal Deficit*, ed. by Mario I. Blejer and Adrienne Cheasty (Washington: International Monetary Fund, 1993).

International Monetary Fund, *The Economy of the Former U.S.S.R. in 1991* (Washington: International Monetary Fund, 1992).

CHAPTER 8

Russian Federation: Economic Reform and Policy Options for Social Protection

Ehtisham Ahmad and Ke-young Chu

This paper analyzes the implications of the present and possible future reform policies for vulnerable groups in the Russian Federation and the role of a social safety net in protecting them during the transition to a market-oriented economy. In view of the rapidity of the changes in economic conditions, policy measures, and institutions, our aim is to sketch broadly the effects of Russia's reform policies on vulnerable groups and to discuss economic aspects of potential social safety net options in protecting these groups. The economic aspects include the implications of the various options for the budget. In discussing the economic situation and institutional arrangements, our starting point in general is December 1991—just before a major increase in prices. We also discuss the developments during the first half of 1992.

Russia is a middle-income country with a large population and a vast territory. It is in the throes of a market-oriented economic reform. While the living standards for a large number of people are deteriorating rapidly, Russia, on average, is relatively better off than many of the other states of the former U.S.S.R. It is nevertheless important to note that, given large pre-reform distortions, major changes in relative prices will have a differential effect on various income groups. Without an effective safety net, the social effects of the reform would be immense, with a potentially severe negative impact on the political viability of the reform process.

The paper is organized as follows. The effects of economic reform measures on vulnerable groups are first discussed, and then the existing social protection measures, their potential role as social safety nets, and their budgetary implications are described. The discussion of the budgetary implications is based on very rough simulations. Next, possible options for reforming the existing social protection measures are assessed, and finally a summary and conclusions are provided.

Ehtisham Ahmad is Deputy Division Chief and Ke-young Chu is Division Chief of the Expenditure Policy Division of the Fiscal Affairs Department. The authors are grateful to colleagues in European II Department for helpful comments.

Economic Reform and Vulnerable Groups

Living Standards and Vulnerable Groups

A Study of the Soviet Economy, published in 1991,[1] estimated Russia's per capita income in 1989 at 10 percent higher than the average—estimated at US$1,800—for the former U.S.S.R. While this level was lower than per capita incomes in the Baltic states, it was above the per capita incomes in most states of the former U.S.S.R., in particular, those in Central Asia. Russia has a large population—150 billion people.

The recent decline in Russia's production suggests that per capita income in Russia, as in the other states of the former U.S.S.R., has declined substantially since 1989. Nevertheless, the common practice of expressing Russian incomes in U.S. dollar terms on the basis of the commercial rate may be misleading. For example, in December 1991, the monthly salary of a typical professional in Moscow was perhaps some rub 1,000, which at the then commercial exchange rate of rub 100 per U.S. dollar was equivalent to about US$10. However, a monthly income of rub 1,000 in Moscow, in spite of the limited use of rubles resulting from great shortages of goods and services, commanded a substantially larger basket of essential goods than US$10 would, for example, in Washington, D.C.

A child dependency ratio[2] of 43 percent and an old-age dependency ratio of 32 percent imply a young-age population of 37 million, an old-age population of 27 million, and a working age population (including the unemployed, college-age students, and housewives) of 75 million. The child dependency ratio in Russia is substantially lower than those in the Central Asian states of the former U.S.S.R., China, and India, but higher than that in the United States; the high old-age dependency ratio reflects both the relatively long life expectancy and the retirement system that allows workers to retire relatively early (Table 1).[3]

In December 1991, the number of employees in the state sector (including state farms) was estimated at 65 million and pensioners at 38 million. The difference between the working-age population of 75 million and the number of employees of 65 million in the state sector is accounted for largely by college students, nonworking housewives, and the

---

[1] International Monetary Fund and others (1991).

[2] This is defined as the ratio between the number of children under age 16 and the number of persons of working age. The old-age dependency ratio is defined as the ratio between the number of the elderly (men over age 60 and women over age 55) and the number of persons of working age. The definition of these ratios for other countries is slightly different (see Table 1).

[3] See Chu and Holzmann (1992), Kopits (1992), Ahmad (1992), and International Monetary Fund and others (1991) for a further discussion of the living standards and the demographic profiles of the former U.S.S.R. and its states, compared with other countries.

Table 1. Russia: Basic Indicators
Compared with Selected Countries, 1989–90[1]

	Population	Per Capita GDP (In U.S. dollars)	Infant Mortality Rate (Per 1,000)	Life Expectancy at Birth	Dependency Ratio	
					Child	Old age
Russia	150	1,980	18	70	43	32
Other states of former U.S.S.R.						
Belarus	10	1,820	12	72	44	35
Kazakhstan	17	1,670	26	69	61	20
Kyrgyzstan	4	1,300	32	69	78	20
Tajikistan	5	970	43	69	95	16
Ukraine	52	1,730	13	71	41	38
Baltic states						
Estonia	2	2,400	15	71	42	36
Latvia	3	2,200	11	70	40	37
Other countries						
China	1,114	350	30	70	40	9
India	833	340	95	59	63	7
Turkey	55	1,370	61	66	57	7
United States	249	20,910	10	76	33	18

Sources: International Monetary Fund, World Bank, Organization for Economic Cooperation and Development and European Bank for Reconstruction and Development (1991),
Vol. I, p. 230; World Bank (1991), Table 26.
[1] The dependency ratios for the states of the former U.S.S.R. and other countries are for
rough comparisons. For the ratios for the former U.S.S.R. states, a child is defined to be age
16 or younger and the elderly to be older than 55 for women and 60 for men. For the ratios
for other countries, a child is defined to be age 14 or younger and the elderly to be older
than age 64.

unemployed. The number of pensioners of 38 million, together with the old-age population of 27 million, implies that 11 million pensioners receive disability and survivors' benefits.

Recent survey data indicate that in the second quarter 1991, between 80 percent and 90 percent of families received a per capita monthly income of rub 360 (about twice the minimum wage) or less. Pensioners were in a particularly difficult position because the increase in the minimum pension had been less than the price rise in 1991. In December 1991, the minimum pension and the minimum wage were both rub 180 a month. By comparison, the average pension was rub 160.[4] With the adjustment of the minimum pension to rub 342 on January 1, 1992, about 95 percent of pensioners received the minimum pension.

---

[4] This figure includes social pensions, which were half of the minimum pension.

Survey data also indicate that, on average, Russia's consumption of bread, meat products, and milk was not substantially below that of upper middle-income countries. The per capita annual consumption of bread, meat products, and milk in Russia during 1991 was 140 kilograms, 72 kilograms, and 390 liters, respectively. By comparison, the per capita consumption of meat products and milk of low-income groups (lowest 20–30 percent income groups) was 38 kilograms and 300 liters, respectively. A comparable figure for bread is unavailable, but, on the basis of the bread consumption levels of various income groups in other countries, it would not be unreasonable to estimate it at 120 kilograms. These levels undoubtedly have been reduced in recent months. While the average consumption of essential foodstuffs is not low in comparison with other middle-income countries, the consumption of low-income groups is considerably lower than the average for some commodities (for example, meat products and milk). In particular, the consumption of meat, even for the poorest groups, is high by international standards (the poorest group in Russia in 1990 consumed as much meat per capita as the richest 20 percent of the population in a middle-income country—Jordan—in 1989). Considering the apparent further decline in their consumption in recent months, some groups (for example, children, nursing mothers, and elderly) are particularly vulnerable to a further large decline in consumption, particularly of milk and milk products.

Economic Reform and Vulnerable Groups

The large pre-reform price distortions imply that any economic reform effort should aim, among other things, at improving both the structure of relative prices and the functioning of the price system. The extent of distorted domestic prices at the end of 1991 can be illustrated by using the example of bread prices and exchange rates. At the end of 1991, the official price of a loaf of bread was rub 0.48, the basic official rate was rub 1.8 per U.S. dollar, and the commercial exchange rate was about rub 100 per U.S. dollar. These implied that the price of a loaf of bread was less than half a U.S. cent at the commercial rate, and, even at the grossly overvalued basic official exchange rate, was as low as 28 U.S. cents. By comparison, the comparable price in Washington, D.C. was between 80 U.S. cents and $1.

In the Government's discussion of price reform, a major issue has been whether the liberalization of prices should precede, or be preceded by, creating conditions for competition, the latter including measures to establish private ownership of properties, including land, to privatize state-owned enterprises, and to break up monopolies. The Government apparently decided, first, to increase prices, perhaps to reduce a large monetary overhang, and, at the same time, to correct, at least to a certain extent, the grossly distorted relative prices.

The Government liberalized and raised a large number of prices. For example, in January 1992, the Government increased essential food prices by a factor of between 3 and 5. Consumer prices subsequently increased further, resulting in a 250 percent increase in the consumer price index (CPI) during the first quarter of 1992. The Government also raised the minimum wage and minimum pensions. The minimum wage was raised from rub 180 a month to rub 342 a month in January 1992, and again to rub 900 with effect from May 1, 1992. The minimum pension was adjusted from rub 180 a month to rub 342 a month in January 1992, but only to rub 800 a month in May 1992, thus effectively breaking the link with the minimum wage.

Although it is unclear to what extent the present relative prices reflect market conditions, the price increases imply substantial reductions in the *real* minimum wage and pension. It is evident that real living standards have fallen, particularly for groups, such as pensioners, dependent on state transfers. For instance, between December 1991 and March 1992, pensions have increased about two times, compared with a price increase of approximately six times.[5] And income distribution data for early January 1992 suggest that the concentration of per capita incomes around the minimum wage has increased relative to the mid-1991 bunching of incomes.[6] Under these circumstances, a lowering of the benefit below the current minimum wage may not be socially acceptable, although there may be some scope for using a lower subsistence minimum in the determination of localized social assistance programs. A substantially higher level of benefits than at present would, however, entail serious budgetary consequences.

The labor market situation is shrouded by great uncertainties. The tight budgetary situation calls for a sharp reduction in enterprise subsidies and transfers; this, in turn, implies the possibility of an increase in unemployment. Moreover, it is likely that a large number of defense enterprises will be restructured, adding to the increase in unemployment. Moreover, defense conversion will have further social implications because of the extensive reliance of some large towns on one or two enterprises for providing social services, such as health and education.

In March 1992, slightly more than 100,000 workers were officially registered as unemployed; on August 1, 1992, that figure was reported to have increased to about 250,000. While low, it represents a substantial increase since the beginning of the year. As there have been no bankruptcies so far, the trend is deceptive, and it is difficult to predict the future course of unemployment. Moreover, there are reports that many workers are not being paid, and are effectively unemployed, although they have not been

[5]Based on the urban CPI.
[6]See Ahmad (1992).

laid off. Others who have been laid off have not been registered as unemployed. Thus, the true extent of unemployment is probably considerably higher than reported. The above figure represents a small proportion of the labor force. As is seen in other transition economies, an unemployment rate of 5–10 percent is not uncommon, and in Russia, an unemployment rate of 5 percent would imply some 3–4 million unemployed workers and 10 percent would imply some 6–7 million unemployed workers.

Children in low-income families are particularly vulnerable. (Further, younger families with children tend to have lower per capita incomes.) Assuming that about one fifth of the 38 million children are infants (two years or younger), some 8 million children, together with their nursing mothers, especially those in low-income families, would be affected by an increase in the price of food. If nursing mothers and pregnant women leave paid employment in the absence of adequate provisions for maternity care, a considerable reduction in household living standards would result.

Existing Social Protection Measures and Implications

Russia has inherited a set of social protection measures from the former U.S.S.R., and shares many of its features with other states of the former U.S.S.R. After liberalizing many prices and discarding the long-established system of fixed consumer prices, the Government delegated the authority to set the prices of a number of essential commodities (such as bread, sugar, energy products, and transportation) to local governments. Some (such as Moscow) have chosen not to retain explicit subsidies; others still retain them. Note that implicit subsidies would still obtain, depending the extent of input subsidies. It is also possible to view the difference between domestic and world prices as an implicit subsidy, as argued above.

In addition to subsidies, the Government maintains a guaranteed minimum wage for those who work, and a set of cash transfers (pensions, family allowances, and unemployment benefits) for those who do not. In principle, the minimum wage sets the floor for wages of unskilled workers, but it is also used as a reference for cash transfers. The pension scheme is a social insurance arrangement for old-age, disability, and the loss of breadwinner. The Pension Fund was established in 1991 to introduce social insurance; however, along with pensions some family allowances were also to be paid from the Pension Fund (see Ahmad (1992)).

The social security system, however, has been changing rapidly. The Government has abandoned the policy of guaranteed employment for all, but introduced the Employment Fund to finance unemployment compensation and retraining programs. Both the Pension Fund and the Employment Fund are financed through payroll taxes. Budgetary transfers are also involved, particularly for some family allowances, and may well have to be incurred also for increased unemployment.

Existing Measures

Generalized Consumer Subsidies

In December 1991, the system of administered prices still existed. The Government controlled both producer and consumer prices. For foodstuffs, the Government compensated for low producer prices through the subsidized provision of inputs, credits, or cash subsidies. Although there had been efforts to reduce cash subsidies, producer prices were set on the basis of the administratively determined consumer prices, with certain allowed margins for the state-owned enterprises engaged in processing and distributing the good, rather than on the basis of the levels that would provide the farmers with adequate incentives. The administratively determined consumer prices did not reflect the scarcity of the goods and were thus much lower than the prices that prevailed at the few free markets allowed to operate in large cities.

This system benefited those consumers who had access to the goods at the administered prices by keeping prices low, but created severe shortages of subsidized goods and imposed a financial burden on the Government for the budgetary subsidies (to compensate for the losses of state enterprises engaged in processing and distributing the goods) together with implicit taxes on the farmers who received unremunerative prices.

The extent of the benefits may be indicated by comparing the official consumer prices of a set of illustrative foodstuffs with those prevailing at Moscow free markets. For example, in December 1991, the official price of milk was rub 0.43 a liter, whereas the free market price was about rub 15 a liter; similarly, the official price of beef was rub 7 a kilogram, whereas the free market price was between rub 80 and rub 100 a kilogram.

A general subsidy for a commodity tends to provide greater benefits to the better-off groups, who consume more of the subsidized commodity than do the poor. In Russia, while the smaller benefits received by the poor from subsidies accounted for a large share of their household expenditure, the system had degenerated in that the well connected continued to have special access to goods, whereas others had to queue for the severely limited supplies at official prices, or buy in open markets at considerably higher prices.

Although consumer price controls have been lifted by and large, the Government still is unable to eliminate subsidies to agricultural producers on the grounds that consumer prices for staples would have to rise. Thus, despite the ostensible removal of subsidies and price controls, an effective generalized subsidy still remains, and its effects are as opaque as the situation in 1989.

Cash Transfers Based on Social Security

Minimum Wage. The minimum wage was set at rub 900 a month in May 1992, compared with rub 342 at the beginning of 1992 and rub 180 at the end of 1991.[7] The Government once contemplated a system of wage indexation to increase the minimum wage fully to compensate for the increase in the cost of living, while increasing the average wage at a lower rate. Because of the linkage of the minimum wage, pensions, family allowances, and unemployment compensation, the increase in the minimum wage has important implications for overall cash benefits and the financial viability of the Pension Fund and the Employment Fund. It remains unclear, however, how nominal wages and social security benefits will be adjusted for inflation.

Pensions and Allowances. To establish a best-practice market-based system, a new pension law was prepared and legislated in 1991, with help from international agencies such as the International Labor Organization.

At present there is a total payroll tax of 37 percent for pensions and allowances and 1 percent for unemployment insurance. Eighty-five percent of the overall payroll tax (or 31.6 percent of the payroll) is allocated to the Pension Fund to finance old-age, disability, and survivors' pensions and to finance a part of family allowances (for infants); the balance (or 5.4 percent of the payroll) accrues to the Social Insurance Fund to finance the social programs, including family allowances for older children, sick leave, maternity leave, and use of sanatoriums; these programs are administered by trade unions.

A major difficulty has been the high contribution rate, of about 37 percent of the payroll, for pensions and family allowances, in addition to 1 percent for unemployment insurance. Given substantial and growing inter-enterprise arrears, enterprises defer payments, and there are considerable lags in collection. Also, the contribution rate paid by those in the agro-prom complex is considerably lower than elsewhere (20.6 percent, compared with 31.6 percent). This differentiation leads to considerable distortions, as enterprises seek to be reclassified as part of agro-prom.

The system of family allowances is extremely cumbersome, with 18 different types of overlapping allowances, and lacks a clear rationale. Moreover, legally many of the allowances are set as multiples of the minimum wage—for example, the lump-sum birth grant is set at three times the minimum wage. In practice, the minimum wage used for the calculation has remained at the 1990 level of rub 70 a month, and a lump-sum compensation for price changes has been made. For the birth grant, this compensation has been rub 140, making for a total grant of rub 350 (compared with the minimum wage of rub 900 in mid-1992).

---

[7]Given the increasing extent of inter-enterprise arrears and a cash shortage, it appears that the minimum wage adjustment was not fully implemented in May as originally envisaged.

Unemployment Benefits. An earnings-related unemployment benefit system is in operation for those who have lost their employment. After a three-month period of severance pay financed by the enterprise,[8] unemployment benefits are 75 percent of the average wage during the most recent pre-unemployment 12 months for the first 3 months following the loss of a job, then 60 percent and 45 percent, respectively, for the subsequent two quarters. The benefit is to be no lower than the minimum wage. For those without a work history, the minimum benefit is equivalent to the minimum wage. Under the present circumstances, the administration of the system is complicated by the calculation of the earnings-related benefit. The authorities believe that the task would become overwhelming if there is an increase in the numbers becoming unemployed.

Budgetary Implications and Trade-Offs

The budgetary implications of the social protection system have several dimensions. The cost of consumer subsidies depends on a number of factors: the producer price, the consumer price, and the quantity of subsidized consumption. There are many trade-offs. Other factors remaining constant, an increase in the producer price would improve production incentives but would increase the budgetary cost of subsidies. An increase in the consumer price would reduce the budgetary cost, but would raise the cost of living for all, including the poor. These dilemmas underscore the importance of reducing the quantity of subsidized consumption to a bare minimum and, if possible, by targeting, for example, on a geographical or categorical basis.

Subsidies are extremely costly. For example, on the assumption that Russia's domestic producer prices were equalized with world market prices, the financial cost of allowing the entire population access to minimum subsidized consumption of bread, milk, and meat products at half the world prices would cost US$7.6 billion annually (Table 2). At a hypothetical exchange rate of rub 100 per U.S. dollar, this amounts to rub 760 billion.

The budgetary cost of cash benefits depends on the deficits of the Pension Fund and the Employment Fund. These deficits, in turn, depend on their revenues and expenditures. Because the revenues derive from the payroll taxes, the total wage bill and the tax rates are two major determinants. An increase in the wage bill or the tax rates would raise revenues, but the former itself—to the extent that wages of government employees are raised—implies an increase in budgetary expenditure, while the latter would have a negative impact on the financial position of

---

[8]In mid-1992, the number of unemployed receiving severance pay was substantial (more than 600,000). They are not included in official unemployment statistics until the cessation of the three-month period of severance pay.

Table 2. Russia: Illustrative Calculations of General Food Subsidies—Bread, Milk, and Meat

| Commodities | Quantity and Price Assumptions | | | Amount of Subsidies[4] | |
	Annual subsidized consumption per capita[1] (In kilograms or liters)	Producer prices[2] (In U.S. dollar per unit)	Number of beneficiaries[3] (Million persons)	(In billions of U.S. dollars)	(In billions of rubles)
Bread	100	0.13	150	0.9	90
Milk	300	0.14	150	3.1	310
Meat	24	2.00	150	3.6	360
Total				7.6	760

Source: Authors' calculations. See also Table 4 for altenative calculations that provide a safety net at lower costs.

[1] Authors' assumptions based on the household income and expenditure survey. The unit is kilograms for bread and meat; liters for milk.

[2] World market prices in early 1992.

[3] Entire population.

[4] The cost of subsidies at official retail price equal to half the levels equivalent to the world market prices. The ruble amount is based on a hypothetical exchange rate of rub 100 per U.S. dollar.

enterprises, unless the enterprise can shift the tax. The shift would result in either an increase in prices, lower wages, lower production or employment, or a combination of these. The fundamental dilemma for the Pension Fund and the Employment Fund in Russia is that the wage restraint, which is inevitable and necessary, will limit the growth of revenues of these funds, but the benefits for a large number of vulnerable groups—particularly minimum social benefits—need to be raised in line with increases in prices. This will aggravate the financial imbalances of these two funds. Thus, the full indexation of benefits with respect to price changes during the transition would be infeasible. However, this will endanger the living standards of the vulnerable. At best, benefits could be adjusted from time to time with respect to the growth in contributions, although formal indexation with respect to wages should be avoided.

These dilemmas underscore the importance of designing the level and structure of the benefits carefully to provide adequate benefits to vulnerable groups and to limit the budgetary cost. Provision of social benefits in excess of minimum levels may not be feasible.[9]

---

[9] Minimum levels of social benefits should be determined to ensure the minimum consumption of basic necessities. See the next section for a related discussion of a subsistence minimum.

The earnings-related benefits structure, differentiating pensions or unemployment compensation in accordance with past earnings of the beneficiaries, may not be feasible on financial or administrative grounds. The benefits should be structured so as not to produce negative incentives to work.

Table 3 illustrates calculations of the cost of providing children, pensioners, and the unemployed with minimal cash benefits: a family allowance equivalent, as of July 1992, to half the minimum wage for each child and a pension or unemployment compensation equivalent to rub 800 a month to each pensioner or unemployed worker. The cost of such provision, without including the benefits being provided through the Social Insurance Fund, amounts to about rub 600 billion. Assuming that the average monthly wage in Russia is rub 4,000, this amount is equivalent to some 20 percent of the wage bill. Assuming that wages are partly indexed (with a coefficient of 0.7) on prices and that the cash benefits are fully indexed on prices, a 50 percent rate of inflation would raise the ratio between cash benefits and the wage bill by more than 2 percentage points. This would worsen the financial balance of the Pension Fund and the Unemployment Fund.

There is a need for a system of social protection that cushions the vulnerable from the effects of major changes in the prices of essential goods. This would reduce the need for adjustments in benefit levels to the full extent of the price change which would have to be met from the payroll contributions and the pension funds. As argued in Ahmad and Schneider (1992), a limited quantity-based system of food stamps (or the cash equivalent) could be viewed as a basic benefit in kind, which would avoid the need for indexation of cash benefits. It is to be emphasized that such a system is mainly relevant for a period of transition with major relative price changes—not as a permanent instrument of social protection.

Social Safety Net Reform Options and Implications

In the Russian context, the transition to a market economy imposes a set of constraints relating, in particular, to the administrative feasibility of several of the measures that might be advocated for a market-based economy. In addition, the reliance of a large section of the population on transfers underlines the need to ensure adequacy of the benefits provided during a period of rapid change. At the same time, the overall costs of the system and the need for fiscal restraint during the transition make it imperative to evaluate the budgetary consequences of various alternatives.

Russia's special conditions need to be taken into account. For example, the severe budgetary constraint and a large population of old people do not allow for generous social benefits. The large population of old people and a vast territory pose special difficulties in designing the administrative arrangements for the delivery of social benefits.

Table 3. Russia: Simulated Social Protection Costs in Mid-1992

	Unemployment Assumptions			
	Two Million Persons		Five Million Persons	
	Base line	50 percent inflation	Base line	50 percent inflation
Number of persons				
Employed[1]	63	63	60	60
Not employed				
Children	37	37	37	37
Pensioners	38	38	38	38
Unemployed[2]	2	2	5	5
Average amount (in rubles a month)				
Wages[3]	4,000	5,400	4,000	5,400
Cash benefits				
Allowances[4]	450	675	450	675
Pensions	800	1,200	800	1,200
Unemployment compensation	800	1,200	800	1,200
Total amount (in billions of rubles)				
Wages	3,024	4,082	2,880	3,888
Cash benefits[5]	584	877	613	920
(In percent of wage bill)	19.3	21.5	21.3	23.7
Allowances	200	300	200	300
Pensions	365	548	365	548
Unemployment compensation	19	29	48	72

Sources: Government announcements and the authors' assumptions.
[1] Total number of state sector employees minus the number of unemployed.
[2] Hypothetical numbers.
[3] Hypothetical number based on authors' observations. It is extremely difficult to obtain precise wage data.
[4] Assumed to be half of the minimum wage.
[5] Sum of allowances, pensions, and unemployment compensation, excluding the benefits financed through the Social Insurance Fund.

Subsidy Reform Options

We will focus our discussion on consumer subsidies for foodstuffs (such as wheat or bread, milk, and meat products), although the analysis could be extended to other subsidized goods or services. Russia's recent introduction of a more liberalized system of market prices is a move in the right direction. The faster Russia moves to a fully functioning system of market pricing, the faster will be the improvement in resource allocation. However, the market-oriented pricing system cannot operate satisfactorily without a liberal external trading regime. Especially with a large number of monopolistic enterprises, allocative efficiency requires vigorous external competition. The domestic price of a tradable good (for example, wheat) should be determined at a level comparable with its world market price at an exchange rate appropriate to ensure a sustainable external payments position. A higher price would imply a protected, inefficient domestic wheat sector and excessive use of domestic resources for the production of wheat; a lower price would imply insufficient production incentives.

The first step in reforming subsidies should be to liberalize producer prices. In the Russian context, this would imply a substantial increase in producer prices. Given the present system of subsidies, which provide unrestricted access by all to the subsidized goods, an increase in key agricultural producer prices to their world market levels would imply (1) an increase in budgetary subsidies (if consumer prices are to be kept low) or (2) an increase in consumer prices (if budgetary subsidies are to be constrained). The first option would add pressure on the fiscal deficit; the second option would add to the cost of living for the poor, implying the need to raise cash benefits. A third option would be to liberalize both producer and consumer prices (for example, for bread), but keep consumer subsidies at a limited level—for example, only for well-specified groups, such as urban residents (or low-income urban residents), who will tend to suffer from a deterioration in the terms of trade for urban area, relative to rural areas, during economic reform. Subsidies to children and nursing mothers can be targeted through the provision of milk. This option can be less costly and more equitable than a system of generalized subsidies. However, the administrative requirements may be demanding. It would be important to assess the existing administrative arrangements for the possibility of simplifying and adapting them as social protection instruments.[10]

Reforming subsidies along these lines would reduce the budgetary burden substantially. For example, on the assumption that bread and meat subsidies are targeted to urban residents and milk subsidies to children, these subsidies could be reduced from rub 760 billion to rub 300 billion (Table 4).

In Russia, the Government appears to have chosen to eliminate budgetary subsidies as quickly as possible. If the elimination of budgetary subsidies is accompanied by a vigorous policy to liberalize both producer and consumer prices, the outcome would be very desirable. If the elimination of budgetary subsidies were achieved simply by eliminating the negative margins between consumer and producer prices, with one or both prices still controlled, the result would not be satisfactory. In any case, a general increase in consumer prices would raise the cost of living for the poor, and the cash benefits would have to be adjusted, keeping in view other protective measures that might also be instituted.

---

[10]Delegating the authority to set prices to local governments, however, will increase geographical inequities, depending on the financial situations of local governments and will also intensify price distortions across regions. The problem may reappear as an increased need for transfers to local authorities.

Table 4. Russia: Simulated Social Protection Costs— Illustrative Calculations of Food Subsidies

Commodities	Annual subsidized consumption per capita[1] (In kilograms or liters)	Producer prices[2] (In U.S. dollar per unit)	Number of beneficiaries[3] (Million persons)	Amount of Subsidies[4] (In billions of U.S. dollars)	(In billions of rubles)
Untargeted[5]					
Bread	100	0.13	150	0.9	90
Milk	300	0.14	150	3.1	310
Meat	24	2.00	150	3.6	360
Total				7.6	760
Targeted[6]					
Bread	100	0.13	75	0.5	50
Milk	300	0.14	37	0.7	70
Meat	24	2.00	75	1.8	180
Total				3.0	300

Source: Authors' calculations.
[1] Authors' assumptions based on the recent household income and expenditure survey. The unit is kilograms for bread and meat; liters for milk.
[2] World market prices in early 1992.
[3] Entire population.
[4] The cost of subsidies at official retail price equal to half the levels equivalent to the world market prices. The ruble amount is based on a hypothetical exchange rate of rub 100 per U.S. dollar.
[5] The same as in Table 2.
[6] Bread and meat subsidies area assumed to be targeted to urban residents; milk subsidies to children.

Social Security Benefits

Russia has an extensive system of benefits for major life-cycle contingencies—old age, disability, unemployment, and so on. Many of the measures have been introduced recently, and there are serious difficulties concerning the administrative and financial viability of some of the funds that have been established.

Pensions and Allowances

The recent reduction in the real pension benefits have tended to reduce pension outlays relative to the contribution base, leading to a substantial buildup of reserves of the Pension Fund. This buildup of reserves, however, may be temporary, and pension benefits should be determined on the basis of longer-term financial considerations, as well as social protection objectives. There may be some scope for the reduction in the portion of the fund allocated for the old-age, disability, and survivors' pensions, although care should be taken to evaluate (1) the aging of the Russian population, and (2) possible re-evaluation of benefit levels, both of which would lead to increased outlays. The savings could be used to finance family allowances, or greater unemployment benefits, thus reducing budgetary transfers.

An amendment was introduced in the Pension Law in April 1992, revaluing the pensions of people who had retired prior to recent increases in nominal wages. This amendment came into effect in June 1992. The revaluation is based on a one-time recalculation of the pension base, as a function of the average wage in the year of retirement relative to the average wage in 1991. People who retired in 1971 or earlier would have their base salary increased by a factor of 11.2. This factor decreases by 0.3 for each year—to 5.5 for 1990 and 2.9 for 1991.

The revalued pension is expected to be indexed to prices in the future, but pension benefits are now restricted to being less than twice the minimum wage,[11] compared with three times the maximum currently in force. It also appears that the calculation of the pension base is being changed to include the greater of the two last years before retirement, or any five-year period of activity. The revaluation, indexation, and change in the calculation of the base are all likely to add considerably to the cost of pensions. The revaluation of existing pensions, while desirable from an equity perspective, might pose problems, particularly if indexation proposals were implemented.

The administrative requirements of the Pension Fund appear to be more structural and institutional. For example, pension administration would benefit from the introduction of individual social security numbers, computerization, and improved administrative, monitoring, and reporting capabilities.

The system of allowances seems to face more challenging tasks. The Government's proposed streamlining of the system of allowances and the introduction of a simplified system is a move in the right direction. The main benefit is to be the child benefit, payable from birth to age 16 or 18 (if the child continues to study). This could be a flat-rate benefit, although supplements would be possible for single parents and abandoned children. The basic child benefit should also replace the benefit paid to children below the age of 18 months using the resources of the Pension Fund. In addition, there would be four other benefits, including pregnancy and maternity benefits, birth grants, and child care and invalidity allowances.

---

[11]Exceptionally, if the person has worked more than 45 years and receives the maximum pension he would be entitled to an additional rub 342—above twice the minimum wage.

Centralized benefits should be uniform throughout the country, although local authorities would have the power to supplement some of the benefits out of their own resources to suit local conditions. The latter appears to be a continuation of current practices (for instance, in Moscow, some of the benefits are augmented through an additional sales tax on tobacco).

The Government's stated objective to tailor benefits to available resources is encouraging. Taking as an indicative guide the 5.4 percent contribution for allowances, now channeled through the trade union-administered Social Insurance Fund, it would appear that the level of the basic child benefit could not exceed half the current minimum wage without major calls on the budget or a substantial increase in the payroll tax. Neither of the above outcomes is desirable and, in addition, a high level of child benefit (for example, at the minimum wage, as proposed) would generate work disincentives. It would be preferable to limit the basic child benefit to a flat rate no greater than half the minimum wage and to provide social assistance supplements in deserving cases.

The system of adjustment of benefits has major implications for the balances of the social security funds. Indexation to prices, when contributions are linked to the growth of the wage bill which is declining in real terms, will quickly lead to deficits.

At present, most family allowances, as well as holidays and other benefits, are provided by the Social Insurance Fund managed by trade unions, financed by the 5.4 percent payroll tax. These resources should be reallocated through the budget to provide for the new system of allowances. Some of the services that are provided by trade unions may continue, but should be financed by the voluntary contributions of members and should no longer form part of the social security system. To guarantee the payment of the allowances and also to impose discipline on the overall level of expenditure on allowances, the 5.4 percent payroll contribution should continue to be earmarked in the medium term to protect the levels of benefits. In the longer term, allowances should be paid directly from the budget without earmarking, the levels thus being determined jointly with the other expenditure decisions of the Government.

Employment Fund and Other Labor Market Intervention

An alternative to the earnings-related system is a two-tier system for providing unemployment benefits.[12] This would simplify the calculation of benefits. For budgetary and incentive reasons, it would be important to reduce the period during which it would be paid. Thus, persons losing their jobs could be paid a flat-rate benefit of 125 percent of the minimum

---

[12]Apparently the Government is considering this option, along with another proposal to relate unemployment benefits to a matrix of earnings and length of service. This would approximate an earnings-related system and would be less cumbersome to administer but more complex than the two-tiered system.

wage for a period of 6 months. There could be a second, lower-tier benefit of 75 percent of the minimum wage payable for 12 months to those without a recent work history. After the 12-month period, there could be other assistance, such as aid to dependents, rent payments, and in-kind benefits. It is important that Russia maintain the basic unemployment support for the transition period, since the simplification of administrative procedures and speedy payments of benefits will be crucial to the overall acceptability of Russia's economic reform program, and would also be less costly than the current legislation.

In the longer term, to generate equity, it may be advisable to revert to an earnings-related system. This issue will become politically important as the variance in earnings levels increases. Further, to improve work incentives and contain overall costs, for the longer-term unemployed, or for fresh entrants to the work force, it would be desirable to require the recipients to retrain or participate in public works.

Arrangements for public works are already under way, with the preparation of documents and the training of personnel. This measure is expected to be particularly useful in defense-oriented "closed towns." The expenditures on public works should be supported in part through the resources of the local communities that benefit directly, topped-up by allocations from the Employment Fund.

Preparations for retraining programs are also in place. Many of the workers of the former defense-based industries are highly skilled, and it is believed that some retraining would make them highly productive members of a market economy. While considerable emphasis is being placed on the retraining aspects of the employment services, the official priorities are clearly to first provide support to those being laid off.

The costs of stipends for retraining purposes, or wages for the participants in public works, could be charged to the unemployment contribution receipts. However, overhead costs of the Employment Services, including staff salaries and building and equipment costs, are likely to be incurred, increasing the expenditures of the Employment Fund above the revenues based on the 1 percent payroll contribution. These expenditures could be met, in part, through external assistance (for example, for automation of the services), but would also require budgetary support. The capital outlays, such as building and equipment costs, should be included in the capital expenditure budget.

Although under present conditions it may be politically difficult to increase the 1 percent payroll tax, or even introduce an individual contribution at this stage, there may be a possibility of increasing the contribution rate allocated to the Employment Fund if there is a more than corresponding decrease in the payroll contribution for other purposes.

During the last quarter of 1991 and the first quarter of 1992, the expenditures of the Employment Services had been a relatively small share of the receipts. Reserves had been invested with a commercial bank—at a substantial rate of return (a 40 percent rate of return is not unlikely) in nominal terms; however, the current level of reserves could be exhausted in a matter of a few months with a higher level of unemployment than at present.

Social Assistance

It will take time to develop criteria and administrative mechanisms for means testing, and such assistance will eventually only be feasible at the local level. It is here that the work on subsistence minimum baskets (which will vary by region) could be of some use. Despite local administration and financing, many of the eligibility and financing criteria should be centrally coordinated, and this would require considerable further work, with the participation in survey work by institutions such as the World Bank.

The use of means testing poses difficulties. The verification of household or per capita income levels and assets is an essential ingredient of a means test—the wage level of an individual member of a household is an important, but by no means sufficient, element in a proper means test. While the identification of wages received by an individual or from a single enterprise is possible, the verification of the total income of the household is quite another matter. It is important not to overburden the stretched administrative resources during the transition period—as seen in the case of provision of unemployment insurance.

Despite the difficulties that are associated with setting up means-tested mechanisms, it is possible to use categorical targeting as a method of providing social assistance. For instance, age, family composition, employment status, and residential location could be some of the criteria for such targeting. Public works participation, at, say, the lower tier of unemployment benefit, could be thought of as an assistance mechanism. The low wage, together with the works test, combine to target the assistance through self-selection to those who really need help.

Concluding Remarks

The issue of appropriate social safety nets and protecting vulnerable groups during the transition from an administered to a market economy is of crucial importance in providing an underpinning of reforms. It is also important to be aware of the budgetary consequences of alternatives. Moreover, policy measures taken with respect to subsidy reduction and price reform will have important implications for the living standards of various groups. This will affect the subsequent need to adjust the "permanent" social security instruments—pensions, allowances, unemployment benefits—and to provide for those who might fall below an acceptable minimum standard.

In designing social safety nets for the transition, in many respects, Russia faces difficulties similar to those in other reforming countries. The budgetary constraint is a problem common to the group of reforming countries with or without the socialist legacy. Russia has inherited a set of social programs and institutional arrangements many other reforming countries outside the former socialist world do not necessarily have. These programs and institutions can provide a basis on which Russia can design a reformed social protection system, but they may also be an obstacle to instituting such a system. In particular, scaling down the inefficient, but extensive social benefits—such as guaranteed employment, generous family allowances, and various employment-related benefits—before the fruits of a market-oriented economic system materialize can meet considerable opposition from present beneficiaries.

Russia's demographic profile is more like those of the Baltic states than the Central Asian states of the former U.S.S.R. While both old-age pensions and family allowances are costly in Russia, family allowances (for children) are relatively less costly in Russia (and the Baltic states) than in some Central Asian states of the former U.S.S.R. (Ahmad (1992)). Russia has a vast territory and a large population. A highly centrally administered, nationally uniform social benefit system would be more difficult to establish in Russia than in some other states of the former Soviet Union, with a smaller population and territory. In Russia, local governments will have to play an important role.

The ability to adjust benefits for the "permanent" social security instruments is constrained by the overall level of the payroll tax, and even maintaining the current level is likely to lead to labor-market disincentives as well as evasion. It is thus important to rationalize benefits and procedures for adjustment. A combination of policy instruments will be needed to provide for social protection of the vulnerable in a cost-effective manner.

References

Ahmad, Ehtisham, "Poverty, Demographic Characteristics, and Public Policy in CIS Countries," paper presented at the forty-eighth Congress of the International Institute of Public Finance, Seoul, Korea, 1992.

———, and Jean-Luc Schneider, "Alternative Social Security Systems in CIS Countries," paper presented at Conference on Fifty Years After the Beveridge Report, York, United Kingdom, 1992.

Chu, Ke-young, and Robert Holzmann, "Public Expenditure: Policy Aspects," in *Fiscal Policies in Economies in Transition*, ed. by Vito Tanzi (Washington: International Monetary Fund, 1992).

International Monetary Fund, World Bank, Organization for Economic Cooperation and Development, and European Bank for Reconstruction and Development, *A Study of the Soviet Economy*, Vols. I, II, and III (Washington: International Monetary Fund, 1991).

Kopits, George, "Social Security," in *Fiscal Policies in Economies in Transition*, ed. by Vito Tanzi (Washington: International Monetary Fund, 1992).

World Bank, *World Development Report, 1991* (New York: Oxford University Press, 1991).

CHAPTER 9

Fiscal Federalism and
the New Independent States

George Kopits and Dubravko Mihaljek

Perhaps the most dramatic economic change in the disintegration of the Soviet Union involves the vertical and horizontal fiscal relations among various levels of government. In fact, there is hardly another area (money, trade) in which centrifugal forces have acted so rapidly and so powerfully since the late 1980s. Further modifications are under way; in practically all the new independent states there is an ongoing search for stable and durable intergovernmental fiscal arrangements.

This chapter highlights the most salient developments in the evolution of intergovernmental relations from those in the former Soviet Union toward the current relations prevailing among and within the new independent states. First, it provides a historical overview of the Soviet budget structure prior to the decentralization process. As part of this overview, the chapter examines the role of state-owned enterprises in intergovernmental relations. Second, it focuses on the disintegration of the former system and the creation of new independent states and, in particular, on the scope for fiscal harmonization and coordination among the states. Third, the chapter discusses fiscal relations as they have evolved within the states, identifying both innovative and unchanged features of the system. Also, an attempt is made to assess the outlook for fiscal federalism in the states.

The discussion tries to draw on broad principles of fiscal federalism—solidarity, subsidiarity, correspondence, benefit—that are reflected in criteria of interregional equity, efficiency, and macroeconomic stabilization, and to examine their relevance to the former Soviet Union and the new independent states.

George Kopits is Division Chief in the Fiscal Affairs Department, and Dubravko Mihaljek is Economist in the Central Asia Department. The authors were, respectively, the head and a member of the fiscal team in the 1990 IMF Task Force on the Soviet Economy, whose findings are published in IMF and others (1991). An earlier version of this chapter was presented at the annual meetings of the American Economic Association, Anaheim, California, January 5-7, 1993. Comments by Jon Craig, Henri Lorie, Charles McLure, Richard Musgrave, and Emil Sunley are gratefully acknowledged.

155

Federalism in the Soviet Union

Background

Associative arrangements among states or regional units span a range of contractual, confederate, federal, and unitary structures. In a confederation, sovereign states unite to pursue joint actions, such as defense or trade, on the basis of the principle of "the general government being subordinate to the regional governments and dependent upon them."[1] This was, for example, the case of the American Colonies' Articles of Confederation of 1777, the 1848 Swiss Constitution, the 1867 *Ausgleich* (Compromise) of the Austro-Hungarian Empire, and the Constitution of the German Empire of 1867–1919. As regards the European Community (EC), the Treaty of Rome, strengthened by the Maastricht amendments, provides a contemporary example of a confederate arrangement. In contrast, a federal structure involves "dividing powers so that the general and regional governments are each, within a sphere, co-ordinate and independent."[2] This principle is enshrined in the U.S. Constitution of 1787—as explained in *The Federalist Papers* by Hamilton, Jay, and Madison—and adopted by many countries around the world.

The position of the former Soviet Union was that of an extremely centralized unitary state, at the very end of the spectrum of intergovernmental arrangements. Contrary to widespread belief, the Soviet Union did not come into existence through the voluntary decision of its member states and was never a genuine federal system, its proclaimed principles of self-determination and free secession notwithstanding.[3] Formally, it was established on two contradictory principles: democratic centralism as the principle of the communist party organization, and federalism as the principle of state organization.[4] While the former required that decisions of central party organs—in theory democratically adopted after free discussion "from the bottom up"—be implemented loyally by regional party organizations on the basis of directives "from the top down," federalism proper required that the powers of government be divided between coordinate, independent authorities operating on behalf of regional or local electorates. In practice, unitary party authority superseded the principle of state federalism in all intergovernmental relations; federalism provided an exterior form without substance.

Historically, the supremacy of the party principle of democratic centralism was the platform of the Soviet state founded by Lenin after the victory of the October Revolution. Lenin, as most Marxists, was a unitarist by

---

[1]Wheare (1964), p. 4. In German, a confederation is denoted as *der Staatenbund*, the alliance of states, as opposed to *der Bundesstaat*, the federal state.

[2]Wheare (1964), p. 10.

[3]See Swoboda (1992).

[4]Kristan (1990), p. 5.

conviction and an advocate of strong centralized states. He adopted a nominal federal structure as a way to resolve the national question after the dissolution of czarist Russia, but only as a transition to a centralized proletarian state.[5] He saw the authority of the party, based on party centralism, as a safeguard against separatist forces within the Russian Empire.

The strategy pursued to install Bolshevik rule in most of the newly independent non-Russian territories was to proclaim the local Bolsheviks as the only legitimate representatives of the Ukrainian, Byelorussian, Latvian, Armenian, and other workers, lend them armed support in their struggle to overthrow the local "bourgeoisie" (non-Bolshevik governments set up locally), replace them with Soviet Bolshevik governments, and create Soviet Republics.[6] At the same time, the right of individual republics to self-determination and free secession was repeatedly recognized, with the understanding that the right could be exercised only by Bolshevik governments.

In 1919, on the occasion of the VIII Party Congress, Zinov'ev noted that it would be impossible to uphold for long the contradiction of "one single centralized party alongside a federation of states," and predicted that of the two principles, the federative principle would yield to the central hegemony of the party. Similarly, Pyatakov stressed on the same occasion the inconsistency of pursuing the economic merger of all the Soviet republics while proclaiming self-determination.[7] Nevertheless, the federative principle was enshrined in the Union Treaty, signed in the Bolshoi Theater on December 30, 1922, exactly 69 years before the formal dissolution of the U.S.S.R.

Matryoshka Dolls Under the Unitary Structure[8]

The state budget in the former Soviet Union was an organic and accounting consolidation of the union budget, including the social security accounts and the state budgets of the union republics. In turn, the state

---

[5]See Kristan (1990).

[6]This strategy was foreshadowed in the following remarks by Lenin on December 5, 1917: "We are told that Russia will disintegrate and split up into separate republics but we have no reason to fear this. We have nothing to fear, whatever the number of independent republics. The important thing for us is not where the state border runs but whether or not the working people of all nations remain allied in their struggle against the bourgeoisie, irrespective of nationality . . . . We are going to tell the Ukrainians that as Ukrainians they can go ahead and arrange their life as they see fit. But we are going to stretch out a fraternal hand to the Ukrainian workers and tell them that together with them we are going to fight against their bourgeoisie and ours. Only a socialist alliance of the working people of all countries can remove all ground for national persecution and strife." Lenin (1960–70), Vol. 26, p. 344.

[7]As quoted in Swoboda (1992), p. 769.

[8]This subsection draws partly on International Monetary Fund and others (1991), Chapter III.2.

budget of each of the 15 union republics was a consolidation of its own budget and the budgets of all lower levels of government under its jurisdiction, which included more than 52,000 oblast, okrug, kray, rayon, city, village, and settlement budgets. Traditionally, despite the formal federal structure of public administration, the formulation and execution of fiscal policy was highly centralized to ensure full conformity with the plan.

The unitary fiscal structure in the Soviet Union was characterized by a concentric configuration of the budgets, much like a large set of *matryoshka* dolls, one at each government level. The minimum revenue, by category, and maximum expenditure, by program, were determined at each level of government for the budgets of the immediately lower level under its jurisdiction. The budgetary aggregates were set by the Gosplan in the context of the annual plan.[9] Deficits at any level could be covered with transfers from the budget of the next higher level government. Some of the transfers from the union to the republic governments consisted of loans, subject to repayment by the republics, and of shares of the proceeds from the so-called lottery bonds. Recourse to horizontal or upward transfers was made only in exceptional circumstances. Budget surpluses were to be returned to the next higher level of government.

Regarding the mechanics of revenue assignment, each year governments at every level were allocated a certain proportion of tax or nontax revenue in a given category collected within their territory, more or less in line with expenditure needs, especially for social purposes. By 1989, the state budgets of the union republics (that is, republic plus all local budgets) obtained, on average, 86 percent of revenue from the turnover tax, 61 percent of revenue from income taxation of individuals, and 39 percent and 93 percent of revenue from income taxation of state-owned enterprises and cooperatives, respectively. Poorer union republics were permitted to retain a higher proportion of revenue (for example, turnover tax retention in Central Asian republics was 100 percent). The union budget received all foreign trade revenue, including external financing, and 61 percent of revenue from state enterprise profits. Revenue from social security contributions, assisted with general revenue, was channeled to beneficiaries through both the union and the republic budgets.[10]

On the expenditure side, fiscal responsibilities were divided broadly along functional lines, under tight centralized control. Union republics and the local levels of government were responsible for social and cultural expenditures (education, health, social insurance, pension and other

---

[9] In another dimension, the Gosplan, as the largest doll, contained the Ministry of Finance, which, as an administrative agency, in turn engulfed a smaller doll, the Gosbank operating largely as a payments and accounting department. For a discussion of fiscal and monetary institutions, see Kopits (1992b).

[10] For a more detailed breakdown of revenue by government level, see International Monetary Fund and others (1991), p. 280.

benefits), and the union government for defense, science, justice and internal security, and subsidies to the foreign trade sector (including financing flows to abroad). Expenditures on the economy (investment, operational expenditures, price subsidies) were split in half between the union budget and republics; the latter were further split in half between the republic and local budgets.

Total intergovernmental transfers amounted to $6^1/_2$ percent of the union budget in 1989, consisting of payments by the union to the republics for meat and milk subsidies (43 percent), repayments by and lending to republics (38 percent), and republic-specific grants (19 percent), channeled almost solely to Central Asian republics. Allocations were subject to yearly variations depending largely on changing needs. Both revenue sharing and transfers were subject to considerable intergovernmental negotiation and discretionary decision.

The combination of chronic commodity shortages and rudimentary financial markets provided an opportunity for covering budget deficits from unspent cash balances deposited by consumers in state banks.[11] Once the size of the budget deficit was known, the State Savings Bank would finance it with the net increase in savings deposits. In addition, state-owned enterprises were obliged periodically to hold various types of government bonds. As long as the stock of forced savings was growing faster than the size of the deficit, this approach was noninflationary.

Clearly, in the unitary centrally planned framework, an all-pervasive solidarity principle was superimposed forcefully on all levels of government. Horizontal equity, defined in terms of expenditure levels, was to be ensured across union republics, oblasts, and various local governments, in line with merit wants as defined by the central party authority.[12] Application of fiscal resources and responsibilities at a given level was entirely under the control of the next higher level of government. The combination of central planning and unitary fiscal structure undermined efficiency in the collection of revenue and its allocation at different levels of government. At the same time, however, the system facilitated macroeconomic stabilization.

Role of the Enterprise Sector

In the former Soviet Union, as in other socialist countries, state-owned enterprises occupied a pivotal place in fiscal policy, including intergovernmental fiscal arrangements. Recent experience shows that these enterprises also play a critical role in the transition from central planning

---

[11]See Birman (1990).

[12]The concept of merit wants found its full expression precisely in communist societies and has become so deeply ingrained that it now presents a formidable obstacle to reforms of social welfare and labor relations.

to market economy and in economic relations among and within the successor states of the U.S.S.R. It is argued herein that fiscal decentralization in the former Soviet Union is critically intertwined with enterprise restructuring. The argument is based on four points.

First, in the Soviet Union, as in other centrally planned economies, the state budget relied excessively on revenues collected through taxation or outright confiscation of enterprise profits, largely for reallocation back to the enterprise sector. As observed in other post-socialist economies that are more advanced in the transition process, it is very difficult to maintain this reliance when enterprises are exposed to an increasingly tighter budget constraint (that is, reduced credit and subsidies) in an environment of weak tax administration and proliferating tax concessions. As a result of enterprise restructuring and decentralization of decision making, a substantial portion of the tax base can evaporate long before other reform measures bear the fruit of improved efficiency and higher growth. The revenue erosion has been particularly pronounced regarding the profit tax and turnover tax, or its successor, the value-added tax (VAT). Because in the short run other revenue sources cannot substitute for enterprise taxation, governments are forced either to accept lower overall revenues, with all the negative consequences for fiscal decentralization and macroeconomic balance, or to raise enterprise tax rates, thus stifling the process of enterprise reform.

The second point involves government ownership and control of the enterprise sector. With increased enterprise autonomy and government decentralization, the paternalistic relations between governments and enterprises become open to question. In the former Soviet Union, for example, union control at the highest level was simply replaced by republic control. As republics proclaimed their independence, they imposed full control over all property on their territory. In a number of cases, this amounted to continuation of the command economy. Republic authorities quickly took steps to regulate enterprises, retaining a higher-than-agreed share of profit taxes, and requisitioning part of their profits.[13] In turn, lower level governments have also asserted their control over some local enterprises.[14] With some exceptions, fiscal decentralization has thus been achieved at the expense of enterprise reform, creating a situation that is untenable in the long run as the economy embarks on market-oriented transition.

[13]In 1991, a higher-than-agreed retention of revenues by the republics was responsible for almost 60 percent (5.9 percent of GDP) of the union budget deficit; see International Monetary Fund (1992a), p. 12. As pointed out by Aleksashenko (1991), p. 23, one centralized economic system was replaced by 15 or more similar, albeit smaller, and in some cases more authoritarian, systems.

[14]In the short to medium run, the actual locus of government ownership and control over enterprises has, of course, important implications for the fiscal jurisdiction as well as for the consequences of privatization, including disposition of proceeds from asset sales.

A third and related point is the high degree—probably the highest anywhere in the world—of industrial concentration of former Soviet enterprises. Prior to the breakup of the union, around one third of industrial output, including services, was produced by single-enterprise industries, and a further one third by two-enterprise industries.[15] The underlying rationale for a concentrated productive structure lies not only in economies of scale and vertical integration, but, perhaps more important, in its usefulness for centralized planning, exercised directly through the industrial branch ministries. Large monopolistic enterprise structures, arching over a number of jurisdictions, or closely linked across jurisdictions, can complicate both the trend toward fiscal decentralization at all levels and the realignment of enterprise control and ownership. Progress on these fronts requires splitting up large enterprises wherever this is technologically and economically feasible.

The fourth major aspect of the relationship between state-owned enterprises and fiscal decentralization involves the provision of public services. Traditionally, socialist enterprises had supplied the population with a major share of local public goods (training programs, culture, health care, housing, child care, and other social benefits). A large portion of infrastructure supplying local public services was operated and financed by enterprises. As they have received some autonomy from the state and as they are increasingly exposed to a hard budget constraint, enterprises are trying to relinquish the burden of providing such services. Thus, some of the first victims of enterprise restructuring were day-care centers, clinics, cinemas, and other nonproductive facilities operated by enterprises. At the same time, the new laws mandated that local governments take over increased expenditure responsibilities.[16] Although initially eager to take over some public services (for example, cinemas, cemeteries, company-owned housing), and in some cases to privatize them along with enterprises—partly because of the potential revenue source—many local governments discovered that they were ill-equipped to organize and finance the supply of such services.

Because enterprises are a significant source of tax revenue and economic as well as political influence for republic and local governments and because they provide basic public services and, in many cases, commodities essential for production within and outside republics, present policymakers face a difficult trade-off on the road to market-oriented enterprise restructuring and fiscal decentralization. At the same time, a discussion of intergovernmental fiscal relations in the former Soviet Union

---

[15]See Hewett (1988).
[16]Article 7 of Russia's Law on the Formation of the Budgets of the Russian Soviet Federated Socialist Republic of 1991, for example, stated that local budgets were responsible for financing expenditures on the maintenance and development of the local autonomy, the implementation of regional programs, and "other programs agreed upon with the appropriate bodies of power."

cannot ignore the traditional structure of state-owned enterprises, in particular those reaching across jurisdictions. The implications of these features for changes in intergovernmental arrangements are a recurrent theme in the following sections.

From Soviet Union to Independent States

Divorce Soviet Style, 1989–91

Fiscal decentralization in the former Soviet Union can be traced to an experiment in 1988, when a small proportion of the payments out of after-tax enterprise profits started to be transferred to local budgets. Increasing shares of various tax categories were being disposed of freely at lower levels of government, given that a proportion of union revenue, including taxes on individuals and profit taxes on enterprises subordinate to union authorities, was earmarked for republic and local budgets. In principle, these shares were intended to give the republics and local governments an incentive to raise tax revenue from enterprises and individuals, and thus to facilitate the introduction of greater financial autonomy.

The unitary system was further relaxed in the way budgets were drawn up for 1990 at various levels of government. Mounting pressures for regional fiscal decentralization led to the enactment in April 1990 of a law that stressed the primacy of the union in determining the tax system—in terms of the type of taxes and their rates—and in managing and financing various broadly defined common functions, namely, defense, debt servicing, public investment programs, and subsidies to enterprises.[17] Union programs were to be financed with mandatory transfers from the republics. In return, republics gained more freedom to determine fiscal policy in their own territory, mainly in the area of public expenditure and investment, acquisition of property, price controls of certain goods, and disposal of profits. However, the republics had de facto already acquired more fiscal powers than were granted belatedly under the law. This legal catching-up has characterized the fiscal decentralization process at all levels of government ever since.

Subsequent events have shown that 1990 was the last year in which republic rights and responsibilities were subordinate to union laws and regulations. It was also in the fall of 1990 that the last attempt was made to establish a rational federal—or rather confederate—fiscal framework, predicated on a meaningful application of both principles of solidarity

[17]See the Law on the Fundamentals of the Economic Relations of the U.S.S.R. and the Union and Autonomous Republics. Further details on intergovernmental relations were laid down in a companion Decree on the Delineation of Powers Between the U.S.S.R. and the Subjects of the Federation.

and subsidiarity. According to one celebrated proposal, most revenue and expenditure functions would have been allocated to the republics, which in return would have made upward transfers to the union budget to finance common expenditures on the basis of the GNP (or GNP per capita) of each republic.[18] This and similar attempts were doomed to failure; by the end of the year, all union republics had declared the sovereignty of their laws over those of the union.

In early 1991, a radical restructuring of the Soviet budget system was already under way. For the first time since the establishment of socialist central planning, the union authorities prepared only the union budget, while some large republics (especially Russia and Ukraine) began to formulate their own budgets. The union retained responsibility only for strictly common functions (defense, union civil service, debt servicing), transferring other functions to republics and union extrabudgetary funds (for example, Stabilization Fund, Pension Fund, Employment Fund, Fund for Social Support of the Population). These funds were to be financed with earmarked republic transfers, social security contributions, and proceeds from privatization, which for the most part never materialized.[19]

Although the union tax laws still had nominal primacy over republic regulations, some republics started to determine their tax rates independently and to retain amounts well in excess of shared revenues. This practice became widespread by midyear. To compensate, union budget transfers to withholding republics were reduced or stopped altogether. Republics also overrode union regulations over republic expenditure responsibilities by pursuing independent investment, subsidy, and social support policies.

Fiscal disintegration accelerated after the failure of the August coup. At that time, virtually all the republics discontinued transfers to the union budget. An extraordinary budget for the fourth quarter of 1991 was approved but never executed, as the Russian Federation took over the central union institutions in Moscow, including the U.S.S.R. Ministry of Finance, and decided to close altogether the union budget in November 1991. In return, Russia agreed to pay for about two thirds of envisaged union expenditures for the months of November and December, both on its territory as well as common expenditures in other republics.[20] Fiscal performance for the year as a whole varied sharply among republics; while Lithuania netted a surplus, all other republics incurred deficits, with the largest one faced by Tajikistan, estimated at more than one half of its GDP.[21]

At the end of 1991, the devolution of fiscal authority to the republics was complete. Following declarations of independence in rapid succession, the

[18]See Shatalin and others (1990).

[19]See International Monetary Fund (1992a), pp. 10–11.

[20]See International Monetary Fund (1992a), p. 11.

[21]For a comparison of fiscal imbalances and monetary conditions in each republic at the disintegration stage, see Aleksashenko (1992).

new states were drafting their first separate budgets and tax laws effective January 1992. Not surprisingly, after seven decades of absolute dependence on union authority, republic governments were technically ill-prepared to conduct fiscal policy in a consistent macroeconomic framework.

Commonwealth of Independent States

From about the middle of 1991, there was at least tacit recognition of the independence of each republic and of the need to form a new treaty among them on a voluntary basis. In late June, a draft treaty was published and endorsed by eight republics. This draft sought unsuccessfully to retain for the union the authority only to implement the union budget, issue money, and maintain foreign exchange reserves; all other responsibilities for the conduct of macroeconomic policy could fall within the sphere of joint union-republic competence. Under a somewhat looser arrangement, in October eight states signed an economic community treaty. In addition to the maintenance of a single currency, a common economic space, and a small common budget, it envisaged limits for member states' budget deficits; sums exceeding these limits were to become a debt vis-à-vis other member states. Interestingly, the proposed limit on the budget deficit seems to have been inspired by a similar fiscal rule adopted by the EC under the Maastricht accord.[22] However, lacking a minimum degree of solidarity and discipline, this treaty quickly became obsolete.

Possibly the most ambitious arrangement that could realistically be accomplished at the time was the Commonwealth of Independent States (CIS), established in Minsk in December 1991 by three Slavic republics of the former Soviet Union. The Minsk accord formally recognized the dissolution of the U.S.S.R. and called for a broad framework to preserve a common economic space among member states (especially regarding trade in raw materials and other essential inputs), to coordinate economic reforms, to use the ruble in interrepublic trade, to consult prior to the introduction of separate currencies, to establish a banking union, to reduce budget deficits, to harmonize taxes, and to agree on defense and environmental issues. One year after agreement in principle by eleven states, the CIS continues to exist as an amorphous body, without a charter or an enforcement mechanism for agreements reached by its members.

---

[22]Whereas the economic and monetary union (EMU) agreement binds EC members to a limit equivalent to 3 percent of GDP, a draft agreement among the new independent states would have imposed a limit equivalent to 5 percent of GNP in 1992, followed by successive annual reductions down to 2 percent of GNP by 1995. It is worth noting that unlike in the EC where four large member countries are surrounded by eight relatively smaller ones, in the former Soviet Union the Russian economy is larger than all the other states combined whereby it would have had to bear the largest share of the adjustment under such rule.

Although relations between two of its most important members, Russia and Ukraine, remain uneasy, the Commonwealth's existence does not seem to be under imminent threat.

The first few months of the Commonwealth were characterized by the euphoria of the new states over independence, which, in some cases, seems to have been unexpectedly thrust upon them. As a result, the centrifugal forces that had led to the breakup of the Soviet Union were enhanced and the remaining economic ties among the republics were further disrupted. A glance at the agreements signed by member states of the CIS seems to indicate that, depending on their willingness to maintain links with Russia—by far the dominant member—a dichotomy is emerging among the states. The inner group is comprised of Armenia, Belarus, Kazakhstan, Kyrgyzstan, Russia, Tajikistan, and Uzbekistan; the outer group is made up of Ukraine, Moldova, Azerbaijan, and Turkmenistan.[23] Among the former Soviet republics, the Baltic states are the only ones not likely to join any part of the CIS.[24]

Fiscal Issues Among the States

As indicated in the preceding discussion, the center of gravity in intergovernmental relations has shifted over the past three years from an extremely centralized unitary state to a stage where the republics abandoned the idea of improving the "union state" and were considering instead the creation of a "union of states," and then further to the stage of complete independence with incipient autarkic tendencies.

Notwithstanding continued tensions in trade relations, introduction of separate currencies, differential price liberalization, control over strategic supplies, and division of common assets and liabilities, there remains considerable scope for maintaining some fiscal coordination and cooperation. Specifically, in view of the existing multistate enterprises, the closer links among enterprises located in different states, the emerging social needs, and the overall costs of breaking up an open economic space, it seems to be in each state's economic interest to address rationally the interstate fiscal issues, regardless of the final form of an associative arrangement among the states. Indeed, it can be argued that recognition of these fiscal issues is instrumental for the economic welfare of the new independent states.

In its present form, the CIS is a very loose contractual arrangement that cannot be regarded as a confederation. However, the efficiency arguments for preserving an open economic space among the states are well

---

[23]See Sheehy (1992).

[24]Georgia has never been a member of the Commonwealth, but the possibility of its joining in the future cannot be ruled out. The Azeri and Moldovan parliaments have not yet ratified the CIS treaty, but it seems that they have not rejected the idea of membership either.

known. Because the new states had been closely linked for a long time and had developed productive structures that are highly specialized across regions, often without regard to comparative advantage and market demand, their situation is comparable in many respects to the case of Siamese twins who cannot be separated overnight without the risk of serious or even fatal injury. To minimize this risk, it would seem essential to identify the necessary conditions for maintaining an open interstate economic space. These conditions include an appropriate interstate trade and payments mechanism as well as a degree of macroeconomic policy coordination.[25] In this regard, we focus on the fiscal conditions.

As a first step, it would be necessary to eliminate any barriers to trade and factor movements that have proliferated in the recent past, mostly in an effort to protect domestic supplies. As a corollary, a certain degree of tax harmonization would help reduce tax-induced allocative distortions.[26] The case for tax harmonization is especially strong given the interstate economic linkages inherited from the past. While a major market-oriented restructuring of the enterprise sector has already begun in a number of states, many large-scale enterprises operating across state jurisdictions have yet to be accommodated by a harmonized system of commodity and company income taxation. For one thing, it would be beneficial to agree on a realistic set of minimum rates for the VAT, excises, the company income tax, and payroll taxes (mainly earmarked for social security). It would be equally important to reach agreement on the definition of tax bases and on the principles of taxation that would govern cross-border commodity and factor movements.

As regards the VAT and excises, the absence of border controls and the importance of multistate enterprises (including vertically integrated ones) argues for the origin principle of taxation on interstate transactions. This approach would not preclude the application of the destination principle, as permitted by the General Agreement on Tariffs and Trade (GATT), on transactions with third countries or former republics that do not wish to participate in the common economic space. A comparable approach is expected to be adopted eventually in the EC, following removal of internal border controls. Concerning company income taxation, it might be administratively easiest to adopt the source principle, instead of the possibly more efficient residence principle with appropriate credit for taxes paid at source. A potential problem may emerge, however, in the allocation among relevant jurisdictions of multistate enterprise income, owing

---

[25]Recent discussions of this issue have been devoted almost solely to the trade and payments arrangements and monetary cooperation, to the neglect of fiscal relations among the states. See, for example, Fischer (1992).

[26]As an alternative to tax harmonization, a system of border tax adjustment would be sufficient, upon imposition of border controls among the states. For a discussion of various approaches considered under the EC's single market, see Kopits (1992a).

in part to undeveloped market-based accounting practices. In such cases, it may be necessary to apply a presumptive apportionment method.[27]

An additional structural issue involves the application of the benefit principle in taxation and provision of public services. In order to avoid potentially ruinous fiscal competition among states seeking to attract foreign investment—for which there are precedents in post-socialist Central and East European countries—the new states would be well advised to agree on a minimum company income tax rate and on developing, and perhaps jointly maintaining, basic infrastructure facilities. Such a qualified application of the benefit principle would prevent excessive revenue erosion and provide the basis for a favorable and stable fiscal environment for private investment.

More generally, the likelihood of preservation of an open economic space would be enhanced by broad fiscal policy coordination among states. With a single currency, there is great temptation for individual states to engage in high rates of credit expansion to finance local budget deficits and enterprise losses. As recent experience in the former Soviet Union shows, the resulting inflation-tax burden spreads quickly over the entire ruble area.[28] To prevent such practices, especially in view of relatively undeveloped financial markets, it would be necessary to abide by fiscal rules in the form of tight limits on budget deficits at the state level. Although for members of a common economic space that do use separate currencies the argument for such fiscal rules may be less compelling, radically different fiscal stances would be untenable—unless accompanied by a flexible exchange rate policy—and could lead to the erection of barriers to trade and capital movements by states experiencing external imbalances.

At this stage, the principle of solidarity among the new independent states is under considerable strain. However, it is conceivable that in the medium to long term, as regional differentials in income and standard of living become more pronounced, given market-oriented enterprise restructuring and liberalization of energy prices, there could be a voluntary rapprochement, at least among states with some cultural affinity. Therefore, for equity reasons, periodic general- or specific-purpose grants could be expected from high-income, resource-rich states to states with low incomes and high dependency ratios.

Looking at the present state of interrepublic relations in the former Soviet Union, it might seem that the stage at which the new states would become interested in fiscal coordination lies in the distant future. In the absence of an obvious single right answer to the many problems of post-socialist transition, one could argue that temporary economic independence is beneficial, as multiple variants of reform processes under

---

[27]Some of the arguments involving the application of formula apportionment in developing countries may be relevant; see Kopits and Mutén (1984).

[28]See, for example, International Monetary Fund (1992b).

experimentation confer benefits of variety, comparison, and competition.[29] In addition, the need for strong and accepted administrative leadership, which is essential for establishing the credibility of transition policies, can be more easily satisfied at the state level. These and other arguments in favor of economic independence notwithstanding,[30] the welfare benefits of cooperation exemplified by the United States, Canada, and, more recently, the EC, are sufficiently large to make the prediction of a centripetal trend of cooperation among the new independent states a safe bet for the long run.

Intergovernmental Relations Within the States

Toward Genuine Federalism

The process of fiscal disintegration at the union level was closely paralleled by similar developments, in some instances of equal strength, within the republics.[31] There too, the geographic expanse of some republics, the ethnic factor and other noneconomic variables, including deep-rooted and long-repressed national consciousness, fueled the centrifugal tendencies that have yet to climax in some regions. Much as in the interrepublic context, within many states the practice of local fiscal autonomy has been and seems to be far ahead of its statutory recognition.

Since late 1990, most states have enacted laws on local self-government even before the formal disintegration of the union. These laws, in combination with statutes on the new tax system and the budget process, represent the initial formal step toward a genuine federal fiscal structure in the newly established states. Although subject to variation across states, especially in terms of implementation, these statutes have a number of broadly common characteristics. The laws endow governments at various levels with considerable fiscal autonomy as regards budget formulation, taxation, and borrowing. At the same time, however, they perpetuate much of the previous government structure, budget process, and tax administration. In most states, this tenuous—in some aspects contradictory—amalgam of fiscal decentralization cast in the former unitary model is not likely to survive in its present form.

Under the new laws, subnational governments at the oblast, provincial, city, and village levels have the authority to formulate and execute their own budgets, disposing of own fiscal resources and of prescribed shares of national revenue. The loci of expenditure responsibilities are defined,

---

[29]See Palei and Petr (1992), p. 8.
[30]See Gros (1991).
[31]For an informative discussion of republic-local fiscal relations during the second half of the 1980s, see Berkowitz and Mitchneck (1992).

but without precision. Outlays on defense, higher education, and major investment projects (in transportation, communication, energy, and the like) that confer country-wide benefits in terms of economies of scale and externalities, fall under national jurisdiction. In contrast, for example, lower levels of professional and secondary education, and construction and renovation of health-care facilities are to be managed at the oblast level, whereas their maintenance is the responsibility of the respective local governments. Primary schools, local roads, and other local facilities are run at the city or village level. Also, subsidies to local enterprises, as well as price subsidies, have to be financed at the local level. Thus, broadly speaking, the principle of subsidiarity—namely, of assigning government functions to the lowest possible level where they can be performed efficiently—seems applicable under the law.

In an important break with the past, the fiscal autonomy of subnational governments is explicitly protected from interference by higher government levels, unless authorized by the national legislature. Accordingly, higher-level governments are not allowed to extract surpluses from lower-level governments.[32] Furthermore, subnational budgets no longer need to be consolidated with higher-level budgets.[33]

In general, revenue accrues to various levels of government through a combination of tax assignment and revenue sharing. Revenue from taxes on personal income, collective farm income, property (such as land, transport, and, in some states such as Ukraine, natural resources) is assigned entirely to subnational levels of government. Revenue from the VAT, most excises, enterprise profit tax, and taxes on foreign transactions, and in the case of Russia, natural resource taxes, accrues to the national or federal government and is shared with subnational governments. In principle, the revenue split between national and subnational levels for each tax is to be determined by the national legislature according to regional need.[34] In fact, however, revenue shares are often subject to intergovernmental negotiation or unilateral adjustment and to variation even in the course of the year. As a further example of fiscal autonomy, subnational governments can authorize preferential tax treatment, including exemption from certain taxes.

In the event of vertical imbalances, that is, when the revenue from own taxes and from the earmarked share of national taxes is not sufficient,

---

[32]See, for example, Article 43 of Russia's Law on Local Self-Government.

[33]Ukraine's Law on Local Self-Government (Article 12) stipulates that "high-level bodies may not interfere in the development, approval and execution of local budgets." Further, it rules out the *matryoshka* doll approach of budget consolidation by stating that "local budgets of single administrative and territorial units may not be included in the local budgets of other units and in the state budget of the republic."

[34]In Russia, for instance, the legal subnational shares range from 60 percent to 80 percent of the tax on petroleum production, and amount to 50 percent of the vodka excise and the enterprise profit tax, and up to 20 percent of the VAT.

additional transfers may be provided by the higher government level, which can then participate in the expenditure decision. In addition, in a number of states, subnational governments are authorized to borrow from bank or nonbank sources to finance budget deficits at their levels. Alternatively, subnational governments may dispose of budget surpluses by depositing them (along with various forms of nontax revenue, including user fees) in own extrabudgetary funds created for that purpose. As indicated above, there are no longer restrictions on the local use of surpluses, and in particular, there is no mandatory return of accumulated surpluses to higher levels of government.

Notwithstanding fiscal decentralization and a strong drive to local government autonomy, the basic structure of government in the former republics—apart from the takeover of union-level institutions—has remained in many respects largely intact. Likewise, the process of budget preparation and appropriation at various government levels has not been altered substantially, except insofar as subnational governments do not act any longer merely as a transmission belt between the higher and lower levels of government. A notable feature left over from the past is that minimum outlays of local governments for specific activities are to be allocated on the basis of budget norms which specify in detail nominal daily expenditure per resident.[35] Budget norms as well as price controls are determined by the national government (for instance, in Russia) or legislature (in Ukraine). Also, as noted, the shares of subnational governments in national tax revenue are to be set by the national legislature. Although tax administration remains centralized at the national level, effective control over branch offices—staffed mostly by local officials—in many regions rests with subnational authorities.

Outstanding Issues and Outlook

In most of the new independent states, intergovernmental fiscal arrangements are internally inconsistent and unsustainable in their present form. The inconsistency stems largely from the lack of correspondence between revenue sources and expenditure responsibilities—in part to be based on budget norms—assigned under the law to each level of government.[36] While the prescribed shares of national revenue can be adjusted periodically to compensate for possible revenue shortfalls at the local level, over time the lack of correspondence is likely to be exacerbated by local pressures for increased expenditures and by inherently weak incentives for local revenue raising.

[35]For example, in Russia, in 1991, the daily hospital food intake for gynecology patients was set at rub 5.60 and for leprosy patients at rub 4.71 for each patient. For a list of health-care budget norms, see Wallich (1992), p. 44.

[36]For an analysis of minimum requirements for a functioning fiscal federal system, see Hewitt and Mihaljek (1992).

In the period ahead, there is bound to be a significant jump in claims on public services. Some tasks, such as environmental cleanup, have been altogether neglected in the past. Others, particularly social assistance, are closely related to the restructuring and privatization of state-owned enterprises which will no longer be able or willing to provide a range of social services, including employment, as in the past. Additional claims also arise from ongoing demilitarization. Although responsibility for these new expenditures remains rather vague, it is being assumed largely by subnational (mainly oblast and city) levels of government, given the regional or local nature of the needs.[37] Meanwhile, attempts at updating and adhering to budget norms in absolute terms impose an additional burden on local jurisdictions.

On the revenue side, it is becoming increasingly difficult to collect taxes from a shrinking base. As in Central and East European economies in transition, revenue performance in the former Soviet Union has deteriorated owing to severe administrative shortcomings, exposure of state-owned enterprises to a hard budget constraint and market forces, and their privatization. Furthermore, local governments have been tempted to offer tax holidays or other preferences to stimulate economic activity on their territory.

As a result, many subnational governments have been unable to balance their budgets. Their response to budgetary pressures has been, in the first place, to push expenditure responsibilities upward to the national level and to negotiate for increasing shares in national taxes. At the same time, some subnational governments have found it convenient to transfer occasional surpluses or nontax revenue (for example, local privatization proceeds) to their extrabudgetary funds. In all, the incentives for efficient allocation of budgetary resources and revenue raising at the local level are very weak.

The prospect of widening vertical imbalances at subnational levels of government is considerable in most of the new independent states. In the absence of an institutional mechanism for intergovernmental transfers there is continued recourse to ad hoc and nontransparent negotiation over grants and revenue shares between different levels of government. In addition, some subnational governments want to exercise their legal right to borrow from the banking system (in part from captive local commercial banks) and nonbank sources, without regard to creditworthiness. Uncontrolled borrowing by large regional and local governments is likely to contribute significantly to consolidated budget deficits, and consequently, to macroeconomic disequilibria.

Not all subnational governments are prone to incur budget deficits. In some states there are jurisdictions endowed with oil, gas, gold, diamonds,

---

[37]As an exception, compensation and cleanup related to the Chernobyl accident have been assumed by the central government in Ukraine, to be financed with a payroll tax earmarked for that purpose.

and other mineral resources, which are likely to accumulate sizable budget surpluses, not necessarily to be shared with the national government.[38] Such budget surpluses can be expected to mount particularly in the event of a domestic adjustment of commodity prices to world market levels. In this regard, a major outstanding question concerns the willingness of resource-rich regions to relinquish, in the near future, an increasing share of the resulting revenue vertically to the national government or horizontally to subnational governments experiencing deficits. The answer to this question may be intimately connected with the ethnic factor and the apparent lack of solidarity across regions. In view of the strong backlash against the former centralized structure, the creation of intergovernmental fiscal arrangements based on horizontal equity criteria seems to be a long way off. In the meantime, the very integrity of some states, especially those with the largest ethnic and resource endowment disparities, such as the Russian Federation, will be subject to considerable strain.[39]

The destabilizing effect of subnational government finances may not be readily apparent. In some cases, large national budget deficits mask excess spending at subnational levels. Indeed, there are preliminary indications that, in the course of 1992, subnational governments in certain states, notably in Russia, have accumulated surpluses because, relative to assumed spending responsibilities, they had ample revenue from assigned taxes and earmarked shares.[40] In response, there are initiatives at the national level to shift more expenditure responsibilities (for health-care services and infrastructure projects, among others) to lower levels of government and, at the same time, to reduce the shares of national taxes (especially the VAT) earmarked to subnational jurisdictions. Elsewhere, as in Ukraine for example, some subnational governments have incurred sizable deficits financed directly by the banking system.

These developments argue, on grounds of efficiency, stabilization, and horizontal equity, for the introduction of a simple and transparent system of unrequited transfers from the central budget to oblast and local budgets. These transfers would be determined by a set of quantitative indicators, specified at the relevant subnational level, reflecting expenditure need (taking into account population and other factors) and potential, rather than actual, revenue (in terms of a proxy for value added, natural

---

[38]In 1992, several resource-rich oblasts have adopted "single channel" arrangements whereby they unilaterally decide to withhold all taxes collected in their territory and to transfer a fixed nominal amount to the federal budget, disregarding statutory sharing provisions. See Wallich (1992).

[39]Although to a much milder extent—absent the ethnic factor and the need for enterprise restructuring—some strains emerged among energy-producing regions and other regions in Australia and Canada, since the oil booms of the mid-1970s and the early 1980s, which have contributed to major changes in intergovernmental fiscal arrangements.

[40]Also, in Russia, subnational governments were barred by decree from exercising their right to borrow.

resource endowment, and so forth).[41] Such a system could accommodate matching grants and bloc grants, either of a general nature or earmarked for specific purposes (for example, to maintain a minimum level of primary education or primary health care, or to finance a large-scale infrastructure project), that confer nationwide benefits through spillovers beyond the spending jurisdiction. Ideally, grants should constitute an addition to rather than a substitute for local resource use. The principle of additionality could be ensured in broad terms, mainly through formula-based equalization transfers.[42] Furthermore, the aggregate level of grants would be determined as part of the overall fiscal stance, in line with economy-wide stabilization and growth objectives. Thus, the transfer scheme could address in a consistent manner horizontal inequities as well as the vertical imbalance.

Equalization transfers would partly obviate an elaborate assignment or sharing of taxes between national and subnational governments,[43] albeit without precluding the imposition of subnational surcharges on the national tax bases according to the benefit principle of taxation. Consensus may be reached over time regarding the assignment of several major taxes—in particular, the VAT—[44] to the national government for regional reallocation through formula-based transfers. However, it must be recognized from the outset that there is virtually no prospect for such a treatment of natural resource taxes; at most, resource-rich subnational governments may be willing to share only a portion of the latter with the national government.

The overall picture of intergovernmental relations that emerges at this time within the new independent states is that of a federal structure characterized by a fair degree of discretion and nontransparent negotiation among different levels of government. The enactment and implementation of the basic statutes on fiscal federalism are in a state of flux and subject to almost continuous review. Such review is essential before the intergovernmental relations are cast in a formal constitutional framework that is both credible and durable. Even then, as the experience of federations such as Australia and Canada shows, intergovernmental fiscal arrangements can be subject to periodic review between the national and subnational governments.

---

[41]See, for example, Economic Council of Canada (1982) for a discussion and evaluation of the Canadian equalization programs. Other countries that rely at least partially on well-functioning equalization grants, based on formulas that reflect both regional need and revenue capacity, include Australia, Denmark, Germany, and Switzerland. For an early theoretical analysis of alternative forms of equalization, see Musgrave (1961).

[42]The difficulty of applying the additionality principle in practice cannot be overstated. See the recent analysis of the allocation of EC Structural Funds in Gordon (1992).

[43]For a critical assessment of the transfer scheme coupled with centralized assignment of revenue, as implemented in Australia, see McLure (1992).

[44]The cases of Argentina and Brazil illustrate the problems of stabilization and efficiency that can arise from a VAT assigned to, or shared with, subnational levels of government.

In sum, the moment of truth for the viability of existing intergovernmental arrangements within the new states will be faced only when they fully embark on market-oriented economic transformation. The transformation is likely to have a considerable differential regional incidence in some states, especially in Russia, exposing wide differences in incomes and wealth across regions. While resource-rich regions with a sparse population would enjoy a marked surge in incomes upon liberalization of energy prices, populated industrial regions would suffer from an increase in poverty and unemployment due to enterprise restructuring under hardened budget constraints—as enterprise restructuring would be, in fact, inevitable under energy price liberalization. Simply stated, the integrity of states undergoing transformation hinges on the adoption of a federal system, based on the broadest possible consensus, that combines a clear allocation of expenditure responsibilities among different government levels, taking into account subsidiarity and interregional spillovers, an explicit set of rules for assignment of tax revenue, and a transparent mechanism of regional equalization transfers based explicitly on need and revenue capacity, that will ensure broad correspondence with the expenditure responsibilities.

References

Aleksashenko, Sergei, "Reform of the Fiscal System in the Soviet Federation: The Main Complexities and Possible Solutions," paper prepared for the Seminar on Intergovernmental Fiscal Relations and Macroeconomic Management, New Delhi, February 1991.

———, "Macroeconomic Stabilisation in the Former Soviet Republics: Dream or Reality?" *Communist Economies and Economic Transformation*, Vol. 4, No. 4 (1992), pp. 439-67.

Berkowitz, Daniel, and Beth Mitchneck, "Fiscal Decentralization in the Soviet Economy," *Comparative Economic Studies*, Vol. 34 (Summer 1992), pp. 1-18.

Birman, Igor, "The Budget Gap, Excess Money and Reform," *Communist Economies*, Vol. 2, No. 1 (1990), pp. 25-45.

Economic Council of Canada, *Financing Confederation: Today and Tomorrow* (Ottawa: Supply and Services Canada, 1982).

Fischer, Stanley, "Russia and the Soviet Union, Then and Now," NBER Working Paper No. 4077 (Cambridge, Massachusetts: National Bureau of Economic Research, 1992).

Gordon, James, "An Analysis of the EC Structural Funds," in *Tax Harmonization in the European Community: Policy Issues and Analysis*, IMF Occasional Paper No. 94, ed. by George Kopits (Washington: International Monetary Fund, 1992).

Gros, Daniel, "Regional Disintegration in the Soviet Union: Economic Costs and Benefits," *Intereconomics*, Vol. 26 (September/October 1991), pp. 207-13.

Hewett, Ed A., *Reforming the Soviet Economy: Equality Versus Efficiency* (Washington: Brookings Institution, 1988).

Hewitt, Daniel, and Dubravko Mihaljek, "Fiscal Federalism," in *Fiscal Policies in Economies in Transition*, ed. by Vito Tanzi (Washington: International Monetary Fund, 1992).

International Monetary Fund (1992a), *The Economy of the Former U.S.S.R. in 1991* (Washington: International Monetary Fund, 1992).

——— (1992b), *Common Issues and Interrepublic Relations in the Former U.S.S.R.* (Washington: International Monetary Fund, 1992).

———, World Bank, Organization for Economic Cooperation and Development, and European Bank for Reconstruction and Development, *A Study of the Soviet Economy*, Vol. I (Washington: International Monetary Fund, 1991).

Kopits, George (1992a), "Overview," in *Tax Harmonization in the European Community: Policy Issues and Analysis*, IMF Occasional Paper No. 94, ed. by George Kopits (Washington: International Monetary Fund, 1992).

——— (1992b), "Fiscal and Monetary Policies in Transition: Some Reflections," paper prepared for the Conference on Democratic Government and the Transition from Plan to Market, University of Twente, Enschede, August 1992.

———, and Leif Mutén, "Relevance of the Unitary Approach for Developing Countries," in *The State Corporation Income Tax: Issues in Worldwide Unitary Combination*, ed. by Charles E. McLure, Jr. (Stanford, California: Hoover Institution Press, 1984).

Kristan, Ivan, "Federalism and Democratic Centralism," *Review of International Affairs*, Vol. 41 (July 5-20, 1990), pp. 4-8.

Lenin, Vladimir Ilyich, *Collected Works*, Vol. 20 (Moscow and London, 1960-70).

McLure, Charles E., Jr.,"A North American View of Vertical Imbalance and the Assignment of Taxing Powers," paper prepared for the Conference on Vertical Fiscal Imbalance and the Allocation of Tax Powers, Canberra, November 1992.

Musgrave, Richard A., "Approaches to a Fiscal Theory of Political Federalism," in *Public Finances: Needs, Sources, and Utilization*, A Report of the National Bureau of Economic Research (Princeton: Princeton University Press, 1961).

Palei, L.V., and Jerry L. Petr, "Integration Versus Independence for the Successor States of the USSR: When Might Economics' 'Right Answers' Be Wrong?" *Comparative Economic Studies*, Vol. 34, No. 1 (Spring 1992), pp. 1-12.

Shatalin, S., and others, *Transition to the Market: The Concept and Program*, Part I (Moscow: Arkhangelskoe, August 1990).

Sheehy, Ann, "The CIS: A Progress Report," *RFE/RL Research Report*, Vol. 1, No. 38 (September 25, 1992), pp. 1-6.

Swoboda, Victor, "Was the Soviet Union Really Necessary?" *Soviet Studies*, Vol. 44, No. 5 (1992), pp. 761-84.

Wallich, Christine, *Fiscal Decentralization: Intergovernmental Relations in Russia*, Studies of Economies in Transformation, Paper No. 6 (Washington: World Bank, 1992).

Wheare, Kenneth C., *Federal Government* (New York: Oxford University Press for the Royal Institute of International Affairs, 4th ed., 1964).

CHAPTER 10

Intergovernmental Fiscal Relations in Yugoslavia, 1972-90

Dubravko Mihaljek

Long before the countries of Central and Eastern Europe and the states of the former Soviet Union became economies in transition, the former Socialist Federal Republic of Yugoslavia had rejected central planning and experimented with market-oriented reforms. As part of this process, a unique system of intergovernmental fiscal relations was developed, combining elements of confederate finance, a decentralized procedure for the provision of public goods, and an interregional transfer scheme based on the principle of balanced growth. This Yugoslav experience is potentially instructive for countries where domestic or external balance between sovereignty and interdependence is being re-examined, whether such countries are strengthening their ties with other states (as in the European Community), loosening their ties (as in Canada), or severing those ties altogether (as in the former Soviet Union and the former Czechoslovakia).

This chapter reviews how balance between sovereignty and interdependence of federal, republic, and local governments was conceived and maintained in Yugoslavia between 1972 and 1990. Like many other elements of Yugoslav economy and polity, the system of intergovernmental fiscal relations developed during this period was idiosyncratic and does not lend itself readily to analytic description and international comparison. In most federations the main issues of fiscal federalism—the extent and criteria for regional redistribution, assignment of expenditure responsibilities and taxing powers to different levels of government, and design of an intergovernmental transfer scheme—are addressed in the federal constitution and resolved within the budgetary framework of the three tiers of government. But in the former Yugoslavia expenditure responsibilities and taxing powers were also assigned to independent fiscal institutions operating outside the budgetary framework, and the main instrument for interregional transfers was an extrabudgetary development fund. Because of the number and importance of independent fiscal institutions (more than 8,000 organizations responsible for two thirds of

Dubravko Mihaljek, Economist in the Central Asia Department, was Economist in the Fiscal Affairs Department at the time this paper was written.

total public spending), this chapter focuses on the institutional structure of fiscal federalism by considering the three subsystems comprising the structure of intergovernmental fiscal relations: federal fiscal relations in the narrow sense, fiscal decentralization, and intergovernmental transfers.

The most interesting aspect of the system of federal fiscal relations was financing of central government activities through republic contributions. Such "reverse transfers" also were practiced in the early American, Swiss, and German confederate tax systems and were considered for the European Community and the Commonwealth of Independent States. The main criticism of reverse transfers is that they contribute to macroeconomic instability (when federal units cannot agree on how to divide the contributions, the center has incentive to borrow and/or finance expenditures through seigniorage). But since republic governments frequently do not entirely trust each other or the federal government, reverse transfers may be the only way adequately to finance the agreed range of federal activities. This paper examines in some detail the macroeconomic performance of reverse transfers and the rationale for their adoption in former Yugoslavia. Relevant parts of the proposal for a model of confederation in Yugoslavia, put forward by the Republics of Croatia and Slovenia in October 1990, also are discussed.

The second subsystem was a network of independent fiscal institutions called self-governing communities of interest (*samoupravne interesne zajednice*, SIZs). Their aim was to decentralize and "de-budgetize" the provision of public goods and services in concordance with the philosophy of local self-government and the idea of the withering away of the state. Public goods and services, such as health care, social security, education, and economic infrastructure, no longer were to be provided by legal fiat and be financed through the budgets of central, republic, and local governments. Instead, the users and providers of public services were to determine the quantity, quality, and price of such services in negotiations free of government's interference and subject only to basic legislation (for example, on mandatory retirement age or eight-year primary education). From the theoretical point of view, SIZs had similarities with the Lindahl theory of public expenditures and taxation. Owing to administrative inefficiencies, however, the system of SIZs developed into a bureaucratic quagmire and was largely abandoned in early 1990 for the traditional system of budget financing. This chapter discusses the way that the system of SIZs had operated and identifies some reasons for its ultimate collapse.

The third subsystem was the scheme for intergovernmental fiscal transfers. In addition to the republic contributions to the federal budget, this consisted of transfers from the federal budget and the Federal Development Fund to the Province of Kosovo and the three less developed republics (Bosnia-Herzegovina, Macedonia, and Montenegro), and transfers from republic budgets to less developed regions within republics. As in other federations, the rationale, the magnitude, and the method by which interregional transfers were effected had been endlessly contested. This chapter provides an overview of the main points of contention and outlines some reasons for the malfunctioning of this transfer scheme.

The paper is organized in four sections. The first outlines the institutional structure of the three federal finance subsystems described above. The second evaluates the functioning of fiscal federalism from a microeconomic and a macroeconomic point of view. The third looks at the historical evolution of the system and identifies the main economic and political forces that shaped it. The paper concludes with remarks on the potential relevance of the Yugoslav experience for other economies in transition.

Structure of the Public Sector

The public sector in former Yugoslavia comprised the three levels of government normally found in all federations (Federal Government at the center, governments of six republics and two autonomous provinces at the intermediate level, and governments of 500 communes at the local level), a collection of some 8,000 self-governing communities of interest, and the Federal Fund for Crediting Faster Development of the Economically Underdeveloped Republics and the Autonomous Province of Kosovo (henceforth, the Federal Development Fund). These three subsystems of the public sector represented, respectively, 10.5 percent, 22.3 percent, and 0.8 percent of gross social product in 1987.

Confederate Finance

The confederate nature of intergovernmental fiscal relations in former Yugoslavia can best be appreciated by considering the pattern of expenditure and revenue assignment in the period 1972-90.

Despite the large number of participants providing public goods and services, the extent of overlap in expenditure assignment across different institutions was minimal. Public goods and services were divided in three broad categories: (1) those intended to satisfy general social needs (operation of government agencies, national defense, and supplementary funds for social activities in less developed regions); (2) those intended to satisfy collective needs in social services, that is, social welfare expenditures (health, retirement, disability, and unemployment insurance; child welfare; public housing) and expenditures on social activities (education, culture, science, physical culture); and (3) public goods intended to satisfy collective needs in material reproduction (public utilities, public transport and communications, water and energy supply, relief funds).[1]

General social needs were the only segment of public sector expenditures provided by government agencies and financed through the budgets. Expenditures on social welfare, social activities, and infrastructure were financed through self-governing communities of interest, so that the size and composition of government budgets was rudimentary by Western standards. The list of expenditures in the federal budget was especially short (Table 1). Nevertheless, the Federal Government retained considerable fiscal power because it determined the tax bases for enterprise and sales taxes and controlled the spending of lower-level governments and self-governing communities of interest via wage, credit, and public investment controls.

The Federal Government had only one own revenue source (tariffs). It shared with republics the proceeds of the federal sales tax and received transfer payments (contributions) from the republics (Table 2). (A special federal defense tax was introduced in 1990 but was collected only that year.) The sharing of the sales tax and the apportioning of contributions were not based on fixed ex ante formulas, although, in principle, contributions were determined by the republics' shares in gross social product, and the amount of federal sales tax a republic could retain was set according to its share in total sales. The allotment of contributions and sales tax shares was decided through annual budget negotiations between republics and the Federal Government. Once agreement was reached, the republics transferred the funds to the federation while collecting their own taxes. The tax collecting agency, the Social Accounting Service, was organized on a republic basis but used a uniform set of rules throughout the country.

In terms of own revenue sources, republics were in a stronger position than the federation. In addition to collecting and retaining a share of the federal sales tax (also known as the "general" or "basic" sales tax), republics levied their own ("special") sales taxes on the tax base determined by the Federal Government, and controlled excises, enterprise income taxes, social security contributions, and part of the wage tax (Table 2). Local governments enjoyed considerable taxing powers, too. They controlled taxes on property, local sales taxes, wage and personal income taxes, and a variety of fees.

Self-governing communities of interest raised their own revenue from enterprise and wage taxes, user fees, and voluntary contributions that citizens voted on in referendums (Table 3).

---

[1] Translated into the usual public finance terminology, the three categories roughly corresponded to the concepts of pure public goods referred to in item (1), public goods for which the exclusion from consumption was possible (in item (2) and partly in (3)), and local public goods, in item (3).

Table 1. Yugoslavia: Public Sector Expenditures, 1987

(In percent)

Budget Financing	31	SIZ Financing	69
Federal budget	52	Social security	56
Defense	66	Health insurance	36
Social insurance of veterans		Retirement and	
and military personnel	20	disability insurance	63
Supplementary development grants	6	Unemployment insurance	1
Federal administration	5		
Other expenditures	3		
Republic budgets	30	Social services	26
Contributions to the federation	36	Education	57
Republic administration	27	Child care	19
Interventions in the economy	20	Culture	7
Social services	11	Science	7
Other expenditures	6	Welfare benefits	7
		Physical culture	3
Local government budgets	18	Economic infrastructure	18
Local administration	78	Energy, transportation	59
Social services	6	Housing, water supply,	
Interventions in the economy	5	other infrastructure	41
Other expenditures	11		

Sources: Federal Statistical Office, *Statistical Yearbook of Yugoslavia*, 1990; and Jurković (1989a).

Thus, all three methods of tax assignment used in modern federations were practiced: tax sharing (of the federal sales tax), tax separation (tariffs were assigned to the Federal Government, property taxes to local governments, taxes on personal and enterprise incomes were assigned separately to republics, local governments, and SIZs), and tax overlapping (republics and local governments levied additional sales taxes on the tax base determined by the Federal Government).

Fiscal Decentralization

The fiscal system of former Yugoslavia could have been characterized as highly decentralized because of the confederate intergovernmental fiscal relations alone. But government budgets played only a secondary role in public finances and, consequently, in fiscal decentralization. The principal vehicle for fiscal decentralization was the network of self-governing communities of interest. Most of the 8,000 SIZs operated at the local level, with regional and republic headquarters coordinating their operations.[2]

[2]The only federal-level SIZ was the Self-Governing Community of Interest for Foreign Economic Relations. Its main purpose, however, was to administer the transfer of revenue from customs duties and other import taxes to export producers for payment of subsidies.

Table 2. Yugoslavia: Public Sector Revenues, 1987

(In percent)

Budget Financing	32	SIZ Financing	68
Federal budget	16	Wage taxes	50
Federal sales tax	51	Enterprise taxes	26
Tariffs	26	Contributions and fees	24
Contributions from republics	21		
Other revenue	2		
Republic budgets	10		
Sales taxes	64		
Republic sales tax	53		
Share of the federal			
sales tax	47		
Enterprise taxes	21		
Wage taxes	5		
Transfers	5		
Other revenue	5		
Local government budgets	6		
Local sales tax	45		
Wage tax	25		
Personal income tax	17		
Property taxes	8		
Other revenue	5		

Sources: Federal Statistical Office, *Statistical Yearbook of Yugoslavia*, 1990; National Bank of Yugoslavia, *Statistical Survey*, 3/1990; Jurković (1989a); and Vranješ (1990).

The SIZ gathered the representatives of citizens and socially owned businesses (the *users* of public services) and the representatives of educational, medical, cultural, scientific, social welfare, and similar establishments (the *providers* of public services). The users and the providers negotiated on the scope and contents of public services to be offered and jointly decided on their financing. This "free exchange of labor" was conceived as a deliberate attempt to bypass arbitrary decisions by the government bureaucracy in such sensitive areas as education, health care, and cultural activities, and in matters of direct economic significance such as power generation and transmission, road construction, water resources management, public housing, and other local and regional infrastructure.

Before the start of negotiations in the SIZ, prices, quantities, and quality mixes of public goods to be supplied were stochastic variables (see Mihaljek (1986)). In some cases, prices (that is, unit production costs) would be announced first, whereupon the three parties (the providers and, on the users' side, the representatives of citizens and business firms) would adjust supplies and demands until an equilibrium was reached. In other cases, the law mandated that a given amount of service be offered to the public, so the three parties would negotiate on the taxes or user fees necessary to finance the given supply until an agreement was reached. All

Table 3. Yugoslavia: Self-Governing
Communities of Interest—Sources of Financing, 1978
(In percent)

	Contributions from Enterprise Income	Contributions from Personal Income	User Fees and Other Contributions
Total	24.5	71.4	4.1
Of which:			
Social activities	21.2	12.4	6.4
Health	7.0	80.2	12.8
Education	34.4	65.6	12.8
Culture	11.1	88.9	...
Science	90.2	9.8	...
Physical culture	36.5	64.5	...
Social welfare	28.1	70.4	1.5
Pensions, disability	23.2	76.7	0.1
Child care	14.1	78.3	7.6
Unemployment	55.2	44.8	...
Welfare payments	4.8	95.2	...
Housing	61.5	35.3	3.2

Source: Bogoev and Jurković (1982), p. 212.

decisions on output and prices had to be made by a consensus in the SIZ. The Government could not formally intervene, but in some cases could assume a supervisory role or act as an arbiter. Once reached, decisions on prices, quantities, and quality mixes became contractual obligations.

Business firms and citizens would typically pay different prices for the same public service. In some cases, citizens would pay a higher cash price (tickets for various cultural events, tuition for continuing education, fees for recreational activities). In others, because of the incidence of taxes, the businesses would bear most of the cost of providing the public good (health care, elementary and secondary education). For some public services, the citizens paid by wage taxes ("contributions from personal income"), and businesses by earmarked payroll taxes ("contributions from enterprise income"). These taxes were withheld at source and transferred to the banking account of the appropriate SIZ each month, which then distributed these funds to providers of public services in accordance with the negotiated production plan.

Business firms and citizens thus financed the production of public services in a quasi-market where they paid different prices for the same services. In this respect, the self-governing community of interest was similar to the Lindahl solution to the problem of determining simultaneously the optimal amount of public expenditure and the distribution of the corresponding tax burden (Lindahl (1919), Johansen (1963)). But unlike the theoretical solution, the self-governing communities of interest turned out to be inefficient. Aside from the perennial problem of measuring the output of public services, the main reasons for inefficiency were high administrative costs and asymmetric incidence of taxes paid by the citizens and firms.

Intergovernmental Transfers

The third subsystem of intergovernmental fiscal relations in former Yugoslavia was inextricably intertwined with the other two. Interregional transfers were effected through three channels: the Federal Development Fund, the federal budget, and the republic and provincial budgets.[3] The Federal Development Fund was established in the second half of 1965 to stimulate faster economic growth in less developed republics (Bosnia-Herzegovina, Macedonia, and Montenegro) and in the Province of Kosovo. This goal, explicitly stated in five-year indicative plans, formed the Fund's operational basis. In 1976–80, for example, the social plan stipulated that the annual growth rate of gross social product (GSP) in the three republics should exceed the national average by 20–25 percent and in Kosovo by 60 percent. Transfers from republic budgets to less developed regions within republics had the same purpose.

Transfers from the federal budget were grants-in-aid, providing supplementary funds aimed at ensuring the normal functioning of social services such as education and health care in republics and provinces that did not have enough resources to support these activities. The republics which qualified for federal transfers would decide the use of development loans and social-service assistance. The 1974 Constitution stipulated that only republics and autonomous provinces, but not their constituent parts, could receive assistance from the Federal Development Fund and the federal budget. This meant that underdeveloped regions in republics that did not qualify for federal funds could receive transfers only from their own republic budgets.

The criteria of underdevelopment were never formally defined; instead, the less developed regions were designated by the law. Because the relative positions of the less developed republics changed over time, the developed republics insisted on the introduction of a formal set of criteria defining the status of underdevelopment and the conditions for graduation from this status. According to the proposal presented by the Federal Government in 1987, a republic or province was to be considered underdeveloped if: (1) the ratio of the book value of fixed assets used in production to the size of the able-bodied work force of the republic or

---

[3]For statistical and planning purposes, assets of the Federal Development Fund were recorded as expenditures on collective needs in material reproduction under the category "other collective needs of the economy." But from an economic point of view the Federal Development Fund had little in common with self-governing communities of interest.

province was 25 percent or more below the Yugoslav average; (2) the number of employed in the republic or province per 1,000 able-bodied inhabitants in the work force was 20 percent or more below the Yugoslav average; and (3) per capita GSP of the republic or province was 30 percent or more below the Yugoslav average. A republic or province would graduate from underdevelopment if it no longer met the third and one of the first two criteria (see Baletić (1989, p. 318)). The graduation would not be automatic; depending on development potential the republic or province would continue to draw on the federal funds, albeit on a reduced scale. The proposal was never accepted because some less developed republics insisted on more favorable terms. The ranking of republics and provinces according to the three criteria is given in Table 4.

Assets of the Federal Development Fund were formed through a compulsory loan subscribed by the entire social sector of the economy (including the socially owned enterprises in less developed republics and the Province of Kosovo) at a rate that varied between 1.97 percent of GSP in 1976–80, and 1.56 percent of GSP in 1986–90.[4] While the amount of compulsory loans was determined by the Federal Government for each five-year period, it was left to republics to legislate how the loans were collected. The amount of supplementary funds provided from the federal budget also varied; in 1986–90 the law mandated annual appropriations of 0.53 percent of GSP for this purpose.[5]

The conditions under which the loans were subscribed to the Federal Development Fund and subsequently granted to the less developed republics and the Province of Kosovo were defined by the law and also varied from period to period. In 1971–75, creditors had their loans repaid over 12 years at an annual interest rate of 4 percent. (The Fund actually issued transferable bonds with 12 equal annual coupons.) At the same time, credits to underdeveloped republics were granted at 4 percent interest for 15 years, with a three-year grace period, and to the Province of Kosovo for 19 years at the 3 percent interest rate (Baletić and Marendić (1982)). These operations created substantial financial liabilities for the Federal Development Fund, which were covered by the federation. Despite the favorable terms of development loans, the repayment record was poor; most of the loans were never collected.

---

[4]The term "economy" denotes enterprises and service establishments directly engaged in the production of commodities (in Croatian, *privreda* or economy). The adjective "social" denotes socially owned enterprises. The "social sector of the economy" thus excludes banking and finance, government administration, education, health care, and the provision of public services (in Croatian, *neprivreda* or "noneconomy"), as well as the entire private sector. For comparative purposes only the exclusion of the private sector is relevant, because the national accounts statistics were not compiled on the GDP basis (that is, services not directly engaged in the production of commodities were not covered). The share of the private sector in GSP was 10.1 percent in 1987.

[5]Notice that the supplementary funds from the federal budget were calculated as a fraction of GSP, whereas the compulsory loan for the Development Fund was calculated as a fraction of the social product of the social sector of the economy.

Table 4. Yugoslavia: Level of Development of
Republics and Autonomous Provinces
(Yugoslavia = 100)

	Per Capita GSP[1]	Assets per Work Force[2]	Work Force Employed[3]
Yugoslavia	100.0	100.0	100.0
Bosnia-Herzegovina	71.3	77.0	81.6
Montenegro	73.5	116.3	93.4
Croatia	126.9	110.8	118.0
Macedonia	62.8	64.3	88.9
Slovenia	224.2	240.4	152.0
Serbia	84.8	83.8	92.5
Serbia proper	90.2	83.6	99.3
Kosovo	29.5	43.3	50.2
Voivodina	118.8	114.0	104.6
Developed regions	124.0	117.2	112.9
Underdeveloped regions	60.9	70.8	78.4

Source: Baletić (1989), p. 317.
[1]Two-year average, 1986–87.
[2]1986.
[3]1987.

The shares of less developed republics and the Province of Kosovo in the resources channeled through the Federal Development Fund and the federal budget were changed from period to period, with the share of Kosovo showing an upward trend. Between 1981 and 1985, Kosovo received 42.6 percent of loans from the Federal Development Fund, Bosnia-Herzegovina 27.9 percent, Macedonia 19.6 percent, and Montenegro 9.9 percent (Jašić (1987, p. 279)).[6] In the same period, Bosnia-Herzegovina received 31.7 percent of transfers from the federal budget, Macedonia 14.5 percent, Montenegro 12 percent, and Kosovo 41.8 percent (Jašić (1987, p. 280)). In per capita terms, Bosnia-Herzegovina received, over the period 1976–80, about three times less transfers than Kosovo, about 2.5 times less than Montenegro, and about 1.4 times less than Macedonia (Baletić and Marendić (1982, pp. 256–57)).

Transfers from the Federal Development Fund and the federal budget represented a substantial source of investment funds and public finance in the less developed part of the country, and a sizable portion of the available social accumulation for the more developed part. Not surprisingly,

---

[6]These amounts represent gross receipts from the Federal Development Fund; in net terms the amounts were lower for the three republics and higher for Kosovo.

interregional transfers were continuously on the agenda of discussions between the republics and the federation. Yet little was achieved by improving the effectiveness of interregional transfers and no better scheme was proposed.

Functioning of Fiscal Federalism

Microeconomic Effects

The high degree of fiscal decentralization was blamed for microeconomic ills ranging from inefficient allocation of resources to destruction of the unified market. In public debates during the 1980s, republic and local governments were frequently accused of manipulating their fiscal powers to improve regional economic performance rather than that of the country (or republic) as a whole, of promoting their own regional economic space by fostering a broadly diversified industrial structure with an emphasis upon high-value-added activities, and of protecting local producers with nontariff barriers to interrepublic as well as intrarepublic trade. Such activities, it was argued, had weakened the common market, reduced the gains from industrial specialization and trade, created wasteful competition for markets, and resulted in suboptimal allocation of capital and labor.

On the public choice level, it was argued that control over major taxes gave the republic and local governments a powerful bargaining tool, which the governments used to affect the choice of investment projects, development programs, employment, income distribution, and other business variables not supposed to be in the domain of public decision making. The outcomes of bargaining (for example, the rapid growth of wages and investment) often compromised the implementation of restrictive measures of monetary policy agreed at the federal level. The belief that distortions in the tax system restricted trade and capital flows between republics and gave rise to rents benefiting special interest groups was also widespread.

Most of these claims were supported by circumstantial evidence only. The few empirical studies analyzing the problem more carefully found no convincing evidence that economic fractures were widening over time. Burkett and Škegro (1988) tested the hypothesis of increasing market fragmentation on a rich sample of industry data and established that, from the mid-1960s to the mid-1980s, there were no significant trends in interregional price dispersion, economic specialization, personal income distribution, or enterprise location. The time series data they examined exhibited fluctuations in response to institutional innovations and policy changes, but without an overall trend. Marković (1991) analyzed interrepublic trade and (after adjusting the data for intra-enterprise trade) rejected the hypothesis that republic economies were closed. Thus, to the extent that markets were poorly integrated, it seems this was the consequence of underdeveloped market institutions (especially the factor markets) and inadequate economic infrastructure rather than the protectionist stance of regional governments.

Regarding the microeconomics of self-governing communities of interest, the main complaints on the users' side were administrative inefficiencies (protracted negotiations, high overhead costs) and the incidence of taxes financing the supply of public services. The providers of public services also complained about administrative inefficiencies (especially the higher average salaries of the employees of SIZs), but often their criticism had to do more with the problems of the public sector in general (insufficient investment for hospitals, schools, cultural activities) than with the SIZs themselves.

The functioning of SIZs had not been the object of a systematic inquiry. As independent public institutions their operations had not been subjected to the same financial control as the operations of budgetary organizations. Because they were nonprofit institutions, the SIZs' accounts had not been audited as closely as the accounts of socially owned enterprises. Thus, by escaping the strictures of both the government and market discipline, the SIZs had little incentive to economize on costs. Indeed, the most common financial impropriety of the SIZs was concealment of operating surpluses, which normally had to be returned to the taxpayers.

The problem of lax financial control could have been relatively easily overcome by better auditing of SIZs and stricter enforcement of laws. A more fundamental problem was the incidence of taxes earmarked for production of public goods. In theory, this was financed by both the citizens and businesses (both socially owned and private) through user fees, the wage tax, and payroll taxes. In practice, few public services were sold for cash, so the share of user fees was small (see Table 3). Because the private sector did not participate in negotiations in the SIZs, it was charged the contributions at special rates. But unlike the socially owned firms, private entrepreneurs only had to contribute to the social security and health insurance SIZs. The private sector's participation in the cost of education, culture, child care, public utilities, and other infrastructure was to be covered from personal income tax. But this was ill-structured, its main aim being to discourage legal private sector activity. This implied that an additional tax burden was placed on the incomes generated in socially owned enterprises.

Theoretically, both the employees and socially owned enterprises as employers shared the cost of SIZ financing.[7] The employees' share was

---

[7]The distinction between the employees' share and the employer's share of payroll taxes was somewhat artificial given that practically all firms were labor-managed and socially owned. The distinction was nevertheless important in practice because different macroeconomic policies (wage freezes, tax changes) were aimed at different accounting categories, thus affecting personal incomes and enterprise profitability in different directions.

calculated as a percentage of their net wage ("personal income"), which also served as the basis for all retirement and benefit calculations. Enterprises paid their share out of a different accounting category, based on the usual definition of the payroll. Changes in the rates of contributions did not affect the net wage, however, so that in terms of the incidence both the employees' and employers' contributions represented part of the labor cost over which enterprises had no control. Furthermore, because of the way the net wage was defined, there was no possibility for enterprises to shift part of the tax burden back onto workers. Because of intermittent price controls and competitive pressures, shifting of contributions forward onto consumers was not always possible. The resulting tax burden on socially owned enterprises was extremely high and remains, to this day, the fundamental problem of public finances in the former Yugoslav republics.[8]

Macroeconomic Effects

Critics of the federal fiscal system in former Yugoslavia advanced two main hypotheses on the system's macroeconomic effects: that reverse transfers contributed to macroeconomic instability and that "excessive" fiscal decentralization paralyzed federal fiscal policy.

On the first point, Tišma established that between 1972 and 1985 contributions by republics were sufficient to cover federal expenditures only in 1972–73 and 1982–84; in all other years the federation had to resort to borrowing, even though federal expenditures were on a downward trend since 1977 (Tišma (1986, p. 270)). Bogoev established that in 1976–80 one third of all increases in central bank credits were used to finance deficits of the federal budget and up to 38 percent of total expenditure in the budget was financed from this source (Bogoev (1989, pp. 630–31)). The National Bank of Yugoslavia would grant loans on very favorable terms, usually for repayment over 20 years, with a 5-year grace period and fixed nominal interest rate of 1 percent. In addition to the crowding-out and inflationary effects, public borrowing of this kind had negative political economy aspects: the Federal Government could avoid raising the taxes and negotiating with republics on higher contributions (Bogoev (1989, p. 631)) and it could avoid political responsibility regarding the nonfulfillment of agreed tasks (Tišma (1986, p. 264)).

On the second point, the main complaint was that the structure of expenditures in the federal budget rendered futile any effort to conduct active fiscal policy. Four budget items (defense, pensions of veterans and

---

[8]Data for the first 11 months of 1990 show, for example, that enterprises in the social sector of the economy paid Din 204 billion in net wages and Din 198 billion in wage and payroll taxes (Social Accounting Service (SDK): *Statistical Bulletin of the SDK*, November 1990).

Table 5. Yugoslavia: Financing of the Federation

Year	Total Revenue	Contri-butions	Customs Duties	Federal Sales Tax	National Bank Credit to Federation	Budget Deficit (−) or Surplus	Contri-butions as a Share of Total Revenue	Customs Duties as a Share of Total Revenue	Federal Sales Tax as a Share of Total Revenue	Share of Other Taxes
	(In millions of dinars)						*(In percent)*			
1981	16.5	6.4	2.6	7.1	—	−0.4	38.8	15.8	43.0	2.4
1982	19.9	8.0	2.8	8.5	8.3	0.0	40.2	14.1	42.7	3.0
1983	26.2	9.7	4.5	11.2	8.3	0.0	37.0	17.2	42.8	3.0
1984	39.1	13.1	8.7	16.3	8.8	0.0	33.5	22.3	41.7	2.5
1985	68.6	25.1	15.0	26.4	10.2	−1.0	36.6	21.9	38.5	3.0
1986	137.4	53.3	32.4	49.1	10.2	0.0	38.8	23.6	35.7	1.9
1987	300.9	62.2	78.9	153.8	72.0	0.0	20.7	26.2	51.1	2.0
1988	813.1	125.0	239.6	427.2	87.1	7.4	15.4	29.5	52.5	2.6
1989	11,376.0	1,570.0	3,241.0	6,241.0	1,169.3	551.0	13.8	28.5	54.9	2.8
1990	97,542.0	5,932.0	34,110.0	54,900.0	—	3,918.2	6.1	35.0	56.3	2.6

Sources: Federal Statistical Office, *Statistical Yearbook of Yugoslavia*, 1990; National Bank of Yugoslavia, *Statistical Survey*, 3/1990; and IMF staff estimates.

military, grants to less developed republics, and federal administration), accounting for 96 percent of federal expenditure, were determined by law or their growth was tied to growth of the nominal GSP and nominal wages, thus precluding the use of the federal budget for stabilization purposes (Bogoev (1987)) or social policy objectives (Jurković (1989a)). When the budget was used to help stabilize the economy, the effects were procyclical (Jurković (1989b)).

The available public finance data do not allow detailed analysis and testing of these hypotheses. The fact that, even at the federal level, there were so many independent public sector agents (the representatives of six republics, two autonomous provinces, and the Federal Government) reveals the difficulty of compiling and classifying the relevant information. For example, data on the payment of contributions by republics were rarely separated from transfers to the federation of the federal sales tax; the purpose, timing, and term structure of central bank credits to the federation were seldom specified; and extending the fiscal year by a month or two, or using a temporary budget, was not unusual. These deficiencies notwithstanding, data in Table 5 show that the weight of reverse transfers as a federal revenue source declined since 1982, while the revenue from tariffs and the federal sales tax became more important. In 1982, more than 40 percent of the federal expenditure was financed by contributions from the republics; by 1990 this had dropped to 6 percent. In the same period the share of tariffs more than doubled, while the share of the sales tax increased by a quarter.

The total amount of central bank credit to the federation rapidly decreased in real terms between 1982 and 1986; in 1987, credit from the National Bank of Yugoslavia increased to Din 35 million (in 1980 prices) and afterward stabilized at about Din 14 million. These data reject, at least for the 1980s, the hypothesis that revenue shortfalls occasioned by the declining share of contributions had to be financed by central bank borrowing. Clearly, tariffs and the sales tax substituted for contributions.

Data on budget deficits in Table 5 also show that in the 1980s the federal budget could not have been a source of macroeconomic instability—as a rule, the budget was balanced. Data on republic and local government budget deficits show that these budgets were generally balanced, too. The available data on budgets of self-governing communities of interest indicate that social security SIZs had chronic deficits, financed by grants from republic budgets, whereas the health care, education, science, culture, and some infrastructure SIZs had surpluses.

Because of possible discrepancies between the timing of expenditures and the collection and transfer of revenues, the role of central bank credit may have been greater than indicated by the data. It is likely that during protracted budget negotiations the Federal Government frequently had to borrow. When fiscal accounts were closed, this operation would not necessarily show up as deficit financing because by that time republics would have transferred the amounts necessary to balance the budget.

Regarding the hypothesis of "fiscal paralysis" at the federal level, to the extent that this was a problem, it was not created by republics at the expense of the federation. Although the revenue position of republics was stronger, the importance of SIZs implied a low share of budget-financing in republic finances (between 17 percent and 24 percent). Consequently, it was difficult even for republic governments effectively to control public spending and monitor the realization of agreed stabilization and social policy objectives.

The apparent absence of deficits at the federal level is the main difference between the Yugoslav and other historical experiences with reverse transfers (America during the period of confederation (1777-89) and the German Empire of 1871-1919). This does not mean that government budgets in Yugoslavia were diligently balanced; public sector deficits may have been concealed in the balance sheets of commercial banks. Eventually these deficits emerged in the form of central bank losses. Fiscal accounts remained unaffected by such losses, however, which may explain why the reform of public finances was never considered a pressing issue.

Turning to the macroeconomics of interregional transfers, in relative terms the resources channeled through the Federal Development Fund and the federal budget were substantial by any measure. In the 25 years since establishment of the transfer scheme, total transfers to less developed republics and the Province of Kosovo had consumed at least 2 percent of GSP annually. Taken together, transfers from the Federal Development Fund and the federal budget accounted for about 12 percent of the GSP of the underdeveloped republics and the Province of Kosovo; the share of transfers in the GSP was about 7 percent in Bosnia-Herzegovina, about 9 percent in Macedonia, 17 percent in Montenegro, and 68 percent in Kosovo (Baletić and Marendić (1982, pp. 256-57)).[9]

The share of allocations from the Federal Development Fund amounted to 5.4 percent of all investments in fixed assets in Yugoslavia in 1976, and to 8 percent of all investments in productive fixed assets; the corresponding figures for individual republics were 13.4 percent and 20.8 percent in Bosnia-Herzegovina, 21.5 percent and 29.1 percent in Macedonia, 30.3 percent and 40.5 percent in Montenegro, and 44 percent and 61.5 percent in Kosovo (Baletić and Marendić (1982, p. 255)). In addition to direct financial assistance, less developed republics and the Province of Kosovo also enjoyed advantages in external borrowing (especially from the World Bank), and they qualified for duty reductions on imports of

---

[9]These figures relate to gross amounts, the share of net transfers being smaller, but not equally so for all these republics.

capital goods and rebates of costs in connection with the operation of the Federal Development Fund.

In the 1980s, the assets of the Federal Development Fund were formed partly through subscriptions of the compulsory loan, and partly through the "pooling of labor and resources" between enterprises in developed and underdeveloped republics.[10] Thus, during 1986–90, 60 percent of the assets of the Federal Development Fund were to be formed through pooling of labor and resources (50 percent for the Province of Kosovo) and 40 percent through loan subscriptions. The annual interest rate paid by the recipients of pooled resources was 11 percent (9 percent for the recipients in Kosovo) (Jašić (1987, pp. 282–83)). In practice, there was little difference between compulsory loans and the pooling of labor and resources; both were mandatory. Though the enterprises from developed republics were formally given the opportunity to realize some gains by pooling labor and resources with compatible enterprises in the less developed republics, their rights were not effectively protected; moreover, the governments of less developed republics had to approve the investors' projects.

The intensity and scope of efforts to achieve faster economic growth in the less developed republics and the Province of Kosovo notwithstanding, the leveling of differences in various development indicators has been slower than expected. The effects of interregional transfers are especially disappointing if one looks at the ranking of republics in terms of per capita GSP, which had remained practically unchanged throughout the quarter century since the introduction of the transfer scheme (see Table 4). The difference between Kosovo and all other republics had increased because of extremely high population growth in the province (3 percent annually). Differences in other indicators (consumption, fixed assets, employment, education) had substantially narrowed over the years. But these improvements in productive capacity had not been matched by increases in the efficiency of use of production factors.

This suggests that, besides the obvious organizational, technical, and political economy weaknesses, the main reason for malfunctioning of the interregional transfer scheme was in the flawed concept of development supported by the scheme. As pointed out by Baletić and Marendić (1982, p. 258), the task of development was treated as a matter of supplementary financing of investments from central funds. This orientation was determined partly by the character of the Yugoslav federal system and partly by the fact that the problem of underdevelopment was reduced to the need to industrialize backward agrarian areas, with the securing of necessary funds being regarded as the core of the problem. As the development

---

[10]The concept of pooling of labor and resources was introduced in the Associated Labor Act of 1976 in an attempt to replace the functions of the capital market, in earlier periods performed by the banking system and planners.

level of the country was rising, the economies of all the republics and provinces, including the lagging ones, were facing increasingly complex development problems. Greater availability of new production technologies demanded that, for efficiency gains to be realized, complex organizational and personnel problems be resolved. Under these circumstances, the strategy which focused on accumulation of physical capital became insufficient to ensure successful development.

The lack of perceptible signs of catching up frustrated all members of the Yugoslav federation. The developed part of the country complained, especially in periods of economic downturn, about the drain of scarce investment resources from their own economies and about the apparent waste of these resources in the underdeveloped south. The less developed republics and the Province of Kosovo criticized the developed republics for their insensitivity with regard to the development problems of the historically less fortunate members of the federation. Interregional transfers came to be viewed as costs (or benefits) of belonging to the federation, and the failure to achieve the proclaimed objectives as one reason leading to the breakup of the federation.

Evolution of Fiscal Federalism

Economic analysis alone cannot identify the rationale for the system of intergovernmental fiscal relations that existed in Yugoslavia between 1972 and 1990. Judged by the usual standards of sound public finance, the system was microeconomically and administratively inefficient, macroeconomically rigid, and relatively unfair from the point of view of individual and, to some extent, regional equity. The only remaining a priori justification for this system—greater political responsibility—must be judged against the background of the historical and political environment in which the Yugoslav federalism had evolved.

Origins of Fiscal Federalism

The system of fiscal federalism in former Yugoslavia had its origins in the political events that took place in 1968–72 (see Rusinow (1977)). In 1968, a power vacuum was felt in the political life of the country. Reformist forces in central organs of the communist party had consolidated their power but were unable to solve the plethora of economic problems brought about by the ill-conceived 1965 reform. At the same time, party organizations in individual republics had become virtually autonomous and some of their leaders were eager to be seen as defenders of interests of their republic against what was perceived as the attempts at exploitation or domination by other republics.

There was little possibility of dealing with economic issues at the republic level because key monetary and fiscal instruments, especially turnover and capital taxes, remained in the hands of the immobilized federal administration. The power of regional authorities was thus almost entirely negative: they could veto federal proposals but they could not implement policies of their own. Of the three possible solutions to the stalemate—recentralization, radical decentralization, and decentralization with an interrepublic consensus mechanism—the second temporarily prevailed, thus opening the view toward a loose confederation. The strongest advocate of this position was the Croatian party leadership, and the process culminated with open demands and prospects for Croatian independence.

In late 1971, President Tito could no longer tolerate the situation and so he forced party leaderships in Croatia and other republics to resign. Central party organs reasserted strict control over republic parties on the basis of the principle of "democratic centralism" that had been abandoned during the late 1960s.[11] The move was followed by the increased involvement of party organs (now under the new leadership) in all spheres of economic and social life, and by ideological attacks on the managerial class that had emerged from the market reforms of the 1960s and was now accused of impeding the development of workers' self-management. The market philosophy of the 1960s was gradually replaced by a completely new set of organizational principles that came to be known as the "contractual economy."

Legislation of the 1970s, in particular the new enterprise law—the Associated Labor Act—reflected many political and ideological concerns of the party. But some of the more radical demands voiced by republic leaderships in the late 1960s ultimately also found their expression in the laws adopted during this period. Because the nationality question was the central constitutional problem and the economic system its most important aspect, the realization of economic sovereignty of nations became the leading principle of the new federal order. This implied control by the republics of investment activity, credit policy, public spending and revenues, foreign exchange allocations, and other key aspects of economic life. As a result, it was no longer possible to maintain a model of federation in which the Federal Government had supremacy over republics in deciding on important economic issues. Instead, the Federal Government could only perform the "joint functions" of federation, that is, those functions that had been explicitly delegated to it by sovereign republics—there was no room any more for "autonomous functions" of the federation. The republics thus became "responsible for their own development as well as the development of the federation" (Gošev (1990, p. 15)). In the same spirit, the 1974 Constitution confirmed the right of republics (but not of autonomous provinces) to secede from the federation. Thus, the third

---

[11] For a discussion of democratic centralism and federalism, see Chapter 9 in this volume.

constitutional model—decentralization with interrepublic consensus mechanism—had eventually prevailed.

In the fiscal sphere, the new concept of federalism implied that the number of fiscal issues about which republics could quarrel at the federal level ought to be minimized. Thus, under the 1974 Constitution, the Federal Government was stripped of all taxing authority save for import tariffs and the federal sales tax (which was shared with republics), most taxing and spending powers were transferred to republics and local governments, a system of self-governing communities of interest was established to provide the bulk of public goods at the most decentralized level possible, and contributions by republics were introduced to finance the federal budget.

From this perspective, the use of contributions seemed the logical solution to the main problem of federal finance—financing the federation. Like contributions of member countries to international organizations, republic contributions were viewed as payment for services offered by the federation. The system functioned relatively smoothly as long as the dominant position of the Communist Party ensured the minimum amount of trust between the republics and the federation. Political developments that took place in 1989 and 1990 (see Rusinow (1990–91)) disproved the expectation that such trust could be established in a post-communist environment. In economic terms, two challenges faced the old federation. First, it was not clear that there was a surplus from integration of six republics and two autonomous provinces into the Yugoslav economic system. Second, to the extent that this surplus existed, all members of the federation argued that it was not distributed in a way acceptable to them.[12]

Proposed Model of Confederation After 1990

Partly in response to these challenges, in October 1990 the presidencies of the Republics of Croatia and Slovenia presented the other former Yugoslav republics with a proposal for a new state treaty establishing the Yugoslav Confederation. The treaty would have established a voluntary alliance of sovereign states united for the purpose of realizing joint interests. The basic premise of the model was that the economic interest—the creation of a common market—lay at the foundation of the new confederation.[13] The transition from the old federation to the new confederation was to be addressed in a separate treaty.

---

[12]For an almost identical characterization of the Canadian federalist quandary in the 1970s, see Maxwell and Pestieau (1980).

[13]Other joint interests included joining the European integration processes, protecting the external borders, protecting human and ethnic rights, and fostering the international position of member countries.

In economic terms the confederation was envisaged as a customs union, a common market, and a monetary union. Three options were presented for the monetary union: (1) each member could have its own currency and coordinate exchange rate policy with other members; (2) members could have their own currencies and set up a payments union; and (3) members could share a common currency and a joint central bank. Members were to apply a common competition policy and coordinate policies in transportation, communications, energy, and agriculture (the alternative was to have joint infrastructure policies).

Joint functions were to be financed in three ways. First, member countries would have provided the necessary facilities and finance for those agencies of confederation that would have been located on their territory. Second, they would have covered the cost of that part of joint defense forces which would have been put under the joint command. Third, other joint expenditures would have been financed by contributions to be determined by a weighted average formula, the weights being the members' shares in GSP (40 percent), territory (30 percent), and population (30 percent). The alternative was for each member to finance the work of its own citizens in joint bodies; other costs would have been covered by contributions negotiated for individual institutions and projects. Equal shares, the benefit principle, and economic capacity were envisaged as apportionment criteria for such contributions.

Given that the confederation would not have been an independent political and economic entity, it would have had no own revenue sources: tariffs collected under the customs union provision would have been distributed among member countries. The distribution key, however, was not specified in the model. It is not clear why tariff revenue was not assigned to the confederation if it was modeled on the image of the European Community. Because of the narrow scope of joint functions it is conceivable that tariff revenue alone would have been sufficient to finance the work of confederate bodies, in which case contributions would not have been necessary. It seems, therefore, that the main reason for insistence on contributions was lack of trust among confederate members. In light of the benefits of confederation (lower cost of providing some countrywide public goods) and its costs (uncertainty about the willingness of other members as well as confederate bodies to deliver on their promises), contributions were once again seen as a convenient second-best solution, preferable to uncertain arrangements on the recycling of tariff revenue.

Concluding Remarks

A key conclusion to emerge from analysis of the Yugoslav experience is that to function properly, the system of intergovernmental fiscal relations must be transparent. The federal order in former Yugoslavia was somewhere between a confederation and a centralized federation.[14] Different tiers of government interacted through a tangled web of rights and responsibilities, frequently, if not necessarily intentionally, encroaching on each other's spheres of competency. The lack of transparency in the delineation of the political, legal, and economic aspects of federalism was compounded by intricate organizational procedures for representing regional interests. Not surprisingly, the outcome was a situation in which the costs of belonging to the federation were easily ascertainable, but the benefits seemed elusive to all parties involved.

The second conclusion is that confederate finances constitute a very fragile structure. While not necessarily contributing to macroeconomic instability, the reverse transfers, the concept of minimum central government, and budgetary procedures based on consensus unavoidably restrict the scope for the use of fiscal policy in the pursuit of stabilization and social policy objectives. This may generate some important benefits that have been neglected in the traditional fiscal federalism literature.[15] At the same time, however, the narrowing of the scope for centralized fiscal policy complicates macroeconomic policymaking. Specifically, in a loose confederate setting regional economic policies have to be carefully coordinated in order to avoid negative spillovers of domestic policies. Moreover, a complex system of interregional fiscal transfers has to be established to prevent the emergence (or the widening) of disruptive differences in regional economic performance. Without this infrastructure of confederate policymaking, monetary and exchange rate policies alone (to the extent they remain centralized) cannot ensure realization of the very objective that forms the logical foundation of confederation—the creation of a common market.[16]

Another conclusion to emerge from the Yugoslav experience is that welfare surpluses from federating (or confederating) cannot be taken for granted. Before asserting that economic integration is always and everywhere preferable to economic independence, policymakers must consider the costs of unity and demonstrate convincingly that factors promoting the formation of economic unions—regional flexibility of factor and commodity prices, industrial diversification by regions, factor mobility,

---

[14]For political science definitions of federation and confederation, see Wheare (1964), King (1982), and Chapter 9 in this volume. For legal definitions see Pajić (1991). Differences between federations and confederations from the point of view of economics are discussed in Hewitt and Mihaljek (1992) and Hardy and Mihaljek (1992).

[15]See, for example, Scott (1964), Wiseman (1965), Haller (1968), and Dafflon (1977). A recurring theme in the work of these authors is a critique of the traditional Musgrave-Oates approach, which argues for centralized control of redistribution and stabilization functions and the assignment to the subcentral level of only the allocation function.

[16]At present, our understanding of positive and normative aspects of economic policy coordination is very limited, though. See Kolm (1989) for some theoretical underpinnings.

openness, and interregional trade—are in place and can be combined with political and cultural factors in a way that makes a given group of countries or regions a promising candidate for economic union. Neither economic analysis nor historical experience can provide unequivocal predictions about compatibility; many arguments on benefits and costs of union will necessarily be based on value judgments. Historical experiences of federations such as the United States, Canada, Australia, Germany, and Switzerland indicate that such judgments are best when made on a pragmatic rather than ideological basis.

Finally, the Yugoslav experience is instructive because it shows that economic efficiency is not necessarily the most important dimension of public policymaking or of citizens' welfare. Neglecting this by insisting on presupposed benefits from economies of scale may easily result in negative-sum economic and social outcomes. When choosing the instruments of fiscal policy, the trade-off between economic and sociopolitical objectives must therefore be realized and considered. Thus, it seems perfectly logical to place a constraint on the operation of policy instruments that would require too much central fiscal power. Since contributions represent one way of placing such constraints, they are likely to be important in the design of future confederate arrangements.

References

Baletić, Zvonimir, "Osnove politike bržeg razvoja privredno nedovoljno razvijenih republika i autonomnih pokrajina" [Foundations of the policy of faster economic development of economically underdeveloped republics and autonomous provinces], in *Problemi privrednog razvoja i privrednog sistema Jugoslavije*, Vol. IV [Problems of economic development and economic system in Yugoslavia, Vol. IV], ed. by Dragomir Vojnić and others (Zagreb: Ekonomski institut-Zagreb, 1989).

_____, and Božo Marendić, "The Policy and System of Regional Development," in *Essays on the Political Economy of Yugoslavia*, ed. by Rikard Lang, George Macesich, and Dragomir Vojnić (Zagreb: Center for Yugoslav-American Studies, Research, and Exchanges at the Florida State University, Ekonomski Institut Zagreb, and Informator Zagreb, 1982).

Bogoev, Ksente, "Osnovne karakteristike savremenih fiskalnih sistema" [Main characteristics of contemporary fiscal systems], *Finansije*, Vol. 44 (November–December 1989), pp. 611–36.

_____, "Fiskalna harmonizacija i fiskalni federalizam" [Fiscal harmonization and fiscal federalism], *Finansije*, Vol. 42 (January–February 1987), pp. 1–38.

_____, and Pero Jurković, "The Fiscal System," in *Essays on the Political Economy of Yugoslavia*, ed. by Rikard Lang, George Macesich, and Dragomir Vojnić

(Zagreb: Center for Yugoslav-American Studies, Research, and Exchanges at the Florida State University, Ekonomski Institut Zagreb, and Informator Zagreb, 1982).

Burkett, John, and Borislav Škegro, "Are Economic Fractures Widening?" in *Yugoslavia: A Fractured Federalism*, ed. by Dennison Rusinow (Washington: Wilson Center Press, 1988).

Dafflon, Bernard, *Federal Finance in Theory and Practice: with Special Reference to Switzerland* (Bern: Paul Haupt, 1977).

Gošev, Petar, "O ekonomskim funkcijama federacije" [On the economic functions of federation], *Ekonomska politika*, Vol. 39 (June 11, 1990), pp. 14-15.

Haller, Heinz, "Wandlungen in den Problemen föderativer Staatswirtschaften," *Finanzarchiv*, Vol. 27 (January 1968), pp. 249-70.

Hardy, Daniel, and Dubravko Mihaljek, "Economic Policymaking in a Federation," *Finance & Development*, Vol. 29 (June 1992), pp. 14-17.

Hewitt, Daniel, and Dubravko Mihaljek, "Fiscal Federalism," in *Fiscal Issues in Economies in Transition*, ed. by Vito Tanzi (Washington: International Monetary Fund, 1992).

Jašić, Zoran, "Poticanje razvitka nedovoljno razvijenih područja u SFR Jugoslaviji i SR Hrvatskoj" [Stimulating development in underdeveloped regions in SFR Yugoslavia and SR Croatia], in *Sistem i politika društvenog financiranja* [System and policy of public finance], ed. by Pero Jurković (Zagreb: Ekonomski institut-Zagreb, 1987).

Johansen, Leif, "Some Notes on the Lindahl Theory of Determination of Public Expenditures," *International Economic Review*, Vol. 4 (September 1963), pp. 346-58.

Jurković, Pero (1989a), *Fiskalna politika u ekonomskoj teoriji i praksi* [Fiscal policy in economic theory and practice] (Zagreb: Informator, 1989).

—— (1989b), "Aktualni problemi reforme fiskalnog sistema" [Current issues in reform of the fiscal system], in *Problemi privrednog razvoja i privrednog sistema Jugoslavije*, Vol. IV [Problems of economic development and economic system in Yugoslavia, Vol. IV], ed. by Dragomir Vojnić and others (Zagreb: Ekonomski institut-Zagreb, 1989).

King, Preston, *Federalism and Federation* (Baltimore: Johns Hopkins University Press, 1982).

Kolm, Serge-Chrisophe, "Cooperative-Game Properties of International Coordination," Working Paper No. 77, Centre d'Enseignement et de Recherche en Analyse Socio-Economique (Paris: Ecole Nationale des Ponts et Chausées, 1989).

Lindahl, Erik, *Die Gerechtigkeit der Besteuerung* (Lund, 1919). Excerpts translated as "Just Taxation: A Positive Solution," in *Classics in the Theory of Public Finance*, ed. by Richard A. Musgrave and Alan T. Peacock (London: Macmillan, 1958).

Marković, Branimir, "Proporcije robne razmjene republika i pokrajina" [Proportions of commodity trade between republics and provinces], *Ekonomska politika*, Vol. 42 (June 10, 1991), pp. 11-12.

Maxwell, Judith, and Caroline Pestieau, *Economic Realities of Contemporary Confederation* (Montreal: C.D. Howe Research Institute, 1980).

Mihaljek, Dubravko, "Financing of Public Services in Yugoslavia: A Lindahl Equilibrium Model for the Labour-Managed Economy," *Economic Analysis*, Vol. 20, No. 2 (1986), pp. 135-68.

Pajić, Zoran, "Yugoslavia and the Confederation Model: International Aspects," *Review of International Affairs*, Vol. 42 (April 20, 1991), pp. 5-7.

Presidency of the Republic of Croatia and Presidency of the Republic of Slovenia, *Model konfederacije u Jugoslaviji* [Model of confederation in Yugoslavia], Zagreb and Ljubljana, October 4, 1990. Published in *Vjesnik, Panorama subotom*, October 4, 1990, pp. 2-3). English Translation in the *Review of International Affairs*, Vol. 41 (October 20, 1990), pp. 11-16.

Rusinow, Dennison, *The Yugoslav Experiment: 1948-1974* (London: C. Hurst and Company for the Royal Institute of International Affairs, 1977).

_____, "To Be or Not to Be? Yugoslavia as Hamlet," *Universities Field Staff International, Field Staff Reports, Europe*, Vol. 40, No. 18 (1990-91).

Scott, Anthony, "The Economic Goals of Federal Finance," *Public Finance*, Vol. 19, No. 3 (1964), pp. 241-88.

Tišma, Toša, "Finansiranje federacije" [Financing of the federation], *Finansije*, Vol. 41 (May-June 1986), pp. 259-78.

Vranješ, Mile, "Aktuelna pitanja lokalnih finansija" [Current issues in local public finance], *Finansije*, Vol. 46 (September-October 1990), pp. 567-77.

Wiseman, Jack, *The Political Economy of Federalism: A Critical Appraisal* (Ottawa: Canadian Royal Commission on Taxation, 1965). Reprinted in *Environment and Planning C: Government and Policy*, Vol. 5, No. 4 (1987), pp. 383-410.

Wheare, Kenneth C., *Federal Government* (New York: Oxford University Press for the Royal Institute of International Affairs, 4th ed., 1964).

CHAPTER 11

Privatization in East Germany
Dieter Bös

The transition of the industrial sector from planning to market orientation is a central problem facing east Germany after German unification. The industrial sector has to be completely rebuilt, and the privatization of viable firms is as important a step in this process as the liquidation of nonviable firms. While these problems have been intensively discussed in all former communist states, it is important to keep in mind the particularities of the German situation. These features explain why policies adequate for, say, the former Czechoslovakia, might not be recommendable for east Germany. Accordingly, this paper begins by highlighting the economic and institutional background of the east German transition.

Then we turn to the transition itself. Currently, privatization in east Germany is carried out by a government property trust, Treuhandanstalt, which has opted for a policy of rapid privatization by low-price sales of industrial firms to investors who present the best business plans for investment and employment. Although the sales figures look impressive, a current policy issue is how the Treuhandanstalt's procedure can be improved. Should general vouchers or vouchers for special groups of the population (for instance, for employees) be introduced? Should the Treuhandanstalt retain part of the shares of privatized companies? Should wages or capital, or both, be subsidized? Many proposals referring to these questions, put forward in 1991, are critically evaluated in this paper.

These are key questions. Even more important, however, is the issue of what will happen as the privatization policy ends when all or most of the attractive firms have been sold. If there are no private bidders for some firms, should the Government (via the Treuhandanstalt) restructure these firms? How much restructuring is desired?

Finally, it is not too early to start thinking about how to end the transition process. To avoid the nightmare of permanent subsidies, policies to liquidate unpopular firms will have to be devised. The Federal Government should announce these policies now as part of a long-term commitment to preclude prolonged bailing-out of nonviable firms.

Dieter Bös is Professor of Economics at the University of Bonn.

East Germany in Transition

Privatization in Germany is different from privatization in, say, the former Czechoslovakia, Hungary, or Poland. In contrast to these countries, only part of this large, Western-style economy is to be privatized. Taking 1988 figures, east German employees would have accounted for 22 percent of the total east and west German work force. East German disposable income would have accounted for only 11 percent of total German disposable income.[1] While in the former Czechoslovakia or Poland the whole economy is to be restructured, the problem facing united Germany could better be compared with the problem of restructuring the underdeveloped parts of a country, like the Mezzogiorno in Italy, or with the problem of revitalizing decaying areas in otherwise flourishing cities.

Being part of the united Germany, the new states and east Berlin now enjoy:

- The west German system of laws and regulations for government and business, which has been well developed over many years of application.
- Instant currency convertibility and, by using a currency with a long-standing reputation for stability, guaranteed absence of hyperinflation as a consequence of price liberalization.
- The benefits of special recovery programs set up and financed from the West for infrastructure, restructuring of old firms, establishment of new firms, and stimulation of investments.
- Access to west German human resources and expertise; west German investors, banks, and insurance companies are available for starting and redeveloping businesses.
- The mature (west) German social security system.
- Direct access to European Community markets.

East Germany is in a privileged position. Using a "parental guidance" model helps explain the transition from a planned to a market economy better than the "help yourself" model, applicable to the former Czechoslovakia, Hungary, Poland, and other countries.

The advantage of having successful parents is not without risk. Risks inherent in a parental-guidance relationship show clearly in the relation between west Germany as the parent and east Germany as the child. East Germany's expectations are often excessively high, be it the 1:1 conversion of the marks of the former German Democratic Republic (GDR) and deutsche mark, or the rapid rise in east German wages to reach the west German level in a few years. West Germany, having simply too much money to spend, may bail out sinking east German firms for too long

---

[1]Calculated on the basis of Sachverständigenrat (1990), pp. 51–52, converting the currencies 1:1.

precisely because workers earn wages that significantly exceed east German productivity. A country such as Poland cannot afford to pay such high wages *and* keep the firms alive; as a result, workers there have to accept low wages. Only a rich parent such as west Germany can opt for a policy of high wages *and* intense subsidization of nonviable firms. This paper warns of such a policy, which, by ignoring the trade-off between wages and jobs, is unacceptably costly.

The background of this policy is the special problem of German internal migration. German policymakers fear two types of migration. First, a high-unemployment migration, brought about by high east German wages, which might force firms out of business; although unemployment benefits are generous, east Germans seem dismayed by the prospect of long-term unemployment and would move to the west despite the difficulties associated with such a move.[2] Second, a low-wage migration where the wage differentials between east and west Germany are the main driving force; this would make it difficult to adjust east German wages in line with the development of labor productivity.

However, any policy of moderate unemployment coupled with moderate wage increases was made impossible by the trade unions, which used the argument of imminent high migration to gain support for a policy of high minimum wages.[3] This shifted the responsibility for the employment policy to the Federal Government, which in turn pushed the Treuhandanstalt to rank job preservation high on the scale of its objectives.

Institutional Background

The Treuhandanstalt, founded by the Government of the GDR in December 1989 and restructured in June 1990, owns most industrial enterprises in east Germany. The privatization or restructuring of east German firms started with this government agency in charge of transforming the east German economy from central planning to "market socialism"; unlike Hungary, there was in east Germany no movement toward "spontaneous privatization." Statistical information on the Treuhandanstalt is presented in Table 1.

In 1989–90, a view of east German industrial firms regarded one third as viable in a market environment, one third as viable after restructuring, and one third as nonviable. Using this triage approach, the Treuhand-

---

[2]According to Akerlof and others (1991), unemployment is more important than wage differentials for the east-west German migration.

[3]The employers' side was presented by former east German officials and managers who themselves were interested in high-wage increases (which also guarantee higher unemployment benefits). The west German employers' representatives did not interfere, most probably because they are not interested in low-wage competitors located within Germany.

Table 1. The Treuhandanstalt in 1990–91

Property in 1990[1]
9,000 industrial enterprises with more than 45,000 business premises
20,000 commercial businesses
7,500 hotels and restaurants
Several thousand pharmacies, bookshops, and cinemas
2.3 million hectares of agricultural land
1.9 million hectares of forest

(Implies responsibility for 3 million jobs)

Privatizations until June 30, 1991[2]

Industrial firms sold	
July–December 1990	408
January–July 1991	2,578
Total number	2,986
Total price	DM 11.6 billion
Small businesses sold	
1990 to end-May 1991	17,000

Liquidations[2]

1990 to end-May 1991	450
Of which: "silent" liquidation	350

Budget in 1991[3]
(In billions of deutsche mark)

Revenues		Expenditures	
Privatizations	15.8	Interest and debt repayment	13.8
Others	1.1	Restructuring of firms	12.9
Debt-financed deficit	20.8	Cost of sale of firms	4.8
		Others	6.2

Note: The deficit is financed by borrowing on capital and money markets. The treaty on German unity limited borrowing for 1990–91 together to DM 25 billion. For 1992, borrowing of DM 32 billion was expected. Since the Treuhandanstalt is a government agency, the Federal Government is responsible for paying any deficit arising from its operation. After the closure of the Treuhandanstalt, interest on and payment of the Treuhandanstalt debt will remain an obligation of the Federal Government.

[1] See Breuel (1991).
[2] Treuhandanstalt (1991).
[3] Institut der deutschen Wirtschaft, *Informationsdienst des Instituts der deutschen Wirtschaft*, Nos. 26, 37, and 43 (1991).

anstalt was supposed to immediately privatize the first group, to restructure and then privatize the second, and to liquidate the third.[4]

This conveniently equal division did not come from empirical research. Moreover, the actual proportions depend on economic development;

[4] Throughout this paper, I exclude the special problems of the administration and privatization of the agricultural land and forests owned by the Treuhandanstalt.

wage increases in 1990–91 have reduced the first and second groups and have enlarged the third. For the argument of this paper the precise levels are unimportant: what matters is the qualitative categorization of the Treuhandanstalt's activities. This reflects planning under perfect information, in which the government agency as benevolent dictator knows perfectly which firms are viable in a market economy, how to restructure other firms, and which ones to liquidate.

It soon became clear that the brief of the Treuhandanstalt was too demanding for a government agency and that political pressures and bureaucratic red tape would interfere with an efficient transition from a state-planned industrial structure to a market-oriented economy. In privatizing, Treuhandanstalt officials typically do not sell for the highest price set by auction bidding, but evaluate the explicit investment and employment plans of potential purchasers. This demonstrates a bias in favor of job preservation. In restructuring, as far as the Treuhandanstalt operates according to business plans formulated by firms that are candidates for restructuring, industrial structures may become fossilized. In liquidating, the job-preservation objectives of the Treuhandanstalt may dictate that many firms that should be liquidated are in fact not liquidated.

Privatization

Should People's Shares or Vouchers Be Recommended for Germany?

The application of people's shares or vouchers has been advocated by many advisors to former communist countries.[5] The German Federal Government never intended to implement a scheme of general vouchers or shares. However, several German reform proposals suggest such a scheme, for instance, an October 1991 program of the German trade union of the metal workers and the reform model of Sinn and Sinn (1991). In practice, the former Czechoslovakia is the first country to apply such a scheme,[6] with other countries to follow. Only Hungary has shown no interest in such a policy.

This is not the place to repeat the details of the various proposals put forward.[7] The basic idea is that the publicly owned firms should not be sold to private bidders, but should be given to the adult population either free of charge or at a very low price. The general population receives shares or vouchers that at some later time can be exchanged for shares. If a direct ownership program is intended, the publicly owned firms must be converted to joint-stock companies and the general population be

---

[5]For a good overview, see Borensztein and Kumar (1991).
[6]Sales of vouchers began in the former Czechoslovakia on October 1, 1991.
[7]For details, see Borensztein and Kumar (1991).

entitled to the property rights of the firms (directly via shares or indirectly via vouchers).[8] But if all the entitlements are given to the general population, there will be no effective management control, at least not in the short run. Because of this, typically, only a smaller percentage is given to the population; the remaining entitlements can be auctioned off to private investors in such a way as to achieve effective management control. Alternatively, such control may be attained by giving part of the entitlements to financial intermediaries or banks or by withholding government participation in the privatized firms.[9] If an indirect ownership program is planned, the ownership of the firms is transferred—free of charge—from the Government to financial intermediaries, and the entitlements in the intermediaries are distributed to the general public. The intermediaries control the firms; they themselves should be controlled by the Government or by competition among themselves.[10]

Defendants of distributive privatization base their arguments on distributive justice.[11] Granting the same number of shares or vouchers to every citizen realizes equal distribution. However, this initial equality will not hold for very long if trading in shares or vouchers is initiated. Trading will quickly destroy the initial equality, and those who favor end-state equality will not be content with the resulting distribution, in which speculators will have gained more than the proverbial man in the street.

In Germany, achieving even initial equality is complicated. Only citizens of the former GDR would be issued vouchers or shares. However, it is difficult to determine which qualifying date should be chosen. Should those who left the GDR before the day of unification also be entitled to get vouchers? Certainly not, if they fled in, say, 1953. What about those citizens who fled between the fall of the Berlin Wall and the day of unification (and, perhaps, returned after unification)? What about those who fled via Hungary in the dramatic days before the fall of the Berlin Wall (after all, it was mainly those refugees who caused the collapse of the hard-line communist regime)? Any qualifying date would be contestable on equity grounds.

---

[8]The value of the firm is determined by issuing vouchers exchangeable for enterprise equity, where bidding by the population establishes an evaluation of the equity relative to the vouchers. The implementation of this convenient theoretical idea would, however, face serious problems (see Borensztein and Kumar (1991), p. 309). Not only would the general population lack the knowledge to bid for equity in exchange of vouchers, but the bidding would require a most complicated *tâtonnement* process.

[9]In some proposals these alternatives are combined. See, for instance, Lipton and Sachs (1990).

[10]One hundred percent ownership given to intermediaries was proposed in Frydman and Rapaczynski (1991) and in Blanchard and others (1991). The Polish mass privatization program suggested 60 percent ownership of the intermediaries—see Poland, Ministry of Ownership Changes (1991). A more sophisticated proposal for Poland was presented in Lipton and Sachs (1990).

[11]Voucher schemes help start privatization in economies lacking purchasing power and avoid the problems of determining the firms' value.

Yet another issue of justice is connected with distributive privatization programs. It has been argued that it is equitable to grant explicit ownership of east German firms to the east German population because before unification they implicitly owned the firms. This argument accepts as legitimate the people's property inherited from the communist system and proposes transforming it into the Western type of individual property.[12] If such a juridical position is taken, as in the former Czechoslovakia or Poland, it could well constitute the basis for giving away people's shares of publicly owned enterprises.

This has certainly not been the German position. In the treaty on German unity, the original owners whose individual property was expropriated by the Nazis or the GDR were explicitly entitled to plead for restitution in-kind.[13] The people's property became extinct on the day of German unity; only the concept of individual property of the original owners matters from a legal standpoint. If the people's property is extinct, it cannot be a legitimate basis for giving away shares or vouchers. It is clear that, given the stipulations of the treaty on German unity, there is no argument for a general scheme of people's shares or vouchers in Germany.[14]

Consider the case of a firm originally owned by an east German who is not interested in restitution in-kind, but prefers monetary compensation. The Treuhandanstalt sells the firm to the entrepreneur who offers the best bid. The original owner is then entitled to receive either the money the Treuhandanstalt received from the bidder, or the market value, whichever

---

[12]The communist concept of people's property differs decisively from the Western concept of individual property. In the communist concept no individual rights result from people's property; in the Western concept an owner has all conceivable individual rights with respect to the goods owned, except some rights removed by governmental regulation and rights voluntarily renounced.

[13]See Article 41 (1) and the joint declaration of the Federal Republic of Germany and the German Democratic Republic of June 15, 1990 (part of the treaty on German unity). However, former owners may be given monetary compensation instead of restitution in-kind, if this is in the interest of prompt economic recovery. See Article 41 (2) of the treaty on German unity, and Vermögensgesetz in the version of April 1991. For political reasons, there is no restitution in-kind for the nationalization in the Soviet-occupied zone of Germany (1945–49). However, as the constitutional court in Karlsruhe ruled in 1991, in these cases the former owners may claim monetary compensation.

[14]Article 10 (6) of the treaty on the German economic, monetary, and social union (GEMSU) and Article 25 (6) of the treaty on German unity do not contradict the hypothesis raised in the text. According to these articles, remaining Treuhandanstalt financial revenue should be passed on to savers who suffered financial loss when part of their savings was converted at 2:1. This accepts an implicit claim by savers to convert all their savings at 1:1; and does not accept a claim of the general population with respect to their former people's property. It refers to the remaining Treuhandanstalt financial revenue "after use of the people's property for structural adjustment of the economy and for reduction of the government budget deficit (Sanierung des Staatshaushaltes)." It postulates an ex-post policy, not a policy of compensations paid to savers, say, in 1991, before it is clear whether there will be any Treuhandanstalt financial revenue. This has been raised by Sinn and Sinn (1991), pp. 110–21. For the opposing view, see Beirat of the Bundeswirtschaftsministerium (1991), pp. 16–28.

is higher. In this way east Germans get a share of the new German economy. Restitution in-kind is particularly applicable in cases of small enterprises nationalized in 1972. A general voucher scheme would not fit into such a privatization process. Giving vouchers to these original owners would mean giving to them twice.

But east Germans might argue that it is not enough that the original owners get their property back or get monetary compensation. They might argue that in the 40-odd years since 1949, west German citizens could establish new firms, acquire ownership of shares, and so on. This would imply an argument by east Germans that financial compensation be paid for lost chances. This argument is plausible and, since everybody has been deprived of chances, justifies a general system of compensation.

There are arguments for and against the application of general vouchers or share schemes for east Germans. I am not convinced that a voucher scheme is a recommendable policy. First, vouchers or shares are not a good distributive device if one cares for end-state equality and, second, the entitlement of original owners is at variance with an entitlement of the general population. However, I can understand how someone could think that general vouchers should be given as financial compensation for 40 years of lost opportunity.

Giveaways and Participation Model

Most former communist countries lack the purchasing power to allow rapid privatization. Estrin (1991) mentions that "in Poland . . . savers could . . . purchase approximately 1 per cent of the capital stock." "Czechs could currently purchase 10 per cent of the state assets . . . and at the current rate of saving would take a further 150 years to purchase the entire capital stock."[15] Giving away the firms solves the problem of the lack of purchasing power and also allows comparatively rapid privatization. In Germany there is more purchasing power than in the former Czechoslovakia or in Poland. Moreover, it may more easily attract foreign capital. However, even in Germany it is uncertain whether all viable east German industrial firms can be sold at prices equal to their estimated value.[16]

Let us next recognize the difficulties in evaluating the firms to be sold. In east Germany, these difficulties are severe, given the lack of information on ownership or on environmental damage that must be rectified. The Treuhandanstalt deals with these problems in the following way. The agency shares with the investor, or even fully bears, the environmental and ownership risks. It also may enter into some agreement

---

[15]Both quotations are from Estrin (1991), p. 171.
[16]See the detailed discussion in Sinn (1991) and Sinn and Sinn (1991), pp. 83–109. Also see, however, Beirat of the Bundeswirtschaftsministerium (1991), p. 17.

about the servicing of former company debts. The agency sells firms at a low price, sometimes at even DM 1, but coupled with investment pledges and job guarantees (with penalties to be paid by those who do not abide by their commitments). This illustrates that the Treuhandanstalt is giving the firms to entrepreneurs and not to citizens or employees and managers—the other possible recipients.

In the trade-off between speed and transparency of privatization, the Treuhandanstalt has opted for speed. This proves advantageous for the transition to a market economy. No time is lost in ensuring that economic decisions are taken by private entrepreneurs. A critical mass of enterprises has been privatized during the still-powerful momentum of unification. But if the privatization process should take too long, bureaucratic hierarchies in the Treuhandanstalt enterprises would take command, and it would prove most difficult to transform these into Western-type managers and employees. Unfortunately, higher speed is always coupled with less transparency, and this has led to allegations of insider trading in the Treuhandanstalt itself.

Sinn and Sinn (1991) suggest combining a giveaway to investors with a giveaway to the population at large.[17] The investor should be granted free of charge the equivalent in shares of his investment and job-guarantee plans for the firm to be privatized. All other shares of the firm should remain with the Treuhandanstalt. These Treuhandanstalt participations should be the basis of a distributive policy where vouchers are given to the east German population. After some time these vouchers could be exchanged for shares of the privatized firms.[18] Priority should be given to those savers who suffered from the 2:1 conversion of part of their savings and to those employees who recommend to their trade union the acceptance of a four-year general wage moratorium in which east German minimum wages would not increase more than their west German counterparts.

The Sinn-Sinn "participation model" combines giving away instead of selling, granting a participation to the Treuhandanstalt, reducing east German wage increases by employees' vouchers, giving general vouchers to east Germans, and helping east German savers. Let us recognize that there is no need to combine precisely these five basic elements.[19] A reader

[17]This proposal is aimed at shareholding companies. For other privatization cases, Sinn and Sinn suggest selling firms or other property at positive prices, but crediting the investor with the payment.

[18]In Sinn and Sinn (1991), p. 114, some alternative scenarios of distributive policies are suggested.

[19]In October 1991, the German union of metal workers' (IG Metall) proposal suggested, among other things, a "Treuhandanstalt property fund" which should hold a 25 percent participation—first, in the Treuhandanstalt, and, after privatization, in the privatized firms. Fifty percent of the shares of this Treuhandanstalt property fund should be distributed to the general public free of charge. (For the remaining 50 percent of the shares, forced sales to higher-income earners were proposed by IG Metall—certainly an element not contained in the Sinn-Sinn package.) See Institut der deutschen Wirtschaft, *Informationsdienst des Instituts der deutschen Wirtschaft*, No. 44 (1991).

accepting the argument in the preceding section would agree that the privatization policy of the Treuhandanstalt should not include general vouchers or the assumed entitlements of savers. Now for the wage policy, which should be linked to the employees' voucher part of the model. First, this policy rests on the assumption that trade unions agree to minimum wage increases that fall below those already negotiated for future years, at least in principle.[20] Second, the wage policy, which is part of the Sinn-Sinn model, requires fine tuning to move east German wages and employment along a path connecting the labor market equilibria before and after the transition of the east German economy. After excluding all these distributive features from the Sinn-Sinn proposal, let us look at the giveaways to investors and the participation of the Treuhandanstalt.

A giveaway policy does not require purchasing power by the recipients. This advantage still applies if a giveaway policy is combined with Treuhandanstalt participation. Such a policy attracts additional investors and relieves the strain on the capital market because investors need not borrow funds to pay for the purchase of the firm, but only for new investments. This allows some acceleration in the privatization process. However, one major advantage of a giveaway policy is lost if this policy is combined with Treuhandanstalt participation in the firm. To determine the extent of Treuhandanstalt participation, the value of the privatized firm must be computed to calculate the equivalent in shares of an investment and job-guarantee plan. Is a business plan of a potential buyer worth 22.17 percent of the shares of the firm or is it 24.23 percent? This determination of the precise extent of Treuhandanstalt participation is difficult and would reduce the speed of privatization.

There has always been some hesitation with respect to any form of partial privatization, since this may imply mixed and therefore unclear responsibilities and ongoing government interference.[21] Let us concentrate on the problem of ongoing government interference. In several of my own publications, I suggested partial privatization to guarantee just such continuing government influence.[22] However, my suggestions referred to the privatization of public utilities in Western economies, where the government would want to regulate the privatized firm and where a continued government influence should be both necessary and certain. Here, a minority participation provides the German Government with additional information that will be useful for regulation.[23] This argument fails to hold in the case of privatization of industrial firms

---

[20]Sinn and Sinn even suggest having this moratorium made retroactive to April 1, 1991 (their book appeared in October 1991).

[21]Of course, this argument does not hold if the Treuhandanstalt is privatized, as in Sinn and Sinn (1991), p. 114. However, in my opinion, we can safely discard this possibility.

[22]These are assembled in Bös (1991a), pp. 135–48 and pp. 219–84.

[23]The remaining shares may be sold at some later time without too much underpricing.

by the Treuhandanstalt.[24] Government interference in those cases refers to Treuhandanstalt activities to ensure that the firm stands by its investment and job-guarantee plans, and it may well imply further lobbying for jobs in the firm. This may deter potential investors. For this among other reasons, in the privatization of industrial firms, such ongoing Treuhandanstalt interference is undesirable.[25]

In view of these reservations, only a modified version of the Sinn-Sinn participation model can be recommended. The modifications refer to two points of criticism. First, the evaluation problem has to be overcome. I suggest that only two categories of Treuhandanstalt participation be introduced—a 25 percent participation and a 49 percent participation. It should not be too difficult to assign a particular business plan of an investor to one of these two categories. Second, continued government (Treuhandanstalt) interference must be excluded. I suggest that the Treuhandanstalt commit itself to a silent partnership in which Treuhandanstalt retains only nonvoting shares. The Treuhandanstalt must also make clear that the private owner will be at risk and that the owner will not be bailed out in case of bankruptcy. Such a commitment certainly is credible in the case of a 25 percent silent participation. I believe it should also work in the case of 49 percent.[26]

Given these two decisive modifications, the Sinn-Sinn participation model can be a recommendable policy. The silent participation could be used as a source of government revenue if the Treuhandanstalt shares are sold at some later time. Alternatively, the participation model could be readily combined with a general voucher system. The advantage of such a silent participation over the present Treuhandanstalt policy is evident: the giveaway is restricted to 75 percent or 51 percent, respectively, of the firm; the present Treuhandanstalt policy increasingly runs the risk of giving away 100 percent.

Wage Subsidies

There is much debate over the payment of wage subsidies to promote the rapid privatization of as many east German industrial firms as possible. This has received much interest because of the prestige of the

[24]This can theoretically be shown for a welfare-maximizing privatization policy. See Bös and Peters (1988) and Bös (1991a), pp. 247-49.
[25]Sales with credited payment, as suggested by Sinn and Sinn (1991) for Treuhandanstalt property other than shareholding companies, avoid Treuhandanstalt minority participation. However, payments finally due would go to the Treuhandanstalt, which then would use the funds to subsidize nonviable firms. This problem would then be met insofar as the funds would not be directed to the Treuhandanstalt, but to the population—for example, to savers, as suggested by Sinn and Sinn.
[26]At one time I thought a 75 percent silent participation of the Treuhandanstalt worth considering. However, I do not believe that in such a case the Treuhandanstalt could credibly commit itself to not bailing out the firm if it goes bankrupt.

Berkeley group which advocated this idea.[27] According to Akerlof and his co-authors, the collapse of the east German economy is due to a price-cost squeeze and to a shift of demand away from east German products. Akerlof's proposal concentrates on the former. The rapid increase in east German wages (with the goal of matching west German wages in a few years) has increased costs to an extent that makes most firms nonviable: at world market prices they could not cover their short-run average variable costs. However, a firm that is not viable cannot be sold by the Treuhand-anstalt. Akerlof and his co-authors calculate that only 8 percent of the east German industrial labor force is employed in viable firms as a result of the present price-cost squeeze.[28] They suggest reducing the short-run variable costs by paying wage subsidies to these firms. Subsidies of 50 (75) percent of total labor costs would imply that 37 (77) percent of the industrial labor force would work in viable firms.[29] Unfortunately, these figures show wage subsidies in too favorable a light; they are static, that is, first-year figures. If wage subsidies go on forever, and nothing else changes, these figures would be always correct. However, the figures should be lower, that is, fewer firms would be viable if, all things being equal, the subsidies decrease over time, which seems to be the only acceptable policy.[30]

The net costs of wage subsidies are lower than the gross costs for the following reasons. If a worker remains employed, the Government saves on unemployment benefits and receives taxes and social insurance contributions. For the first year of unemployment, some 79 percent of the employee's gross compensation is saved by a job-preserving wage subsidy.[31] Hence, the authors suggest subsidies up to 75 percent of total labor costs. In a perfect bidding for Treuhandanstalt-owned firms, the wage subsidies are fully capitalized in selling the firm and so pay for themselves.[32] At least part of this capitalization might also hold in practice.

Firms made viable by wage subsidies should be promptly sold by the Treuhandanstalt to the highest-bidding private investor. There is no need to sell firms to purchasers who propose the most appealing investment and job-preservation plans. Jobs are preserved through wage subsidies

---

[27]See Akerlof and others (1991). See also Begg and Portes (1991).

[28]The authors obtained a set of cost data, previously used for GDR planning, which they adjust to the present situation by (1) removing all profits, interest, and depreciation in excess of repairs necessary for current operation; and (2) taking into account changes in the tax structure, in the cost of imported intermediate inputs, and in wages. The resulting modified short-run average variable costs are then compared with the respective world market prices.

[29]See Akerlof and others (1991), p. 28.

[30]How many firms are viable in case of decreasing wage subsidies depends on the time schedule of subsidy reductions, on the discount rate applied by the investors, and on investors' expectations of the east German economic development.

[31]Akerlof and others (1991), p. 71. Gross compensation is gross wage plus employer's contribution to social insurance.

[32]Akerlof and others (1991), p. 72.

that correct for the distorted price of labor, keeping both unemployment and migration from east to west Germany low.[33]

The job-preserving bias of the Akerlof plan constitutes one of its weaknesses. Although wage subsidies are offered to all private industrial employment, so supporting both old and new jobs, the Akerlof proposal "risk[s] fossilizing the status quo in production and employment."[34] It is the declared intention of the Akerlof proposal to make artificially viable two thirds of the former GDR industry.[35] Market forces must be allowed to eliminate firms that stand to be abolished (even at the cost of higher unemployment and migration) because of the permanent shift of demand away from tradable east German goods. This requires restructuring the economy and establishing new firms.[36] Wage subsidies directed toward saving jobs in old firms are not the adequate instrument to apply to the transition from a planned to a market economy.

There are further serious objections against wage subsidies. The trade unions would push for higher wage increases[37] and would oppose the granting of such subsidies to profitable Western firms that invest in east Germany.[38] Some investments would be shifted to east Germany only to obtain wage subsidies.[39] Finally, the Akerlof plan would in all likelihood turn out to be more expensive than previously thought by its authors.[40]

The German labor market policy does not include a general wage-subsidy scheme of the kind advocated by Akerlof. However, wage subsidies are granted indirectly to all firms still under Treuhandanstalt ownership because any deficits of these firms are paid by the Treuhandanstalt.[41] If Treuhandanstalt privatization and liquidation policies are slow, these wage subsidies could go on for quite a while. To reduce the official figures of unemployment, wages—at a reduced rate—are paid to employees who work short time, which is sometimes a euphemism for working

---

[33] Surveys conducted by Akerlof and others showed that unemployment is the main reason for migration to the West. See Akerlof and others (1991), pp. 45-55.

[34] Dornbusch (1991), p. 89.

[35] See Akerlof and others (1991), p. 27: firms that employ 77 percent of the industrial work force are viable if wage subsidies of 75 percent are granted—the alternative favored by the authors. In the absence of wage subsidies, only 8 percent work in viable firms.

[36] If it were a temporary shift only, wage subsidies would perhaps be an adequate instrument (see Guitian (1991), p. 93).

[37] Akerlof and others (1991) suggest a "self-eliminating flexible employment bonus program" where wage subsidies are inversely linked to wage increases. The authors claim that "in simple maximizing models of union behavior, the . . . plan usually makes wages sticky when unemployment exists" (p. 81). It may be doubted that such a program would work in practice (see Guitian (1991), pp. 97-98).

[38] This argument was decisive for the retraction of a German trade unions' plan for east German wage subsidies. See Akerlof and others (1991), p. 72.

[39] This might even require some subsidization of west German, for example, west Berlin firms—see Akerlof and others (1991), pp. 84-85.

[40] See Guitian (1991), pp. 97-98.

[41] There are proposals that the Government should set up enterprises that are considered "employment companies." These proposals should be rejected. If there is any need for new firms, private entrepreneurs should enter the market.

zero time. In east Germany, this short-time work schedule was applied until the end of 1991. This was particularly important for nonviable Treuhandanstalt firms. The payment of short-time benefits is not contingent on training employees, although employers are supposed to make it possible for workers to undergo vocational training and although higher short-time benefits are paid to workers during retraining.

As these special short-time provisions for east Germany expire, other measures of the German Employment Promotion Law (Arbeitsmarkt-förderungsgesetz) will become more important.[42] First, the Government pays a maintenance allowance during times of occupational retraining (and east Germans qualify more easily than west Germans for such courses). The Government also pays the costs of the training course. Second, there are two schemes of wage subsidies: one to allow the occupational integration of the unemployed (40–50 percent[43] of local wage paid up to six months; in exceptional cases, up to two years), and another to promote additional jobs (grants of 50–100 percent of the wages for a maximum of one year; in exceptional cases, up to three years).

The wage subsidies of the Employment Promotion Law are short-run, marginal subsidies; they are not applicable to all employees. In contrast to the Akerlof proposal of general, not necessarily short-run, wage subsidies, they are much better shaped for the recovering east German economy. The transition from short-time labor pay to the wage subsidies of the Employment Promotion Law moves from a policy that subsidizes workers "who would be fired in the absence [of the subsidy]" to one that subsidizes those "who would not be hired in the absence [thereof]."[44] This is a consistent policy change: the first policy aims at mitigating the collapse of the economy, the second at promoting the recovery. If early 1992 began the recovery of the east German economy, the swing from one type of policy to the other will have been timed correctly.

The policy of retraining—promoting human capital—should be intensified to increase labor productivity to catch up with higher wages. Labor productivity will, of course, also increase because more capital of recent vintage will be invested in east Germany. The scale effect of capital incentives (investment premiums, tax credits, accelerated depreciation) makes them an alternative to wage subsidies, implying a tendency toward increased employment. Capital subsidies increase the relative price of labor, however, which in the present situation of very high east German wages leads to an even more extensive substitution of labor by capital, implying overly capital-intensive industries[45] and a tendency toward reduced employment. This is an imminent danger in east Germany, since

---

[42]An overview of these measures is given in Germany, Federal Ministry of Economics (1991), pp. 94–100.

[43]In special cases, 50–70 percent.

[44]See Kopits (1978), p. 497.

[45]See Sinn and Sinn (1991), pp. 165–70.

generous capital subsidies have been provided for investment in east Germany. The Government and trade unions hope that eventually the scale effect of capital subsidies will outweigh the substitution effect, thus solving the employment problem in spite of the high wages. This hope is overly optimistic.

Future German economic policy will require a delicate balance between the retraining schemes and the wage subsidies against the capital subsidies. Unfortunately, the trade union policy of high minimum wages makes achieving this balance even more complicated. I share the opinion of a 1991 report of the Federal Government's commission on deregulation, which recommends relaxing the strict German minimum wage regulations if too-high minimum wages are coupled with long-term unemployment.[46]

Restructuring

Restructuring is the second priority in the threefold catalogue of Treuhandanstalt strategies. Restructuring—preparing an industrial firm for privatization—includes the following activities.

- The breakup of large conglomerates, the so-called Kombinate. The Treuhandanstalt has been active in this.
- The dismissal of former managers who are politically incriminated or lacking in managerial skills. By the end of June 1991, the Treuhandanstalt had replaced over half of its force of enterprise managers; approximately 20 percent of the new managers came from west Germany.
- The reduction in the labor force; here the Treuhandanstalt has acted cautiously.
- The development of new investments to render the firms more attractive to private purchasers; here, the Treuhandanstalt has not accomplished much to date.

The following discussion refers in particular to active firm management by the Treuhandanstalt, which entails some degree of direct government investment, and job planning.

A theoretical view argues that restructuring by the Treuhandanstalt is futile and that the Treuhandanstalt should only privatize or liquidate. If a firm is viable after restructuring,[47] there is some price at which it can be

---

[46]If such relaxations became possible, it should be made clear that the Treuhandanstalt also applies them. Otherwise, privatized firms offering lower wages would not be competitive with Treuhandanstalt firms, which can pay higher wages because their deficit is always covered. See Sinn and Sinn (1991), p. 189.

[47]This definition of viability differs from Akerlof's. Viability after restructuring is given if the present value of revenues from sales minus the present value of costs, including costs of restructuring, is positive. In this definition, revenues and costs are as calculated by the private investor, not by the Treuhandanstalt.

sold; restructuring can be executed by the private purchaser. According to this view private purchasers are generally more competent at restructuring than the Treuhandanstalt, since they are directly interested in the value of the firm and well informed on both the prospective chances of the firm and its internal organization. The Treuhandanstalt faces a principal-agent problem. Its knowledge typically comes from the firm to be restructured, whose managers and employees have vested interests and will not inform the Treuhandanstalt as forthrightly as required.[48]

However, this theoretical argument stresses all the informational problems of the Treuhandanstalt and places private investors in a first-best world of perfect information and incentives. There are some arguments in favor of Treuhandanstalt restructuring. First, the very definition of viability after restructuring by a private investor excludes taking account of externalities, productivity spillovers, and so on. From a general economic point of view, explicit consideration of these effects may be worthwhile and restructuring by the Treuhandanstalt would be the appropriate consequence. Second, the Treuhandanstalt can pool the risks of restructuring many firms, including environmental damage to be repaid, property claims by previous owners, and unexpected demand developments. The Treuhandanstalt can wait until the necessary infrastructure has been set up and the administration has become reliable. Third, the Treuhandanstalt may enjoy economies of scale and of scope in restructuring. The more firms are restructured, the more experience is acquired. Fourth, Western private investors are better informed on how to sell in Western markets and on the organizational aspects of a firm to be privatized. However, the Treuhandanstalt might possess informational advantage with respect to the east German scene[49] concerning the treatment of east German employees, and so on. Fifth, the Treuhandanstalt may have political advantages in restructuring. As a government agency, it has direct channels to other government agencies and could, for example, arrange better coordination between the restructuring of firms and setting up of infrastructure. Treuhandanstalt could exert political pressure to modify laws that inhibit the restructuring of firms.

These arguments look convincing from the point of view of second-best theory. One could easily think of theoretical models in which these advantages of the Treuhandanstalt more than outweigh its principal-agent relationship with the firm to be privatized. However, the second-best economic theories miss the point, which is eminently political. I do not think that a large state-owned holding company is a good choice for restructuring. The second-best arguments restore the very theories of

---

[48]This is the predominant opinion in Germany. See Sachverständigenrat (1991) and Beirat of the Bundeswirtschaftsministerium (1991). See also Sinn and Sinn (1991), pp. 85–86.
[49]See Möschel (1991).

planning which we want to eliminate.[50] A Treuhandanstalt in full command of restructuring would not act according to a second-best model. Under political pressure, the Treuhandanstalt would try to preserve firms that should be liquidated. Restructuring is often used as a label to disguise subsidization of nonviable firms. In particular, the Treuhandanstalt would try to preserve jobs because this is the Government's mandate.

For these political reasons, I think that restructuring should be removed from the responsibilities of the Treuhandanstalt. Its activities should be reduced to privatization or liquidation. If the Treuhandanstalt is only able to sell around 4,000 firms a year, some firms known to be viable will have to wait another year or more. Restructuring in such a framework would mean keeping these firms afloat until they are privatized.

Liquidation

If privatization proves impossible, the Treuhandanstalt will have to liquidate the firm.[51] In spite of early closure of some prestigious firms, such as Interflug and Wartburg, the Treuhandanstalt is generally cautious in closing down firms. Two reasons for this policy are job preservation and the need to obtain additional information on the viability of east German firms.

By the end of, say, 1993, the picture will be much gloomier than at the end of 1991. In 1991 the easier privatizations had taken place, the pace of privatization had slowed. By the end of 1993 the Treuhandanstalt will own only firms that private investors are unwilling to take over. Shipyards and steel, coal, and chemical industries will constitute the core of the doomed remnants of the former GDR economy.

The Treuhandanstalt is unlikely to liquidate all those firms by January 1, 1994. I am afraid that by subsidizing such firms for the next ten or so years, the mistakes of the Bremen shipyards or the Saarland coal mines will be repeated.[52] Of course, the logical decision for the Treuhandanstalt is to liquidate those firms that have not been sold by, say, the end of 1993. How can we make sure that such a policy is actually applied? Unemployment in east Germany will be high in December 1993, even without closure of all the remaining Treuhandanstalt firms, and the Federal Gov-

---

[50]The October 1991 reform proposal of the union of the metal workers (IG Metall) speaks of "volkswirtschaftliche Sanierungsfähigkeit" (restructuring which is justified from a general economic point of view, that is, not necessarily profitable for a private investor).

[51]In the United States the huge government bailout of the savings and loan industry led to a problem similar to the Treuhandanstalt liquidation. The Federal Deposit Insurance Corporation and its affiliate agency, the Resolution Trust Corporation, are in charge of liquidating many government-owned banks and savings and loan institutions. The Resolution Trust Corporation is scheduled to end in 1996. Unfortunately, such a clear end-date has not been set for the Treuhandanstalt liquidation activities.

[52]See Streit (1991), pp. 175–76. The same mistakes were made in other countries; the IRI in Italy is an example.

ernment will be eager to capture votes for the end-of-1994 election of the Bundestag. Given these conditions, the Treuhandanstalt will be under pressure not to liquidate too many firms.

At that stage, the Treuhandanstalt will have become a liability. What can be done to abolish it by then? Let us consider some options.

(1) Incentive wages for employees of the Treuhandanstalt could depend on the number of both privatized and liquidated firms; no incentive would be given for restructuring. This scheme should be introduced now, when the number of firms to be privatized is still high and the proposed incentive wage is a politically attractive way to reward Treuhandanstalt employees for every case ultimately settled. Over time, this would become a scheme that rewards staff for liquidation. Then the scheme will accelerate the liquidation of nonviable firms and constitute a trade-off for Treuhandanstalt employees—if they liquidate fast, they get the bonus earlier, but lose their basic income earlier. In the absence of an incentive wage, only the latter would hold and employees might postpone liquidations to keep their jobs. The rewards and incentives could be formulated to fully compensate employees for the earlier loss of basic income.

The incentive wage should depend on the number of liquidated firms, not on the number of employees or on the monetary value of the firms. The number of employees should not be a factor since it would give the Treuhandanstalt an incentive to keep as many employees as possible just before privatization or liquidation. The value of the firm cannot serve as a basis for an incentive payment because, in case of liquidation, it is nil or negative or impossible to determine. The number of firms is a neutral indicator, if the figures of mid-1991 are taken, perhaps allowing large conglomerates to count as more than one firm. The strategic breakup of firms would then be avoided. There could still be some moral hazard because the incentive scheme would promote the privatization and liquidation of smaller, easy-to-handle firms, delaying the privatization and liquidation of larger firms whose cases would be complicated to settle. If this becomes a problem, the incentive wages should be related to weighted numbers of firms, the weights depending on the size of the firms.

(2) Another option would be to lower the Treuhandanstalt borrowing limit. Limits that continually decrease over time should be published now. The decreasing limits should be set to equal zero by the year 2000, thus signaling the Government's determination to end Treuhandanstalt activities by that time. It could be questioned whether the Government can credibly commit itself to such a policy of decreasing the financial means of the Treuhandanstalt, in particular since the credibility of the present Government has severely suffered from broken promises, such as the introduction of an income-tax surcharge in spite of earlier promises that the German unification would take place without tax increases. The financial means to be distributed by the "fund on German unity" were originally defined to decrease from 1991 to 1994. However, these

financial means have been increased, so as to achieve a nondecreasing pay schedule.[53] Would not this tend to discredit an announced intent to decrease the financial means of the Treuhandanstalt? However, even then the original law on decreasing Treuhandanstalt finances would signal the Government's intention not to let the Treuhandanstalt go on forever, and would present a political barrier against easy increases in Treuhandanstalt finances.[54]

(3) Liquidations will be more readily accepted by the east German population if the laid-off employees are quickly re-employed. If new firms are set up near the firms to be closed, there would be less opposition to such closures (even if high wages and low productivity would prevent re-employment of all employees of a liquidated enterprise). However, the Treuhandanstalt cannot be requested to restructure the entire economy. It is far beyond its restructuring strategy to take primary responsibility for the establishment of new firms.

Much remains to be done by the federal and state governments to provide opportunities for the private establishment of new firms,[55] for instance:

- Improving the infrastructure;
- Improving the public administration;
- More rapid processing of property right claims;
- Increasing bank flexibility for granting loans to potential new entrepreneurs;
- Training east German managers to promote the entrepreneurial spirit;
- Retraining east German employees to stimulate occupational changes;
- Relaxing minimum wage provisions; and
- Diluting labor market rigidities.[56]

Conclusion

The present policy of the Treuhandanstalt consists of privatization by low-price sales or giveaways of industrial firms to those investors who present the best investment pledges and job guarantees. This policy has been successful in 1990–91: privatization of 2,500 industrial firms in the

---

[53] See Institut der deutschen Wirtschaft, *Informationsdienst des Instituts der deutschen Wirtschaft*, No. 43 (1991).

[54] At an informal meeting some months ago, I proposed that the Treuhandanstalt should set a date, say, January 1, 1994, at which time it will give away the remaining nonprivatized firms to the firms' managers (including partial employee participation). However, I now believe that moral hazard makes this a bad proposal.

[55] See Bös (1991b).

[56] See Bös (1991b), p. 16.

first six months of 1991 is more than the former Czechoslovakia or Poland achieved during the same period. However, this paper argues that the extent of giving away national property could be reduced by applying a modified version of the Sinn-Sinn participation model, making the Treuhandanstalt a silent partner of the private investors. The Akerlof proposal of a general scheme of wage subsidies would lead to undesirable consequences; the existing German system of retraining and wage-subsidy schedules seems preferable.

By the end of 1993, the Treuhandanstalt may have degenerated into a government-financed subsidization trust to keep alive nonviable firms. As a consequence, I argue against restructuring by the Treuhandanstalt and propose setting decreasing limits on Treuhandanstalt finances for the years following 1994, and publishing these limits now. The decreasing financial inflow will force the Treuhandanstalt to close firms, and will signal the commitment of the Government to liquidate the Treuhandanstalt itself by, say, the year 2000.

References

Akerlof, George A., Andrew K. Rose, Janet L. Yellen, and Helga Hessenius, "East Germany in from the Cold: The Economic Aftermath of Currency Union," *Brookings Papers on Economic Activity*, Brookings Institution, Vol. 1 (1991), pp. 1–105.

Begg, David, and Richard Portes, "There Is a Better Way to Help Germany's New Länder Catch Up," *International Herald Tribune* (June 19, 1991).

Beirat of the Bundeswirtschaftsministerium, "Probleme der Privatisierung in den neuen Bundesländern," *Studienreihe*, Bundesministerium für Wirtschaft (Bonn), Vol. 73 (1991).

Blanchard, Olivier, Rudiger Dornbusch, Paul Krugman, Richard Layard, and Lawrence Summers, *Reform in Eastern Europe* (Cambridge, Massachusetts: MIT Press, 1991).

Borensztein, Eduardo, and Manmohan S. Kumar, "Proposals for Privatization in Eastern Europe," *Staff Papers*, International Monetary Fund, Vol. 38 (June 1991), pp. 300–26.

Bös, Dieter (1991a), *Privatization: A Theoretical Treatment* (Oxford: Oxford University Press, 1991).

———— (1991b), "Privatization and the Transition from Planned to Market Economies: Some Thoughts About Germany 1991," *Annals of Public and Cooperative Economics* (Liège), Vol. 62 (1991), pp. 183–94.

————, and Wolfgang Peters, "Privatization, Internal Control, and Internal Regulation," *Journal of Public Economics*, Vol. 36, No. 2 (July 1988), pp. 231–58.

Breuel, Birgit, "Der Auftrag der Treuhandanstalt," *Wirtschaftsdienst* (Hamburg), Vol. 71, No. 4 (1991).

Dornbusch, Rudiger, "Comments and Discussion," *Brookings Papers on Economic Activity*, Brookings Institution, Vol. 1 (1991), pp. 88-92.

Estrin, Saul, "Privatization in Central and Eastern Europe: What Lessons Can Be Learnt for Western Experience?" *Annals of Public and Cooperative Economics* (Liège), Vol. 62 (1991), pp. 159-82.

Frydman, Roman, and Andrzej Rapaczynski, "Markets and Institutions in Large-Scale Privatization: An Approach to Economic and Social Transformation in Eastern Europe," in *Reforming Central and Eastern European Economies: Initial Results and Challenges*, ed. by Vittorio Corbo, Fabrizio Coricelli, and Jan Bossak (Washington: World Bank, 1991).

Germany, Federal Ministry of Economics, *Economic Assistance in the New German Länder* (Bonn), May 1991.

Guitian, Manuel, "Comments and Discussion," *Brookings Papers on Economic Activity*, Brookings Institution, Vol. 1 (1991), pp. 92-98.

Hemming, Richard, "Privatization of State Enterprises," in *Fiscal Policies in Economies in Transition*, ed. by Vito Tanzi (Washington: International Monetary Fund, 1992).

Institut der deutschen Wirtschaft, *Informationsdienst des Instituts der deutschen Wirtschaft* (Cologne), Nos. 26, 37, 43, and 44 (1991).

Kopits, George F., "Wage Subsidies and Employment: An Analysis of the French Experience," *Staff Papers*, International Monetary Fund, Vol. 25 (September 1978), pp. 494-527.

———, "Fiscal Reform in European Economies in Transition," IMF Working Paper No. 91/43 (Washington: International Monetary Fund, April 1991).

Lipschitz, Leslie, and Donogh McDonald, eds., *German Unification: Economic Issues*, IMF Occasional Paper No. 75 (Washington: International Monetary Fund, 1990).

Lipton, David, and Jeffrey Sachs, "Privatization in Eastern Europe: The Case of Poland," *Brookings Papers on Economic Activity*, Brookings Institution, Vol. 2 (1990), pp. 293-341.

Möschel, Wernhard, "Ein Staatskonzern im Angebot," *Frankfurter Allgemeine Zeitung* (Frankfurt), January 26, 1991.

Poland, Ministry of Ownership Changes, *Mass Privatisation: Proposed Programme* (Warsaw), June 1991.

Sachverständigenrat, *Zur Unterstützung der Wirtschaftsreform in der DDR: Voraussetzungen und Möglichkeiten*, Sondergutachten (Wiesbaden), January 20, 1990.

———, *Marktwirtschaftlichen Kurs halten: Zur Wirtschaftspolitik für die neuen Bundesländer*, Sondergutachten (Wiesbaden), April 13, 1991.

Schmieding, Holger, and Michael J. Koop, *Privatisierung in Mittel- und Osteuropa: Konzepte für den Hindernislauf zur Marktwirtschaft*, Kiel Discussion Papers, No. 165 (Kiel: Institute of World Economics, February 1991).

Siebert, Horst, *The Economic Integration of Germany*, Kiel Discussion Papers, No. 160 (Kiel: Institute of World Economics, 1990).

Sinn, Gerlinde, and Hans-Werner Sinn, *Kaltstart: Volkswirtschaftliche Aspekte der deutschen Vereinigung* (Tübingen: J.C.B. Mohr, 1991).

Sinn, Hans-Werner, *Macroeconomic Aspects of German Unification*, NBER Working Paper No. 3596 (Cambridge, Massachusetts: National Bureau of Economic Research, 1991).

Streit, Manfred E., "Ordnungspolitische Defizite der deutschen Vereinigung," *Wirtschaftsdienst* (Hamburg), Vol. 71, No. 4 (1991).

Treuhandanstalt, *Privatisierung* (Berlin, July 1991).

CHAPTER 12

Privatization: Trade-Offs, Experience, and Policy Lessons from Eastern European Countries

Gerd Schwartz

Just as state-owned enterprises lie at the heart of planned economies, privately owned enterprises lie at the heart of market economies, and privatization is central to the transition from plan to market. While for market economies the fundamental argument for privatization is that it improves allocative and productive efficiency (Hemming and Miranda (1991)), for economies in transition three other arguments have been suggested: creating a market economy, establishing a political system based on private property rights and individual freedoms, and boosting state revenue (Dhanji and Milanovic (1990)). While privatization and efficiency gains are usually thought to go hand in hand, evidence from recent large-scale privatizations in Eastern Europe indicates that efficiency gains may have to be obtained particularly at the expense of privatization proceeds (Schwartz and Silva Lopes (1993)).

Given vastly overextended public sectors, both goals and methods of privatization in economies in transition are fundamentally different from those in market economies. While many enterprises may remain state owned for a while, several economies in transition, notably some of the early reformers in Eastern Europe, have already achieved significant progress in privatizing their economies. In reviewing this experience, this chapter outlines some fundamental problems encountered in large-scale privatizations, discusses unresolved policy choices, and draws preliminary conclusions regarding the desirable properties of privatization schemes for economies in transition. Like the other chapters in this volume, it presents a case study, but unlike the others it does not primarily focus on fiscal issues. However, privatization policies have important fiscal implications, which arise not so much from the direct budgetary impact of asset transfers, but more from the indirect macroeconomic consequences of the selected speed and scope of privatization (Hemming (1992)). Given that many state enterprises have grown used to soft budget constraints, privatization has become an important mechanism for consol-

Gerd Schwartz is an Economist in the Fiscal Affairs Department. He gratefully acknowledges helpful comments and suggestions by Tessa van der Willigen, Mark Lutz, and Mark Stone.

idating the financial discipline imposed on the state enterprise sector during stabilization and transformation.

After examining the general trade-offs encountered by all policymakers, this chapter reviews the general experience with privatization in several Eastern European countries. It concentrates on issues that affect the quality of privatization schemes, such as the role of privatization in the process of transition, the selection of privatization goals and tools, property rights and corporate control, bank restructuring, and the problem of large enterprises. Following this discussion, the final section offers some preliminary conclusions regarding the desirable properties of privatization schemes for economies in transition.

Constraints and Trade-Offs

It has been argued that policymakers, faced with having to initiate large-scale privatizations, typically tend to define privatization policy objectives broadly (Maurer and others (1991)), thereby running the risk of creating a set of mutually inconsistent policies. This section argues that these broadly defined objectives frequently obscure the trade-offs all policymakers face.

The definition of a "good" privatization scheme strongly depends on a country's specific economic, political, and social conditions; the policymaker's objective function has to be adjusted according to the particular circumstances of each country. With privatization schemes having been promoted in countries with public sectors of very different size (Table 1), it has become clear that there can be no standard recipe for privatization. As a result, the experience of one country may be of only limited use in another country with a state-owned enterprise sector that is significantly different in size and scope.

Still, independent of a country's particular circumstances, its policymakers are likely to have objective functions that comprise a fairly large number of general privatization objectives. The declared goals of selected Eastern European privatization schemes, shown in Table 2, may be considered typical. In Poland, for example, following an initial criticism that the Government's privatization program was devoid of any clearly identifiable goals (Gruszecki and Winiecki (1991)), the Ministry of Privatization put forward eight specific privatization objectives (Table 2). A proliferation of goals naturally leads to the question of mutual compatibility.

In general, typical policymakers may initially want to (1) privatize the economy in the shortest possible time, (2) maximize privatization proceeds, (3) select the "right" buyers, (4) safeguard employment, and (5) obtain investment guarantees. It is a well-known argument that in order to meet all five objectives—speed, proceeds, ownership, employment, and new investment—the number of independent policy tools has to equal the number of goals. If this is not the case, trade-offs may be

Table 1. Share of State Sector in Selected Economies

	Percent of Value Added	Percent of Employment
Eastern Europe		
Czechoslovakia (1986)	97.0	. . .
East Germany (1982)	96.5	94.2
Soviet Union (1985)	96.0	. . .
Bulgaria (1990)	92.0	. . .
Poland (1985)	81.7	71.5
Hungary (1984)	65.2	69.9
OECD economies[1]		
France (1982)	16.5	14.6
Austria (1978–79)	14.5	13.0
Italy (1982)	14.0	15.0
Turkey (1985)	11.2	20.0
West Germany (1982)	10.7	7.8
United Kingdom (1983)	10.7	7.0
Portugal (1976)	9.7	. . .
Denmark (1974)	6.3	5.0
Greece (1979)	6.1	. . .
Spain (1979)	4.1	. . .
Netherlands (1971–73)	3.6	8.0
United States (1983)	1.3	1.8
Sweden (early 1980s)	. . .	10.6
Finland (early 1980s)	. . .	10.0
Norway (early 1980s)	. . .	6.0
Other economies		
China (1984)	73.6	. . .
Venezuela (1978–80)	27.5	. . .
Tunisia (1978–79)	25.4	. . .
Malawi (1984)	25.0	8.0
Malaysia (1985–88)	25.0	. . .
Singapore (1983)	25.0	. . .
Jamaica (1984)	21.0	11.0
Sri Lanka (1988)	20.0	40.0
Trinidad and Tobago (1985)	16.0	13.0
Kenya (1984)	15.0	15.0
Bolivia (1974–77)	12.1	. . .
India (1978)	10.3	6.0
Papua New Guinea (1989)	10.0	. . .
Niger (1980s)	10.0	. . .
Korea (1981–83)	9.0	7.0
Pakistan (1974–75)	6.0	2.8
Paraguay (1978–80)	3.1	. . .

Sources: Milanovic (1989); Adam and others (1992); and data provided by the World Bank.

[1] Excludes government services, but includes state-owned enterprises in commercial activities.

Table 2. Typical Goals of Privatization Programs[1]

Former Czechoslovakia[2]
The aims of the privatization program are both political and economic. Among the political aims are changes in the social structure. The economic aim of privatization is to increase the ability of the economy to adapt to external conditions.

Germany[3]
The German privatization program has three primary objectives:
  (1) Restructuring viable enterprises in order to make them competitive under market conditions.
  (2) Privatizing enterprises.
  (3) Promoting de-monopolization in order to provide eastern Germany with an efficient market structure.

Hungary[4]
The principal aim of the Hungarian privatization scheme is to create a real market economy. It is the Government's objective to reduce the share of state-owned enterprises in the sphere of industry, trade, banking, and other economic activities from 90 percent to 30–40 percent in a few years.

Poland[5]
The Polish privatization program is based on the following objectives:
  (1) Move the economy from a centrally planned system to a competitive market system which would encourage the creation of a profitable private sector.
  (2) Improve the performance of enterprises through a more efficient use of labor, capital, and management skills.
  (3) Prevent possible distortions of the privatization process, such as the sale of state assets to foreign investors at unduly low prices.
  (4) Reduce the size of the public sector and the burden on the public budget and administration.
  (5) Generate funds from the sale of enterprises or their shares.
  (6) Ensure a wide diffusion of ownership of privatized assets.
  (7) Provide an effective system of corporate governance.
  (8) Commence the program of exchanging the country's external debt into equity of privatized enterprises. The privatization program will transform Poland's ownership structure to resemble that of Western Europe within five years, with approximately half the state-owned assets to be transferred into private hands within the first three years.

[1] The goals listed here do not necessarily represent the current policy objectives of the various privatization agencies.
[2] Czechoslovakia, Ministry of Finance (1991).
[3] Maurer and others (1991).
[4] Hungary, State Property Agency (1991).
[5] Poland, Ministry of Privatization (1991b).

inevitable, and they may occur in different ways. For example, when it is decided to privatize an economy within the shortest possible time, any constraint imposed on the other four variables will tend to slow down the process of privatization. Conceptually, it may be useful to think of privatization policies as constrained optimization processes, where one variable is optimized subject to constraints on all other variables. This implies that a government that wants to pursue more than one policy objective at the same time may have to group state-owned enterprises, and define separate policy goals and policy constraints for each group of enterprises to be privatized.

Given multiple and not necessarily independent goals, it is no surprise that actual privatization schemes are usually multidimensional and operate with multiple privatization tools (Table 3) that are separately applied to individual subgroups of enterprises. Specific privatization tools are often closely related to specific privatization objectives. For example, mass privatization schemes, designed to transfer ownership rights of a large number of state-owned enterprises to the population at large, can easily be associated with speed objectives. Speed being dominant, constraints on proceeds, ownership, employment, and investment will have to be set carefully to avoid jeopardizing the main objective. Similar conclusions hold for other privatization tools, such as one-by-one asset auctions, which are probably most appropriate when policymakers wish to maximize privatization proceeds, or special employee or management buy-out or leasing schemes, which target specific groups of potential buyers.

Experience with Privatization

Ever since the rapid demise of socialism, the new governments of Eastern Europe have been busy transforming their economies into market-based economies. Fischer (1991) has argued that advice on how to privatize Eastern Europe has rapidly converged on a standard approach: small firms should be privatized fast; larger firms should be corporatized quickly, put under the direction of independent corporate boards, and their shares should be distributed to some combination of current workers, current management, mutual funds, holding companies, banks, insurance companies, pension funds, citizens, and the government. But even though the issues addressed by the various existing privatization schemes necessarily show a number of important commonalities, privatization policies (and successes) differ significantly across Eastern Europe. Drawing upon the privatization experience of selected Eastern European countries, this section discusses five aspects of privatization policies with an important bearing on the eventual success or failure of privatization schemes: (1) the role of privatization in the process of transition, (2) the selection of privatization goals and tools, (3) property rights and corporate control, (4) banking sector reform, and (5) the problem of large enterprises.

Privatization in Economies in Transition

Across Eastern Europe, privatization is commonly viewed as a prime mover of transition from plan to market. Still, as Hare and Grosfeld (1991) have argued, the virtual absence of well-established and functioning financial markets and the lack of an established and well-understood legal and regulatory framework require great care in determining the role of privatization and its place in the sequence of transition. In spring 1992, some countries, such as Bulgaria and Romania, were still in the early stages of setting up a fully defined privatization scheme, while others, notably the former Czechoslovakia, Hungary, and Poland, appeared to have their basic systems in place, even though changes, refinements, and amendments were frequently found to be necessary.

Initially, the discussion of the role of privatization focused on the speed of transition and privatization; it was far from clear whether privatization should lead, accompany, or follow the process of transition. Proponents of slow privatization put forward three main arguments. First, macroeconomic stabilization, domestic price liberalization, and current account convertibility have to precede privatization because efficient decisions can only be made on the basis of correct relative prices. Second, the introduction of competition policies and current account convertibility has to precede privatization to prevent monopoly profits. Third, the introduction of modern tax systems and accounting procedures, and reforms of financial and capital markets have to precede privatization to allow for proper enterprise valuation (Keating and Hoffman (1991)). In contrast, proponents of fast privatization pointed toward the broader macroeconomic consequences of continuing to burden the economy with a large and inefficient state enterprise sector for decades to come (Hemming (1992)).

It is widely accepted now that the transition from plan to market and the urgently needed improvements in enterprise efficiency are unlikely to occur without extensive and rapid privatization (Hemming (1992)). This view is reflected in the mass privatization programs set up or proposed in countries such as Poland, Romania, and the former Czechoslovakia, which was the first country to advance mass privatization to an operational stage, when the shares of over 1,400 state enterprises went on offer to the public in mid-May 1992. Poland, the first country to embark on a comprehensive approach to macroeconomic reform, has mostly been experimenting with one-by-one privatizations that involve valuations, prospectuses, subscriptions, and underwritings, but, after experiencing very slow progress, decided to broaden the approach in summer 1990 (Gruszecki and Winiecki (1991)).[1] However, the mass privatization program currently envisaged will only comprise a maximum of 400–600 enterprises, the main selection criterion being that they are bigger and in better financial shape than the average Polish enterprise.

In general, the rapid progress achieved in devising mass privatization schemes that allow rapid divestiture of state assets while delaying the

---

[1]See C. Wellisz (1991) for a detailed account of the problems of enterprise valuation experienced in Poland.

Table 3. Privatization Tools

Bulgaria

Restitution of agricultural land, small shops, some industrial property, and residential properties.

Small enterprise privatization involving the auctioning of small shops and gasoline stations.

One-by-one privatization using a multi-track approach that includes public offering, public auction of shares, publicly invited tender, and publicized private placement. Shareholding schemes allow for some minority shareholding by employees (who can purchase nonvoting shares at a discount), and establishing of mutual funds. Privatization is preceded by commercialization.

Former Czechoslovakia

Restitution of land and of commercial and noncommercial properties.

Small enterprise privatization in the form of auctioning or leasing small business units with priority being given to domestic investors.

Large enterprise privatization in the form of:
• Direct sales to foreign or domestic investors.
• Mass privatization with no provision for minority shareholding by employees is carried out via vouchers and competing investment funds.

Germany

Restitution of land and of commercial and noncommercial property.

One-by-one privatization via trade sales, in whole or in parts, to domestic and foreign buyers, but also via management buy-outs, management buy-ins, and worker buy-outs. Simplified privatization rules for small enterprises.

Hungary

Restitution of agricultural land; compensation for nonagricultural property given in the form of partial compensation via securities.

Small enterprise privatization via direct sale to domestic individuals of selected small commercial units, mostly in retail trade, services, and tourism.

One-by-one privatization, alternatively through:
• Public share offering or trade sales to domestic or foreign investors of selected medium to large enterprises; the program is initiated by the privatization agency which brings companies to the market simultaneously in small groups of 20 to 40.
• Self-privatization in the form of management- or worker-initiated privatization proposals that are supervised by the privatization agency; this may involve management buy-outs, management buy-ins, or worker buy-outs, or trade sales to foreign or domestic investors.
• Investor-initiated privatization, supervised by the privatization agency.

Poland

Small enterprise privatization involving the direct sale to domestic buyers of small commercial properties, mostly in retail trade, services, and tourism.

Commercialization path: after being transformed into a joint-stock or limited-liability company wholly owned by the state treasury, enterprises may be privatized in one of the following ways:
• One-by-one capital privatization in the form of public share offering or trade sale to domestic or foreign investors.
• Mass privatization with a provision for employees to become minority shareholders, but with details still to be defined.
• Sectoral privatization primarily as a support for decision making, but also as a way to "package" weaker companies with stronger ones.
• Privatization with restructuring to assist small to medium-sized state-owned enterprises to prepare for eventual privatization.

Table 3 *(concluded)*

Liquidation path: after being liquidated as a legal entity (small to medium size) enterprises are either sold or leased. This may involve:
- Sale, in whole or in parts, in the form of management buy-outs or worker buy-outs, purchase by a joint venture, or direct purchase by domestic or foreign investors.
- Leasing, in whole or in parts, but typically in the form of an installment sale to the employees of the former state-owned enterprise, where employees pay a leasing fee until the company is paid for in full.
- Restitution still to be decided.

Romania
Small enterprise privatization via leasing, management contract offers, or sale to domestic buyers of up to 75 percent of the total asset value of small commercial units, mostly in retail trade, services, and tourism.
Early privatization of 30 commercial enterprises in good financial condition.
Mass privatization with no provision for minority shareholding by employees.
Privatization of land: establishing a land reform program that is to privatize about 80 percent of all agricultural lands.

Source: Information provided by the privatization agencies.

question of asset valuation significantly strengthened arguments in favor of speedy and comprehensive privatization. In addition, with all Eastern European countries implementing bold macroeconomic reform and stabilization policies, arguments for delaying comprehensive privatization were further weakened.

Privatization Goals and Tools

Having broad policy objectives, and recognizing a general need to match the number of goals with the number of independent policy tools, policymakers in most Eastern European countries have decided to apply separate policy tools to separate subsets of state-owned enterprises. Accordingly, new owners are carefully selected for some enterprises, prices are maximized for others, a strict timeframe is pursued for a third group, and investment guarantees or employment are safeguarded in a fourth. This has led to a range of privatization tools, including special programs for small enterprise privatization, enterprise liquidation with asset sale or auction, leasing of state assets, management/employee buy-out/buy-in, direct sale (by either trade sale or public share offering) to foreign or domestic investors, restitution to previous owners, and mass privatization. While the strategy of pursuing a variety of policy goals by applying different policy tools to separate parts of the existing portfolio of state assets tallies well with the highly differentiated demand for state assets, it has also made the meaning of "privatization" complex and often ambiguous. Privatization schemes in many countries are characterized by complicated economic and legal relations that may sometimes impede the clarification of property rights and the transformation to a market economy (Frydman and Rapaczynski (1993)).

The case of Poland may be used to illustrate the broadness of privatization objectives and the differentiation of privatization tools. According to the Ministry of Privatization, Poland's privatization program is based upon "a multi-track approach comprising separate privatization paths for the various categories of the enterprises, often with a simultaneous use of different techniques of privatization within a category" (Poland, Ministry of Privatization (1991b)). Consequently, enterprises are separated along the lines of size, demand, perceived economic and financial viability, level of state ownership and clarity of legal situation, quality of labor relations between management, workers, and unions within the enterprise (Poland, Ministry of Privatization (1991b)). In principle, privatization is then carried out as a two-step procedure. In the first step, enterprises that have applied for privatization are either "liquidated" in the legal sense or "commercialized," that is, transformed into joint-stock or limited-liability companies wholly owned by the State Treasury and governed by the commercial code. The second step consists of applying one of the various possible privatization tools (see Table 3).

While the Polish case may be extreme in its degree of compartmentalization, it is not unlike the schemes operated by other countries (see Table 3). In fact, all Eastern European privatization programs show important common features such as separate arrangements for privatizing small enterprises, early privatization of enterprises in "good financial health," and special procedures for restitution.

Small enterprises, such as retail stores, hotels, restaurants, gasoline stations, small service enterprises, and cinemas, have faced a strong domestic demand in all Eastern European countries. Governments reacted to this strong demand by devising simplified procedures; private savings were often sufficient to purchase individual units. As a result, privatization of small enterprises has been very successful. In Hungary, the "pre-privatization" law of September 1990 requires the privatization agency to auction off all catering establishments with fewer than 15 employees and all shops with fewer than 10 employees. By February 1992, the privatization agency had sold over 35 percent of all units it had identified for sale (European Bank for Reconstruction and Development (1992)). In Germany, by the end of February 1992, close to 80 percent of all small commercial entities of the former German Democratic Republic had been sold (Table 4). In the former Czechoslovakia, the privatization of small enterprises began in January 1991; foreigners were barred from participating in the program at least during the first round of sales. While unclear property rights and the need to resolve reprivatization questions initially resulted in a more cautious approach to selling small enterprises and to an extensive use of leasing arrangements, auctions of small enterprises were being held as often as four times a week throughout the country. By March 1992 over 25,000 small enterprises had been leased or sold. In Romania, since November 1990, many small enterprises have been sold or leased to domestic individuals and to joint ventures between domestic and foreign partners (Demekas and Khan (1991)). In mid-1992, auctions of assets of about 3,600 small public sector enterprises were expected to start soon, with foreigners not being allowed to bid in the first round of the auctions but being free to participate thereafter.

Enterprises in good financial health usually have no difficulty in attracting potential foreign and domestic investors. While only Romania has developed a separate early privatization program for enterprises thought to be in good financial condition, it is clear that all Eastern European privatization programs have found it easier to privatize well-run, profitable enterprises than to privatize perpetual loss makers. Eventually, all privatization programs will have to face up to the problem of enterprises that are unlikely to sell at any positive price. Not only in Germany, where privatization has already reached an advanced stage, this has led to a renewed debate on industrial policy and on the need for extensive enterprise restructuring, which typically is used as a euphemism for artificially keeping alive nonviable enterprises (Bös and Kayser (1992)).

All Eastern European privatization programs address the issue of restitution. While restitution may be justified on moral grounds, it implicitly favors people who used to possess real estate over those who used to possess financial assets or human capital (Hinds and Pohl (1991)). Some countries, like Hungary, have chosen a moderate financial compensation over a direct return of the physical assets; others, like Germany and Bulgaria, use extensive in-kind restitution as an integral part of their privatization programs.

In eastern Germany, where large parts of all buildings and land are subject to restitution claims, the issue of restitution has tended to obscure property rights, slow the process of privatization, and give disincentives to potential investors. As a result, the German privatization agency, the Treuhandanstalt, was given permission to use financial compensation instead of in-kind restitution when it deems this solution to be indicated by an overriding public interest.

In Bulgaria, where the National Assembly passed three laws providing for the restitution of large areas of agricultural land, small shops and warehouses, some industrial property, and residential and urban properties confiscated during the communist government, there is a clear danger that restitution questions will further delay privatization.

In general, Eastern European countries have favored less extensive restitution or financial compensation than Germany or Bulgaria. In the former Czechoslovakia, the Government limited restitution by imposing a strict deadline for filing claims and by restricting restitution to property that was nationalized under communist rule, that is, between 1948 and

Table 4. Results of Privatization

Bulgaria
Size of state sector
 3,356 large state enterprises at end-1991, of which 1,891 industrial sector enterprises.
 An unknown number of small enterprises (retail stores, cinemas, restaurants, hotels, etc.).
 4.6 million ha. of agricultural land.

Privatization results (until end-January 1992)
 (1) Industry

Privatized	0	(—)
Commercialized, to be privatized	1,320	(69.8%)
Status unchanged, commercialization under way	571	(30.2%)
	1,891	(100.0%)

 (2) Other
  Auctions of retail stores and gas stations were suspended in June 1991; the program is expected to be continued with 1,500 small enterprises being prepared for privatization.
  589,000 restitution claims received for 1.9 million ha. of agricultural land.

Former Czechoslovakia
Size of state sector
 Small enterprises (mostly retail stores, cinemas, hotels, and restaurants): originally about 120,000 units.
 Large enterprises: 5,482 units.

Privatization results (until March 1992)
 (1) Small enterprises
  Leased and sold, mostly via auctions: approximately 25,000 units (over 20 percent of all small enterprises); many more restituted (number unknown).

 (2) Large enterprises

To be mass privatized or sold in a first round that started May 1992	2,285	(41.7%)
To be mass privatized or sold in consecutive rounds	1,844	(33.6%)
To remain state-owned	1,271	(23.2%)
Listed for liquidation	82	(1.5%)
	5,482	(100.0%)

Restitution
 Potential restitution affects only about 6 percent of the total value of state assets. Actual restitution will be in the form of physical restitution; financial compensation will be in cash (up to Kčs 30,000) or securities. Close to 100,000 restitution claims for properties and land had been filed by the end of 1991.

Eastern Germany
Size of state sector
 (1) Industry
  270 Kombinate (vertically integrated state holding companies).
  8,000 individual industrial enterprises.
 (2) Other
  14,800 restaurants, retail outlets, cinemas, and tourist facilities.

Table 4 *(continued)*

Privatization results (as of February 29, 1992)
  (1) Industry
      Break-up of the Kombinate and of individual companies increased the
        total number of enterprises to 11,447; these can be categorized as
        follows:
      6,779 privatizations, partial privatizations, and re-privatizations au-
        thorized until March 1992, with the following breakdown:

Totally privatized	3,038	(26.5%)
Restitution (re-privatization)	711	(6.2%)
Majority privately owned	589	(5.1%)
Majority state-owned; most to be privatized further	2,441	(21.3%)
	6,779	(59.2%)

496 enterprises were turned over to local authorities, liquidated, or
  temporarily administered by a third party:

Turned over to local authorities	193	(1.7%)
Liquidated	247	(2.2%)
Administered by third party	56	(0.5%)
	496	(4.3%)

4,172 enterprises remain fully owned by the privatization agency, of
  which:

To be given to local authorities	101	(0.8%)
To be liquidated	1,079	(9.4%)
Privatization to be initiated	2,992	(26.2%)
	4,172	(36.4%)

  (2) Other
      About 80 percent (close to 12,000) of all restaurants, retail outlets,
        cinemas, and tourist facilities sold by March 1992.
      About 3 percent (700 out of 24,300) of all land parcels sold by March
        1992; privatization of land has been slow because of restitution
        claims.

Hungary
Size of state sector (end-December 1989)
  2,399 industrial sector enterprises.
  10,200 small businesses eligible for privatization.

Privatization results (during 1990–91)
  (1) Industry

Industrial firms privatized	246	(10.3%)
No privatization procedures initiated	1,517	(63.3%)
Privatization in progress (as of end-1991) via:		
Self-privatization	353	(14.7%)
Investor-led privatization	176	(7.3%)
State-initiated	107	(4.5%)
	2,399	(100.0%)

  (2) Small enterprises

Fully privatized	2,120	(20.8%)
Identified for sale	3,911	(38.3%)
No clear action proposed yet	4,169	(40.9%)
	10,200	(100.0%)

Table 4 *(concluded)*

Poland
Size of state sector (as of end-1990)
  (1) Industry
      8,453 fully state-owned enterprises.
      1,135 partially state-owned enterprises.
      32 municipal enterprises.
      248 enterprises owned by the State Treasury.
  (2) Other
      An unspecified number of small enterprises (retail stores, hotels, restaurants, cinemas, etc.).

Privatization results (as of end-1991)
  (1) Industry
      Commercialization path:

Completed privatizations	26	(0.3%)
Commercialized and to be privatized	218	(2.6%)
	244	(2.9%)
Liquidation path:		
Completed privatizations	198	(2.3%)
Liquidation due to bad financial standing; to be privatized	490	(5.8%)
Liquidation due to nonfinancial reasons; to be privatized	262	(3.1%)
	950	(11.2%)
Other enterprises (details on current status not available)	7,259	(85.9%)
	8,453	(100.0%)

Romania
Size of state sector
  A total of 6,320 large state-owned enterprises.
  An indeterminate number of small enterprises (retail stores, restaurants, hotels and tourist facilities, etc).

Privatization results (as of March 1992)
  (1) Large enterprises

Undergoing privatization	30	(0.5%)
Listed for privatization	5,970	(94.5%)
To remain state-owned	320	(5.0%)
	6,320	(100.0%)
(2) Small enterprises		
Units identified for sale	4,409	

Sources: Information provided by the countries' authorities and Fund staff estimates. All data are approximations.

1989. Notwithstanding that most nationalizations of large industrial enterprises were carried out under the democratic government between 1945 and 1948, about 6 percent of state assets were affected by restitution (Organization for Economic Cooperation and Development (1992)).

In Hungary, the Government has decided to compensate rather than to restitute former owners or their direct descendants. A key problem of direct financial compensation is that, in its economic effects, it is equal to an untied transfer from the state budget to households; that is, it may either be used for savings or consumption, and its effects on investment are uncertain. In Hungary, this problem has been solved by offering compensation in the form of property vouchers that can only be used for certain purposes such as buying stocks or acquiring land, apartments, or commercial properties. While at first it was planned to provide compensation only for the loss of private property that occurred after June 1949, the Hungarian Constitutional Court ordered a revision of the initial draft legislation to address illegal confiscations of private property between May 1939 and June 1949. This has caused a large number of properties to be subject to compensation claims—about 830,000 compensation applications were filed by the end of February 1992—and the amount of financial compensation for individual properties via the property vouchers had to be strictly limited (Okolicsanyi (1991)).

In Poland, the issue of restitution remains unresolved; in early 1993 legislation still had not been passed by parliament. Poland's large state budget deficit appears to make direct monetary compensation that would go beyond a symbolic gesture unfeasible (Górska and Henderson (1992)). In any case, it can be expected that restitution or financial compensation will not encompass a major portion of state-owned enterprises, and that, even when it eventually will be permitted, in most cases, no legitimate claimants will exist (S. Wellisz (1991)).

While there are certainly many common features, there also exist marked differences among the privatization programs in Eastern European countries. Examples include the acceptance of mass privatization, the openness to foreign investors, and the involvement of foreign institutions in the privatization process. Given that domestic credit in Eastern Europe is severely constrained, particularly compared with what is available to potential Western buyers, a rejection of mass privatization implies that extensive sales to foreign investors are almost unavoidable if privatization is to proceed. In Hungary, for example, the nonuse of mass privatization has brought about a broad openness to foreign investment. In addition, Hungary has effectively privatized the privatization process by granting permission to around 400 enterprises with fewer than 300 employees to deal directly with potential foreign and domestic buyers. The supervisory responsibility for these transactions, as well as for decisions on asset valuation and transformation, was delegated to 80 predominantly foreign consultants selected by the Hungarian privatization agency. An individual enterprise is free to choose any consultant from the list; only a final review is carried out by the privatization agency. Other countries, particularly those in which mass privatization is expected to play an important role, have usually placed more restrictions on foreign investment and foreign involvement. Stricter controls on foreign investments have often been justified by the need to ensure congruence of interests between enterprises and nations regarding long-term corporate strategies (Carlin and Mayer (1992)). Poland, for example, requires foreign investors to obtain formal approval by the Agency of Foreign Investment when the par value of the shares they want to acquire exceeds 10 percent of the share capital of the enterprise (Poland, Ministry of Privatization (1991a)).

Property Rights and Corporate Control

Eastern European governments have sometimes been reluctant to mandate changes in enterprise behavior, be it through privatization, the development of restructuring and business plans, or participation in technical assistance programs. This has been attributed to a desire to avoid charges of centralized control over firms, which had been blamed for the economic crisis under the communist governments (Kharas (1991)). In Poland and Hungary, for example, privatization is largely carried out on a voluntary basis, and at least in Poland, a fundamental clarification of property rights has yet to take place. More generally, the lack of action in defining property rights has slowed the creation of a modern system of corporate control, and contributed to a severe lack of enterprise guidance and supervision during the first few years of transition.

In principle, two models of corporate control are available: the *outsider model*, which is found in the United Kingdom and the United States, and the *insider model*, which is found in most of Western Europe and in Japan. The outsider model is characterized by (1) dispersed ownership and separation of ownership from control; (2) little incentive for outside investors to participate in corporate control and consequently weak commitments of outside investors to long-term strategies of firms; and (3) friendly and hostile takeovers and frequent market entrance and exit. In contrast, the insider model is characterized by (1) concentrated ownership and association of ownership and control; (2) corporate control exercised by shareholding parties (banks, other firms, employees), with outside interventions being limited to periods of clear financial failure; and (3) absence of takeovers, and infrequent market entrance and exit (Corbett and Mayer (1991)).

Under the outsider model, commercial banks rarely hold equity shares and play no active role in management; enterprises rarely hold substantial equity stakes in their suppliers or customers. Instead, commercial banks hold enterprise debt, while equity shares are held by a wide range of individuals and financial and nonfinancial institutions, with few stakes being large enough to ensure a controlling interest (Hare (1991); Corbett and Mayer (1991)). In the outsider model, exit (for individual shareholders) and friendly and hostile takeovers are the main mechanisms for ensuring management discipline: if an enterprise is perceived to be poorly managed, individual investors will either sell their equity shares quickly, or put together a group that will attempt to acquire the enterprise and introduce changes and adjustment measures (Hinds (1991); Borensztein (1991)). Under the insider model, mutual funds, commercial banks, and other interest groups make up the core investors who hold substantial equity, and enterprises are frequently interlinked through extensive cross-shareholding. In this model, core investors are active participants in enterprise management as it is considered the most effective way of protecting and increasing the value of their stake (equity plus debt) (Hare (1991)).

After first considering the "British model" of privatization via initial public offerings, the governments of the former Czechoslovakia, Poland, and Romania began to advance mass privatization schemes; in Hungary, Bulgaria, and Germany mass privatization was never actively considered. Under mass privatization the core investor principle can be preserved in a number of ways, and each possibility involves mutual funds that act as core investors and which are owned by the general public. Lipton and Sachs (1991) envision core investors to be created by the government, which would endow them with initial equity holdings and appoint their first directors. In contrast, Frydman and Rapaczynski (1991) propose free entry into the mutual fund market and competition among mutual funds to obtain shares from the public. While Sachs (1991) argues against allowing mutual funds to gain a majority stake in individual enterprises, Frydman and Rapaczynski (1991) propose auctioning enterprises to the different mutual funds in such a way as to ensure a few large initial shareholders. Clearly, countries that consider mass privatization with mutual funds have, implicitly or explicitly, given an important role to the insider model of corporate control. However, Bolton and Roland (1992) question whether this approach has yielded beneficial results, arguing that, in practice it has tended to create an environment that is too favorable to incumbent management. In their view, the mass privatization program in the former Czechoslovakia, for example, has led to the privatization of cash-flow claims without establishing effective corporate control. This view, however, seems excessively narrow for three reasons. First, there is a danger of failure to establish corporate control under any method of privatization, not only under mass privatization. Second, fully developed systems of corporate control will take years to establish, and it is clearly too early to derive strong general policy recommendations from the less than one year of mass privatization in the former Czechoslovakia prior to the country's split-up. Third, outright rejection of mass privatization may prolong the agony where the old system, in which corporate control is exercised by the state, continues to prevent rapid efficiency gains. Particularly because Eastern European governments have little experience with regulating the private sector in a nonintrusive way, the design of a simple and unambiguous system of corporate control should be a priority task, which can proceed only when privatization gets under way.

Bank Restructuring and Privatization

This section discusses proposals to use privatization as an instrument of banking sector reform. Eastern European banks were traditionally agents of the central authorities, part of the mechanism for plan implementation. Abolishing central plans has left the commercial banking sector of Eastern European countries disoriented and virtually paralyzed. While it would be difficult to make a compelling argument for privatization to precede banking sector reform, this is what is currently happening in Eastern Europe.[2]

Svejnar (1991) has argued that the limited availability of commercial credit caused by Eastern Europe's underdeveloped banking sectors has been the single most important hindrance to the growth of private sector activity. Failure to undertake comprehensive banking sector reforms has meant that the role of banks in the emerging corporate structures of Eastern Europe remains yet to be defined. In addition, given extreme differences in the amount of credit available to foreign and domestic investors, it becomes arguable whether privatization via sale of enterprises allocates ownership and control appropriately (Carlin and Mayer (1992)).

Comprehensive banking sector reform in Eastern European countries has four main elements: (1) restructuring and possibly consolidating state-owned banks; (2) enacting a banking law that provides for establishing new private banks; (3) adopting and implementing modern banking supervision standards; and (4) resolving the problem of nonperforming loans in bank portfolios. Of these four, probably the most difficult problem to resolve concerns nonperforming bank loans to enterprises. The magnitude of the outstanding bad loans was estimated to be in the range of 15–20 percent of total loans to enterprises in Hungary and the former Czechoslovakia, and may be 30 to 40 percent in Poland and Bulgaria (Bruno (1992)). While there are different ways to address this problem,[3] for the purpose of this chapter, proposals that link bank recapitalization to privatization are clearly most important.

One way to address the problem of nonperforming enterprise debt to banks is to earmark the cash proceeds from privatization for bank restructuring. This solution was adopted in the former Czechoslovakia. Another option currently under discussion in various Eastern European countries is to provide banks with shares of newly privatized enterprises. Both solutions address the recapitalization needs of banks and facilitate writing

---

[2]Corbett and Mayer (1991) have suggested that, in the minds of most people, capitalism is synonymous with stock markets, and that the creation of domestic stock markets epitomizes the break with socialism more than anything else. This may help to explain why most Eastern European governments first addressed the politically visible task of opening a stock market (on which there is still hardly anything to trade), but have delayed comprehensive banking sector reform.

[3]See Bruno (1992) for an in-depth discussion.

off nonperforming assets in bank balance sheets. Fischer (1991) has pointed out that, since part of the nonperforming bank assets are loans to the same firms that are being privatized, there is some logic in compensating the banks in advance.

This solution, however, is not without controversy. One problem is that it may just replace one bad asset (nonperforming loans) with another bad asset (shares of bankrupt enterprises), and hence simply fail to resolve the issue of bank recapitalization altogether. More fundamentally, however, bank participation in privatization also means bank participation in the exercise of corporate control over enterprises, which takes us directly back to the issue of property rights and corporate control. While providing banks with enterprise shares has been advocated by several authors, such as Lipton and Sachs (1991) in the case of Poland, others have strongly opposed it, arguing that it causes inequities, misallocation of resources, increased financial instability, and potential conflicts of interest. Borensztein (1991), for example, on the basis of evidence presented by Hinds (1991) and by Lipton and Sachs (1991) for the case of Chile, suggests caution in establishing close relationships between banks and their clients. Similarly, Kornai (1991) has argued that putting a sizable proportion of industrial shares in the hands of large banks is premature in Eastern Europe, particularly when banks are still state owned. He suggests that banks, as shareholders of large stock companies, may fail to apply regular business criteria to the stock companies in which they hold a stake, and generally share the interest of the stock companies of being bailed out and artificially sustained. This argument is supported by Schwartz (1991) who, citing evidence from Hungary, has pointed out abuses of close bank-client relationships. The need for unambiguous incentive structures has led McKinnon (1991) to propose an extreme solution, where privatized firms are given no access to credit from the traditional banks, which implies that they would have to finance investments either from retained earnings or by raising funds in capital markets from the nonbank public.

All this points to the urgency of a comprehensive reform of the banking system, and to the specific problems related to the recapitalization of banks. Using shares of privatized enterprises to recapitalize banks is highly controversial. Hence, it should not be considered as a general solution, but also not be completely ruled out from the outset. If it is decided to use privatization in the recapitalization of banks, mechanisms and incentive structures need to be designed carefully. The solution that was adopted by the former Czechoslovakia, earmarking cash proceeds from privatization, is less controversial than the direct provision of enterprise shares to banks, but may fail to generate sufficient funds. An alternative, proposed by Fischer (1991), would be to hold the shares earmarked for banks in a separate general fund, which would be used at a later stage to infuse funds into banks, and to restructure bank balance sheets with safer assets. In general, privatization policies can provide valuable support, but are no substitute for a comprehensive bank restructuring scheme.

The Problem of Large Enterprises

The privatization of small enterprises, mostly retail stores and enterprises in trade and services, has proceeded rapidly and successfully across Eastern Europe; privatization of large enterprises, such as mines, steel mills, shipyards, petrochemical complexes, and textile mills, has been much slower (see Table 4). There are two main reasons. First, many large enterprises have an obsolete capital stock and use outdated production technologies and are therefore unlikely to attract interested buyers at positive prices (C. Wellisz (1991)). Second, large enterprises account for a major share of employment and production in the economy, and privatization, particularly to foreigners, or shut-down may run into strong popular opposition,[4] with arguments ranging from a potentially strong adverse impact on output and employment to a perceived antagonism between foreign ownership and national interests (Applebaum (1992)). Still, it is clear that ultimately there may be only two solutions for these enterprises: massive investments to modernize the capital stock, or shut-down, liquidation, and asset disposal. Given that few local individuals have the financial resources to make the necessary investments, governments have three basic choices, each of which will move problem enterprises out of their responsibility: (1) find ways to attract foreigners on a large scale, (2) establish diluted share ownership by local individuals via mass privatization, and (3) break the existing large-scale enterprises into smaller units that can be privatized separately.

Eastern European governments have not yet tackled the question of large enterprises comprehensively. Instead, governments have begun to build privatization policies around the possibility that many enterprises remain state owned for a while. Usually, this involves the construction of "halfway houses," which may come in different forms, but usually involve putting the enterprise under the control of an independent board of executive directors, and transforming it into a joint-stock or limited-liability company.

In Hungary, for example, property rights were redefined to make the State Property Agency the sole owner of all state enterprises; the enterprises were then given boards of directors who required them to produce properly audited balance sheets, and independent contractors were brought in to help with supervision. More recently, the Hungarian Gov-

---

[4]In Poland, for example, the top 400 enterprises, ranked by sales, accounted for 36 percent of total employment in 1990 (Lipton and Sachs (1991)). Given that employment in some regions depends heavily on large industrial enterprises, shutting down these enterprises may severely strain the economies of these regions, particularly since there is a severe housing shortage that reduces labor mobility.

ernment has begun to create a separate supervisory board, the State Ownership Institute, which is to oversee the activities of commercialized enterprises. In Poland, the concept of commercialization is similar in that it legally transforms state-owned enterprises either into limited-liability companies or into joint-stock companies wholly owned by the state treasury. A basic difference between the Hungarian and the Polish concepts is that in Hungary commercialization is independent of the intent to privatize, while in Poland commercialization is a possible outcome of a voluntary enterprise decision to be privatized. As a result, most state-owned enterprises in Poland remain under the control of individual ministries; the Polish privatization agency has concentrated its efforts almost exclusively on profitable enterprises, leaving the problem of unprofitable enterprises to be resolved by the ministries.

In Romania, commercialization has been pursued vigorously since August 1990. With the exception of enterprises in strategic sectors such as telecommunications, mining, and defense, most enterprises were required to become commercialized, to inventory and value their assets, and then to transfer 30 percent of their value to five private ownership funds which would use these shares for the mass privatization program. Under the mass privatization program each eligible citizen will receive a share in each of the five private ownership funds. The remaining 70 percent will be retained by the Government in a state ownership fund for future sale.

The former Czechoslovakia adopted a more radical position; the speedy transfer of ownership rights to the private sector was thought to alleviate the need for halfway houses. Accordingly, mass privatization was championed as the main tool of privatizing large enterprises.[5] Bruno (1992) has argued that halfway houses to privatization are generally inevitable, unless one is willing to take the line that what cannot be privatized instantaneously had better be junked immediately. While commercialization entails a number of problems, the perceived advantage is that state-owned enterprises start being covered by normal commercial law and obtain corporate governance through a professional board of directors (Sachs (1991)). Recent evidence from Poland suggests that commercialization is superior to the present self-governance structure that is dominated by the Workers' Council, and which clearly conflicts with long-term restructuring and profit maximization considerations (Pinto and others (1992)). The empirical finding that managers of state-owned enterprises in Poland are an important source of change has strengthened arguments in favor of an expanded role for commercialization, where power is delegated to managers, where managers are empowered to make all operational and most strategic decisions without prior consultation with government officials,

---

[5]For a detailed description of the mass privatization program of the former Czechoslovakia, refer to Aghevli and others (1992).

and where managers are given contracts that link their compensation to the long-run value of the firm and its privatization (Pinto and others (1992)). In addition, it somewhat weakens the argument by Bolton and Roland (1992) that incumbent management is necessarly inefficient.

Still, commercialization and other halfway houses do not solve the problem of privatizing large enterprises; they may often be unavoidable, but are certainly not sufficient for successful privatization. In particular, halfway houses fail fully to expose state-owned enterprises to a uniformly hard budget constraint that implies the risk of bankruptcy (Kopits (1991)). In addition, they do not fully alleviate concerns about decapitalization by the firms' managers (Bruno (1992)), and the government may easily find itself in a position where it either has to provide bailouts or let enterprises go bankrupt. Halfway houses may allow governments some breathing space, but eventually decisions that are more far reaching will have to be made.

Preliminary Policy Lessons

The Eastern European privatization experience presents some preliminary policy lessons for governments of other economies in transition wishing to reduce an overextended public sector. The following five policy considerations should provide a nucleus around which further discussion on privatization policies in economies in transition may be focused.

First, privatization is a key mover of the transition from plan to market. Hence, it must be accomplished in a speedy and comprehensive fashion. Rapid creation of a legal framework that defines ownership rights clearly facilitates public understanding of privatization, stimulates broad-based ownership, prevents abuses of power, and speeds up privatization. Given a variety of policy objectives and a highly differentiated demand for the portfolio of state assets, a diverse set of privatization tools will be needed. Separate programs for small enterprises targeted at domestic buyers should be part of any privatization scheme. Settling questions of restitution has both a moral and a practical dimension. In general, favoring people who used to own real estate over those who used to own financial assets or human capital should be avoided. Generous restitution programs are likely to result in a flood of claims that will strain administrative capacities and impede the clarification of property rights. Direct financial compensation will add further adverse pressure on state budgets. In practice, restitution should be limited to a symbolic gesture. Exclusive reliance on one-by-one privatization is time-consuming and unnecessarily slows down the transition to a market economy. Problems of valuing enterprise assets are no reason for delaying privatization. Mass privatization schemes and other techniques that allow changing the structure of property rights without necessarily requiring prior asset valuation should be given due consideration. While broad-scale commercialization should be accomplished rapidly, mass privatization should be used to prevent halfway houses from becoming costly semipermanent solutions. Foreign investment should generally be welcome; there is little economic rationale for placing an upper limit on the share of state-owned property that foreigners may buy.

Second, people are more willing to bear an inevitable burden if they can expect tangible benefits. To enhance social acceptability, any privatization scheme should have a distributive component. Creating broad-based ownership rights, as envisaged under the various mass privatization programs, facilitates the formulation of incomes policy and aids efforts to reform social policy. For the same reason, it is useful to encourage leveraged buy-outs by management and employees, and partial employee ownership schemes. It is unlikely that creating broad-based ownership rights will jeopardize macroeconomic stabilization efforts by fueling consumption. Still, distributive questions have to be handled carefully. For example, many people would be excluded from employee ownership schemes because they do not work for the companies that are privatized. Given strong quality differences across the various state assets, employee ownership schemes are generally inequitable. This can easily lead to tensions. While offering a minority share to workers can be useful, preferential treatment, in particular with respect to purchase prices, has to be avoided.

Third, for privatization to be successful, financial sector reform is crucial. Reasons for this include the significant investments required to make Eastern European industries competitive and the problem that property rights may not be reallocated efficiently if potential buyers have no access to credit. Credit should be given on "hard" terms as this signals from the outset that potential owners need to be willing and able to take on risks, and that privatization is not just a legal procedure where the ownership is transferred to the private sector while the financial risks remain with the public sector. A central element of financial sector reform is banking sector reform. Comprehensive banking reform has three main elements: (1) restructuring and possibly consolidating state-owned banks, (2) enacting banking laws that provide for establishing new private banks, and (3) resolving the problem of nonperforming loans in bank portfolios. The latter issue remains highly controversial, because some of the proposed solutions, like providing banks with shares of privatized enterprises, have direct implications for questions of corporate control. Given the potential problems that may arise from close cooperation between banks and enterprises, great care has to be used in the design of control mechanisms and incentive structures. It is clear that comprehensive banking sector reform has to be accompanied by the creation of an efficient system of bank supervision, the creation of a deposit insurance scheme, and the creation of market structures that facilitate trading financial assets and stocks.

Fourth, since Eastern European governments have little experience with regulating in a nonintrusive way, particularly in the context of a market environment, the design of a simple and unambiguous system of corporate control is a priority task. The two main Western systems of corporate control, the insider model and the outsider model, each have advantages and disadvantages for economies in transition. For Eastern Europe, most advice has favored the insider model, characterized by (1) concentrated ownership and association of ownership with control, (2) corporate control being exercised by shareholding parties (banks, other firms, employees) with outside interventions being limited to periods of clear financial failure, and (3) absence of takeovers and infrequent market entrance and exit. Explicit or implicit acceptance of the insider model implies that banks and nonbank financial institutions become closely involved in privatization and in issues of corporate control over enterprises.

Fifth, the problem of large enterprises has to be tackled early. Given that it will be difficult to sell many of the large industrial enterprises at any positive price, and given the employment implications of forcing these enterprises into immediate bankruptcy, solutions may take time. One way to address the problem is large-scale commercialization, which provides state-owned enterprises with an improved system of corporate governance and subjects them to the regular commercial code. While commercialization provides some breathing space to governments, it remains a halfway house—not a permanent solution. In particular, commercialization alone may not provide the hard budget constraint needed to improve overall efficiency; governments may still be forced to offer bailouts to commercialized companies. But eventually, governments may face a credibility crisis and will have to let some enterprises go bankrupt. Bankruptcy decisions, however painful in the short run, are best made before a credibility crisis arises.

References

Adam, Christopher, William Cavendish, and Percy S. Mistry, *Adjusting Privatization* (London: Curry, Heinemann, and Randle, 1992).

Aghevli, Bijan B., Eduardo Borensztein, and Tessa van der Willigen, *Stabilization and Structural Reform in the Czech and Slovak Federal Republic: First Stage*, IMF Occasional Paper No. 92 (Washington: International Monetary Fund, 1992).

Applebaum, Anne, "Econophobia," *The Washington Post* (Washington), February 16, 1992, pp. C1–C2.

Bolton, Patrick, and Gérard Roland, "Privatization in Central and Eastern Europe," *Economic Policy*, No. 15 (October 1992), pp. 275–303.

Bös, Dieter, and Gunter Kayser, "The Last Days of the Treuhandanstalt," Discussion Paper (Bonn: University of Bonn, November 1992).

Borensztein, Eduardo, "Comments on David Lipton and Jeffrey Sachs, 'Privatization in Eastern Europe: The Case of Poland,'" in *Reforming Central and Eastern European Countries—Initial Results and Challenges*, ed. by Vittorio Corbo, Fabrizio Coricelli, and Jan Bossek (Washington: World Bank, 1991).

Bruno, Michael, "Stabilization and Reform in Eastern Europe," *Staff Papers*, International Monetary Fund, Vol. 39 (December 1992), pp. 741-77.

Carlin, Wendy, and Colin Mayer, "The Treuhandanstalt: Privatization by State and Market," paper presented at the NBER conference on Transition in Eastern Europe (Cambridge, Massachusetts, February 26-29, 1992).

Corbett, Jenny, and Colin Mayer, "Financial Reform in Eastern Europe: Progress with the Wrong Model," *Oxford Review of Economic Policy* (Vol. 7), No. 4 (Winter 1991), pp. 57-75.

Czechoslovakia, Ministry of Finance, *Kupónová Privatizace [Information booklet, voucher privatization]* (Prague, 1991).

Demekas, Dimitri G., and Mohsin S. Khan, *The Romanian Economic Reform Program*, IMF Occasional Paper No. 89 (Washington: International Monetary Fund, 1991).

Dhanji, Farid, and Branko Milanovic, "Privatization in East and Central Europe—Objectives, Constraints, and Models of Divestiture," paper presented at the World Bank Conference on Privatization and Ownership Changes in East and Central Europe (Washington, June 13-14, 1990).

European Bank for Reconstruction and Development, *Quarterly Reports on Economic Developments in Central and Eastern Europe* (London, March 1992).

Fischer, Stanley, "Privatization in East European Transformation," NBER Working Paper No. 3703 (Cambridge, Massachusetts: National Bureau of Economic Research, May 1991).

Frydman, Roman, and Andrzej Rapaczynski, "Markets and Institutions in Large-Scale Privatization: An Approach to Economic and Social Transformation in Eastern Europe," in *Reforming Central and Eastern European Countries—Initial Results and Challenges*, ed. by Vittorio Corbo, Fabrizio Coricelli, and Jan Bossek (Washington: World Bank, 1991).

———, "Privatization in Eastern Europe: Is the State Withering Away?" *Finance & Development*, June 1993 (forthcoming).

Górska, Ewa, and Yolanda K. Henderson, "Tax Aspects of Privatization in Poland" (unpublished; Warsaw, May 1992).

Gruszecki, Tomasz, and Jan Winiecki, "Privatization in East-Central Europe: A Comparative Perspective," *Aussenwirtschaft*, Vol. 46, No. 1 (1991), pp. 67-100.

Hare, Paul G., "The Assessment: Microeconomics of Transition in Eastern Europe," *Oxford Review of Economic Policy*, Vol. 7, No. 4 (Winter 1991), pp. 1-15.

———, and Irena Grosfeld, "Privatization in Hungary, Poland, and Czechoslovakia," CEPR Discussion Paper No. 544 (London: Center for Economic Policy Research, April 1991).

Hemming, Richard, "Privatization of State Enterprises," in *Fiscal Policies in Economies in Transition*, ed. by Vito Tanzi (Washington: International Monetary Fund, 1992).

———, and Kenneth Miranda, "Privatization," in *Public Expenditure Handbook*, ed. by Ke-young Chu and Richard Hemming (Washington: International Monetary Fund, 1991).

Hinds, Manuel, "A Note on the Privatization of Socialized Enterprises in Poland," in *Reforming Central and Eastern European Countries—Initial Results and Challenges*, ed. by Vittorio Corbo, Fabrizio Coricelli, and Jan Bossek (Washington: World Bank, 1991).

———, and Gerhard Pohl, "Going to Market—Privatization in Central and Eastern Europe," World Bank Working Paper, WPS 768 (Washington: World Bank, September 1991).

Hungary, State Property Agency, *Privatization and Foreign Investment in Hungary* (Budapest, March 1991).

Keating, Giles, and Jonathan Hoffman, "Privatisation Theory: Hold Back for a Swift Advance," *Central European* (April 1991), pp. 32-34.

Kharas, Homi J., "Restructuring Socialist Industry—Poland's Experience in 1990," World Bank Discussion Paper No. 142 (Washington: World Bank, December 1991).

Kopits, George, "Fiscal Reform in European Economies in Transition," IMF Working Paper No. 91/43 (Washington: International Monetary Fund, April 1991).

Kornai, János, "The Principles of Privatization in Eastern Europe," Harvard Institute of Economic Research Discussion Paper No. 1567(Cambridge, Massachusetts: Harvard University, September 1991).

Lipton, David, and Jeffrey Sachs, "Privatization in Eastern Europe: The Case of Poland," in *Reforming Central and Eastern European Countries—Initial Results and Challenges*, ed. by Vittorio Corbo, Fabrizio Coricelli, and Jan Bossek (Washington: World Bank, 1991).

Maurer, Rainer, Birgit Sander, and Klaus-Dieter Schmidt, "Privatisierung in Ostdeutschland—Zur Arbeit der Treuhandanstalt," *Weltwirtschaft*, No. 1 (1991) pp. 45-66.

McKinnon, Ronald I., *The Order of Economic Liberalization* (Baltimore: Johns Hopkins University Press, 1991).

Milanovic, Branko, *Liberalization and Entrepreneurship* (New York: Sharpe, 1989).

Okolicsanyi, Karoly, "Hungary: Compensation Law Finally Approved," *Report on Eastern Europe* (September 6, 1991), pp. 22-25.

Organization for Economic Cooperation and Development, *OECD Economic Surveys: Czech and Slovak Federal Republic, 1991* (Paris, January 1992).

Pinto, Brian, Marek Belka, and Stefan Krajewski, "Microeconomics of Transformation in Poland: A Survey of State Enterprise Responses," World Bank Working Paper, WPS 982 (Washington: World Bank, September 1992).

Poland, Ministry of Privatization (1991a), *Guide to Foreign Investment in Poland* (Warsaw, September 1991).

—— (1991b), *Privatization in Poland—Program and Achievements* (Warsaw, December 1991).

Sachs, Jeffrey, "Crossing the Valley of Tears in East European Reform," *Challenge* (September–October 1991), pp. 26–34.

Sadowski, Zdzislaw, "Privatization in Eastern Europe: Goals, Problems, and Implications," *Oxford Review of Economic Policy*, Vol. 7, No. 4 (1991), pp. 46–57.

Schwartz, Gerd, "Privatization: Possible Lessons from the Hungarian Case," *World Development*, Vol. 19, No. 12 (December 1991), pp. 1731–36.

——, and Paulo Silva Lopes, "Privatization: Expectations, Trade Offs, and Results" (unpublished; Washington: International Monetary Fund, March 1993).

Svejnar, Jan, "Microeconomic Issues in the Transition to a Market Economy," *Journal of Economic Perspectives*, Vol. 5, No. 4 (Fall 1991), pp. 123–38.

Wellisz, Christopher, "Privatization in Poland: The Problem of Valuation," *The Journal of International Affairs*, Vol. 45, No. 1 (Summer 1991), pp. 247–70.

Wellisz, Stanislaw, "Poland Under 'Solidarity' Rule," *Journal of Economic Perspectives*, Vol. 5, No. 4 (Fall 1991), pp. 211–17.

PART III

Asia

CHAPTER 13

China: Prolonged Reforms and the Weakening of Fiscal Control

Mario I. Blejer

Starting in 1979, China has carried out wide-ranging economic reforms with the specific aim of accelerating the rate of output growth by increasing productivity and improving the allocation of resources. The nature and design of the reforms in China differ from those of the reforms taking place in many Eastern European countries. These differences should be kept in mind in analyzing the fiscal implications of the Chinese reforms.

First, the reforms were never explicitly designed, nor implicitly conceived, with the objective of fully or partially dismantling the socialist system. Therefore, the issue of privatization of state-owned enterprises, as well as the more general problem of ownership rights, has not played a central role in the Chinese reform scheme. Instead, some peculiar arrangements, such as the "contract-management responsibility system," had to be introduced to provide incentives similar to those prevailing in a predominantly private system. Second, the Chinese reforms were largely "experimental," in the sense that they were concentrated in specific areas of the economy, starting in agriculture, and did not cause wide systemic disruptions. On the contrary, they achieved the objective of rapidly accelerating the overall rate of growth and, in this manner, they tended to overheat rather than to depress the economy. This initial success, however, neither required nor resulted in an enhanced ability of the Government to conduct supporting fiscal and other macroeconomic policies. Third, more than in any other country (with the possible potential exception of the former U.S.S.R.) reforms in China were largely grounded on regional decentralization with the—unintended—consequence that much of the power of the Central Government to manage the system at the macroeconomic level (including the ability to raise revenue) has been lost to local and provincial governments. Fourth, unlike in the U.S.S.R. and in most of the Eastern European countries, the Chinese reforms were started and proceeded over a long period in an environment of (at least apparent) macroeconomic stability. Therefore, the conundrum of se-

---

Mario I. Blejer, a staff member of the Fiscal Affairs Department, is temporarily assigned to the World Bank as Senior Economic Adviser in the Europe and Central Asia Department.

quencing and combining adjustment with structural reforms was, in principle, absent. Macroeconomic imbalances, however, developed strongly in the second half of the 1980s, but it could be argued, as is done below, that much of the imbalances might be attributed to how the reforms were implemented rather than to the initial macroeconomic conditions.

Although these differences are indeed significant, China provides the longest continuous instance of a reforming socialist economy. Its experience, interesting in itself, can also provide important insights into the general patterns of macroeconomic performance during the transformation process. Moreover, the systemic changes that have taken place in China during the last decade have changed the functions and objectives of all major policy instruments, requiring their adaptation to the new demands. This evolution has been particularly marked in the case of fiscal policy, and the prolonged experience of China may contribute to the understanding of the evolving role of the budget in a reforming economy.

As a framework for discussing the fiscal implications of the Chinese reforms, this chapter first presents a summary of the evolution of the overall reform process, followed by an account of the main budgetary developments since the inception of the reforms. The next section analyzes the fiscal implications of the reforms, stressing the elements in the reform process that have affected the ability of the Government to collect revenue and to use fiscal instruments for effective macroeconomic management. Final remarks conclude the chapter.

Synopsis of Reforms

In 1979 a set of radical agricultural reforms were started across China.[1] They ended the commune system, increased the size of allowed private plots, and legalized the informal markets for farm products in rural areas. These reforms increased the rate of growth of agricultural output from an average of about 2 percent a year during 1958–78 to about 8 percent a year in 1979–84.[2] The rapid increase in productivity displaced labor from the agricultural sector, but large-scale migration to the cities was effectively prevented by the implementation of an additional reform: the elimination of the restrictions on nonagricultural activities in the rural areas. This led to the creation of a large number of individually or collectively owned enterprises—the so-called township and village enterprises—that by 1987 accounted for nearly one fourth of the gross value of industrial output and employed about 17 percent of the labor force.[3]

---

[1] The literature on the reforms in China is vast. For a survey, see Perkins (1988). On the macroeconomic dimensions of the reforms, see Blejer and others (1991) and Hussain and Stern (1991).

[2] On the effects of agricultural reforms see, for example, McMillan, Whalley, and Zhu (1989) and Perkins and Yusuf (1984).

[3] See World Bank (1989).

The second stage of the transformation began in 1984 by extending some of the agricultural reforms to the cities. At the core of the urban reforms was the enterprise reform, and its main feature was to allow enterprises to retain part of their profits. Before 1984 all profits of enterprises were fully remitted to the budget while, by 1986, almost all profits were subject to partial taxation with the net of taxes profits (and the depreciation allowances) being retained by the enterprises to finance their investments and for wage bonuses and incentive payments to management. In addition, the number of products allocated through the central plan was largely reduced, bringing the share of industrial output and retail sales subject to the plan to 30 percent by 1989, compared with close to 70 percent in 1979. Collectives and some private firms (mainly in services) were also permitted in the cities, and their share in retail sales rose from less than 10 percent in the late 1970s to more than 50 percent in 1987.

Partial price reforms also took place. Price liberalization began with the introduction of a two-tier price system, first implemented in rural areas and slowly expanded to include a number of industrial products. The system allows producers to sell their output, above a set quota, at free market prices. Many other commodities, however, remained subject to price guidelines, while the prices of a large portion of inputs and consumer goods were kept tightly controlled. Part of these controlled prices were administrated through budgetary intermediation, in the form of direct subsidies that cover the difference between procurement and retail prices.[4]

An important result of both the rural and the urban reforms was that a large fraction of the economy was diverted away from direct government control. Remarkably, the rates of aggregate growth reached unprecedented levels. During 1978–89 the average annual growth rate of per capita income was about 8 percent, with industrial output growing more than 16 percent a year on average in 1985–88.[5]

The reform measures were not, however, accompanied by strong financial policies, which resulted in large increases in aggregate demand that were compounded by the ability of enterprises to grant large raises in wages and bonuses and to borrow heavily in order to expand capacity. As will be discussed later, the particular way in which the reforms were implemented led to a deterioration in the budgetary accounts and, more important, to a loss in the ability of the Central Government to maintain macroeconomic discipline. In the second half of the 1980s, inflation increased rapidly and the external accounts deteriorated. By September 1988, inflationary expectations caused a rash of panic buying and bank

---

[4]On the two-track price system see, for example, Wu and Zhao (1987).

[5]Real GDP grew at an average of about 11 percent a year over the same period (1985–88), while the growth of industrial output exceeded 20 percent in both 1985 and 1988.

runs that prompted the Government to adopt stabilization measures that were rather incompatible with the spirit of the reforms. Thus, credit was largely restricted and redirected to state-owned enterprises, stemming the development of the nonstate sector. Further, price controls were reimposed, and the decentralization of foreign trade was halted.

Following these measures, inflation fell to about 2 percent in 1990 but growth almost collapsed (output grew at less than 5 percent in 1989–90). Despite this partial retrenchment, however, reforms did not fully stop and there are indications of a current shift toward renewed liberalization. Export and consumer subsidies are being phased out, only one eighth of all farm produce is sold at procurement prices set by the Government, and the importance of the nonstate firms in industrial output continues to expand.[6]

Contrary to what is widely believed, the events of June 1989 were not the immediate cause of the apparent reversal of the Chinese reforms, but only strengthened a trend toward increased recentralization that had already started almost a year earlier. This observation is important because it demonstrates that the reforms ran into serious problems not for political reasons but rather for macroeconomic reasons. This strengthens, therefore, the need to consider in detail the interactions between microeconomic reforms and macroeconomic stability.

Budgetary Developments

The major developments since the inception of the reforms are described briefly below. The discussion refers to the consolidated state budget that covers both the Central Government and all levels of local government.

One of the most salient features of the evolution of government finances since the beginning of the reforms has been the continuous decline of the total revenue-GDP ratio, from more than 34 percent in 1978 to below 20 percent at the beginning of the 1990s (Table 1). The main reason for this trend has been the steady fall in revenue from the enterprise sector (direct taxation plus remittances) that plunged from 20 percent of GDP in 1978 to an estimated 4.5 percent in 1992.[7] Although part

---

[6]In 1978 state-owned enterprises accounted for about 80 percent of industrial output. In 1990 the figure was 54 percent and it is expected that it will not exceed 50 percent by the end of 1991. In 1990 the output of state-owned industries grew by 3 percent, while that of collectives was up by 20 percent and foreign joint ventures raised their industrial output by more than 50 percent (from a very low base). See "China's Economy," *The Economist* (1991).

[7]The statutory profit tax rate that applies currently to most of large and medium-sized enterprises is 55 percent and, in addition, they may also be subject to an enterprise-specific income adjustment tax that is imposed to adjust for the differential endowment of assets inherited from the pre-reform period. Most of these enterprises, however, negotiate their tax liability in the context of the "contract responsibility systems" (see below). Small state-owned enterprises, as well as collective enterprises, are subject to a nonlinear tax schedule with a marginal tax rate equal to 55 percent. Since tax rates vary with the size and the type of ownership of the enterprises, this makes the revenues from enterprise taxes vulnerable to changes in the structure and ownership of enterprises.

Table 1. China: Government Revenue

(In percent of GNP)

	1978	1979–81	1982–84	1985–87	1988–89	1990–91	1992 (Prel.)
Total revenue[1]	34.4	30.0	27.0	24.8	20.6	19.1	16.4
Revenue from enterprises[2]	20.6	17.1	12.5	8.3	6.9	6.0	4.6
Taxes on							
Income and profits[3]	21.5	17.8	13.3	7.9	5.4	4.9	3.7
Goods and services[4]	11.3	10.6	10.1	10.6	9.2	8.6	7.8
Of which: VAT	. . .	. . .	. . .	2.1	2.7	2.2	2.0
International trade	0.8	0.9	1.1	1.8	1.2	0.9	1.0
Other taxes[5]	. . .	. . .	1.5	3.2	3.0	3.3	3.0
Nontax revenue[6]	0.8	0.8	1.0	1.3	1.8	1.9	1.2
Net budgetary contribution of enterprises[7]	19.6	16.2	11.2	5.4	3.4	3.0	2.6

Source: Ministry of Finance.

[1] Total revenue, including nontax revenue.

[2] Profit remittances and profit taxes, plus special levies on enterprises (tax on extrabudgetary construction), and tax on extrabudgetary receipts.

[3] Includes profit remittances.

[4] Includes product, value-added, and business taxes.

[5] Other taxes include the wage bonus tax, estate taxes, and the tax on the income of foreign-related enterprises (joint ventures and foreign owned).

[6] Excludes profit remittances.

[7] Revenues from enterprises minus subsidies to loss-making enterprises (from Table 2).

of this fall has been the intended outcome of the decentralization process, the declining trend also reflects, as discussed in the next section, the unintended tax consequences of the institutional framework within which the reforms were carried out.

Contrary to the performance of profit taxes, revenue from indirect taxes held rather well during the period. In 1984 four separate indirect taxes—the product tax, the value-added tax (VAT), the business tax, and the urban maintenance and construction tax—were introduced to replace the previous consolidated industrial and commercial tax.[8] In China, however, indirect taxes are directly collected from enterprises and, unlike in market economies, they can rarely be shifted forward because of price controls. They became, therefore, akin to a profit tax as their incidence falls fully on the enterprise. Moreover, in addition to their revenue-generating potential, indirect taxes are largely used to compensate for perceived variations in enterprise profitability arising from the incomplete nature of price reforms. Indirect taxes contain, therefore, a discretional component that translates into a wide range of rates.

---

[8] For a full review of the Chinese tax system at the end of the 1980s, see World Bank (1990).

As in other centrally planned economies, individual income taxation and taxes on international trade do not account for a large share of Chinese revenues. However, efforts have been made to tax individual incomes that have increased substantially following the reforms.[9] Consequently, receipts from personal income taxes, as well as receipts from foreign-related enterprises (foreign owned and joint ventures) have increased in importance after 1987.[10]

The reforms also had a profound impact on public expenditure, which, as a ratio of GDP, fell from 34 percent in 1978 to an estimated 19 percent in 1992 (Table 2). Most of the reduction took place in capital outlays, although the level of defense spending has also fallen sharply, as the Government demobilized about one million persons and converted a considerable number of military plants to civilian use. Capital expenditures declined rapidly (from 15 percent of GDP in 1978 to less than 5 percent by the beginning of the 1990s), as a result of reduced intermediation by the Government, larger profit retention by the enterprises, and because enterprises were required to use their own funds and bank loans to finance their investments.

Subsidies, after rising substantially in the early years of the reforms, remained broadly unchanged at approximately 6 percent of GDP in the 1980s, falling further in 1990-92. There are two types of budgetary subsidies in China: consumption subsidies and enterprise subsidies. Initially, consumption subsidies rose sharply as the Government compensated urban consumers for price increases arising from the agricultural reforms and the lifting of agricultural price controls. Subsequently, these subsidies declined (from 5.4 percent of GDP at the beginning of the 1980s to about 2 percent of GDP by 1990), following the policy of relying on increases in productivity and wages rather than on subsidies to maintain and enhance living standards. On the other hand, subsidies to cover enterprise losses have increased steadily from about 1 percent of GDP at the start of the process to 3.5 percent in 1988-89, being slightly reduced by 1990-91. Essentially, higher enterprise losses have arisen from the rigidity of administered prices in the face of increasing costs.[11] The pressure on the fiscal accounts from the impact of the reforms on the budgetary contribution of enterprises is highlighted by the rapid drop in the net budgetary yield of

---

[9]There are two types of individual income taxation: a long-standing individual income tax levied, in practice, on foreign residents, and the personal income adjustment tax, introduced in 1987, which is applied to Chinese citizens at rates varying from 20 percent to 60 percent.

[10]The receipts from personal income taxes and from taxes on foreign-related enterprises are included in "other taxes" in Table 1. Wholly foreign-owned enterprises are subject to a progressive schedule ranging from 20 percent to 40 percent and a local surcharge of 10 percent. There is also a 10 percent tax on dividend remittances. Taxation on joint ventures is rather complicated, depending on the equity participation of the Chinese partner. The receipts from these taxes should, in fact, be added to the revenues from enterprises but no separate data were available.

[11]See below for a discussion on the factors affecting enterprise profitability under partial reforms.

Table 2. China: Government Expenditure
(In percent of GDP)

	1978	1979–81	1982–84	1985–87	1988–89	1990–91	1992 (Prel.)
Total expenditure	34.1	33.2	28.5	26.4	22.8	21.5	18.7
Current expenditure	19.3	22.0	21.1	19.0	17.8	17.0	14.8
Defense	4.7	4.5	3.0	2.1	1.5	1.6	1.5
Subsidies	3.2	6.2	6.8	5.9	5.9	5.0	3.2
To enterprises[1]	1.0	0.9	1.3	2.9	3.5	3.0	2.0
Other[2]	2.2	5.4	5.5	3.0	2.4	2.0	1.2
Capital expenditure	14.9	11.2	7.4	7.4	5.1	4.5	3.9

Source: Ministry of Finance.

[1] Data prior to 1981 may be less than a full accounting for subsidies because certain subsidies to enterprises were subtracted from taxes rather than shown as expenditure. Available information does not permit reclassification for those years.

[2] Includes price subsidies on consumption goods (daily necessities) and subsidies to agricultural inputs.

enterprise activities, measured by the difference between revenues and subsidies to loss-making firms (Table 1, bottom line). The net contribution fell dramatically from more than 19 percent of GDP in 1978 to less than 3 percent by 1992.

Prior to the reforms, balanced budgets were emphasized and, in fact, the government budget recorded small surpluses almost every year for three decades. The evolution of the budget deficit over the 1980s, as a percentage of GDP, is presented in Table 3. After a few years of budget deficits averaging about 2 percent of GDP, there was a shift toward stabilization and tighter macroeconomic control. As a result, the deficit, while fluctuating from one year to another, fell to as low as 0.5 percent in 1985. However, from 1986 until 1989, the deficits rose again, reaching 2.4 percent of GDP in 1988, as revenue again tended to fall faster than expenditure. In the early years of the reforms, more than 80 percent of the deficits were financed by the central bank. In 1981, the Government began issuing bonds, which have financed an increasing proportion of the deficit and reflect the institutional changes brought about by the development of financial markets. Foreign borrowing has also become an important source of finance, averaging about 30 percent of the total yearly financing needs.[12]

The fiscal deficits in China were not very large by international standards and could not, without further elucidation, constitute the main explanation for the rise in inflationary pressures. However, the measured deficit understates the correct magnitude of the macroeconomic impact of budgetary developments. Because government-financed investments

---

[12]See Blejer and others (1991), Table 8.

Table 3. China: Consolidated Budget Deficits
(In percent of GDP)

Years	Deficit
1980–82	1.9
1983–85	1.2
1986–87	2.0
1988	2.4
1989	2.3
1990	2.1
1991	2.5
1992 (prel.)	2.3

Source: Ministry of Finance.

declined fast, pressure grew on the publicly owned banking system to increase credit to enterprises so as to facilitate the financing of their investment.[13] Loans to enterprises and individuals grew by more than 20 percent a year during 1985–88. This extension of excessive bank credit undermined monetary control after the mid-1980s and compounded the expansive effects of the rising budget deficit.[14]

Faced with inflationary and balance of payments pressures the authorities implemented, starting in the last quarter of 1988, a number of austerity measures. Spending guidelines were introduced to slash state investment outlays by 20 percent in 1989, and the budget deficit was actually reduced by almost 1 percent of GDP. In addition, the central bank adopted highly contractionary monetary policies that resulted in a rapid deceleration of inflation and output growth. A further reduction in the deficit took place in 1990, based on additional cuts in public investment. Credit policy, however, was relaxed in late 1989 and 1990, mainly to bail out inefficient enterprises and avoid the deepening of the recessionary trends. Despite further cuts in expenditures, deficits grew again in 1991–92, largely due to continuous depressed revenues.

Fiscal Dimensions of Reforms

The reform process resulted in significant changes in the objectives and mechanisms of fiscal policy. Under strict central planning, fiscal policy aims to allocate resources administratively by regulating the rate of investment and by maintaining household incomes at a level consistent with the

---

[13]This pressure was sometimes intensified by the ability of local governments to obtain additional financial resources for the enterprises they own in order to induce them to invest in infrastructure projects in their localities.

[14]See McKinnon (1991).

availability of consumer goods. Tax policy as such does not fulfill a major function, since there is no private sector participating in the production process and state enterprises are required to remit all their surpluses to the government. The primary instrument of fiscal policy is, therefore, the level and composition of government expenditure. Government funds are channeled back to the enterprises through the financing of investment and the provision of working capital and, in many cases, in the form of subsidies. The level of expenditures is largely determined by the guidelines implied by the quantitative plan and, if the need for aggregate demand adjustments arises, cutbacks in expenditure are the main instrument for reducing inflationary and balance of payments pressures.[15] These were the characteristics of fiscal policy in China until the early 1980s. As market-oriented reforms started to be implemented, two important issues became relevant: first, the direct and indirect budgetary consequences of the reforms, or, more precisely, the type of built-in elements in the reform process that tend to create fiscal imbalances; and second, the ability of fiscal policy to perform an effective macroeconomic role under the prevailing circumstances. These issues are, of course, pertinent in the context of all reforming economies but they take a distinctive turn in the Chinese setting given the specificity of some of the measures adopted and the particular institutional and organizational arrangements within which the reforms became operational.

The central goal of the Chinese reforms, both rural and urban, was to improve productive efficiency. In order to reach this goal it was deemed necessary to increase the autonomy of economic agents, to reinforce their managerial capabilities, and to decentralize the economic decision-making process. The Government, however, did not intend to transfer the ownership of most of the means of production and, although private businesses and joint ventures were allowed in some sectors, public ownership of virtually all large enterprises was to be preserved. An institutional mechanism was therefore necessary to make government ownership compatible with the enhancement of productive incentives. The chosen mechanism had two components: a disengagement of enterprise finances from the fiscal budget and the adoption of the contract management responsibility system that was supposed to drive enterprises, in practice, toward a system in which they make their productive decisions "as if" they were privately owned.

The first component implies a reduction in the intermediation role of the budget: the profits of enterprises will be only partially taxed but they will become responsible for the financing of their investments as well as their working capital. This, of course, means that the observed decline in both government revenues and expenditure relative to national income

---

[15]For a discussion on the role of the budget in centrally planned economies and its evolution during the transition, see Tanzi (1991).

was an integral component of the reforms. However, the second component, the contract responsibility system, led to continuous and *unintended* reductions in revenues, compounded by an erosion in enterprise profits arising from the incomplete nature of the reforms. The outcome was a fall in revenues much larger than expected and it exceeded the cut in expenditures, resulting in wider fiscal imbalances. Moreover, the system has involved widespread discretion, detracting from the predictability and effectiveness of fiscal policies. In addition, the manner in which the growing decentralization of fiscal authority to lower levels of government has been implemented has tended to reduce the revenue that is transferred to the Central Government, a development that has serious implications for macroeconomic management. These aspects of revenue developments, as well as some expenditure issues associated with the reforms, are discussed here in detail.[16]

Revenue Consequences of Contract Responsibility System

The contract responsibility system was introduced in the industrial sector in 1984 and currently covers more than 90 percent of large and medium-sized state-owned enterprises. It consists of a contractual arrangement between the management of an enterprise and the Central Government (or the local government) that owns it. The contract usually covers up to five years and provides for a minimum amount of profit to be realized or tax to be paid to the government each year.[17] The contracted amount is typically the amount realized in the year preceding the signature of the contract or some fixed rate of increase over that amount. Profits in excess of the contracted amount are retained fully by the enterprise or are taxed at a lower rate. Firms that fail to reach their profit target are supposed to meet the contract from their reserves. However, when it is clear that the enterprise cannot meet the contract, the government is forced to reduce the contracted amounts since this would not be considered sufficient grounds for bankruptcy.

The contract system was supposed to expand the tax base by improving considerably the performance of the enterprises. However, the way the contracts set the tax obligations resulted, in practice, in an opposite effect. Since below-quota profits are subject to a flat tax while above-quota profits are taxed at a lower (or zero) rate, enterprises retain an increasingly larger share of their profits as output and profits expand, resulting in a continuously decreasing average tax rate and in an income elasticity of less than unity for the enterprise profit tax. The lack of buoyancy that is introduced by this system was aggravated by the absence of

---

[16]For a more detailed discussion of these issues see Blejer and Szapary (1990).

[17]Usually, for large and medium-sized enterprises, the tax rate applied to the "agreed profits" is the statutory 55 percent rate.

provisions for inflation, since in most of the multiyear contracts the tax is based on estimated profitability under an assumed standard inflation rate; if actual nominal income exceeds the estimates embodied in the contract (as was the case in 1988–89 when inflation was high), the effective tax rate declines further. This tends to reduce macroeconomic built-in stabilizers and to introduce a procyclical aggregate demand element into the tax system: after-tax profits of enterprises rise when growth and inflation are higher than the trend rates and fall when these rates are low.[18]

The contract responsibility system not only has tended to reduce the tax-GNP ratio (Table 1) but has largely impaired the flexibility of tax policy as a macroeconomic instrument. This is so because long-run contracts constrain the ability of the government to introduce new revenue measures in a timely manner and to change current policies in order to address unforeseen emergencies or to achieve stabilization targets.

Besides introducing serious microeconomic distortions, the high degree of discretion that arises from the contract system weakens the ability of the budget to perform an active and predictable macroeconomic function. The system has involved case-by-case negotiations of taxes between the government and the enterprises with the consequence that the government does not, in fact, assess and enforce taxes, but rather bargains for them. This leads to taxation rules that vary from one enterprise to another and which are very costly to change once the long-term contracts are signed. The discretion entailed in the bargaining process makes fiscal policy less effective in the macroeconomic sense, but it also detracts from the benefits of the reforms because it tends to validate the distortions in the system that could ultimately eliminate the incentives that the reforms intended to provide. This is so because the efficiency in the allocation of resources will not improve if decisions at the level of the firm continue to be made under a soft budget constraint. Discretion is bound to soften the budget constraint, thereby working against allocative efficiency.[19]

Erosion of Enterprise Profits

The negative impact of the contract system on government revenue was magnified by the shrinking of the tax base itself, caused by the decline in enterprise profits. Although there are no available data to esti-

---

[18]The contracts also seem to result in "ratchet effects" because if enterprises expect that the target rate of profit in the next contract, and therefore the effective tax rate, would depend on their current performance, this would have a strong negative impact on the current enterprise behavior. Hussain and Stern (1991).

[19]The Chinese authorities are currently experimenting with a different form of enterprise taxation, under which a flat, nonnegotiable tax rate of 35 percent of total profits is the norm. The enterprises then negotiate with the government (the "owner") the distribution of posttax profits. This has limited coverage: no more than 20 cities are said to have implemented it so far with enterprises participating on a voluntary basis. Experiments of this type are expected to continue.

mate precisely the evolution of enterprise profits, there is strong evidence that these have indeed diminished over time.[20] Within the contract system, the decline in the profit-GDP ratio causes the tax-GDP ratio to fall at a compounded exponential rate.[21] The main cause behind the decline in enterprise profits is the incomplete nature of the reforms. Thus, an important factor lowering taxable profits in China has been the maintenance of price controls on final products, which has prevented many enterprises from shifting increased costs to prices. The higher costs have a number of causes: higher input prices (since prices of a number of raw materials were not tightly controlled), the depreciation of the exchange rate, and higher indirect taxes that cannot be shifted forward. In addition, the autonomy granted to enterprises regarding various aspects of wage policies, in the context of soft budget constraints arising from largely accommodating credit policies, led to a quite rapid increase in wages, benefit payments, and bonuses, which tended to reduce profits. Moreover, enterprises are allowed to treat both interest and loan repayments as deductible expenses in the calculation of taxable income, giving rise to an inverse relationship between the tax base and the level of indebtedness.[22]

Budgetary Repercussions of Regional Decentralization

Regional decentralization of fiscal powers was seen as an integral part of the economic transformation of China. The types of reforms adopted in this area, however, made tax revenues less buoyant and eroded the amount of revenue transferred to the Central Government. In China, local governments, mostly provincial and city governments, are in charge of collecting virtually all major taxes. The revenue is then shared upward with the next level of government. The sharing arrangements are not uniform, are subject to negotiation, and may vary from one case to another. Over the years, the revenue-sharing arrangements have undergone many changes, but, since the inception of the reforms in the late 1970s, the trend has been toward granting local governments more fiscal authority and allowing them to retain more revenue.

Regional decentralization reduced revenue collection, particularly following the introduction of the contract responsibility system for enterprises. Although in China tax policy is nominally set at the national level by the Central Government, local governments are responsible for negotiating contracts with the enterprises that they own. As this negotiation

---

[20]See Blejer and others (1991), p. 27.

[21]For a proof, see Blejer and Szapary (1990), Appendix I.

[22]This policy was envisaged to be transitional and intended to put enterprises that have to rely on bank loans and those that continue to benefit from budgetary grants to finance investments on an even footing. Although this practice is being phased out slowly, it is still the prevalent system. Under the experimental system described in footnote 19, loan repayments are no longer admissible as a deductible expense.

proceeds, local authorities have the power to set effective tax rates (as opposed to the statutory rates dictated from the center) through the establishment of quota profits and the rate of taxation of above-quota profits. Further, given the sharing rules between the center and the local governments, the latter have a clear stake in keeping as much financial resources as possible within their territory. In order to attain this objective, local governments are keen to grant generous tax treatment to their enterprises in the context of the negotiated contracts. In this way, resources remain within the local jurisdiction and local authorities can then tap these resources through "voluntary" contributions from enterprises to local projects—contributions that, of course, are not shared with the Central Government. Thus, while the effective tax burden on the enterprises is not reduced, explicit tax revenue, especially the budgetary revenue of the Central Government, is seriously eroded.

In order to address this problem and to provide incentives for local governments to collect and remit taxes, in 1988 the Central Government entered into contracts with each of the provinces. These contracts feature a quota arrangement, somewhat similar to the contract responsibility system for enterprises. The regional contracts replace the retention system previously in operation and specify the manner in which the resources raised in the provinces would be allocated between central and local governments. Typically, local governments contract to remit to the higher level of government a predetermined amount of revenue and retain all or part of the revenue above the quota.[23]

For two reasons, this type of revenue-sharing agreement weakens further the control of the center over fiscal policy and its ability to use it for macroeconomic purposes. First, the relatively low incremental revenue transfers that these contracts appear to set leave increased amounts of resources in the hands of local governments, which tend to generate higher local expenditures (that are difficult to control at the central level) and do not contribute to the improvement of the consolidated budget. Second, the fixed increment featured in the quota arrangements implies that the revenue transmitted to the Central Government is not affected by the underlying economic conditions, which affect only the revenue accruing to the local government. Since local governments usually do not consider themselves as responsible for country-wide demand management,

---

[23]As with enterprises, the quota is usually calculated as the revenue remitted in the year prior to the signing of the contract plus a fixed increment. There are however five types of contracts: (1) localities retain a specified proportion of any revenue that is within a certain percentage growth from the previous year and retain any excess of this growth rate; (2) a specific proportion of all revenue is remitted to the center; (3) a certain proportion of revenue is retained up to a quota, and then a usually higher proportion of revenue is retained in excess of the quota; and (4) a given transfer to the center is contracted for the first year. In subsequent years the initial amount is contracted without changes over time. In addition, the center has entered into contracts to provide specified transfers to deficit or poor provinces.

the quota arrangement tends to compound the procyclical bias of the fiscal system generated by the enterprise contract system.[24]

Some recent information on the financial flows between the Central Government and local governments indicates that, indeed, a large proportion of the funds raised in the localities remain there, strengthening the constraints faced by the Central Government (Table 4) and restricting its ability to utilize fiscal instruments to attain global macroeconomic goals.

Inflexibility of Public Expenditure

Although, as discussed above, the reduction in public expenditures as a proportion of GDP has been indeed significant, the question arises, in view of the trends in government revenues, whether the pace of spending cuts is consistent with the maintenance of macroeconomic balance. The decline in government expenditures has been constrained, in practice, by the interaction of the following: (1) the incomplete nature of reforms, particularly price reforms, that has required a sustained increase in budgetary subsidies to cover operating losses of enterprises; (2) the perceived need to raise consumer subsidies in order to avoid sharp increases in the prices of basic consumer goods that result from agricultural reforms; and (3) the limited success of the Government in transferring investment responsibilities to enterprises in an appropriate relation to the increase in their ability to retain profits.

In addition to these problems, further reforms now being considered or implemented also tend to put upward pressure on government expenditures or, at least, to limit their downward flexibility. In particular, a resumption of price reforms is likely to raise government spending since, in addition to the impact on the direct purchase of goods and services, and probably on wages, the demand for consumer subsidies will probably rise. On the other hand, freeing prices may allow many enterprises affected by price controls to become profitable and reduce the need for enterprise subsidies. Further pressure on expenditure will come also from the need to increase capital spending to relieve major bottlenecks in transportation, energy, and agriculture, or, at least, to limit their downward flexibility.

As a whole, therefore, much room for major contraction in the levels of expenditures cannot be realistically expected . Therefore, to prevent the emergence of serious fiscal imbalances it is crucial to address the revenue problems discussed above and, in particular, to streamline the tax system and the revenue-sharing arrangements so as to enhance the elasticity of revenue and strengthen the ability of the Government to use tax policy efficiently.

---

[24]For further discussion on the fiscal dimension of regional decentralization, see Wong (1990).

Table 4. China: Budgetary Operations
of Central and Local Governments

(In billions of yuan)

	1989	1990	1991	1992 (Budget)
Central Government				
Receipts of Central Government	155.8	185.0	189.0	183.6
Central government revenue collection	110.5	136.8	140.0	130.6
Profits remitted from localities	45.2	48.2	49.0	53.0
Outlays of Central Government	166.7	195.8	207.2	196.6
For central government expenditure	110.5	137.3	151.8	150.0
Central government financing of local expenditures	56.2	58.5	55.4	46.6
Local governments				
Receipts of local governments	240.5	253.0	276.6	260.3
Local revenue collection	184.2	194.5	221.1	213.7
Transfers from Central Government	56.3	58.5	55.5	46.3
Outlays of local governments	238.7	256.1	278.6	259.7
For local expenditure	193.5	207.9	229.6	206.7
Transfers to Central Government	45.2	48.2	49.0	53.0

Source: Ministry of Finance.

Concluding Remarks

The economic reforms taking place in centrally planned economies have brought risks and challenges that require a constant effort to monitor experience and find new strategies. Meeting these challenges necessitates the development of new policy instruments, or the modification of existing ones, to make them suitable to the changing circumstances that arise as a direct consequence of the reforms.

The central elements of economic reform in China have been granting greater decision-making powers to enterprises and enhancing the role played by market forces, while preserving the basic framework of socialist ownership. These changes require the development of instruments for indirect control over the behavior of increasingly autonomous economic agents. Among these instruments, fiscal policy plays a central role since it could be useful both for controlling aggregate demand and for affecting resource allocation. For these purposes, however, fiscal policy has to be transformed into an indirect lever of economic management rather than remaining a tool for the administrative allocation of resources.

In this paper, the evolution of fiscal policy over the course of the Chinese reforms has been examined with the objective of analyzing the main reasons for the major budgetary developments and assessing whether fiscal policy, under the conditions created by the reforms, can fulfill effectively its new macroeconomic role.

With respect to the first issue, the impact of reforms on the evolution of fiscal accounts, the Government is faced with a policy conflict. The goal of allowing enterprises to retain and freely dispose of a larger proportion of their profits means, at least in the short run, less revenue. However, the success of the reforms necessitates the maintenance of macroeconomic stability which entails a broad measure of fiscal balance. This, in turn, requires that the Government either divest itself further of spending responsibilities or redress the erosion of revenue elasticity that has arisen from the institutional framework associated with the reforms. While there is some scope for further reduction in spending, it is indeed quite limited and, therefore, ways must be found to enhance the elasticity of government revenue. This objective can only be attained, however, if the discretionary elements of tax policy are reduced.

The high degree of discretion, as well as the inflexibility entailed in current practices, particularly regarding the bargaining elements embodied in the contract systems, also limit the ability of the Government to exercise efficient fiscal control. The regional revenue-sharing arrangements, by leaving increased resources in the hands of local governments and by increasing their powers to set tax rates effectively, have eroded the command of the center over the mobilization of resources and have reduced its capacity to predict the outcome of policy measures.

Fiscal policies can and must play an important role in hardening the budget constraints during the transition from a centrally planned system. However, for this purpose a compromise should be found to solve the conflict between decentralization of decision making and maintenance of macroeconomic control and flexibility. Decentralization of decision making does not mean decentralization of macroeconomic instruments, which have to remain under firm government control. The need to adopt more transparent and flexible fiscal rules while developing the instruments for appropriate macroeconomic management seems to be an important lesson from the Chinese experience for other economies undertaking market-oriented reforms.

References

Blejer, Mario I., and Gyorgy Szapary, "The Evolving Role of Tax Policy in China," *Journal of Comparative Economics*, Vol. 14 (September 1990), pp. 452–72.

Blejer, Mario I., David Burton, Steven Dunaway, and Gyorgy Szapary, *China: Economic Reform and Macroeconomic Management*, IMF Occasional Paper No. 76 (Washington: International Monetary Fund, 1991).

"China's Economy: They Couldn't Keep It Down," *The Economist* (June 1, 1991), pp. 15–18.

Hussain, Athar, and Nicholas Stern, "Effective Demand, Enterprise Reforms and Public Finance in China" *Economic Policy*, No. 12 (April 1991), pp. 141–86.

McKinnon, Ronald I., "Taxation, Money, and Credit in a Liberalizing Socialist Economy," paper presented at the IPR-IRIS Conference, Prague, March 1991.

McMillan, John, John Whalley, and Lijing Zhu, "The Impact of China's Economic Reforms on Agricultural Productivity Growth," *Journal of Political Economy*, Vol. 97 (August 1989), pp. 781–807.

Perkins, Dwight H., "Reforming China's Economic System," *Journal of Economic Literature*, Vol. 26 (June 1988), pp. 601–45.

———, and Shahid Yusuf, *Rural Development in China* (Baltimore: Johns Hopkins University Press, 1984).

Tanzi, Vito, "Mobilization of Savings in Eastern European Countries: The Role of the State," IMF Working Paper No. 91/16 (Washington: International Monetary Fund, 1991).

Wong, Christine, "Central-Local Relations in an Era of Fiscal Decline: The Paradox of Fiscal Decentralization in Post-Mao China," Working Paper No. 210, University of California, September 1990.

World Bank, *China: Rural Industry—Overview, Issues, and Prospects* (Washington: World Bank, 1989).

———, *China: Revenue Mobilization and Tax Policy—Issues and Options* (Washington: World Bank, 1990).

Wu, Jinglian, and Renwei Zhao, "The Dual Pricing System in China's Industry," *Journal of Comparative Economics*, Vol. 11 (September 1987), pp. 309–18.

CHAPTER 14

Viet Nam: Constraints on Fiscal Adjustments During Economic Reforms

Howell H. Zee

Centrally planned economies undertaking comprehensive market-oriented reforms frequently experience significant difficulties in managing their public finances during the period of reform. The difficulties could stem from pressures on both the revenue and the expenditure side of the budget; from a lack of monetary discipline in financing budget deficits and losses of state enterprises that invariably lead to other macroeconomic imbalances; and from an inadequate legal framework (especially that pertaining to property rights and bankruptcy laws), incomplete or incorrect accounting principles, and a deficiency in the administrative machinery to accommodate drastic changes in how an economy is organized and functions.

In these economies, the state sector (usually comprising all levels of government and state-owned enterprises) is particularly vulnerable to reform, since under central planning almost all economic activities directly or indirectly revolve around that sector. Alteration or dismantlement of existing relationships and arrangements among economic units can put the institutional structure of the state sector under severe strain. While the pace of, and the demand for, reform in many areas of the economy could develop rapidly and urgently, such as those related to price and trade liberalization, the institutional changes necessary to support those reforms—to render them meaningful and sustainable—are by nature slow to materialize. Thus, the institutional shortcomings often become the binding constraint, at least in the short to medium term, of market-oriented reform programs. In the state sector, this can lead to a significant deterioration in fiscal imbalances, which, if compensating domestic policy measures, as well as external assistance, are not put in place in a sufficiently timely fashion, may endanger the success of the overall reform effort.[1]

Howell H. Zee is a Senior Economist in the Tax Policy Division of the Fiscal Affairs Department.

[1]See Tanzi (1991a) for a broader discussion of fiscal issues relevant for economies in transition.

The reform experience in Viet Nam in 1989-90 brought into sharp focus the constraints imposed by institutional factors in an economy facing rapid economic change. It also underscored the difficulties in making the requisite fiscal adjustments during the transition of moving a centrally planned economy to a market-oriented environment. This paper first gives a summary background to recent economic developments in Viet Nam leading up to the 1989-90 reforms. It then describes the structure of the public finances and their relationship to the rest of the economy prior to those reforms. This relationship is used to discuss the fiscal consequences of the measures implemented during the reform period. Lessons are drawn to illustrate the institutional dimension of the fiscal adjustments necessary to underpin reform objectives. Some concluding remarks complete the paper. An appendix updates tax reform measures undertaken in 1990-91.

Background to Recent Economic Developments

The Sixth Party Congress, in December 1986, marked a turning point in Viet Nam's economic development by ushering in a more forward- and outward-looking approach to economic reform. Although partial and piecemeal reforms, as well as open debate on economic policies based on the DRV (Democratic Republic of Vietnam) model of development, a model that has its origin in the Soviet-style central planning in the 1930s, were already evident in the period prior to the Sixth Party Congress (largely in response to the 1979-80 economic crisis of severe shortages in food, consumer goods, and raw material inputs to agriculture and industry), there was no attempt at a comprehensive program of reform that would address the deteriorating external and internal imbalances. The DRV model stressed direct control of individual economic units by the state, through the establishment of quantitative output targets, centrally directed allocations of inputs, and fixing of prices and exchange rates at levels divorced from market demand and supply conditions. The DRV model also emphasized fixed capital formation as the primary engine for economic growth, without, however, paying sufficient attention to the efficient utilization of the capital stock once it was in place. As a result, the economy experienced widespread misallocation of resources, sectoral imbalances in favor of heavy industries over agriculture and light industries for consumer goods, and large trade deficits.

The period prior to the Sixth Party Congress was also characterized by a severe deterioration of the fiscal position, stemming largely from the lack of resistance to pressure for wage and price hikes in the face of spiraling inflation, which led, among other things, to an ever-increasing burden on the state budget of consumer subsidies. The root cause of the high rates of inflation lay in the large expansion of domestic bank credits, particularly those used to finance deficits of the state budget and state enterprises. In the absence of meaningful price signals, many state enterprises were operated with noticeable inefficiency and sustained largely by budgetary support and easy recourse to bank financing, or, to use a phrase made popular by Kornai (1986), by soft budget constraints. Indeed, some loss-incurring enterprises would not have survived had the monetary stance not been so accommodating.

Recognizing that the deteriorating economic situation was not sustainable, the Sixth Party Congress laid the foundation for a comprehensive framework of economic reform comprising an investment strategy emphasizing agriculture, consumer goods production, and exports; a provision for greater scope in decentralized decision making for individual economic units, particularly with respect to production and pricing policies of state enterprises; and a general direction to give price signals a greater role to play in the process of resource allocation. While these elements of reform were reaffirmed and amplified later in a number of Plena of the Central Committee, no effective measures to reduce the fiscal imbalance and to instill tight monetary discipline within an integrated macroeconomic framework were put in place in the two years following the Sixth Party Congress. A comprehensive market-oriented reform program to arrest the growing macroeconomic imbalances was not launched until 1989.[2]

The Structure of Public Finances in the Pre-Reform Period[3]

In common with most other centrally planned economies before embarking on comprehensive reforms, the Vietnamese economy was divided broadly into two sectors: state (comprising all levels of government and state enterprises) and nonstate (comprising cooperatives and private enterprises), corresponding to the division between production within and outside the central plan. Being predominantly an agriculture-based economy, about 40 percent of Viet Nam's GDP originated from agriculture, whose production derived almost entirely from cooperative and private farms. While output from state enterprises technically accounted for less than one fourth of total GDP, production outside the central plan was nevertheless to a large extent centrally directed because of its limited access to officially controlled raw materials and bank credits; agricultural production was governed by a contract system in which a specified number of plots of land and quantity of inputs would be exchanged for a fixed

---

[2]See Beresford (1988; 1989), Fforde and Paine (1987), and Wiegersma (1988) for historical accounts and analyses of political and economic developments in Viet Nam. Extensive reviews of the Vietnamese economy prior to the 1989–90 reforms can be found in Fforde and de Vylder (1988), Drabek (1990), and Kimura (1989).

[3]All statistical references to the pre-reform period, unless otherwise specified, correspond to five-year averages for 1984–88. As will be discussed below, some reform measures were actually implemented as early as mid-1988.

share of output. The overall structure of production in the economy was further guided by a two-tier price system: a set of official prices applicable to most essential industrial and agricultural goods and a set of "market" prices applicable to goods produced outside the central plan and surplus goods within the plan (goods whose production had exceeded plan targets). Although official prices were adjusted more frequently to movements in the "market" prices following the Sixth Party Congress in late 1986, the pricing system remained severely distortive until the 1989-90 reforms.

Given the pervasive influence of the state sector on the economy, fiscal operations in Viet Nam in the pre-reform period were in line with those typically found in other centrally planned economies: they were largely related to supporting state-directed objectives for employment, subsidies, investment, and defense by means of what amounted to centrally determined appropriations of the national output. As a result, the structure of revenue and expenditure of the state budget, which consolidated the transactions of the central, provincial, and district governments, was ill-equipped to respond speedily, flexibly, and effectively to institutional shocks in the economy. Table 1 provides some details of the composition of the state budget before and during the reforms.[4]

Revenue

The revenue base of Viet Nam's state budget prior to the reforms had consisted primarily of transfers from state enterprises amounting on average to almost 8 percent of GDP, or well over two thirds of total revenue. These transfers technically consisted of four components: a turnover tax included in the selling price of each enterprise; various commodity taxes (excises); a tax on profits, defined as sales less cost of production (inclusive of all other taxes levied) and allowable contributions to various enterprise funds; and the remittance of depreciation allowances to recoup past government investments in the state enterprises. The distinction among the components had, however, little analytical significance, given the substantial official control over input and output prices and the limited degree of enterprise autonomy. Moreover, the amount of transfers to be collected from each state enterprise was frequently subject to negotiation between the Government and state enterprises (through varying the prices or tax rates, or both)—with the negotiations being influenced by the latter's financial positions. Since many state enterprises were, as noted earlier, heavily dependent on a multitude of distortive government policies, the basis of their fiscal contributions was precarious at best.

---

[4]All references to GDP ratios below are based on budgetary data provided by the Vietnamese authorities, and nominal GDP estimates by IMF staff, which are different from those of the authorities.

Table 1. Viet Nam: Budgetary Operations

(In percent of GDP)

	Pre-Reform Period 1984–88 average	Reform Period 1989	1990
Revenue	10.8	11.9	11.5
Of which:			
Enterprise transfers	7.8	5.6	3.9
Crude oil exports	—	1.0	1.8
Nonagricultural taxes	1.2	1.3	1.5
Agricultural tax	0.5	0.9	0.6
Trade taxes	0.5	1.1	1.6
Current expenditure[1]	10.6	11.5	11.9
Of which:			
Wages	0.9	3.9	3.3
Subsidies	3.9	—	—
Unidentified item[2]	4.0	5.0	6.3
Capital expenditure[3]	5.8	7.1[4]	4.5
Overall deficit (–)	–5.5	–6.8	–4.8
Of which financed by:			
Domestic sources	3.3	5.2	3.5
Foreign sources	2.2	1.5	1.3

Sources: Budgetary data provided by the Vietnamese authorities; GDP ratios are based on IMF staff estimates of nominal GDP.
[1] Exclusive of maintenance expenditure.
[2] Inclusive of defense expenditure.
[3] Inclusive of maintenance expenditure.
[4] Inclusive of special rice stock purchases of 1.1 percent of GDP.

The remaining sources of budgetary revenue principally consisted of taxes on agriculture, trade, and (nonagricultural) cooperatives and private enterprises. These sources contributed a little over 2 percent of GDP in revenue, or only about one fifth of total revenue collected. Hence, the state budget's overwhelming reliance on (largely negotiated) contributions by state enterprises made it all but inevitable that a comprehensive reform of the tax system—by necessity a complicated and time-consuming task—would be required if economy-wide market-oriented reforms were to bear fruit.

Expenditure

The expenditure side of the state budget prior to the reforms comprised four main categories: wages to government workers (exclusive of employees of state enterprises); various subsidies to consumers, state enterprises, and exporters; capital and maintenance expenditure; and a large but (formally) unidentified category, the bulk of which consisted of defense spending. It came as no surprise to find later, during the reform period 1989–90, that the extent to which these expenditures could be reduced quickly and in a manner consistent with the overall objectives of the reform program was extremely limited. Indeed, overcoming institutional rigidities necessitated expenditures in new areas.

The structure of government wages was complex, since total remuneration for a government worker comprised both cash and subsidized goods and services. Average remuneration was linked to the price index of six basic commodities (rice, sugar, pork, fish sauce, soap, and kerosene), and minimum remuneration was linked to the (official) price of rice. Hence, the total wage bill in the state budget, which partly reflected the cash component of government wages,[5] was intertwined with the pricing and subsidy policies of the government, rendering it difficult to be controlled independently.

Substantial budgetary resources in the pre-reform period were devoted to subsidies, which averaged about 4 percent of GDP, or over 30 percent of total current expenditure. Consumer subsidies, usually accounting for about two thirds of total subsidies, arose from keeping the official prices of rice, kerosene, and a range of foodstuffs below procurement costs; export subsidies, associated with the maintenance of unrealistic official exchange rates, were next in importance; finally, subsidies were given to state enterprises to assist in their production costs. Given their nature, these subsidies could not be easily reduced without, at least in the short run, compensating measures elsewhere, or even outside, the state budget.

Although capital and maintenance expenditure averaged almost 6 percent of GDP prior to the reforms, limited budgetary resources and rising wage and subsidy outlays steadily eroded such expenditure in real terms over the pre-reform period; for example, it fell from about 9.5 percent of GDP in 1985 to about 4 percent of GDP in 1988. While investments in key industrial and energy projects, such as fertilizer and cement production, and, in particular, hydroelectric power generators, were maintained throughout this period, the decline in capital and maintenance expenditure further impinged on the infrastructure needs of Viet Nam, especially those in the transport sector, in which the extremely poor condition and strained capacity of most roads, bridges, and rail links imposed a severe bottleneck to growth and national economic integration.

An average of 4 percent of GDP, or more than a third of total budgetary resources, was devoted to an "unidentified" category of expenditure that encompassed all military-related spending (inclusive of remuneration for soldiers, which was not classified as part of the government wage bill). Such expenditure was clearly driven as much by political as by economic factors, and, even if a favorable political environment were to develop—

---

[5]The other part of the wage bill reflected government contributions to a social security fund for retirement and assorted social benefit payments.

as it did during the reform period of 1989-90—institutional factors would render an appreciable reduction in its level difficult to achieve in the short run.

Financing of Budget Deficit

The manner in which deficits in the state budget were financed in the pre-reform period is important to understanding fiscal developments during the reform process. Like many other centrally planned economies, monetary policy in Viet Nam prior to the reforms played a role essentially subservient to the central plan, and was by and large conducted passively to accommodate the needs of the state sector. Indeed, domestic credit expansion by the banking sector to the state budget and state enterprises, which increased at a rate exceeding 300 percent in 1987 and 400 percent in 1988,[6] had been the primary contributing factor to high rates of inflation (at annual rates exceeding 300 percent) in the same period.

More than half the deficit in the state budget was financed by the domestic banking sector; the rest was met almost entirely by foreign financing, the bulk of which consisted of Soviet commodity aid in the form of productive inputs and raw materials that the Government sold to state enterprises at the dong equivalent of the ruble price, as well as in the form of machinery and equipment for capital expenditure. Prior to 1989, exchange rates used in converting transferable ruble costs to dong prices were fixed at artificially low levels, thus providing state enterprises with hidden but significant budgetary subsidies. This linkage between government fiscal operations and state enterprises had important implications for public finances in the reform period.

All Soviet commodity aid to Viet Nam, which represented the bulk of the latter's trade with the Council for Mutual Economic Assistance (CMEA) members, was entirely channeled through the state budget under official trade protocols between the two countries. Even at the substantially overvalued dong exchange rates against the transferable ruble, foreign financing in dong terms still covered about 40 percent of the deficit in the state budget, which is an indication of how much the Vietnamese economy had relied on Soviet assistance in the pre-reform period. Such reliance foreshadowed later fiscal difficulties when financing from this source was drastically reduced.

A final aspect of how the state budget deficits were financed in the pre-reform period was the extremely limited extent to which private domestic savings were utilized as a financing source—government debt covered less than 10 percent of the deficit in this period. The unavailability of adequate institutional arrangements and financial instruments for the Government to mobilize private savings directly—a not uncommon charac-

---

[6]Monetary data prior to 1986 were inadequate for analytical purposes.

teristic of centrally planned economies—was also to become a major constraint later in its attempt at an effective anti-inflation policy to support the economic reforms.[7]

Fiscal Impact of Reform

The reform program launched by Viet Nam in 1989 (with certain measures already implemented in mid-1988) was not only intended to transform the economy into one more compatible with a market-oriented, outward-looking environment, but also contained strong policy initiatives for macroeconomic stabilization, in particular to reduce triple-digit annual inflation rates to a low double-digit range. The scope of the reforms was comprehensive, encompassing almost all sectors of the economy: agriculture, trade, the financial sector, and state enterprises. Apart from those of a structural nature, the reforms included an overall liberalization of prices as well as significant devaluations of the dong to more realistic levels. Not surprisingly, this wide-ranging reform program exerted a fundamental impact on the Government's fiscal operations and illuminated the Government's difficulties in overcoming institutional rigidities inherent in the fiscal system over the transitional period.

Impact on Revenue

The weakness in the state budget's revenue base became all too apparent in 1989, as state enterprises, bearing the initial brunt of the reforms, found themselves unable to adjust to radically different economic circumstances and consequently suffered heavy losses. The rapid deterioration in their financial position could be attributed primarily to three factors. The first was major realignment of exchange rates. In line with the unification, in March 1989, of the then multiple exchange rates between the dong and the U.S. dollar at a level close to the parallel market (implying a fivefold average increase in the price of foreign exchange relative to the rates prevailing in October 1988), the dong also depreciated dramatically against the transferable ruble—by more than 100 percent in 1989 from the average 1988 level, and by a further 80 percent in 1990. These realignments in the dong-transferable ruble exchange rate implied that the state enterprises suddenly faced drastic jumps in prices for their inputs. The second factor was severe reduction in direct budgetary support. Since 1989, as an increasing number of commodity prices have been allowed to be determined more by market and cost considerations than by central planning, all direct budgetary subsidies have been eliminated (with the exception of small working capital contributions to newly established

---

[7]Tanzi (1991b) discusses the importance and difficulties of mobilizing savings in centrally planned economies undertaking reforms.

state enterprises). At the same time, the Government has also been phasing out budgetary support for enterprise investments in nonkey industrial projects. The third factor was the significant tightening of bank credits. A principal instrument in the Government's anti-inflation package was a sharp upward revision, in March 1989, in the structure of interest rates to positive real levels, which markedly slowed the growth in bank lending to state enterprises from over 350 percent in 1988 to less than 150 percent in 1989; the relatively tight credit conditions generally continued into 1990, albeit with some slippage.[8]

Although the above developments transpired in an environment in which state enterprises were given increasing autonomy in production, investment, employment, and pricing decisions, the rapidity of their onset virtually ruled out the possibility that the state enterprises could fully compensate for such adversities through immediate adjustments in operational efficiency. Indeed, only about a third of all state enterprises actually managed to report an operating profit in 1989. Consequently, enterprise transfers to the state budget dropped precipitously—by an annual average of 2 percentage points of GDP in 1989–90.

The erosion of enterprise transfers of this magnitude, over such a short period, would have been disastrous for the state budget had it not been for contributions—partly also as a result of the reforms—from other revenue sources. A series of agricultural reforms that began in mid-1988 and included such measures as lengthened land tenure, increased retainment of output in the hands of the farmers, and the decontrolling of agricultural prices, provided strong incentives for cooperative and private farms and dramatically boosted agricultural production;[9] they also led to a substantial improvement in the performance of the agricultural tax in 1989 (a 50 percent agricultural tax relief was subsequently announced for both 1990 and 1991). Reforms in the trade sector, which included the elimination of trade quotas and the restructuring (twice) of the import and export duties, led to significant increases in trade with the convertible area; this, coupled with large exchange rate depreciations, caused a surge in trade taxes. Finally, but most important, exports of crude oil produced under a joint venture between Viet Nam and the former Soviet Union became a major item in 1989–90 and yielded substantial revenue for the state budget.

While the sharp drop in enterprise transfers seemed to have been compensated for, at least in the short run, by higher revenue elsewhere in the

---

[8]As inflation declined during 1989, lending rates were adjusted downward more rapidly than deposit rates in the second half of the year, in response to enterprise difficulties. However, most lending rates turned negative by March 1990; they were further eased even as inflation began to pick up again.

[9]Viet Nam has been transformed from a rice importer in 1987 (importing over 400,000 tons) to the rank of the world's third largest rice exporter in 1989 (exporting over 1.4 million tons).

state budget, it still constrained the Government's ability to mobilize additional revenue to underpin its macroeconomic reform and stabilization program.

Impact on Expenditure

It is rarely possible for an economy in transition to carry out fiscal adjustments by relying on (appropriate) expenditure reductions, and Viet Nam is no exception. The initial impact of the elimination of all direct budgetary subsidies was offset to a large extent by the necessity of incorporating some consumer subsidies into the wage bill as part of a comprehensive reform of the wage structure of government workers. This wage restructuring, implemented at the beginning of 1989, essentially involved the "monetization" of workers' remuneration from a combination of cash payments and an assortment of subsidized goods and services into all cash payments and was intended to render the composition of the wage bill more transparent and therefore easier to control. Although a government-wide nominal wage freeze was put into effect immediately following the wage reform and remained in effect in 1990 despite continued, albeit lower-than-pre-reform, inflation (thus effectively delinking the minimum wage to the price of rice that had existed before), the combined impact of subsidy elimination and wage reform on expenditure was small.

Additional spending pressures surfaced as a result of other reform efforts. For example, as part of an overall strategy to rid the state sector of its excess labor, employment centers were set up nationwide to assist displaced workers to find alternative employment in the private sector by providing them with retraining and relocation services. Although this new employment policy succeeded in, among other things, reducing the government work force by over 15 percent over 1989–90, budgetary allocations were required to provide partial start-up funding for the employment centers as well as one-time financial assistance to displaced workers. In a similar vein, although the military withdrawal from Cambodia in the second half of 1989 seemed to offer an opportunity for cuts in defense-related expenditure, the need to provide financial assistance to demobilized troops not only rendered significant savings in this area unlikely in the next few years, it might have actually led to a temporary increase in such expenditure in 1990.

A structural reorientation of the state budget's capital expenditure was also carried out in 1989 when the Government announced that all state enterprises, except those involved in key industrial projects, would be required to finance their investment needs from their own resources or from commercial credits. Apart from spending on health and education, budgetary allocations for capital and maintenance expenditure would be limited to projects related to selected industries considered vital to the economy and to infrastructure, such as road and bridge construction, energy, irrigation, water works, and communication. As noted earlier, the existing infrastructure in Viet Nam is grossly inadequate, and future growth potential will be impaired if resources are not directed toward its improvement. Yet, in 1990, severe budgetary constraints forced a sharp reduction in such expenditure, clearly an adjustment in the wrong direction.

Impact on Deficit Financing

While the Government's macroeconomic stabilization efforts did achieve notable early success in reducing the annual inflation rate from the triple-digit range in the pre-reform period to the mid-double-digit level in 1989–90, it fell short of the stated goal at the outset of the reform period.[10] The anti-inflation effort was hampered to a large extent by the continuing need to finance sizable deficits in the state budget from bank credits, as economy-wide systemic reforms rendered any increase in revenue mobilization exceedingly difficult, if not impossible, to achieve in the short run. The financing needs were also made more acute by the sudden and sharp decline in Soviet commodity aid—between 1988 and 1990, such aid dropped by almost three quarters in ruble terms. Thus, despite massive devaluations of the dong against the transferable ruble, total foreign financing still decreased in dong terms by a substantial margin in 1989–90 compared with the pre-reform period.

Institutional Dimension of Fiscal Adjustments

It is clear that Viet Nam's market-oriented economic reforms exerted a profound impact on the structure of its public finances: the reforms fundamentally altered the composition of both the revenue base and the expenditure pattern in the state budget. At the same time, the experience during 1989–90 compellingly illustrated how difficult it was to carry out successfully, within a short time, the fiscal adjustments—mobilizing additional revenue and reducing expenditure in an appropriate manner— necessary to underpin the overall reform effort and pave the way for future growth and macroeconomic stability. Constraints to rapid fiscal adjustment primarily stemmed from the need to implement measures that have, unavoidably, a broad institutional dimension, and thus by their very nature would require time to yield results. Measures of such a dimension are common to most economies in transition; in Viet Nam they fell most conveniently into four areas.

---

[10]Wood (1989) provides a review of Viet Nam's experience in reducing inflation at the early stages of recent reforms.

Tax Reforms

The tax system in Viet Nam in the pre-reform period, given its sole function as a device by which the state could appropriate national output under the central plan, is clearly incompatible with a decentralized economic environment. The problems associated with its complex structure (a multitude of rates and schedules) and narrow base (excessive reliance on transfers from state enterprises) were compounded by a system of pervasive price controls under which it functioned, as well as by the taxpayers' frequent ability to negotiate their tax liabilities with the Government ex post—a phenomenon that undoubtedly stemmed from the peculiar role of the state as both tax collector and taxpayer. Hence, a complete overhaul of the tax system would seem to be one of the most important and urgent tasks in ensuring the success of the reform program.[11]

Tax reform efforts began in earnest in 1989; the key objectives included: (1) replacement of the existing tax regime, which had been largely based on decrees and regulations, by a system with explicit legislation of tax laws; (2) uniform tax treatment for the state and nonstate sectors of the economy; and (3) greater revenue mobilization through base broadening, in particular by bringing the burgeoning private and trade sectors properly into the tax net. Substantial progress in this regard was made with the passage by the National Assembly, in July 1990, of new laws on the business income (turnover), profits, and special consumption (excise) taxes. Major revisions to the structure of export and import duties also took place in April 1989, and again in January 1990. Numerous other tax measures are being considered for implementation after 1990, the most notable of which include the planned introduction of a personal income tax, a natural resource tax, and a new agricultural tax law.

Apart from the above tax legislations, it was also recognized that the tax administration and collection machinery would have to be significantly revamped and strengthened if the new tax system were to be effective in a market-oriented economy. In the pre-reform period, most taxes were collected at the provincial and district levels, resulting in frequent unauthorized tax concessions granted by local authorities to the state enterprises and in delinquent remission of revenue to the Central Government. Consequently, various special committees were set up during 1989–90 to address administrative aspects of the tax system and to propose measures to enforce tax collection and ensure that national tax polices would not be circumvented at the local level.[12]

---

[11] The necessity for reforming the tax systems in economies in transition is discussed in greater detail in Tanzi (1991c).

[12] An update to tax reform developments in 1990–91 is provided in the appendix to this paper.

Enterprise Reforms

A critical factor in determining the feasible pace of fiscal adjustments is the financial performance of state enterprises. Beginning in 1988, these enterprises were given increasing autonomy; by 1990, such enterprises were virtually free from direct central control, following successive governmental decrees spelling out the rights and responsibilities of enterprise managers. Together with the concurrent liberalization of prices, these measures were intended to expose the state enterprises to market forces, thus underpinning the transformation of the economy from a centralized into a decentralized setting.

As has already been pointed out in earlier discussions, the sudden and drastic hardening of their budget constraints as implied by the reforms led a significant number of state enterprises into severe financial difficulty, particularly those that predominantly used imported inputs to produce output for the domestic market, such as manufacturers of tools and machinery. Although prices were liberalized, enterprises were unable to pass on rises in their input prices (brought on by large exchange rate depreciations that propelled raw materials costs to world-market levels) to output prices (because of poor product mix and quality and intensified competition from imports). These developments helped to underscore the fact that reforms intended to improve enterprise efficiency could not be expected to yield immediate results, as efficiency can be gained only through a combination of acquisition of new technology, adequate shedding of excess labor,[13] adoption of a new managerial structure, and the proper functioning of market signals—all of which require considerable time to accomplish. For some enterprises, alternative but equally time-consuming courses of action, such as privatization and closure, could be the only feasible solution.[14]

In addition to reforming the state enterprises, the ability to sustain the necessary fiscal adjustments would also depend on enlarging the scope of private sector activities, which in turn would require putting in place an adequate legal framework for conducting business. To this end, a company law was passed in December 1990 containing provisions for property ownership, establishing legal recognition of private enterprises, and affirming equal treatment of all businesses. Preliminary bankruptcy legislation is being drafted.

Infrastructure Investment

Viet Nam's involvement, over the past three decades, in internal and external military conflicts has left its infrastructure in serious disrepair,

---

[13]Recent estimates suggest that up to 30 percent of the 2.7 million workers employed by the state enterprises are in this category.

[14]A limited experimental program of converting some state enterprises into shareholding companies was initiated in May 1990.

severely hampering government efforts to reform and develop the economy. While damage to roads, bridges, power plants, and other transportation and communication facilities during the war years prior to 1975 is a major cause of the infrastructure's current dilapidated state, troop deployment in Cambodia in recent years has further deteriorated the infrastructure by absorbing a significant amount of resources otherwise available for capital and maintenance, which is now at a bare minimum. Indeed, the present size of the public investment program in Viet Nam is smaller than it is in most countries with a similar level of income and economic development.

In addition to the transport sector, already identified in earlier discussions as most critically in need of upgrading, major infrastructure deficiencies may also be found in the electric power supply, which has a limited network and frequent outages, impeding effective water control where irrigation depends on electrical pumping; in communication facilities, which are primitive or nonexistent in many parts of the country; and in the distribution and procurement system, which is poorly organized, resulting in pervasive theft and inadequate quality control.

Although the Government is cognizant of the country's infrastructure needs and has in fact given priority to the completion of major hydro-electric power projects in Tri An and Hao Binh, as well as to improving transportation links between Hanoi and Saigon, it is clear that investment in infrastructure is one area of fiscal adjustment to which significantly more resources should be devoted in the course of economic reforms.

Financial Sector Reforms

At first glance, it would seem that financial sector reforms have little to do with fiscal adjustments. But market-oriented reforms in centrally planned economies can rarely succeed without a concurrent transformation of their financial institutions from being passive accommodators of the central plan to being active contributors to macroeconomic stability under decentralization. Monetary discipline, for example, cannot be instilled unless and until the central bank is granted some independence in conducting monetary policy. This, in turn, has fundamental implications for the financing of state budget and enterprise deficits from domestic credit creation. In Viet Nam, additional significance for its fiscal operations could also be derived from financial sector reforms, considering the complete lack of monetary instruments (in the pre-reform period) by which the Government could effectively mobilize domestic savings. The development of such instruments, and of the requisite institutional framework to support them, would go far to ease the severe budgetary constraints the country will be facing in the period ahead.

Some progress in establishing a market-oriented banking system has been achieved. Two decree-laws were introduced in October 1990: one provided the State Bank of Viet Nam legal powers and responsibilities in line with those assumed by central banks in decentralized economies; the other spelled out the scope of commercial banking activities. However, to give substance to these laws will require comprehensive legislation on collateral, bankruptcy, and private property rights.

Concluding Remarks

While Viet Nam has achieved impressive results with its comprehensive economic reforms in a relatively short time, its experience has also clearly illustrated that the requisite fiscal adjustments to a changed economic environment are important binding constraints in meeting reform objectives and achieving macroeconomic stability. Being largely institutional in character, these constraints are difficult to overcome in the short run without external assistance. Yet, precisely in this period its traditional source of foreign financing—commodity aid from the former Soviet Union—was drastically reduced, with no realistic prospect of its restoration. Thus, while its commitment to continuing with the reforms—and there are important structural measures yet to be implemented—is undiminished, Viet Nam will surely find the road ahead to be a rocky one if no alternative sources of financial assistance become available.

Appendix: Tax Reform in 1990–91

The scope and nature of tax reform in Viet Nam in 1990-91 are vast and highly complex, involving fundamental change in the structure of the tax system and its administration. This appendix briefly describes and assesses some of the more important of these developments.

Import and Export Duties

Enacted as a tax law and effective in January 1988,[15] the structure of import and export duties has gone through two major revisions since implementation of the economic reform program in 1989. In April 1989, the number of commodities subject to export duties was reduced from 30 to 12, together with a lowering of most duty rates; the number of commercially imported commodities subject to import duties was reclassified from 124 to 80 categories, with an effective expansion of the base and a

---

[15]The law on import and export duties is the only tax law enacted prior to the 1989 reform program. Tax laws, as opposed to tax ordinances and decrees typically issued by the State Council and Council of Ministers, require the approval of the National Assembly.

rationalization of the rates. In January 1990, further base broadening and rate revisions on commercial imports were put into effect, although imports of most capital goods and raw materials are still duty exempt. Other recent changes include an increase in the import duties on petroleum products in March 1991 in response to a sharp decline in the international oil price and a reduction in the export duty on rice exports, together with the exemption from import duties on inputs used in the production of exports.

Turnover Tax and VAT

Enacted as a tax law and put into effect in October 1990, the turnover tax replaces the structure of a similar tax (the state business tax) that had existed for decades. All business transactions are subject to this tax, except those involving (1) agricultural products subject to the agricultural tax, (2) products subject to the excise tax (at those stages of production where the excise tax applies), and (3) exports. Its rate structure, revised (lowered for most items, but the number of rates was increased) in October 1991 to adjust for its impact on the pattern of enterprise profitability during its first year of implementation, is highly differentiated. Most activities are taxed at 13 different rates, ranging from 0.5 percent to 16 percent; a few selected activities, such as dancing and shipping services, are taxed at the high rates of 30 percent and 40 percent. Because the tax rates are expressed as percentages of tax-inclusive prices, the corresponding rates are higher when expressed as percentages of prices net of tax (as is common). The base of the tax on imported items is inclusive of their import duties (if any).

October 1991 also saw the introduction of an important change to the turnover tax system. Wholesalers and retailers who meet certain bookkeeping requirements can register with the Government and elect to be taxed only on their value added, calculated as the difference between sales and purchase costs, with rates ranging from 4 percent (for example, on salt) to 16 percent (for example, on petroleum); on most other items the standard VAT rate of 14 percent applies. With a view to eliminating the cascading effects of the turnover tax, the authorities have further proposed to the Council of Ministers to extend the VAT backward to the manufacturing stage, selecting seven industries (cement, sugar cane, bicycles, clothing, electricity, and imports and exports) for experimentation.

Excise Tax

Enacted as a tax law and put into effect in October 1990, the excise tax (officially referred to as the special consumption tax) applies to six categories of mainly domestically produced consumption goods and re-places the previous commodity tax levied on 22 items. The tax is applied at the manufacturing stages of the excisable goods, with a VAT-like tax credit mechanism provided for excise taxes paid on inputs used in earlier stages of production. Sample rates of this tax, as revised in October 1991, are 20 percent to 50 percent on both tobacco and alcoholic products and 70 percent on fireworks, playing cards, and votive offerings (rates on all domestically produced cigarettes and spirits were lowered, and imported filtered cigarettes became subject to tax). As with the turnover tax, the tax rates are expressed as percentages of the tax-inclusive prices, and the base of the imported filtered cigarettes is inclusive of import duties (other imported tobacco and alcoholic products are not subject to the excise tax, but are instead subject to import duties of 80 percent to 100 percent on the basis of their c.i.f. values). As noted earlier, the turnover tax is exempted at those stages where the excise tax applies. Neither luxury consumer goods, such as cars, color television sets, high-fidelity electronic equipment, and jewelry, nor retail sales of petroleum products, which are subject to relatively low import duties by international standards, are currently included in the excise tax base.

Profits Tax

Enacted as a tax law and put into effect in October 1990 for the non-state sector and in January 1991 for the state sector, the profits tax replaces and unifies the erstwhile separate taxation of profits of state and nonstate enterprises. The base of this tax is defined as sales (the base for the turnover tax) less indirect taxes paid and expenses incurred in the normal conduct of business, such as labor and material costs and depreciation charges. The law provides no details on how deductible expenses are to be determined, but appeals to vague concepts such as their "reasonable" or "rational" levels. There are three main tax rates. Generally, heavy industries are taxed at 30 percent, light industries at 40 percent, and services at 50 percent. A one-year loss carryforward is allowed, and there is an investment credit (up to 50 percent of total tax liabilities) for profits reinvested in certain sectors deemed in need of investment.

A special provision for small household enterprises with average monthly turnover below certain specified thresholds stipulates that the applicable tax rates, which range from 1 percent to 3 percent (differentiated according to type of business), are to be assessed on turnover rather than profits. Household enterprises whose monthly taxable profits exceed D 6 million are subject not only to the regular applicable rates of the profits tax, but are also liable to a surtax of 20 percent on the excess profits. The surtax is designed to compensate for the fact that household enterprises are not covered by the personal income tax.

The profits tax applies to all sectors of the economy, except agricultural production subject to the agricultural tax (see below). It does not apply, however, to enterprises with foreign-invested capital (joint ventures with minimum of 30 percent foreign participation), whose tax obligations are governed by the law on foreign investment (adopted in 1987 and amended in 1990) and decided by the State Committee on Foreign Investment in consultation with the Ministry of Finance. In general, joint ventures are taxed at substantially preferential rates on their profits, ranging from 10 percent to 25 percent according to type of activity and share of foreign investment. Losses incurred by joint ventures can be carried forward for up to five years. The profits tax on the foreign partner is proportionately reduced by the share of after-tax profits the partner reinvests in Viet Nam for at least three years. There is a remittance tax (ranging from 5 percent to 10 percent) on profits remitted abroad.[16]

Capital User Fee and Depreciation Allowances

State enterprises, besides being liable to the profits tax, are assessed two additional charges for use by the state budget. Depreciation allowances, which are supposed to recoup the Government's past contributions to the capital assets of state enterprises, have been in effect for a number of years. A second charge, known as the capital user fee, which was introduced on the basis of a decree issued by the Council of Ministers, has been in effect since January 1991. The fee is assessed on the net value of government-contributed fixed assets, and on the gross value of government-contributed working capital, at monthly rates ranging from 0.2 percent to 0.5 percent according to type of industry. Unlike the depreciation allowances, the capital user fee is supposed to simulate the interest cost of funding the state enterprises from budgetary resources, and is intended, ostensibly, to promote the efficient utilization of their capital. For the purpose of introducing this fee, a comprehensive asset valuation exercise for the state sector was undertaken in 1990.

Personal Income Tax

Introduced in April 1991 as an ordinance of the State Council, the personal income tax differentiates incomes from regular (salaries, wages, bonuses, perquisites, and so on) and irregular (gifts from abroad—which has been repealed temporarily—lottery winnings, royalties for transfer of technology or technical designs, and so on) sources. Incomes excluded from the base include social pension and insurance payments, interest

---

[16]Vietsov Petro, a joint venture between Viet Nam and the former U.S.S.R. on crude oil production, has special status and is governed by separate agreements as to tax obligations and profit-sharing between the two.

payments from savings accounts and public debt, dividends, and incomes of household enterprises subject to the profits tax.

Incomes from regular sources are taxed, beginning at a level of D 500,000 a month, at marginal rates rising from 10 percent to 50 percent at intervals of 10 percent. Vietnamese whose total regular income exceeds D 5 million a month are also assessed a supplementary income tax of 30 percent on the excess income. Irregular incomes exceeding D 1.5 million are taxed on a per occurrence basis at marginal rates ranging also from 10 percent to 50 percent at five even rate intervals. However, incomes associated with technology transfers in excess of D 1.5 million and lottery winnings in excess of D 10 million are taxed, respectively, at flat rates of 5 percent and 10 percent. Foreigners with incomes from domestic sources are also subject to the tax at the same rate structure as the Vietnamese, but with different, and much higher, brackets (for example, taxable monthly income begins at D 2.4 million); they are, however, exempted from the supplementary income tax. There is a provision for adjusting the income brackets and threshold levels whenever the cumulative depreciation of the dong against the U.S. dollar exceeds 20 percent. No other exemptions and deductions usually associated with this type of tax are provided.

Proposed Agricultural Tax

The structure of the proposed agricultural tax as specified in the recent draft law is extremely complex. Farm land is classified into five grades based on a weighted average of five indicators (quality of soil, gradient of land, weather condition, water condition, and distance from market). Different grades of land are taxed differently, and the nature of the tax applicable to a particular grade also differs according to type of crop. The tax on short-term crops is specified in fixed quantities of paddy (one quantity for each grade of land) converted into value terms by its price that varies across different regions of the country. For long-term crops, ad valorem tax rates (one rate for each grade of land) are applied to the value of output. The tax is progressive (over grades of land) for both types of crops. There has been much debate in the National Assembly on both the appropriate degree of progressivity of the agricultural tax and the appropriate tax burden on the agricultural sector as a whole, as well as on the desirability of retaining in the agricultural tax some characteristics of a land tax as provided for in the law on land (hence the specification of the tax on short-term crops in terms of quantities of paddy).[17] A satisfactory resolution of these issues is obviously of considerable importance in formulating an appropriate structure for this tax.

---

[17]The National Assembly, which had rejected an earlier version of the draft law in July 1990, again did not approve the present version in September 1991.

Other New Taxes

Two additional new taxes have been introduced recently. A natural resource tax, which came into effect in July 1990 as an ordinance of the State Council, stipulates that the exploitation of mineral deposits (metallic and nonmetallic), forest products, and fish and marine products is subject to this tax at rates ranging from 1 percent to 40 percent (of value) depending on the nature of the exploited resources, except where such exploitation is carried out by joint ventures whose tax obligations are governed by the law on foreign investment. The ordinance also provides other exemptions and reductions at the discretion of the Council of Ministers. A property tax on the assessed market values (to be conducted every two years) of buildings and land, at the annual rates of 0.3 percent and 0.5 percent respectively, was put into effect in January 1991 also as an ordinance of the State Council. The tax covers both the state and nonstate sectors and applies to both residential and commercial buildings, but exempts agricultural land.

Tax Administration[18]

To support and administer the reformed tax system, a new Tax Department has been organized vertically with the General Tax Department subject to the Ministry of Finance, the 49 Provincial Tax Departments subject to the General Tax Department, and the 547 District Tax Departments subject to the Provincial Tax Departments. Each level is given an annual revenue target and is monitored on a monthly basis. The various departmental levels are organized into divisions by type of tax or type of taxpayer and by various administrative functions such as planning and personnel. However, the Tax Department has taken a first step toward a more functional structure (as is common with most modern tax administrations) by ensuring that three separate tax officials perform the estimation, collection, and supervision functions with respect to any taxpayer.

Brief Assessment

The establishment of a firm legal basis for much of the Vietnamese tax system, the inclusion into the tax net of the rapidly growing private sector, and the more uniform tax treatment between the state and nonstate sectors are commendable achievements of the ongoing tax reform process. However, the current tax system in many ways still falls far short of the generally accepted requirements of a market-oriented economy. In particular, the structures of many of the taxes, such as those of the

---

[18]Information on tax administration contained in this section is provided by Charles L. Vehorn, to whom I am grateful.

turnover tax and the profits tax, remain overly complex and highly distortive; they lack the neutrality commonly aimed for in market-oriented tax systems and their implementation continues to result in frequent ex-post negotiations over tax liabilities between the taxpayers and the Government.

Proper implementation of the tax system at present is also being rendered difficult because uniform accounting principles have barely been introduced and record-keeping requirements have only just begun to be recognized. Under these circumstances, the introduction of potentially superior market-oriented taxes, such as the VAT, is administratively premature.[19] Instead, the priority at this juncture of tax reform should be placed on the simplification of many of the existing taxes, and on making a determined effort to enforce tax policies by rule of law rather than by discretion and negotiation.

References

Beresford, Melanie, *Vietnam: Politics, Economics and Society* (London: Pinter Publishers, 1988).

——, *National Unification and Economic Development in Vietnam* (London: Macmillan, 1989).

Drabek, Zdenek, "A Case Study of a Gradual Approach to Economic Reform: The Viet Nam Experience of 1985–88," IDP74 (Washington: World Bank, 1990).

Fforde, Adam, and Suzanne H. Paine, *The Limits of National Liberation* (London: Croom Helm, 1987).

Fforde, Adam, and Stefan de Vylder, *Vietnam: An Economy in Transition* (Stockholm: Swedish International Development Authority, 1988).

Kimura, Tetsusaburo, *The Vietnamese Economy, 1975–86* (Tokyo: Institute of Developing Economies, 1989).

Kornai, János, *Contradictions and Dilemmas: Studies on the Socialist Economy and Society* (Cambridge, Massachusetts: MIT Press, 1986).

Tanzi, Vito (1991a), "Fiscal Issues in Economies in Transition," in *Reforming Central and Eastern European Economies: Initial Results and Challenges*, ed. by Vittorio Corbo, Fabrizio Coricelli, and Jan Bossak (Washington: World Bank, 1991).

—— (1991b), "Mobilization of Savings in Eastern European Countries: The Role of the State," in *Economics for the New Europe*, ed. by Anthony B. Atkinson and Renato Brunetta (London: Macmillan, 1991).

---

[19]A narrowly based VAT, such as that contemplated under the VAT experiment, would in any case be a misguided tax design even under the best circumstances.

────── (1991c), "Tax Reform and the Move to a Market Economy: Overview of the Issues," in *The Role of Tax Reform in Central and Eastern European Economies* (Paris: Organization for Economic Cooperation and Development, 1991).

Wiegersma, Nancy, *Vietnam: Peasant Land, Peasant Revolution* (London: Macmillan, 1988).

Wood, Adrian, "Deceleration of Inflation with Acceleration of Price Reform: Vietnam's Remarkable Recent Experience," *Cambridge Journal of Economics*, Vol. 13 (1989), pp. 563–71.

CHAPTER 15

Mongolia: Opportunities for Simplicity in Tax Policy Design and Implementation

Jacques Baldet and Geoffrey Walton

In the past two decades many developing countries have embarked on reform programs aimed at overhauling their trade regimes and supporting their tax systems. The impetus for these reforms has been fueled by a growing acceptance of the contribution of transparent, neutral, and well-coordinated tax systems to economic growth, welfare, and fiscal stability. On the whole, the successful programs were forthrightly implemented and relied on single, transparent policy instruments for the achievement of each policy goal. The successful programs were accompanied by a practice of maintaining competitive real exchange rates and budget deficits were kept smaller in relation to output than in the less successful programs. These lessons of experience are no less relevant for the economies in transition from central planning to market orientation than they are for those market economies attempting to dismantle distortive policy regimes that have failed to promote efficiency and structural change.

As one of the more recent countries in transition from a centrally planned to a market-based economy, Mongolia[1] is in a unique position to gain from the hard-learned experience of others, including its Eastern European counterparts, many of which are by now well advanced in their reform efforts. Several important characteristics distinguish Mongolia from the other case studies. First, it is a vast, landlocked, sparsely populated country, bordered by two large economies, Russia and China. Both of these neighboring countries are themselves undergoing economic transformation. Mongolia's command economy, dating from the late 1930s, was characterized by increasingly strong economic and political ties with the then U.S.S.R. Its current geopolitics represent a considerable challenge to the reforms now under way, because the old economic bonds will need to be replaced by a widened integration into the world trading community. Second, reliance on the state enterprise sector for government revenues (essentially through a number of budgetary trans-

---

At the time this paper was written, Jacques Baldet was an Advisor in the Fiscal Affairs Department. Geoffrey Walton is a consultant in the same department.

[1]Following student protests in early 1990, a new reform government was formed to lead the country toward its first multiparty elections and to develop a market-based economy.

fers) has been extremely heavy, representing nearly half of GDP in recent years. Third, opportunities for growth and structural change in the private sector will be constrained in the medium term by poor infrastructural development that cannot support even moderately increased trade with the West and by the currently narrow base of economic activity that relies on animal husbandry and rudimentary processing of animal by-products.

In spite of the challenges inherent in these characteristics, the Mongolian authorities have shown a propensity for openness and progressiveness in the reform initiatives taken to date. This has been no less evident in tax policy. This case study will focus on how Mongolia has faced these challenges by seeking to plan and implement, from the outset, a simple tax system as an integral component of its overall reform efforts that avoids many of the costly mistakes made by other developing countries in the past. The paper first provides a brief background to the recent economic developments in Mongolia and describes the pre-reform structure of government revenues. It then examines the main features of the tax reform pursued during the initial phases of the transition period. Finally, it examines directions for future reforms.

Pre-Reform Situation

Economic Developments Leading to Reform[2]

In 1985, the then Government of Mongolia instituted modest steps to improve economic management and reduce central control, while permitting some internal political openness. These changes were accompanied by similar restructuring taking place in what was then the U.S.S.R. Although the policy of political openness was formally established in 1987, political and economic developments in the U.S.S.R. and economic reforms in China during the 1980s outpaced Mongolian restructuring, leading to intensified socioeconomic tensions and, finally, to the establishment of a new reformist Government in March 1990.

The Government in office in 1985 sought to expand agricultural production, improve food supplies, extend electrification, and create a metalworking sector. During 1986, it took modest steps to strengthen public sector finances and to increase trade with the convertible currency area. Wholesale prices were raised to take into account past increases in production costs and higher import prices and to maintain budget revenues from import price differentials.[3] The adverse effect of the price reform on

---

[2]For an expanded account of recent economic developments, see Milne and others (1991).

[3]Import price differentials constitute a tax paid by state foreign trading enterprises and warehousing firms based on the difference between the domestic wholesale price and the foreign trade contract price of the good.

selected industries was ameliorated by a reduction of domestic turnover taxes and an increase in selected production subsidies. Profit taxes were reduced so that a larger share of enterprise investment could be financed from retained earnings.

In 1987, a new strategy of economic restructuring, framed on the Soviet policy of perestroika, was implemented. Under this policy, the role of state planning was limited to setting overall investment policy, while the ministries and state committees were responsible for its implementation. Similarly, state enterprises were accorded increased autonomy, although production, profits, and distribution remained centrally planned. During 1988-89, the pace of reform quickened, although measures continued to aim principally at improving the efficiency of the command economy. During this period the decentralization of revenue collection and expenditure decisions to the local level intensified. Local authorities' control over revenues and expenditures rose to almost half of the total by 1989. Although farmgate prices remained unchanged, agricultural production (except for meat) that exceeded state delivery quotas could be marketed freely. A new law permitted the formation of cooperatives, with private sector participation. To encourage surrender of convertible currencies to the State Bank, the authorities introduced a preferential rate of Tug 20 per U.S. dollar, compared with a commercial rate of Tug 3 per U.S. dollar.

Key reforms during 1989-90 further reduced the number of controls and operating norms over state enterprises. These included the introduction of limited price flexibility, the elimination of monopolies enjoyed by state foreign trading companies, an increase in the amount of foreign exchange that could be retained by state enterprises, and the introduction of differential price incentives for producers to promote exports to the convertible currency area.

The Government that took power in March 1990 embarked upon a comprehensive program of economic transformation toward a market economy. The envisaged three-year program—now in progress—aims at expanding the role of the private sector, diversifying the economic base, promoting exports, generally increasing trade with the convertible currency area, and introducing indirect forms of economic management.

As a first step, the Government eliminated all restrictions on private ownership of herds and announced increases in farmgate prices with effect from January 1991. Selected retail prices were to be freely determined within a set range. In January 1991, most retail prices were doubled with compensating adjustments in civil service wages, pensions, and other benefits. The reforms also included the promulgation of a Foreign Investment Law to encourage investment in the private sector with various incentives, the establishment of a Customs Affairs Department for introducing a tariff system, changes in the system of taxation of corporations and individuals to incorporate the expanding role of the private sector, and the creation of a new Incomes and Taxes Department within the Ministry of Finance to focus on tax administration.

Pre-Reform Structure of Government Revenues

In Mongolia, the basic taxes used in the pre-reform phase included a personal income tax, a company income tax, so-called import and export price differentials, and domestic turnover taxes. Table 1 provides details on the structure of government revenues obtained from these and some other relatively minor taxes at the outset of the reform.

The personal income tax existing prior to the reform consisted of two different rate schedules applicable to wage or salary income and self-employment income. In 1989, revenues from this tax amounted to about 1 percent of total general budget revenues. The personal income tax on wages and salaries was levied at low and barely progressive rates ranging from a minimum of 2.6 percent to a maximum of 2.9 percent. Numerous exemptions reduced the yield of this tax. Administratively, payments of the tax were made via a withholding mechanism and were considered final. No personal tax returns were required. All collections entered local budgets directly. The self-employed were taxed under schedular rates far different from those imposed on wage and salary incomes. The tax rate schedule, compared with that for wages and salaries, was wide and rapidly progressive, ranging from a minimum rate of 4 percent to a maximum rate of 65 percent. Tax payments were made on a quarterly basis according to self-assessments made by taxpayers. The bias against private economic activity, typical of many economies in transition, is clearly evident.

In 1989, the company income tax generated more than 40 percent of total budget revenues. It was divided into four components: the profit deduction, the so-called fund payment to the state budget, labor payments, and the scientific and technological development fund. The first component generated just over 75 percent of planned profit tax revenues and was levied on profits, after the state budget payment. Rates of profit deduction were also enterprise specific. The second component, levied at industry-specific rates ranging from 3 percent to 12 percent, was based on the value of enterprises' fixed assets. This contributed about 20 percent of planned profit tax revenues in 1989. The remaining parts of the company income tax were of minor revenue importance.

Of the three types of indirect taxation in Mongolia, import price differentials were the most important contributor to state budget revenues. These amounted to about one third of revenues in 1989 and represented transfers to the budget by state foreign trading enterprises on their sales of imported goods. Again, typical of the experience of economies in transition, these implicit taxes were based on the difference

Table 1. Mongolia: General Government Budget Revenues, 1989

Revenue Source	Consolidated Budget Amount (In percent of GDP)	Percentage Distribution
Profit taxes	21.2	43.4
Profit deduction	16.3	33.3
Fund payments	4.2	8.6
Labor payments	0.1	0.3
Development fund	0.6	1.2
Import price differentials	16.2	33.2
Export price differentials	1.5	3.1
Domestic turnover taxes	4.8	9.7
Taxes on individuals	0.5	1.0
Wages and salaries	0.2	0.6
Childless persons	0.1	0.2
Self-employed	—	—
Other	—	0.2
Agricultural cooperatives	0.5	1.1
Natural resource use	0.2	0.5
Social security	2.4	4.8
Stamp taxes and fees	0.2	0.6
Other	1.3	2.6
Total revenue	48.9	100.0

Source: Ministry of Finance.

between negotiated foreign contract prices and fixed retail prices.[4] Prior to 1986, wholesale prices were fixed using a 1974 base. In January 1986, wholesale prices were increased by an average of 12 percent to account for changes in production costs and foreign contract prices. Wholesale prices remained at their 1986 levels until the beginning of the reform period.

Export price differentials accounted for about 3 percent of government revenues in 1989. These were determined as the difference between an "adjusted" producer price[5] and the foreign contract price. Profits arising from a positive differential between the contract price and the adjusted producer price were remitted to the budget, whereas losses were covered by transfers from the budget. In January 1986, the adjustment coefficients were abolished, although some were reintroduced in 1989. At the beginning of the reform period, export coefficients were applied only to trade with member countries of the Council for Mutual Economic Assistance.

[4]Some margins and discounts were allowed at various points in the distribution chain.
[5]The adjustments were somewhat arbitrary and were used selectively to subsidize some exports and tax others.

Domestic turnover taxes contributed almost 10 percent of government revenues in 1989. These were levied on a number of generally nonessential goods and services and, as such, more closely resembled excise taxes than a multistage tax on gross receipts. The turnover tax mechanism apparently had several functions, the two most important of which were revenue generation and retail pricing policy. Other less explicit functions of the tax were to form a system of financial planning and control, to influence income distribution (by controlling retail prices), and to act as an instrument for balancing commodity supply and demand.

Initial Period of Transition

As an integral part of their overall efforts toward economic transformation, the Mongolian authorities embarked upon a reform of their tax system in late 1989 after some seven decades of economic planning. The key elements of the reform included revision of the policies and laws relating to the taxation of companies and individuals, the introduction of explicit import duties and export taxes to replace gradually the dual price differential regime, and the rationalization of "turnover" taxes into an explicit schedule of excise taxes. A policy decision was also made early in the reform program to introduce a sales tax at the manufacturing or import level. These changes required a substantial shift in the overall policy design of the fiscal system, the introduction of legislation to support the new fiscal objectives, and important changes in tax administration. The measures taken to date are outlined below.

Recognizing the ability of taxes on international trade to generate revenues quickly, the Mongolian authorities moved forthrightly to create a Customs Affairs Department as early as October 1990 to prepare for the introduction of a tariff system. Customs legislation was prepared soon after and enacted by parliament in March 1991. A customs tariff was enacted in conjunction with the law. In its original form, it contained two schedules: one for the application of explicit export taxes to selected commodities (designed to replace the export price differentials) and the other for the imposition of import duties (designed eventually to replace the import price differentials).

Export taxes, ranging from 5 percent to 25 percent, were applied for a short period to livestock, meats, hay, various types of minerals and ores, animal skins and hides, cashmere, logs, sawn timber, and scrap metal. However, export taxes were subsequently eliminated from the trade policy regime.

The transitional tariff system, adopted in March 1991, applied duties to 29 broad commodity groups at rates ranging from 5 percent to 100 percent. Because more than half of the rates were levied at either 5 percent or 15 percent, the resulting average tariff was estimated to be about 13 percent,[6] with fairly narrow dispersion around the average. While few items were zero rated (children's food and clothing), approximately one third of imports were exempted from payment of duties. These exemptions were primarily afforded to Soviet joint-venture operations, although a number of others were granted, and heavily utilized, under the Foreign Investment Law.

When measured against the experience of countries moving to liberalize their highly distortive trade policy regimes, the Mongolian tariff system was, even in its embryonic form, rather simple with minimal inherent distortion to relative prices. However, the Mongolian authorities have taken the further desirable step of unifying the tariff into a single 15 percent rate for all imports and are considering ways of reducing the number of exemptions.

Because of the importance of import price differentials as a contributor to budget revenues, these have not been replaced by the tariff but rather the tariff has substituted for part of the differential. As a transitional measure this probably has some merit, as it allows importers time to adjust to the new form of taxation without increasing their total tax burden. However, the sooner the differentials are phased out the sooner will the tariff be able to perform its intended policy function of providing a moderate amount of protection to domestic economic activity while at the same time generating much-needed revenues.

Since 1992 a manufacturing or import level sales tax has been levied in conjunction with selective excise taxes. The sales tax is a transitional revenue measure that could, in the long term, be transformed into a full-fledged value-added tax (VAT). It is seen as an important element in the overall tax package, since it would facilitate the rationalization of existing domestic turnover taxes and prepare the taxpaying community for the eventual transition to a VAT system. The sales tax applies to all goods (both domestically produced and imported) and employs a credit mechanism for tax paid on inputs. This credit mechanism gives the sales tax features of a VAT. Export sales are zero rated and are entitled to input tax credits.

As of October 1991, excise taxes were levied on gold and silver jewelry, vodka, and beer. However, other products were being considered for excise coverage, again to help meet the country's urgent revenue needs.

As regards direct taxation of individuals and corporations, new legislation was approved by parliament early in 1991 and was subsequently amended later in the year. The new personal income tax eliminated schedular income taxation by unifying all income into one rate schedule and adopted a broad concept of taxable income by covering wages and salaries, self-employment income, dividends, interest, inheritances, unemployment compensation, income from contract work, and noncash

[6]IMF staff estimates.

incomes. Tax rates range from 1.25 percent in the lowest income bracket to 50 percent in the highest. The uppermost rate, while somewhat high, is broadly in line with rates used in market-oriented economies, and for the present is set at an income level that will be reached by very few taxpayers. Thus, the rate structure and the tax base go well along the road to meeting the criteria of equity and transparency.

The proposed company income tax is intended to unify the fourfold system of taxation described above into a single profits tax that will be applicable to all types of enterprises that have more than five employees. Tax rates will range from 8 percent to a maximum of 60 percent, using the bracket method. Taxable income is defined as gross sales less all material costs, labor costs, and depreciation. Enterprises with foreign capital participation are to be taxed at the lower rate of 40 percent.

Directions for Future Tax Reform

Reforms Planned

As explained in the previous section, since late 1989 a number of important changes to Mongolia's tax system have been introduced. Indeed, Mongolia has made remarkable progress in implementing a tax system more in tune with the requirements of market-oriented economies. In the direct tax field, the previous system of compulsory transfers from the state enterprise sector to the budget is being gradually replaced by income taxation that will treat state-owned and private enterprises equally. In the indirect tax field, the authorities have introduced a simplified customs tariff and a uniform rate sales tax with VAT features. Excise taxes on selected products are also in place.

Even at this early stage in its transition, Mongolia has the unique advantage of having adopted a simple and sound system of indirect taxation, which will be easy to administer and have a high revenue potential. This has been made possible principally because of the determination of its open-minded, coalition Government which has become aware that relatively simple taxes have the potential to meet large revenue requirements without defeating efficiency and equity objectives.

The new tax laws were conceived by policymakers only for the transition period, and some were prepared hastily. Thus, it is not surprising that legislation needs to be improved considerably. The authorities intend to amend the relevant laws as quickly as feasible, with technical assistance from specialized international agencies. They are also well aware of the need for a basic administrative infrastructure to implement a modern tax system. The small customs administration should be able to administer the simplified customs tariff, but the newly created Income and Taxes

Department is not strongly positioned to perform the assessment, collection, and audit functions that will be required to administer income and sales taxation.

Although further refinement of legislation and supporting administrative reform will take time, there are pressing needs for new revenues. Like many other economies in transition, as Mongolia moves ahead with price liberalization and privatization, traditional sources of budget revenue[7] are expected to decline rapidly and worrying signs are evident already. At the same time, the need to maintain a tight fiscal policy stance leaves little room for revenue to decline. This means that substantial receipts will have to be generated quickly from new taxes to cover a sustained level of budgetary spending, even after allowing for some government disengagement in economic activity.

Constraining Factors

Meeting the required revenue effort will constitute a formidable challenge, considering the many economic and institutional constraints. On the economic side, the main constraint will be the pace at which completion of price liberalization can proceed, considering the inevitably high social costs associated with accelerated liberalization. At the time of writing, prices of a number of final consumer goods were still controlled. Even a partial liberalization of prices, whereby input or wholesale prices are free while retail prices remain fixed, would jeopardize the profitability of public and private firms. Moreover, because of the low levels of income and financial savings in Mongolia, and only modest prospects for foreign investment, the privatization program can only proceed slowly. As experienced by countries in similar situations, such slow progress will also have a dampening effect on government revenue. Further, most new enterprises in the private sector will be small and medium-sized units with little, if any, experience in modern accounting practices. Therefore, until such practices can be adopted throughout the emerging private sector, it will be difficult to tax these new enterprises.

On the institutional side, Mongolia is still in the formative stages of developing basic banking, property rights, and business accounting legislation. A new banking law has been enacted, providing the legal and statutory framework for the establishment of a two-tier banking system designed to separate the commercial and central banking activities of the State Bank and to specify the modalities of the key central bank functions. Six commercial banks have also been established. Much remains to be done, however, with regard to the regulatory and administrative

---

[7]Namely, import and export price differentials and compulsory transfers from the state enterprise sector to the government budget, which together still account for more than 70 percent of total government receipts and as much as 37 percent of GDP.

framework for commercial banking and the monetary and exchange rate management tasks of the central bank. Privatization is itself constrained by a lack of private ownership legislation. Laws to protect private ownership rights and facilitate property transfers are being drafted. Uniform business accounting rules defining, in particular, the notion of net economic profits, also need to be formulated and legislated. This will be essential if the privatization program and the increased financial autonomy recently granted to state-owned enterprises are to succeed.

Finally, the Mongolian tax administration is still at an early stage. As mentioned earlier, a Customs Affairs Department was created in October 1990. But this department will face increasing difficulties as foreign trade gains momentum. In January 1991, with the enactment of the Income Tax Law, a very elementary administrative apparatus was put in place, comprising a tax policy unit and collection unit within the tax department, staffed by 22 officers. Although the authorities have drafted legislation for a manufacturing stage sales tax, much work needs to be done to put in place an administrative structure for the collection of this tax.

Agenda for Institutional Reform

During the transition period, the absence of a proper tax administration has been a major impediment to aligning the Mongolian tax system to the requirements of a market-oriented economy. Clearly, the development of a well-structured and adequately staffed tax and customs departments should be of priority for the authorities in the coming years. The organizational features of an efficient tax administration, however, depend greatly on the type of taxes that will be put in place. Therefore, the first priority should be to formulate a carefully articulated medium-term policy strategy.

Medium-Term Objectives for Tax Policy

The main tax policy objectives for the medium term should aim at the following:

- Consolidating the tariff reform by reducing the number of exemptions;
- Establishing a broad-based sales tax with VAT features;
- Improving the existing income tax legislation; and
- Introducing real estate taxation.

Because its industrial sector is still largely uncompetitive and heavily dependent on consumer imports, Mongolia should make extensive use of import taxation to raise revenue. The levying of customs duties is a fairly easy way to tax consumption with relatively low administrative and compliance costs and high revenue potential. The uniform and low rate of tariff now adopted should have relatively few distortionary effects on resource allocation, provided exemptions are kept to a minimum.

As explained above, the authorities are replacing domestic turnover taxes with a coordinated system of indirect taxation consisting of a single-stage manufacturing sales tax with a credit mechanism for taxes paid upstream, complemented by excise taxes on selected commodities. Both apply equally to imports and domestically produced goods, confining the protection function to customs duties. Excises are currently imposed on jewelry, vodka, and beer. For revenue and equity purposes, their coverage should be extended to products such as gasoline, tobacco, and motor vehicles.

A desirable long-term objective for Mongolia should be to implement a full-fledged VAT—a broad-based sales tax on the value added by all the productive sectors of the economy, including the services and distribution sectors. The VAT is now used around the world and has recently been introduced in a number of Southeast Asian countries. The main reasons for its wide acceptance are that it generates proportionally more revenue as GDP grows and that it can be applied at relatively low rates given its broad base. Single rate VATs, with few exemptions and a turnover threshold to eliminate small-scale enterprises, are relatively simple to administer.

The income tax legislation, enacted in 1991, is a step in the right direction to place on equal footing public and private enterprises and to separate corporate and individual incomes for tax purposes. However, since it has several shortcomings, there is ample room for improvement. For instance, for taxing corporations, a single rate not exceeding 40 percent should be substituted for the present multiple-rate structure since the latter introduces unwarranted discrimination across economic sectors. For personal income taxation, the rate structure could be rationalized and, in the longer term, provision could be made for capital gains taxation.

Finally, the possibility of developing some form of land property taxation should be explored, as real estate tends to be a preferred investment for those high income earners prone to income tax evasion. Modern techniques, based on aerial photography, should ease the establishment of simplified fiscal cadastres that can be used for property tax assessment.

Strengthening Tax Administration

Until recently, the Customs Affairs Department relied on approximately 200 customs officers (40 at headquarters and 160 in the field) to carry out its tasks. Field officers currently control 20 border crossing points, and 24 others are staffed by the military police. Prior to the enactment of the new customs law, customs staff were responsible for the clearance of passengers at train stations and at the Ulaanbaatar airport. The Customs Affairs Department plans to recruit about 100 new officers to cope with the tasks mandated by the new legislation. It will need new skills to administer the customs law with respect to commercial operations, which are expected to expand rapidly. Extensive training programs will have to be implemented to master the techniques required to handle tariff classification, valuation, fraud investigation, and the administration of exemptions. Headquarters' responsibilities should be restructured to ensure effective and efficient management, and customs procedures should be computerized early enough in the reorganization process so that these can be coordinated with similar efforts in the sales and income tax administrations. The customs law also needs amending to deal more effectively with valuation problems and the physical and documentary control of goods.

The tax offices in the Ministry of Finance, which were responsible for the administration of the revenue system under the previous regime, are neither organized nor equipped to administer Western-type taxes. Staff lack accounting expertise, as well as basic training in assessment, collection, and audit techniques used in modern tax administrations. Mongolia is currently engaged in establishing new organizational structures and training to remedy this situation. The required reforms in sales tax administration are all the more manageable at this stage since the taxpayer community comprises only about 400 state-owned enterprises, including trading companies. Therefore, taxpayer identification and registration systems should be developed without delay, returns should be prepared, and a taxpayer master file should be established and possibly computerized to allow for the rapid processing of late filers' and nonfilers' forms. The collection function should also be organized quickly, possibly with the direct involvement of banks. Here again, recruitment and extensive training programs should be implemented as early as feasible, possibly with external technical assistance.

Concluding Remarks

At this stage in its transition toward a market economy, Mongolia should enjoy a substantial advantage in taxation, compared with many other former centrally planned economies. To capitalize on these advantages will require the authorities to pursue with determination a reform process that replaces the current revenue system with simple indirect taxes, requiring fairly modest administrational and compliance costs. Later in the transition, or possibly after the transition, Mongolia will need to strengthen its income tax legislation to capture the surplus of economic agents, particularly those in the emerging private sector. Therefore, the coalition Government's initial impetus must be sustained and the reform's emphasis on simplicity preserved.

In any society experimenting with democracy, there is a tendency to yield to pressure groups to try to satisfy conflicting interests. Failure to resist these pressures will lead to the acceptance of an ever-increasing number of exemptions that will hastily erode the tax base and result in a complex, costly-to-administer tax system. The erosion of the tax base will also create the temptation for tax rate increases and pressures for further concessions that will distort the price system and ultimately impede economic growth.

References

Calvo, Guillermo A., and Jacob A. Frenkel, "From Centrally Planned to Market Economy: The Road from CPE to PCPE," *Staff Papers*, International Monetary Fund, Vol. 38 (June 1991), pp. 268–99.

Milne, Elizabeth, John Leimone, Franek Rozwadowski, and Padej Sukachevin, *The Mongolian People's Republic: Toward a Market Economy*, IMF Occasional Paper No. 79 (Washington: International Monetary Fund, 1991).

Mitra, Pradeep, *The Coordinated Reform of Tariffs and Domestic Indirect Taxes*, World Bank Working Paper No. 490 (Washington: World Bank, 1990).

Papageorgiou, Demetris, Armeane M. Choksi, and Michael Michaely, *Liberalizing Foreign Trade in Developing Countries: The Lessons of Experience* (Washington: World Bank, 1990).

Tanzi, Vito, "Tax Reform in Economies in Transition: A Brief Introduction to the Main Issues," IMF Working Paper No. 91/23 (Washington: International Monetary Fund, 1991).

———, ed., *Fiscal Policies in Economies in Transition* (Washington: International Monetary Fund, 1992).

CHAPTER 16

Transition and Transformation: Fiscal Sector Issues in Kazakhstan

Parthasarathi Shome

As in all states of the former Soviet Union, Kazakhstan, in its transformation to a market economy, is facing multiple hurdles. These reflect its geography, the structure of its economy, and the rigid institutional arrangements associated with unpredictable rules, regulations, and financial obligations typical of a command economy. There are no institutions that can provide a basis for the smooth operation of a market economy, and economic agents at present lack sufficient understanding of market systems. Transformation will have to be based on a spread of education and awareness of the rudimentary operating rules of market systems, the steady building of market-oriented institutions, the easing of rigid rules and regulations with the burden of responsibility assigned clearly, clarity and simplicity of obligations to the state, for example, in tax laws, and a reorientation of the economy from an overt dependence on the former U.S.S.R. to a trading system more open to the rest of the world.

This paper focuses on fiscal issues and assesses the structure of economic activities and the overall macroeconomic setting so as to place those fiscal issues in context. First, it describes the structure of the Kazakh economy. Then it outlines the macroeconomic setting and fiscal sector operations before and around the beginning of the transformation process. Next, the paper assesses the factors, including those that have emerged from the reform process, that can be expected to affect short-run economic performance. This is followed by a fiscal strategy for future tax and expenditure policies and, finally, some concluding observations.

Structure of the Economy

Kazakhstan has a population of 17 million, of whom 7 percent of men and 16 percent of women were old enough to claim pensions in 1990.[1]

Parthasarathi Shome is Chief of the Tax Policy Division in the Fiscal Affairs Department. The author would like to acknowledge many useful comments from his colleagues, Luis Valdivieso and Howell Zee.

[1] Life expectancy in the former Soviet Union is 64 years for men (72 in member countries of the Organization for Economic Cooperation and Development (OECD)) and 73 for women (78 in the OECD).

Further, the population aged 50 to 54 is currently much larger than those in the preceding or following age groups, which implies a heavier burden on the pension system in the near future.[2]

Kazakhstan comprises 2.7 million square kilometers and has one fifth of the arable land of the former Soviet Union. Its net material product (NMP) derives primarily from agriculture—wool, grain, meat—followed by mining and manufacturing. Table 1 compares selected states of the former U.S.S.R. representing a Central Asian state, a Baltic state, and three other economically dominant states. Kazakhstan has substantial mineral reserves of chrome, lead, copper, zinc, coal, and oil. The Tengiz oilfield—one of the largest in the world—alone has 25 billion barrels of oil, a third of which is recoverable, and is planned for exploitation over 40 years with foreign collaboration. Metallurgy, heavy machinery, and petrochemicals are major components of manufacturing. Consequently, Kazakhstan's trade pattern indicates its specialization in mining and heavy manufacturing: half of its final goods are imported, and three fourths of its exports consist of intermediate goods and raw materials. State enterprises are responsible for 80 percent of output, and the state owns 90 percent of fixed assets. The remaining assets are divided about equally between the cooperative sector and the private sector.

In the transition phase, agriculture and heavy manufacturing—albeit using static technology—might be expected to continue to dominate production, but the role of energy in ensuring the smooth functioning of production and distribution is especially important. After transformation, mining, reflecting rapid exploitation of mineral resources, as well as services, reflecting the growth of market-based economic activity, may be expected to grow in importance. The crux here is the pace at which the transformation takes place and the length of the transition phase. These will determine the strategic planning of the pace of privatization of state enterprises and state assets, changes in the mechanisms and rules for revenue generation for government, and the composition of appropriate macroeconomic policies. Institution-building and structural change have to proceed hand in hand with the implementation of that strategy.

Recent Fiscal Operations

Macroeconomic Setting

Under the regime of strictly administered prices, production and trade followed a pattern guided by the Gosplan. The Union Government created and allocated credit, which helped bridge any fiscal gap of the Kazakhstan Government through substantial transfers. Under this regime, a

---

[2]In 1990 there were almost a million people between ages 50 and 54, and slightly over half a million between ages 55 and 59.

moderate sustained rate of growth with very little inflation took place in 1985–88.

Transition has led to increased prices but has also reduced the number of administered prices across sectors. By January 1992, 80 percent of retail prices on goods and services were freed, and the prices of those that remained administered were increased threefold to fivefold. State assets, including business property, are slowly being privatized. In 1991, 380 enterprises were sold, mainly services (representing gross assets of about rub 1 billion), out of about 34,400 enterprises in Kazakhstan (total of rub 200 billion of assets). By May 1992, 1,540 enterprises (5 percent of the total) had been privatized or transformed into joint ventures. Less organized changes in contractual and other economic and financial arrangements, such as in wages and pension benefits, are bound to have taken place. The Government has felt the pressure to accommodate many of these changes with softer financial policies. In turn, the partially managed price system has continued to give mixed signals to the production and distribution systems. As a result, growth was negative beginning in 1989, inflation soared beginning in 1991, and the trade balance, which had been negative in recent years, did not improve (Table 1 presents comparative information on these aspects). In addition, widespread structural bottlenecks have appeared.

Fiscal Sector

With the increasing market orientation of the economy, and the reversal of the Union revenue-sharing mechanisms, the entire fiscal system in Kazakhstan is having to change dramatically, leading to an immediate fiscal disequilibrium. The fiscal balance of 1989 rapidly moved to a deficit of 8 percent of GDP in 1991 (Table 2), an experience similar to that in Ukraine. This reflected a fall in tax revenue from 26 percent of GDP to 19 percent even while nontax revenue and expenditure remained stable at about 9 percent and 36 percent, respectively. It is important to assess carefully the changes in tax policy instruments and in the institutions on which tax collection is based.

Revenue Sources[3]

As in most states of the former Soviet Union, in recent years the two largest sources of revenue in Kazakhstan have been taxes on income and profits and taxes on turnover and sales, each accounting for about a third of total revenue. Revenue from the individual income tax has accounted

---

[3]My colleague, Yuichi Ikeda, helped develop the information on revenues and expenditures.

Table 1. Kazakhstan: Comparative Indicators of Output and Sectoral Distribution

	Kazakhstan	Azerbaijan	Belarus	Latvia	Russian Fed.	Ukraine
			(In millions of rubles)			
Net material product (NMP) (1990)	28,088	10,582	28,700	8,854	425,200	118,000
			(Percentage distribution)			
Total	100	100	100	100	100	100
Industry	28	35	47	51	43	42
Agriculture	40	38	22	22	18	28
Construction	15	12	12	8	12	10
Transport and communications	9	5	4	8	8	6
Trade, supply, and other	8	10	15	11	19	14
			(In percent)			
NMP growth rate						
1988–89	5.8	5.2	12.3	8.7	7.1	6.9
1989–90	-1.3[1]	-7.8	1.4	16.0	3.0	8.3
Retail price index (1980 base)						
1980	100.0	100.0	100.0	...	100.0	100.0
1985	105.4	104.2	105.2	...	105.0	104.2
1990	114.1	...	116.3	...	122.3	113.5
1991	208.8	...	210.7	...	231.2	207.2
			(In percent of GDP)			
Trade balance						
1987	-21.6	8.3	3.6	-9.5	...	-4.5
1988	-18.6	7.6	6.0	-7.0	...	-2.1
1989	-20.2	12.5	2.5	-5.7	...	-4.6

Source: IMF staff estimates.
[1]Agriculture was a positive 4.7 percent, but industry, construction, and transport were negative.

Table 2. Kazakhstan: Comparative Indicators of Fiscal Balance of the General Government, 1989–91

(In percent of GDP)

	Kazakhstan	Azerbaijan	Belarus	Latvia	Russian Fed.	Ukraine
1989 performance						
Total revenue and grants	36.6	22.3	...	51.8	...	28.4
Tax revenue	25.0	18.6	...	39.9	...	...
Government expenditure	36.6	24.4	...	51.0	...	27.9
Fiscal balance	—	−2.0	...	0.8	...	0.5
1990 performance						
Total revenue and grants	34.7	26.4	38.2	46.1	...	27.4
Tax revenue	21.9	21.1	30.4	37.5	...	...
Government expenditure	33.4	31.9	34.7	44.0	...	28.0
Fiscal balance	1.3	−5.5	3.5	2.1	...	−0.6
1991 performance						
Total revenue and grants	27.6	32.1	42.9	45.5	25.5	31.8
Tax revenue	18.5	24.5	29.8	46.6	...	...
Government expenditure	35.6	37.4	40.6	39.4	36.8	46.1
Fiscal balance	−8.0	−5.2	2.2	8.0	−11.3	−14.4

Source: IMF staff estimates.

for about 15 percent and other taxes—mainly social security—have accounted for the remainder (Table 3).[4]

Table 3. Kazakhstan: Government Financial Operations

(In percent of GDP)

	1987	1988	1989	1990	1991
Total revenue and grants	35.6	35.4	36.6	34.7	27.6
Tax revenue	27.6	25.2	25.0	21.9	18.5
Of which:					
Income profits tax	11.8	10.6	10.5	8.3	10.7
Of which:					
Individual	4.9	4.8	5.2	2.7	3.4
Corporate	6.9	5.8	5.3	5.6	7.4
Social security					
contributions	3.9	3.8	3.7	3.5	—
Taxes on property	—	—	—	—	—
Taxes on production					
and consumption	11.7	10.6	10.6	9.7	6.8
International trade taxes	—	—	—	—	—
Other taxes	0.2	0.2	0.2	0.4	0.9
Grants—Union transfers	7.1	9.6	11.0	11.9	6.5
Total expenditure	35.7	34.6	36.6	33.4	35.6
National economy	18.9	18.8	20.7	17.7	11.9
Social and cultural programs	14.3	13.8	13.9	12.7	15.4
Of which:					
Social security	4.2	4.2	4.1	3.9	4.7
Transfers to Union budget	1.8	1.3	1.2	2.0	2.0
Other expenditure	0.7	0.7	0.8	1.0	6.3
Revenue and					
grants (–) expenditure	–0.1	0.8	—	1.3	–8.0
Memorandum item:					
GDP (in millions of rubles)	35,000	39,000	42,000	51,000	92,000

Source: IMF staff estimates.

The Kazakh revenue structure reflected the characteristics of a centrally planned economy. A large portion of the budget revenue was collected through the public enterprise sector, directly in the form of profits tax, or less directly in the form of turnover tax, which might eventually be paid by households but was collected and paid by public enterprises.

Until 1990, the profits tax system was configured on centrally established "norms" for contributions to the budget, payments to workers, and the plan-determined investment needs of the enterprises. These enterprises had little autonomy in their investment and financing decisions; their finances and indebtedness were intertwined with the finances and indebtedness of the Government's budget.

---

[4]Except for a relatively small portion, payroll tax is not included in the budget but in extrabudgetary funds set up for social security programs.

The turnover tax presupposed government control over the prices of inputs and outputs. The tax resulted from the difference between producer prices and retail prices, both controlled by the Government, which constantly monitored, and frequently increased or decreased, the turnover tax rates applicable to individual commodities to clear the commodity markets and support unprofitable sectors through tax reliefs (see Tanzi (1991)).

The new market orientation of the Kazakh economy renders the old revenue system obsolete. The conventions of profits tax and turnover tax cannot exist unmodified in a market-oriented economy; the new tax system must not thwart private initiative and enterprise and must be consistent with a liberalized price system.

The Kazakh authorities launched their revenue system reforms in 1991. Effective July 1991, comprehensive income tax laws were introduced, subjecting enterprises to profits tax at proportional rates and wage earners and the self-employed to progressive income tax. Although a sales tax was levied on the consumption of commodities in 1991, much remains to be accomplished.

Expenditure System

About half of expenditure was accounted for by "expenditures for the national economy," which included outlays for subsidies to individuals as well as for subsidies and transfers to public enterprises (see Table 3). Although it captured profits of the public enterprises as budget revenue, the Government was also forced to support this sector, burdened as it was with economically inefficient monopolies, through a variety of open or hidden subsidies and transfers, which dominated the expenditure pattern of the Government. The price controls called for large outlays on consumer subsidies and subsidies to industrial and agricultural inputs.

The "socio-cultural expenditures," which include outlays for social security, health, education, culture, and arts, accounted for about a third of total expenditures. Social security by itself has accounted for slightly over 10 percent of total expenditures. However, most of the social security programs were—and still are—administered by such extrabudgetary funds as the pension fund, social insurance fund, and employment fund.

With the emergence of the market economy, public expenditure policies have to be reoriented from direct investment in, or subsidy of, production and distribution activities to providing social and economic infrastructure to facilitate private production and distribution. Government could play a strategic role in removing the bottlenecks to production and distribution, especially in the transition phase. In lieu of social support programs in the form of consumer subsidies and transfers to public enterprises, appropriate social safety nets have to be created for vulnerable groups.

Fiscal Relations with the Union

The Kazakh fiscal system was closely tied to the fiscal system of the former Soviet Union. Most major fiscal decisions, including those on tax legislation, were made at the Union level, and the republic simply implemented them. At that time, Kazakhstan was fiscally a net recipient of the Union subvention. Transfers from the Kazakh Republic—about 5 percent of total expenditure—which included the transfer of a certain portion of its revenue determined by the Union laws, as well as transfers related to all Union projects, were more than offset by the subvention from the Union budget. Up to 1990, any deficit in the republic's budget was covered by transfers from the Union without any interest obligations. Since 1991, the deficit has been financed through credit from the Gosbank, but at low interest rates.

Factors Affecting Future Economic Performance

Price and economic reforms should help the economy to grow over the medium to long run. In the transitional period, however, the Kazakh economy confronts difficult macroeconomic conditions since the reforms could be expected to have an unfavorable impact on the economy—high inflation, decline in output, and unemployment have occurred. These have implications for fiscal performance, on both revenues and public expenditures. The severance of fiscal ties with the Union carries important consequences. The formulation of future macroeconomic-fiscal policies would need to recognize all these factors.

Balancing the macroeconomic disequilibrium will depend on many factors, including the nature and direction of future interstate economic relations. For example, the extent of pass-through of energy pricing—applicable to the trade between Kazakhstan and the rest of the states of the former Soviet Union—could carry important consequences for the terms of trade of Kazakhstan, depending on how the relative prices of oil and coal (which Kazakhstan produces and exports) move in relation to prices of consumer goods (which Kazakhstan imports). Movements in consumer goods prices would be strongly affected by price movements in the Russian Federation. To the extent that other states fail in macroeconomic management and thus suffer from high inflation, Kazakhstan would "import" such inflation, given a continuing high incidence of trade among the states of the former Soviet Union.[5]

Policies within Kazakhstan would also affect the overall macroeconomic picture. Domestic output could continue to decline and remain

---

[5]Equivalently, of course, Kazakhstan could also export the effects of its own policies to the other republics.

low in the transitional period, owing, on the real side, to enterprise restructuring and subsequent liquidation and closure of firms and, on the financial side, to an adherence to prudent credit and budgetary policies to contain inflation. Given these conditions, the real income level of Kazakhstan may be expected to decline further in the short run. Enterprise profits could decline substantially, while wages could not be raised as fast as prices. Last, opening up the economy to trade and investment with the rest of the world may take considerable time since this involves the removal of many structural rigidities and developing and producing products that meet standards of international competitiveness. These factors call for extraordinary measures to arrest the decline in output. Such measures can be implemented only if the Government takes the lead in the transition phase.

The short-run impact of price reform during the transition phase can be especially stringent. On the expenditure side, the move toward free market prices results in a major reduction in the real value of subsidies to the population and enterprises because of the tendency, at least initially, for prices to rise sharply. But the reduction in real income of the population as a result of higher prices would cause increasing demands on the budget for social security outlays, especially to safeguard the position of vulnerable groups in society. The higher price level, together with pressure to increase wages, would increase budgetary expenditure for purchases of goods and services and wage payments to civil servants.

On the revenue side, the higher price level increases the nominal value of revenue from taxes on commodities. However, it is possible that a large increase in prices would change the expenditure pattern of households, forcing them to spend less on consumption items, with a possible negative impact on revenue from consumption taxes, namely, value-added tax (VAT) and excises. The higher price level would also increase the nominal value of revenue from profits and income taxes but, again, the assessment of the impact is not straightforward. An increase in energy prices and production would have a positive impact on revenue through higher tax collection and royalty payments. But if higher inflation continues to bring recessionary episodes and further declines in output and employment, it would have a serious negative impact on revenue. In addition, as a result of possible collection lags, the Tanzi effect is likely to operate in that inflation would continue to exert a negative impact on the real value of tax revenue.

We may suppose that a rearrangement of the Union system of revenue sharing could turn Kazakhstan into a net payer—from a net receiver—of economic resources to the former Soviet Union and could increase its defense and education expenditures. The pressure on expenditures would tend to increase with a breakup of the revenue-sharing mechanisms, again calling for added fiscal effort to close the fiscal gap.

Strategic Planning and Fiscal Policies

Overall Strategic Planning

Similarities between the current experience of Kazakhstan and the experiences of several East European countries during their recent transition and transformation to market economies are striking. These include starting the transition with a large government deficit and rapid inflation; a markedly different inherited tax system from that of market economies; and guarantees of social benefits at least as ample as in most of the developed market economies. Thus, some experiences—notably Poland—may help in strategic fiscal planning for Kazakhstan.

There are also many likenesses to the economic conditions faced by Japan just after World War II: a sudden decline in military-demand-led output, economic infrastructure in disrepair owing to low wartime investment, and high and rising inflation caused by low output and high debt service. At least, Kazakhstan has not suffered from a lack of natural resources or from a dramatic loss of national wealth as Japan did. Japan's strategic planning in the postwar period may provide important lessons for Kazakhstan.

A fiscal strategy has to be developed within the context of overall economic strategy because fiscal policies cannot function in the absence of other sound stabilization and structural policies. Ota and others (1992), using the Japanese postwar experience as a guide, suggest that the Government's primary task in the initial reconstruction phase was to halt a further decline in output by embarking on a selective interventionist policy aimed at emergency economic stabilization. Such a policy would identify bottlenecks in the production-distribution chain and direct resources to sectors that would help remove them, such as infrastructure (steel), energy (petroleum), and, for social stabilization, food production.[6] A strategy that includes maintaining the health of important segments of the agricultural sector is essential because of the large share of NMP accounted for by agriculture. The worst policy would be to diversify investment in an all-out manner; the authorities should be selective in the choice of leading sectors. To encourage their growth and halt output decline, the authors recommend preferential treatment in credit policy (low-interest loans),[7] tax policy (tax incentives and even earmarking if needed), pricing policy (maintaining energy prices at an "appropriate"

---

[6]Unlike Kazakhstan, Japan also faced trade restrictions.

[7]Calvo and Coricelli (1992) have also emphasized the need to maintain the real value of credit at the initial point of change, in order to prevent an "output collapse." They suggest additional measures such as swapping public enterprise debt with government debt, the latter presumably being more acceptable as collateral for private market borrowing (provided such a market exists); and a slower removal of subsidies (provided hyperinflation is not feared) and a smoother increase in input prices so that enterprises have time to build liquidity.

level), wage policy (maintaining higher levels of wages in priority sectors to keep workers from leaving, while granting lower-than-inflation wage increases in other sectors), and trade policy (exporting oil to import industrial facilities and equipment). Subsequently, as the picture turns around, such a priority production program could be extended sequentially to include other infrastructure and materials industries, such as electricity, railways, and fertilizers. Of course, this strategy would also affect the expenditure composition of the Government.

Regarding structural policy, Ota and others (1992) emphasize that privatization without accompanying structural measures could not capture the full benefits of a private sector economy. Thus, monopolies would have to be broken up simultaneously and equally with the development of markets. Product diversification would be encouraged to step up competition by breaking existing production patterns in which most products are produced by only a few companies. Vertical integration would have to be discouraged and new entry encouraged to promote competition among suppliers of materials and components. The breakup of vertically integrated monopolies would be called for, following the Japanese model of carefully orchestrated divisions of particular manufacturing oligarchies. Such structural reforms reflecting an interventionist style would complement price liberalization and privatization efforts aimed at generating supply-side responses.

Interventionist policies seem to have worked in other selected East Asian economies, notably Taiwan Province of China, Korea, and Singapore. In these economies the respective governments played a major role in development by providing economic and social infrastructure, for example, through differential wage policy and substantial investment in technical education, as well as by promoting economic growth through the vigorous promotion of an export-oriented strategy (see Tanzi and Shome (1992)). The importance of an active government role in the transition and transformation of the Kazakh economy to a market-based economy has to be assessed in the light of these important examples.

Fiscal Strategy

Fiscal policies form part of the Kazakh economy's overall strategic planning. From the fiscal viewpoint, strategies would have to be developed on both the revenue and expenditure sides. For example, consequences of the transition would include a decline in revenue in real terms. To offset this, the tax base would have to be expanded even as the index of economic activity declines. This can be done only if the incomes of new entities emerging as a result of economic liberalization and privatization can be successfully brought into the tax net (although revenue collections from such sources would be small at initial stages). The importance of the pace of privatization and the prevalence of right price signals to encourage private economic activity cannot be ignored. Slack in such structural transformation would necessarily imply a slowing in the conversion of macroeconomic instruments toward market-oriented credit policies as well as tax and expenditure policies.

Because of the tight fiscal constraints, social expenditure programs have to be streamlined and targeted so that social benefits are efficiently provided to the most needy. Much institution-building is necessary in all these efforts, which cannot be achieved overnight. For example, even though institutions geared toward meting out social benefits with broad coverage are in place, the establishment and activation of targeted programs that reduce net cost to the Government will involve considerable time and resources. Analyzing the experience of Hungary, Newbery (1991) points toward the considerable difficulties in setting up the necessary infrastructure for administering social safety net benefits while breaking up schemes for benefit payments (administered through public enterprises) that went primarily to the employed, middle class.[8] The impact on social stability of reducing net benefits to particular groups will have to be recognized at this pivotal point in Kazakh history.

Strategy for Tax Revenue Maintenance

A strategy may be developed benefiting from the experience of Eastern Europe. The average profit rate of Polish firms jumped from 19 percent in 1988 to 46 percent in 1989, when prices exploded. In 1990, it was still high at 30 percent, but fell to 8 percent as nominal interest rates shot up with inflation and true profits were understated as a result of nominal interest deductions (Gordon (1992)). Business income tax revenue paralleled the profits path, growing moderately in real terms in 1989 and 1990 but collapsing in 1991. This experience points in the direction of correcting for inflation-induced biases in the measurement of profits for tax purposes.

Several additional strategic elements should be borne in mind. If tax incentives are to be used as a part of an interventionist strategy, these have to be extremely selective and be geared toward very few leading sectors with the revenue loss being made up from other sources. This is because experience teaches that broad use of tax incentives leads to revenue loss, inefficiences in resource allocation, and bureaucratic growth. Yet, in Kazakhstan, a major role for infrastructure sectors, such as energy, cannot be denied. Here, of course, foreign investment has to be encouraged. However, the authorities would have to design finely tuned

---

[8]Newbery (1991) rightly alludes to the political viability question in that such redistributive policies mean that social benefits will be switched from the middle class to the poor, while simultaneously allowing an entrepreneurial, upper economic class to grow rapidly to encourage quick, private capital accumulation and growth.

tax structures to minimize the possibilities of foreign and joint ventures devising plans to reduce their tax liabilities by setting up lightly taxed subsidiaries, using transfer pricing, and the like. Many European countries do not tax foreign-source income, and many U.S. firms already benefit from excess credits. Thus, foreign investment would not necessarily be attracted by generating additional credit. These matters would need careful examination. It would not be prudent to consider new and untried forms of taxation, such as the cash-flow tax, with unpredictable revenue effects, at this crucial transition phase.[9]

The rapid incorporation of modern methods in tax administration is equally important, for example, through training of officials in acceptable accounting standards and selective auditing of firms. This is especially important given the scarcity of banks and accounting firms. Improvements in accounting and auditing are important for large firms. But improvements in tax administration with the goal of controlling newly emergent small private firms in various sectors are equally important. Otherwise, tax revenue from the private sector will certainly shrink as it did in Poland even as the number of private sector firms increased. If withholding is used to capture as many sources of income as possible within the tax base, the focus of tax administration could be laid on improving other important areas.

Foreign tax advisors must be prepared to accept radical concepts of tax bases at least in the short run. Thus, a corporate "income" tax, incorporating profits plus wages in the tax base, may have to be accepted to discourage managers of state enterprises from giving themselves high wage payments from what would otherwise be taxable profits.[10] Or, a long list of excise taxes may have to suffice during the initial period of price reform and continuing need for greater revenue by government. Indeed, in the initial reform phase, high and changing tax rates may be needed to close the fiscal gap, itself fluctuating with inflation. As the economy transforms to a predominantly market economy, the focus should turn toward improving the efficiency of the tax system, for example, by more methodical implementation of nondistortive taxes such as a consumption-type VAT.[11]

Turnover taxes fixed in specific terms must be quickly transformed to an ad valorem basis. Otherwise their real value could fall dramatically, as it did in Poland in 1990. As high tax rates depress the incentive to invest as

[9]Mintz and Tsiopoulos (1992) have demonstrated that the argument that the cash-flow tax would provide greater incentive for investment cannot be supported for U.S. corporations operating in Central and East European countries because of excess tax credits. See Tait (1992) on related issues.

[10]A tax-based incomes policy has been introduced in Kazakhstan. It disallows exemption from calculation of corporate income tax of any amount of the wage bill over four times the minimum wage times the number of employees.

[11]While the VAT is already on the tax statutes of Kazakhstan and other states of the former Soviet Union, focus cannot perhaps be removed entirely from the continuing interim role of a long list of excise taxes.

well as reduce consumption, it must be recognized that there is a limit to taxation, to arrest any downward spiral of economic activity.[12] Here, the relief has to come from opening the economy, as rapidly as possible, to trade and foreign investment.

Strategy for Expenditure Policies

On the expenditure side, government policies have to be targeted toward reducing the net subsidies to firms and households, desisting from commandeering goods and services at below-market prices, and attracting foreign investment for investment expenditures. These objectives should be reflected in a change in the composition of government expenditure, from broad-based subsidies to enterprises to selected investment in industrial infrastructure. Thus, firms should be allowed to face market prices both on the cost and receipts sides (this should be an integral part of the price reform) and government receipts should be based on properly defined—albeit some distortionary—taxes, rather than through dictating terms to the production sector on transfers.

Households are complex entities. There is no doubt that household subsidies have to be reduced in the net to accommodate the acute need for closing the fiscal gap. However, if strong adverse reaction from households is to be successfully contained, the expenditure policy package geared toward household benefits needs to be carefully designed. This can be achieved by converting the current mix of social welfare programs to a social safety net program for the most vulnerable, including low-income pensioners and children of low-income families. The retirement age could be raised, and contributions be required on a sound actuarial basis.[13] The remaining pensioners (under a revised system) could even be accommodated at a higher real income level. Unemployment compensation can be financed through a specific program funded by the employed rather than through the general budget.[14] The system of family allowances can be targeted to include only low-income families with children, comprising the most vulnerable groups. Other social expenditures, including health care, can be made subject to cost-sharing. While there seems ample room for reductions in subsidies to households, and such reductions are of paramount importance, the actual sequencing of the reduction and removal of particular programs, while replacing them with well-targeted, cost-saving programs for the vulnerable, will need to be handled with great care.

---

[12]For methods of improving the structure of particular taxes such as the turnover tax or profits taxes, see Tanzi (1991) and Gordon (1992).

[13]This could take time because of lack of information and of professionals who could develop appropriate contribution tables from actuarial data.

[14]In 1991, the authorities created an Employment Fund to be financed by enterprise contributions and to be self-financing at least in the short run. They also separated the Pension Fund from the general budget. See Kapur and others (1992).

Concluding Remarks

This paper surveyed the nature of Kazakh economic and fiscal reform in its own macroeconomic setting, during its transition and transformation to a market economy. The objective was to focus attention on the best fiscal strategy. However, such a strategy has to be placed in the context of an overall economic strategy. The experiences of postwar Japan and the development process in some East Asian economies point toward the government playing a strong complementary role—through selective interventionist policies—in fostering a market economy.

Turning to the long-term goal of fiscal reform in the states of the former Soviet Union: neutral, nondistortionary taxes with a wide revenue base and low, overall tax rate structure, assuring stability in revenue productivity, have been widely written about. Certainly, a broad-based consumption-type VAT—rather than a distortionary structure that does not allow credit for capital goods and machinery—would be preferable; an appropriately defined system of selective excises—on alcoholic beverages, tobacco products, and petroleum products—in addition to the VAT, would be desirable; personal income tax cannot be ignored; and ultimately a corporate income tax has to have a sound conceptual basis, rather than hybrid definitions suited for a particular short-run revenue objective. Streamlined payroll taxes would be important in the overall tax structure.

Rather than calling into question the appropriateness and suitability of the specified tax structure, this paper has looked at the important elements of an interim strategy; it has asked what the strategic tax-expenditure policy mix is, and how it is to be differentiated from the ideal, long-run policy package. What are particular concerns that must be kept in mind by fiscal experts in formulating interim tax-expenditure policies to avoid a possible collapse of revenues or an alarming erosion of real values of government expenditures, especially in the social category? What are specific areas in which some compromises—from the long-run optimal package—might be necessary to correct negative rates of growth, rapidly rising prices, and high fiscal deficits?

In its quest for interim fiscal policies, the paper identified selected tax-expenditure measures, in view of recent experiences of Poland and Hungary. Such tax policies would at times result in the maintenance of current structures for certain taxes—albeit only in the short run—in order to prevent the collapse of revenues experienced in Poland. While a consumption-type VAT would be the least distortionary, the existing production-type VAT, which does not allow credit for capital goods and machinery, coupled with a list longer than usually recommended of excisable items, may have to be accepted in the short run for revenue considerations. This might be necessary for macroeconomic stabilization.

On the expenditure side, transition policies would have to identify ways of reducing budgetary subsidies to firms (synchronized with allowing market prices to prevail on their receipts side), while allowing for selective preferential treatment of leading (infrastructure) sectors. This has to be done notwithstanding the significant state ownership of productive assets, superimposed on a monopolistic organization of production. Expenditure policies would have to address the changing needs of households. Government would have to be aware of the possible social consequences of drastic, one-shot reductions in the prevailing subsidies to households. While the objective must be to target the most vulnerable sections of society, the less vulnerable who are more visible still have to be taken into account when making sensitive policy decisions: Hungary provides a case in point; the reductions may have to be gradual.

Finally, despite the belt-tightening measures, a fiscal gap may still remain. That can be filled with foreign financing, flowing primarily into investment activities. It is clear that the search for external resources, especially private resources, will remain an important element of strategic fiscal planning during the transition period.

References

Calvo, Guillermo A., and Fabrizio Coricelli, "Output Collapse in Eastern Europe: The Role of Credit," IMF Working Paper No. 92/64 (Washington: International Monetary Fund, August 1992).

Gordon, Roger H., "Fiscal Policy During the Transition in Eastern Europe," paper presented at Conference on the Transition in Eastern Europe, National Bureau of Economic Research, February 26–29, 1992.

Kapur, I., L. Valdivieso, S. Geadah, K. Warwick, A. Furtado, R. Vaez-Zadeh, and X. Maret, *Kazakhstan—Economic Review* (Washington: International Monetary Fund, May 1992).

Mintz, Jesus, and T. Tsiopoulos, "On the Effectiveness of Corporate Tax Incentives for Foreign Investment in the Presence of Tax Crediting: An Application to Central Eastern European Countries," paper presented at Trans-Atlantic Public Economics Seminar, National Bureau of Economic Research (University of Munich, June 11–13, 1992).

Newbery, David M.G., "An Analysis of the Hungarian Tax Reform," Discussion Paper Series No. 558 (London: Center for Economic Policy Research, May 1991).

Ota, F., H. Tanikawa, and T. Otani, "Russia's Economic Reform and Japan's Industrial Policy," paper presented at symposium on "Unification of Europe," June 1 and 2, 1992, Research Institute of International Trade and Industry (MITI) and Japan Industrial Policy Research Institute.

Tait, Alan A., "A Not-So-Simple Alternative to the Income Tax for Socialist Economies in Transition," *The World Bank Research Observer*, Vol. 7, No. 2 (July 1992), pp. 239–48.

Tanzi, Vito, "Tax Reform and the Move to a Market Economy: Overview of the Issues," in *The Role of Tax Reform in Central and Eastern European Economies* (Paris: Organization for Economic Cooperation and Development, 1991).

―――, and Parthasarathi Shome, "The Role of Taxation in the Development of East Asian Economies," Chap. 2 in *The Political Economy of Tax Reform*, ed. by Takatoshi Ito and Anne O. Krueger (Chicago and London: University of Chicago Press, 1992).

PART IV

Africa

CHAPTER 17

Algeria: A National Approach To Market-Oriented Tax Reform

Ernst-Albrecht Conrad

In many respects Algeria can be described as a country in transition. In the mid-1980s, as the command economy began to exhibit severe strain, a political consensus emerged for a gradual move to a market-oriented system. Most observers would agree, however, that Algeria's point of departure for this transition was different from that of most other centrally planned economies.

Several factors called for a national approach to the transition, particularly as regards taxation. The command system, while fully established in the heavy industrial and oil sectors, had not completely penetrated the rest of the economy. Algeria was among the first centrally planned economies to embark on a broad reorientation toward a market system and, as a major member of the Organization of Petroleum Exporting Countries (OPEC), had benefited from and had become dependent on the inflow of external resources. Moreover, throughout the socialist period it had preserved the financial structure of the former French government.

Nevertheless, Algeria was confronted with many of the same basic issues that other centrally planned economies have had to deal with: how could a gradual path toward transition best be chosen, and how could reforms of the major economic policies effectively be coordinated? The latter issue was particularly important for domestic resource mobilization. It was recognized at an early stage that tax reform needed to be handled as an integral part of the transition. Economic liberalization required the tax system to shed its interventionist role, and, equally basically, reform of the major taxes on income and production made sense only if incomes and prices were liberalized.

This paper first draws a broad picture of these specific national factors and then discusses the principal issues in tax reform. The paper concludes by describing the program for strengthening the tax administration.

Ernst-Albrecht Conrad is an Advisor in the Fiscal Affairs Department.

Setting for Transition

Historical Background and Reorientation of the Economy

When Algeria became independent in 1962, it was suffering from the trauma of a costly civil war that had ended nearly a century of its special status as a French territory. Understandably, the political leaders were strongly motivated to move away from Western European tradition, which may help explain Algeria's initial swing toward the East under Ben Bella. In the subsequent decade, however, President Boumédienne added a more genuine ideological dimension to Algeria's socialist policies.

On the economic side, the creation of a vast hydrocarbon sector helped centralize industrial power. This process was reinforced through the establishment of public enterprises in most other industrial sectors, the nationalization of financial institutions and of medium- and small-scale industries, and the conversion of private farms into state-run agricultural conglomerates. In parallel, the control function of the market was gradually replaced by the central planning of production, by control of prices and labor markets, and, more generally, by the establishment of the system of intervention in most areas of economic activity that constituted a common feature of the centrally planned economies.

In spite of these developments, a core element of a free-market economy remained intact. Both domestic and foreign observers often express surprise at the size and pervasiveness of the parallel economy in Algeria. This shadow economy was not limited to the small-scale informal sector, but apparently also permeated the production and distribution activities of the socialized economy. In addition, imports outside the licensing system were officially tolerated under certain conditions. In the 1980s, the shadow economy further gained in importance as it helped enterprises and consumers to obtain critical materials and goods when the central distribution system began to weaken. This may have helped the transition.

In 1986, Algeria embarked on a broad but gradual program to promote a market economy. Privatization was initiated in the agricultural sector by leasing land to farmers. Real estate, including residences and apartments held by the Government, was sold, mostly to the tenants. Subsequently, the industrial and service sectors were granted more autonomy, while the capital assets of many large enterprises were regrouped in eight holding funds. In addition, transformation of the labor market commenced with the introduction of a new set of laws governing the organization and activities of trade unions. Exchange reform was initiated and a more liberal pricing system was introduced, which limited the use of administered prices to a few essential consumer items while margin controls remained in force for certain other goods and services. The regulatory framework was also gradually dismantled.

In all, progress toward a market system is now clearly apparent, although the transition remains to be completed and many structural economic problems, including creation of employment and effective decentralization of industry, remain to be solved. Tax reform is in a relatively advanced stage of implementation.

At the political level, a program for democratic reforms, including the establishment of a multiparty system and free elections, was initiated concomitant with the economic transition program. However, severe civil disturbances were reported in the 1980s and early 1990s. A fundamentalist movement emerged and dominated local elections in 1990, as well as the first of two rounds of national elections in late 1991. In early 1992, the President resigned under pressure from the military, and elections were suspended. These events have, at least temporarily, distracted attention from economic reform.

Early Start of Transition

Algeria's economic reforms were set in motion a few years ahead of those in many other centrally planned economies. Moreover, they were conceived as an evolutionary process, as opposed to the revolutionary or sudden events that later occurred in Eastern Europe and the former U.S.S.R. Because this transition was initiated within the framework of unchanged political institutions and political leaders and senior civil servants remained at their posts, the change in direction was less abrupt.

To what extent has this gradualism accelerated or slowed the pace of economic reform? As regards taxation, the first indications are that a core of experienced senior officials made it possible to design reforms swiftly and to introduce even major changes (such as the structural reorganization of the service) within a tight timeframe. On the other hand, because the political framework changed only gradually, less radical tax reforms were adopted than those chosen later by Eastern European countries. In particular, the rate structures of the new value-added tax (VAT) and of the new global income tax clearly show a continued emphasis on social objectives.

Availability of External Resources

Following the two increases in oil prices in the 1970s, the share of foreign-generated resources in budget revenue expanded sharply and reached about half of total receipts in the early 1980s. As in other OPEC countries, the availability of foreign resources imparted a disincentive to the tax system. There was no compelling need and little public support for vigorously tightening tax provisions and modernizing the tax administration. This factor also contributed to the very visible degradation of the material facilities of the tax administration and the neglect of training and other efforts to upgrade the skills of the service.

Role of Former French Tax System

During the war and following independence, there was an exodus of those who opted to live in France, including many senior civil servants and technicians. The remaining staff struggled with an administrative apparatus designed to function as part of a developed country rather than to serve the needs of a newly independent nation.

In this difficult situation, French administrative tradition, which predates Napoleon, continued to provide welcome support for public sector management. Like other Francophone countries in North and sub-Saharan Africa, Algeria continued to operate within this framework. However, while the neighboring countries remained open to the evolutionary process in government finance and tax systems, Algeria followed a route of relative isolation. Although the tax laws were modified each year and some new levies were added, basic tax provisions and administrative techniques were left relatively untouched during the last three decades.

Algeria's tax administration is highly decentralized. Although based on French tradition, decentralization is also a common element in the Maghreb countries and the Mediterranean area in general. It is motivated by the belief that the tax officials should be able to closely observe the taxpayer.

There can be little doubt that a Western-style tax system, even if antiquated and administratively decrepit, helped Algeria to push through tax reform legislation and a basic overhaul of the tax service within a short time.

Selected Policy Issues in Tax Reform

Role of National Tax Reform Commission

The National Tax Reform Commission (NTRC), established in 1987, was charged with a comprehensive review of Algeria's tax system to adapt it better to a market economy. It was headed by a former minister and included representatives of the relevant agencies. The IMF was requested to provide policy advice to the Commission in 1989 and a staff team was invited to participate in some of the meetings.

The NTRC began by analyzing the purposes of the tax system and by defining objectives for its reform. The market-oriented objectives included promoting private savings and investment. The NTRC also anticipated the impact that liberalization of prices and the expansion of the private sector would have on the tax system. The proposed basic direction for tax reform was identical to what later became the standard package for countries in transition, namely, the introduction of a personal income tax, a separate corporation tax, and a VAT. The need for further decentralization of taxing power to the local authorities was also recognized.

In addition to the NTRC, a Committee, composed of members with different ideological backgrounds, also met during the early phases of the transition. The Committee wanted the tax system to continue to intervene in the market mechanism. In particular, it continued to place a high priority on such objectives as promoting vertical equity. The Committee was aware, however, that the gradual transition would entail the added difficulty of dealing for a longer time with the inconsistencies between the two economic systems.

As a compromise, the Committee recommended graduated rates for the VAT, sector-specific rates for the corporation tax, and a strongly progressive schedule for the individual income tax. Although these recommendations were somewhat watered down in the ensuing debate and political process, the rate structures actually introduced (see below) clearly emphasize social objectives at the expense of economic efficiency and administrative ease.

Reform of Taxes on Income and Profits

Algeria had preserved schedular taxes on income, a common feature of the traditional French system. They were meant to facilitate assessment and to promote vertical equity when the tax administration was believed not to be equally efficient with regard to different sources of income. The Algerian tax on wages and salaries was legally a monthly levy. This eliminated the need for filing an annual return by individuals with no other sources of income and for processing refunds, which are seldom processed in developing countries. The income tax on business and industrial profits applied to corporations with a flat rate (with preferential rates for reinvested profits) and to individuals with a progressive rate. Assessment based on verifiable accounts (real system) was limited, however, to incorporated businesses and large private enterprises. The bulk of small businesses was assessed on the basis of an estimate by the tax administration, which relied on the value of purchases and certain external signs of the size of the business (*forfait* system).

The reform of the income tax is now nearly complete. A new law, providing for a global income tax on individuals and a separate tax on corporations, was published in late 1990 and became effective in fiscal year 1991/92. The rate schedule for the individual income tax continues to be strongly progressive, with 12 brackets up to 70 percent. The corporation tax rate is 42 percent on distributed profits and 5 percent on reinvested profits. Other features of the new taxes (for example, family allowances and depreciation rules) are more closely aligned to the prevailing systems of Western European countries. One notable exception is that the income taxes (as well as the VAT) retain the standard assessment of small business, which appears to have worked relatively well in Algeria and is adapted to the cultural and economic environment and to the decentralized structure of the tax administration.

Reform of Taxes on Production and Services

Throughout the socialist period, Algeria had maintained a turnover tax on imports and production (TUGP), which provided for credit on the tax paid on purchases and investment. It had nine rates ranging from about 7 percent to 670 percent (on a tax-exclusive base), with the higher rates serving an excise function on such products as tobacco and alcoholic beverages. On services, a sister tax (TUGPS) was used, which did not provide for credit and used seven different rates.

These taxes were different from the turnover taxes used in most other centrally planned economies and again reflected French tradition. They were based on ex-factory prices (rather than administered retail prices). The number of rates was not as high as in most Eastern European countries, and the credit feature was a precursor for a VAT. Nevertheless, the spread of tax rates was substantial and resulted in an intended differential effect on prices. In this latter regard, the TUGP was similar to the turnover taxes that were used in other centrally planned economies.

There was general agreement that the two turnover taxes should be replaced by a VAT, but the design of the tax rate structure was the subject of some debate. Two points were made by the NTRC. First, while simplification was one of the stated objectives, the reduction in the number of rates from 16 (for the two turnover taxes) to 5 for a VAT was considered a major and sufficient step in this direction. Second, maintenance of a number of rates with a significant spread between them was seen as desirable on equity grounds.

Some Algerian and foreign advisers argued for a simpler rate structure on grounds of economic efficiency and administrative simplicity. Simulation studies showed that a single rate in the 10–12 percent range could be revenue neutral if exemptions were limited to those needed to protect the poor. These studies also indicated a negligible distribution effect of differentiated rates because income and consumption patterns across households were rather similar (if survey data could be relied on), as would be expected in a socialized economy. Moreover, nearly half of all products, including most basic food items, were exempt from the TUGP or the TUGPS. The use of additional excises was recommended instead of an increased VAT rate. However, in the national debate, neutrality and administrative simplification were not considered of the highest priority.

The VAT law was adopted and published in late 1990 and the tax became effective in April 1992. The law provides for four tax rates, namely reduced rates of 7 and 13 percent, a standard rate of 21 percent, and an increased rate of 40 percent on a few luxuries and excisable products.

That the TUGP already had features of a VAT is expected to facilitate the changeover. Taxpayer information campaigns have been undertaken. However, automation for the processing of a huge number of returns will need more time to be developed.

Fiscal Federalism

The decentralization of resources and the deconcentration of tax administration had been objectives in Algeria in the socialist period (when they formed uncharacteristic elements of a centrally planned economy) and received new attention in the context of the present reform. The provinces (*wilayate*) and municipalities benefit from shares in several taxes. More important, two transactions-based taxes, the TAIC (2.55 percent) on industrial and commercial activity and the TANC (6.05 percent) on noncommercial activity, are entirely earmarked to the local authorities. In addition, the latter receive the revenue from the property tax and the sewage tax, and there are a few minor locally administered fees. In all, the local levels of government receive fiscal revenues of as much as 9 percent of GDP, an unusually high ratio.

At present, there are three principal issues in fiscal federalism in Algeria. First, the distribution of revenue at the local levels is clearly uneven and not in line with the needs for essential services, although equalization devices, such as special redistribution funds, have been used. Second, the local authorities have little political say and no part in the assessment and collection of these receipts. Third, some of the taxes, namely the TAIC, overlap with the base for the VAT, and there is a need for harmonization. The authorities have established a working group and hope that proposals can be developed in time for implementation in 1993. Another working group is reviewing the legislation for miscellaneous taxes and fees (*Code de l'Enregistrement*).

Institutional Constraints

Although the Algerian tax reform process had started from the policy side, the authorities soon realized that they also needed to strengthen the tax administration to pursue effectively the new policy objectives. In fact, it became clear that what was needed was no less than a basic overhaul of the tax administration, covering (1) the development of a strategy for reform, (2) the reorganization of the structure of the service, (3) the streamlining of working procedures, (4) the development of training programs, and (5) the adoption of improvements in data processing.

The following sections focus on selected issues from each of these broad areas.

Planning for Reform

A point of general significance for economies in transition appears to be the need to first create awareness of the importance of addressing the conceptual issues in administrative reform and then to establish an adequate capacity for dealing with these issues. Ideally, a task of the planned magnitude and complexity should be based on a master plan for reform. The major objectives for strengthening the tax service should be identified, taking into account the policy orientations that the new system is to serve, and priorities should be set and the sequencing of reforms should be worked out. On a more technical level, it would be necessary to design the specific measures and to define the resource requirements in terms of both material resources and know-how.

In reality, centrally planned economies typically lack the time and resources to approach administrative reforms in a strictly systematic way. Algeria, while departing from a relatively favorable basis, used a pragmatic approach. Although basic priorities were established and timetables for some of the tasks were laid down, these efforts still fell short of a comprehensive, well-coordinated, and generally agreed plan for reform. As the entire process would take several years to complete, it became clear that it could best be handled flexibly in the light of changing circumstances.

Algeria asked for and received technical assistance to supplement the national capacity. The IMF followed up on its advice on tax policy with assistance on the reform of the tax administration. With the help of the United Nations Development Program (UNDP), a technical assistance project was formulated for which the IMF agreed to act as executing agency. In addition, technical as well as financial assistance was negotiated with other agencies and donors in such specific areas as computerization.

The priority for technical assistance in tax administration was to assist in the planning of reform. As a matter of urgency, a steering committee was established at the ministerial level with subcommittees for reorganization, training, and data processing. These were staffed with senior officials of the tax department who provided the counterpart structure for external assistance. In addition, the tax department organized a large seminar to which senior tax officers from throughout the country were invited and in which senior headquarters staff and external experts outlined the scope for reform and solicited broad support.

One of the most critical constraints the authorities faced at this stage was the shortage of suitably qualified and diversified staff. Most of the members of these committees had other commitments and were able to devote only a fraction of their time to these tasks.

Review of Organizational Structure

The analysis of the organizational structure of the tax service revealed a poorly defined headquarters function and a far too decentralized network of local offices.

Headquarters Function

At the ministerial level, the functions and powers that usually make up the headquarters of the tax service were dispersed among several departments. The department in charge of running the tax administration (Tax Control) was not responsible for the development of tax policy options and the drafting of laws and regulations. These functions were entrusted to a small separate department (Tax Legislation). Most important, the budget of the tax service, including responsibilities for personnel matters, maintenance of buildings, and the supply of office materials, was handled by the general administration department of the ministry. The Secretary General of the ministry was the lowest ranking official in whom all these functions converged. He had no supporting staff and had to allocate his time between tax-service matters and other responsibilities. By contrast, the Customs Department, coming from a paramilitary tradition, was organized as a separate, unified, and rather independently managed service.

The central office of the tax administration department was a small unit at the ministerial level with four divisions. It was difficult to draw a clear line between its headquarters functions and its involvement in operational matters. Several divisions of the central office dealt directly with taxpayer files, such as the assessment of large public enterprises and the handling of certain appeals. The staff was also accessible to important individual taxpayers. These responsibilities left little time for conceptual issues and the management of the service. Moreover, because personnel and material resources were handled elsewhere, it was difficult to maintain an overview of the operational needs of the service and to redirect resources according to priorities.

Neglect of the headquarters function appears to be a common problem for the tax administration of centrally planned economies. Many observers of economies in transition have been struck by the fact that, in spite of the focus on central planning, management in a corporate sense had been largely absent in public administration.

In the tax reform reorganization of the central office became a high priority of the Algerian authorities. In early 1990, a new headquarters organization was implemented that elevated the tax service to a General

Directorate with authority over all aspects of the service that formerly were dispersed, including the tax policy formulation function, personnel administration, and authority over all other budgetary resources. At the same time, the headquarters function was separated more clearly from the operationally oriented decentralized services, and the central office ceased to deal with matters related to individual taxpayers. These were decisive initial steps. It must be realized, however, that to build an effective management capacity is an involved process that requires years of determined effort for its completion.

Local Level

At the decentralized level, a number of organizational issues were identified, including the need to concentrate the service in fewer local offices and the desirability of assigning functions in a more efficient way. In all, the reforms that have been set in motion will, over time, result in the complete reorganization of the field services.

The Algerian tax administration continues to be characterized by a high degree of decentralization. It is well known that taxpayer attitudes in the Mediterranean countries make it difficult for the authorities to assess income for tax purposes. Scholars of the Maghreb have pointed out that in this region paying taxes also carries the stigma of being considered a form of tribute to the ruler and is therefore seen as being an expression of submission. In Algeria, as in other countries, these taxpayer attitudes have caused the tax service to focus on assessment and especially on the full discovery of income. As a consequence, the Algerian tax administration is organized to maintain close proximity to the taxpayer.

There are some 1,300 tax and collection offices, some staffed with only very few officials serving a small number of taxpayers. Although decentralization had always been a tradition in Algeria, the number of tax offices was increased further in the last two decades, because the number of provinces was nearly doubled to 48 with the concomitant creation of additional circles (*diara*) and municipalities. As a matter of principle, tax offices were then established in each new circle and in the large townships or groups of municipalities. The motivation may have been political (to demonstrate the presence of government) rather than the result of a critical analysis of actual need for a tax office.

The second issue relates to the basic pattern of organization. The old French system (which has since been abandoned in France and some Francophone countries) provided for the organization of the tax service on a tax-by-tax basis. In Algeria, local tax offices were always created in pairs (that is, one for direct taxes and one for indirect taxes). In addition, a third office was usually established for tax collections. However, the cashiers offices usually also assisted the Municipal Councils in administering their budgets and were also often in charge of maintaining the accounts of certain local enterprise units, especially hospitals.

The new organizational plan, now being implemented, calls for a restructuring of offices by type of taxpayer rather than type of tax, and for the transfer of the extraneous functions to the Treasury. This is to permit the service to focus more clearly on priority tasks. In particular, more attention can be given to the largest enterprises, which often account for the bulk of tax collections. Another obvious advantage of this organizational principle is that the information available for one tax could also be used in the assessment and audit of another. The same applies for information on tax collection. Especially for taxes collected monthly, such as the VAT, a separation between assessment and collection is clearly impracticable. Even in France, where traditionally the Treasury has been in charge of the collection of most direct taxes, the VAT is collected by the tax administration.

As an initial step toward reorganization along these lines, a unified tax service that reports to one director has been created in each province. The complete reorganization down to the local office level will require more time to complete. In early 1992, 698 tax inspectorates still existed, excluding collection offices.

The re-establishment of an intermediate administrative level linking the headquarters to the district office was another important step toward streamlining the organizational structure. Although Algeria's administrative structure does not recognize regions as political entities, the tax service established nine regional directorates in mid-1991. These have supervisory and other management functions and will represent the highest level within the tax service at which individual taxpayer matters, including appeals, are handled.

In all, the structural reorganization of the tax service is now nearly complete, encompassing the headquarters function at the ministerial level, the establishment of regional directorates, and the reorganization at the local level. This reorganization will permit the gradual application of more efficient procedures and should facilitate administration of the new taxes. However, it will take several years until material facilities are upgraded to the requisite levels, full use is made of automation, all staff members are trained to face up to their new tasks, and the number of tax offices is reduced in line with efficiency requirements.

Streamlining of Procedures

As regards assessment and collection, the previous French system had remained largely intact during the socialist period. Nevertheless, some procedures had deteriorated, partly because of the weak management structure and the lack of sufficient instructions, documentation, and training of staff. In the framework of administrative reform, these issues were approached from different sides.

First, the establishment of the intermediate management layer at the regional level and the streamlining of the organizational structure under a single director at the provincial level have provided a much-improved basis for administrative guidance and control of field offices.

Second, the authorities intend to issue a revised set of regulations to clarify questions of interpretation of the tax law and to prepare a comprehensive and detailed procedural manual for the service. The latter would need to deal with a broad range of matters where, in the past, field officers had been given leeway to devise their own procedures. It would need to cover file management, methods to detect quickly late-filers and stop-filers, control of penalties, and the timely follow-up on pending issues. A few local offices had on their own initiative installed microcomputers and developed applications to deal with some of the above tasks.

Third, material support will be needed in the form of upgrading office accommodations and providing equipment. The administration has embarked on a far-ranging program for these purposes that will require a number of years to complete. Training is another major aspect, along with office automation and improved support of tax administration in general (see the following two sections for more detail).

Fourth, as an expedient for reorganization as well as for improvement of procedures, a census of the tax administration was initiated in an earlier phase of reform. Based on a detailed questionnaire to be answered by each field office, it called for information on the number and type of tax files, structure and qualifications of staff, and other matters. A preliminary evaluation of answers showed considerable variation in workloads from one office to another. The establishment of realistic workload standards will be useful for streamlining the service.

For the reasons discussed above, the tax administration in Algeria, as in most other Mediterranean countries, monitors the affairs of the taxpayer closely so as to be able to assess income as comprehensively as possible. Self-assessment in the form practiced in the industrial countries of Anglo-Saxon origin is generally not used in this area, although the administration, which determines tax liability, relies in most cases on the declaration by the taxpayer. Full and general reliance on self-assessment appears premature, but it could be considered for certain groups of taxpayer corporations, if supported by effective audit procedures.

Development of Training Programs

The initial analysis of the tax administration revealed a critical need for training and the enforcement of job standards in filling vacancies. Senior officials reported that in the last few years, officers had, in fact, been hired with very little formal training. Within the service, there was no structured system of on-the-job training. As public sector salaries had become unattractive, there were vacancies in spite of the relaxation of hiring standards. A survey by the service had shown that some 7,000 tax officers, of a total of some 13,000, were in urgent need of training in one form or another. The initial training of tax inspectors on various levels had been handled by the National Institute of Finance, which addressed all training needs of the Ministry of Finance and some other organizations. Training in tax matters was confined to a special course for prospective staff of this service, which had a total capacity of about 250 students a year.

In order to redress the situation, the authorities are implementing programs at two levels: (1) creating a specialized training institution for the tax service, and (2) introducing systematic on-the-job training.

In 1990, a separate tax-service school was established as an intermediate step toward the creation of a National Tax Academy that could satisfy the requirements of the service in the long run. A particular short-term need was the expansion of senior staff, as only about 2 percent of all serving officers had a university degree. As an emergency measure, more than 1,000 university graduates were hired in 1990 and put through a one-year crash course.

As to in-service training, courses conducted by senior staff are being organized at the regional and local levels. In Algeria, a remaining small group of highly trained and qualified officials is nearing retirement age. It is therefore of particular importance that suitable individuals from this group be used to provide in-service training in their specialization.

Better Integration of Data Processing into Tax Administration

Taxpayer identification is a prerequisite for successful computerization of the tax administration. Algeria used locally issued taxpayer numbers, often based on geographic criteria, but had no national identification scheme in use by the tax service. It was recognized that a nationwide system is a basis for a taxpayer master file, which becomes indispensable when the income tax system is moved to a global basis and the system of product taxes is changed to a VAT. Therefore, the establishment of a taxpayer identification numbering system, and subsequently a master file, became one of the early priorities in the tax reform process. An agreement was reached to use a common identification scheme based on birth records. In addition, a system for the identification of business was constructed. Implementation of these measures was nearly complete in early 1992.

The authorities, recognizing the need for improvement in data-processing facilities early in the reform, created a working group for this purpose. The administration had reduced staffing of the computer center to the minimum needed to maintain ongoing operations, and a sufficient number of competent private sector companies had not been established. Most local expertise was concentrated in two public enterprises, which had many clients and found it difficult to focus on the specific needs of the tax administration. Algeria obtained technical assistance for analyzing options, including the degree of decentralization, the integration of microcomputers, and the use of on-line access.

The development of a comprehensive and internally consistent strategy or master plan for the use of data processing in the tax administration proved more difficult than had been expected. In the early stages of the process, the precise features of the new taxes had not been agreed upon, the numbers and the types of taxpayers, their reporting requirements, and the treatment of certain types of income and transactions had not been determined, and organization, staffing, and operational procedures of the tax service had not been spelled out in sufficient detail.

Other countries in transition are likely to face similar problems. It is safe to conclude that computerization becomes the acid test of tax reform planning. Frequently, there is pressure to push ahead with the procurement of hardware. But it is difficult to develop a satisfactory concept for electronic data processing support before basic tax policy decisions have been taken and the scope and timeframe of administrative reform have been determined.

Algeria is now establishing three regional tax processing centers, which will replace the outdated single facility in Algiers. It plans to create a microcomputer-based system of decentralized administrative support for the treatment of the monthly VAT returns and payments.

CHAPTER 18

Angola: Improving Fiscal Institutions

Isaias Coelho

Angola is going through a complex political and economic transformation, similar to developments in other parts of the world. The end of a long civil war necessitates a huge reconstruction effort. "Democratic centralism" has been replaced by multiparty democracy, and general elections were held in September 1992. The economy is being reoriented toward a decentralized price system, albeit slowly, and it is hoped that Angola, a country with great potential, will finally take the road of sustained development.

This chapter reviews recent progress made by Angola, with technical assistance from the IMF and cofinancing by the United Nations Development Program (UNDP), in strengthening its institutional capability to manage public finances. The following section covers briefly the main developments in the post-independence period, until the beginning of the IMF-UNDP project. The next section describes in some detail the various components of the project. The final section suggests further steps to improve public finance management in Angola.

Background

On November 11, 1975, Angola became independent and adopted a constitution that called for a centrally planned economy. Most productive facilities were nationalized, not only on ideological grounds but also for pragmatic reasons of national reconstruction in the wake of the economic disruption brought on by the long, armed struggle for independence. A protracted civil war that followed independence resulted in large-scale flight of capital and of entrepreneurial skills, as well as in a massive exodus from rural communities to the cities, especially to Luanda, where the quality of public services declined markedly. Economic activity was then organized around large state enterprises, often monopolies, and prices were administratively fixed. An informal economy developed, despite attempts to repress it, and exchange rates in the black market became higher than the official rate.

Isaias Coelho is a Senior Economist in the European II Department. At the time the paper was written, he was a Senior Economist in the Fiscal Affairs Department.

Angola is rich in petroleum, and the Government's pragmatic oil policies partly made up for the poor performance in other sectors of the economy. Exploration concessions, which produced sizable tax and production-sharing revenue, were negotiated with major international oil companies. Fluctuations in petroleum prices and the U.S. dollar, however, generated financial instability, made worse by the lack of criteria for the allocation of the foreign exchange. For example, the rapid decline of oil prices in the early 1980s forced the Government to make severe cuts in the public investment program. The war raised the priority for defense and internal security expenditures at the expense of social and economic infrastructure outlays, both for operation and maintenance.[1]

The 1986 fall in oil prices, which tightened the external constraint, imparted momentum to major economic reforms. Finally, when a major economic policy reversal was announced in 1987, it was a slow-moving process, but a new orientation nevertheless. The motto that annually proclaimed the major concerns for the year was in 1987 "The Year of the Party's Tenth Anniversary and Consolidation of Popular Power" and in 1988 and 1989 was, respectively, "The First and The Second Year of Economic and Financial Restructuring."

The economic and financial restructuring program (SEF) announced in 1987 was rooted in decisions taken in the Second Congress (1985) of the official MPLA-Workers' Party, in favor of greater economic liberalization. By 1988, a SEF Secretariat was coordinating various task forces engaged in the design of economic reforms. Yet, the SEF was not an executive agency but an advisory team, which proposed policy and structural measures in the financial area, especially in taxation, budget, and banking. An ambitious program of reform was established for 1988 and 1989 of which only a modest part was carried out. The disappointingly scanty results obtained with the SEF were in great part attributable to the scarcity of trained personnel, a lack of effective budgetary and financial controls, and weaknesses in the design and implementation of financial policies. Nonetheless, the SEF created awareness for the much-needed reforms and established a starting point for discussions with the Paris Club on debt rescheduling and with international organizations on financial and technical support for reforms.

Significant reforms began in 1988. Price controls were removed from the trade in unprocessed vegetables, and the *kandongas* (informal markets) were accorded greater toleration, so that in 1989 there were 10 official markets and 31 parallel markets in the city of Luanda. For state enterprises, new legislation was enacted aimed at achieving greater managerial and financial freedom while curtailing reliance on the budget to finance working capital and investment. At the same time, a new law was

---

[1]Defense expenditures have exceeded the combined expenditure in education, health, and social assistance.

passed to attract direct foreign investment. In 1988, studies began for a wide-ranging reorganization of the Ministry of Finance, and a working group was set up for the creation of a treasury.

While the SEF still had momentum, an economic recovery plan (PRE) was designed as a specific plan of action for 1989-90. Its objective was to achieve greater decentralization by redefining the scope for private activity, providing a new statute to state-owned enterprises, restructuring the foreign exchange system, and revising the regulations of foreign investment and the banking system. In the state enterprise sector, the plan included measures to reduce subsidy entitlements, to subject enterprises to the income tax on an equal footing with private businesses, and to clarify their financial position regarding debts and arrears. At the same time, the promotion of private initiative and ownership in certain sectors of the economy was also begun.

In September 1990 a government action plan (GAP) was adopted. Pricing policy was revised and three price regimes (fixed prices, fixed markups, and free prices) were established as a first step toward further price liberalization. The price control authority was transferred to the Ministry of Finance with a view to limiting it, over time, to only a handful of goods. The currency was first devalued in March 1991.[2]

In November 1991 new measures further liberalized prices and foreign trade, payments in kind to civil servants were discontinued, and the currency was devalued a second time along with the introduction of a multiple exchange rate system. In 1991 and 1992, large fiscal deficits occurred in connection with the democratization process and the implementation of the peace accord, which called for the withdrawal of troops from the war zones and their subsequent demobilization. In the first months of 1992, inflation was running at a rate of about 15 percent a month.

General Thrust of the Reforms

As part of the admission of Angola into the IMF, a team from the IMF's Fiscal Affairs Department visited Luanda in May 1989 to assess public finance management, make recommendations for reform, and identify critical technical assistance requirements. The IMF staff soon became aware of the need for a concerted effort to reform public finances and budgetary procedures and, more generally, to provide the Angolan authorities with tools for carrying out economic policies, including access to reliable and timely data. Later in the same year, the Fiscal Affairs Department developed a plan for establishing a treasury.

In 1989, the IMF also sent to Luanda teams of experts from the Monetary and Economic Affairs and Statistics Departments and from the IMF

---

[2]The exchange rate had been kept unchanged since independence in 1975. As a result, the ratio between the parallel and official rates came to exceed 100:1.

Institute to prepare similar studies in their respective areas. These studies concluded that a considerable gap existed between financial management in Angola and standard practices in the rest of the world. In particular, for the Angolan authorities to exercise financial discipline there was a need for a clear definition of responsibilities for the various aspects of financial policy, improved coordination of policymaking, and enhancement of technical and institutional aspects of the main policy instruments.

The Angolan authorities agreed with these assessments and asked the IMF and the UNDP to design and implement such a program. In early 1990, the three parties agreed on a technical assistance project cofinanced by the UNDP and executed by the IMF. The project contemplated assistance in the following areas during its initial 18 months.

- Improving budgeting, expenditure control, and accounting procedures;
- Strengthening financial control over public sector operations through the establishment of a national treasury;
- Improving tax policy and its administration;
- Establishing an integrated and comprehensive set of fiscal statistics;
- Creating an autonomous central bank capable of effectively managing monetary policy and supervising the operations of commercial banks; and
- Providing training by the IMF Institute in financial programming techniques to create the capacity within the Government to design macroeconomic adjustment programs.

Each component of the project comprised advisory services to revamp procedures, update legislation, and computerize services and to develop human resources through on-the-job training, seminars, structured courses, and a small number of scholarships abroad. Given the depth of the reforms, as well as the large training needs, it was decided to assign resident advisers, instead of relying on periodic visits. A chief technical adviser was designated to coordinate the administrative work, who would also advise on the budget. The Ministry of Finance provided space for the project administrative office, and the various agencies concerned, including the National Bank of Angola, provided office space for the experts. Each adviser was to work closely with his national counterpart and share his knowledge of new techniques so that the reforms would be sustainable after the period of assistance was over.

The National Bank, which functions as both a central bank and a commercial bank, was assigned two experts. One expert was to develop a new accounting plan and establish a proper institutional and administrative framework for accounting and control procedures. In particular, this expert was asked to help separate the commercial and central bank accounts of the National Bank, as a first step toward creating a central bank. The other banking expert was to assist the authorities in planning and establishing a bank supervision department, to operate initially within the National Bank and later at the new central bank. This task included the design of an accounting plan for commercial banks and accounting criteria for commercial banks and other financial institutions. In addition, an expert in fiscal statistics was assigned to the Economic Analysis Department of the Ministry of Finance.

Reforms in the Ministry of Finance

During the socialist years, the Ministry of Finance had been relegated to a secondary role with regard to economic policies, which were decided by the Economic Committee of the Party and the Ministry of the Plan.[3] Hard currency, for example, was allocated by the plan and the National Bank with a minimal participation of the Ministry of Finance. Outside Luanda, the operations of the Ministry were hampered by the joint subordination to the local commissariats. The low prestige of the Ministry was reflected in the deterioration of its key institutions, especially the departments in charge of budgeting, accounting, and tax administration, which were unable to attract talented employees. To halt and reverse such a deteriorating trend was the most urgent task.

Budget

During the pre-reform period, budgetary management weakened, and off-budget expenditures grew, predominantly in the defense sector, but also elsewhere. As a result, the Government as a whole borrowed from the National Bank well beyond the already high levels of officially approved deficits. The poor performance of state enterprises contributed decisively to the bleak financial situation by requiring sizable budgetary transfers. In fact, the state enterprise sector not only needed substantial transfers from the budget but soon gained access to the National Bank's credit for financing recurrent losses.

Over time, the budget became more and more irrelevant for policy purposes, as foreign grants were allocated outside the budgetary process, and the budget excluded transactions realized in foreign currencies. Because of the scarcity of foreign exchange, the foreign exchange budget, handled by the National Bank without well-defined rules, had become the relevant allocative instrument. Also, the foreign exchange budget was prepared for shorter periods—usually a quarter—and its forecasts were so unreliable that, in practice, foreign currency was allocated with great discretion.

The revamping of budgetary procedures started with a review of the spending units, which were re-registered with the Budget Department

---

[3]Until 1991, only one political party was allowed to operate, the People's Movement for the Liberation of Angola-Workers' Party (MPLA).

and given a code number. At the same time, the existing budgetary classification was revised to bring it closer to international standards. The new classification was implemented in the budget for 1991.

While the change in the classification of revenues was straightforward, to facilitate policy management expenditures were classified by economic type (investment and current expenditure, together with a breakdown of the latter into wages, goods and services, and so forth) and government function (health, education, public administration, and so forth). The budgetary classification also facilitated presentation by agency, region, and the source of financing. The process of compilation, review, and adjustment of the budget proposals presented by the spending units, as well as the preparation of summary tables and the final budget proposal, was greatly helped by the introduction of computerization in preparing the state budget.[4]

The new budgetary procedures required an important training effort in the Budget Department, the various regional offices, and the main spending units. Along with the training offered by the project advisers, about 100 middle-level budget officers were trained through the UNDP's Management Development Program, whose project for Angola was adjusted to dovetail with the IMF-UNDP project.

To ensure the comprehensiveness of the budget, the authorities, assisted by the budget adviser, conducted a painstaking but successful effort to bring into the realm of the budget all public revenue and expenditures previously kept separately, notably foreign grants and loans, interest on foreign debt, and military outlays. The public sector component of the foreign exchange budget was also incorporated into the state budget, although on the basis of the best available projections.[5] The budget documents introduced columns to specify the amount of spending in domestic currency, in foreign exchange (converted to domestic currency at the relevant exchange rate), and the sum of the two. This simple procedure allowed the National Bank to make available hard currency to the budget, within the agreed limits, in global amounts, leaving to the finance authorities the distribution of these global amounts according to the priorities established in the budget law and in line with the budgetary policies.[6] How effectively such a scheme will work will depend, however, on political considerations, such as the willingness of the National Bank to

---

[4]In 1991, computer specialists from the IMF advised Angola on the computerization strategy, to ensure systems compatibility in the Ministry of Finance's computerization program.

[5]While the state budget covers one (calendar) year, the foreign exchange budget has been traditionally prepared for shorter periods. Of course, in the first years of incorporation into the state budget, the forecasts for expenditures in foreign exchange are highly tentative.

[6]When exchange markets are fully liberalized in Angola, with the budgetary sector behaving as a net buyer or seller of foreign currency, the indication of the budget's foreign currency component will help to assess the impact of exchange rate variations on public expenditure.

relinquish piecemeal management of the foreign exchange allocation to the budgetary sector.

The new procedures were fully put into place with the 1992 budget. As a result of the greater availability of information introduced into the budget, the recorded fiscal deficit has jumped in 1991 and 1992 compared with previous years, but the budget has become a worthwhile instrument for assessing the pressure of the public sector over the economy. To make the budget more useful for the conduct of microeconomic and macroeconomic policies, it is necessary to better coordinate it with the plan (especially at the preparation stage) and with the foreign exchange budget (both in their preparation and execution). The lack of a system for ranking public investment proposals according to established priorities and for monitoring the execution of multiyear investment projects is a weakness of the existing planning procedures. The absence of a public investment program has a negative effect on the quality of the investment component of the budget. The budget should also benefit, in the future, from a better screening of personnel expenditures. Now that the war is over, it is possible to conduct a census of public employees, both civilian and military, and to introduce adequate control mechanisms on this important expenditure item.

The authorities decided to introduce the new budgetary methods based on executive orders, in part to speed up implementation, in part because it would have been difficult to incorporate into a previous law various matters that arise during implementation. Since the procedures are already in place—the 1992 budget was the second to be prepared under the new rules—a draft framework law on the budget system has been prepared and is expected to be presented to the National Assembly in the near future.

Treasury

The Treasury was set up to perform the cash management functions of the budget, administer the public sector external and domestic debt, and supervise the financial relations between the state budget and state-owned enterprises. The design and implementation of a system of cash management was given priority. The Treasury does not directly receive or pay any revenue or expenditure. Instead, it uses the National Bank as the financial agent of the budget.

As a result of the cooperative work of the Treasury, the Budget Department, and the National Bank, all accounts kept by spending units with the banking system were closed, and on the same day new accounts were opened in line with the new system. Each spending unit was assigned an account at the National Bank.[7] The number of this account matched the code number assigned by the Budget Department to the spending unit.

---

[7]In fact, a double account, for the separate recording of transactions in domestic and foreign currency.

The banking system was forbidden to open new accounts for any spending unit without authorization of the Budget Department. These new accounts were, in reality, subaccounts of the single account that the Treasury opened at the National Bank.

The single account of the Treasury at the National Bank works as follows. All budgetary revenues are credited to the account. Each spending unit has two subaccounts, one for operations in domestic currency and the other for foreign exchange operations. Each month, on the basis of the expected development of budgetary revenues, the budgetary authorizations, and the forecast of spending needs, the Treasury transfers funds from the Treasury account to the subaccounts. Since this operation consists of a zero-sum transfer between subaccounts, the Treasury's indebtedness to the National Bank is not affected by the release of funds. The spending unit draws on the balances available on its subaccount. At the time these operations are performed, the system provides an automatic record of the cash execution of the budget.

The main advantage of using a single government account for the cash execution of the budget is to economize on average holdings of bank balances, and thus on the cost of servicing the public debt.[8] Idle bank balances are minimized through the elimination of inactive accounts with positive balances and, more important, through a better matching of cash needs and availabilities. In the past, the budget figures were divided into 12 installments, and each installment was transferred at the beginning of the month to the account of the spending unit. As a result, redundant balances were kept in some accounts, while other spending units starved for resources.

Also, under the previous rule, the execution of budgetary expenditures did not take into account revenue developments during the year. The authorities provided the newly created Treasury with two minicomputers and peripheral equipment, plus attendant software, which allowed nearly full computerization of the system of cash management (by the Treasury) and control of the cash execution of the budget (by the National Bank). As a result, a small team can prepare—for the Minister's approval—and execute cash programs for the budget and provide up-to-date and complete reports on the cash execution. Training has been provided, operation manuals have been prepared, and hands-on experience has been acquired by the Angolan counterpart team so that outside assistance is no longer needed in the technical aspects of cash management of the budget.

At the time this chapter was written, systems were being developed to register, monitor, and service the public debt, both domestic and external. In addition, the authorities are receiving assistance for better forecasting of budget revenues, which is still unsatisfactory. These forecasts need also to be coordinated with the credit and foreign exchange policies of

---

[8]The Government now pays interest on National Bank financing.

the National Bank. Foundations have been established for a systematic control of financial relations of the budget with state enterprises, including the receipt of dividends and the payment of subsidies and financing items, notably lending, onlending, and equity participation.

Accounting

During the first tripartite review of the project in May 1991, it was agreed to extend the project to provide long-term technical assistance for the organization of the National Accounting Department, to be created shortly thereafter, and for the introduction of updated accounting methods. This plan aims at strengthening the control of budget execution and generating a consistent set of data on the public finances.

Work on this component of the project began in November 1991, and the Accounting Department is already in operation, although on a provisional and nuclear structure. The classification schemes introduced earlier in the Budget Department and the Treasury were used to compile the 1991 accounts, a task recently completed. Progress already achieved is remarkable, and 1991 is the first date in many years to see adequate bookkeeping undertaken in Angola.

At present, Angola is receiving assistance for the preparation of a new government accounting code, to provide consistent record keeping for the three accounting subsystems, that is, the budgetary (to control budgetary allotments), the financial (to record the cash execution of the budget), and the patrimonial (to keep track of the state's assets and liabilities). Unlike in other countries where public accounting is a time-consuming and repetitious work, under the system designed for Angola, the Accounting Department, through the use of compatible computer systems, will utilize the same data entered in the Budget and Treasury Departments.

This approach should permit a lightly staffed department to prepare timely accounting reports that will be a valuable source of fiscal statistical information. Indeed, a major goal of the new budgeting and accounting system is to compile government finance statistics consistent with data on the monetary accounts, the balance of payments, and the external debt.

Tax Policy and Administration

The deteriorating trend of the economy, the failure of the state enterprises to generate surpluses, the restrictions on private activities, and the neglect of tax administration contributed to dwindling tax revenues. Public finances have become increasingly dependent on petroleum revenues, which now represent more than two thirds of budget revenue.

The tax system, itself inherited from colonial times, by 1975 was already in need of modernization. Under the MPLA regime, however, the system was only marginally modified, and no innovations were introduced except extirpation of the "national defense tax" and a few other colonial remains. Time made the tax structure increasingly inadequate.

Shortcomings in tax administration were even more serious than obsolescence of the tax system. Lacking a clear role in a centrally planned economy, the tax service was left to languish through nonreplacement of human and natural resources and was isolated from developments in tax administration techniques in market economies. As in the Soviet Union during the 1960s and 1970s, the Angolan tax service lost cadres, equipment, prestige, and enforcement power.

In 1989, IMF experts suggested simplifying the tax system, reducing distortions, and increasing non-oil revenue and assisted the tax authorities in designing a number of these measures and in drafting the corresponding legislation. Indeed, by June 1992 legislation had been enacted introducing the first set of tax measures, which rationalized rates for the individual income tax, included customs duties in the base of the consumption tax levied on imported goods, introduced greater uniformity in consumption tax rates, and replaced the stamp duty levied on some commercial transactions by an equivalent tax based on accounting records and paid monthly.

Other tax measures enacted in July 1992 eliminated the popular resistance tax (a graduated supertax levied on the bases of three other taxes), greatly simplified the rate structure of the gifts and inheritance tax, and significantly reformed the enterprise profits tax, including the assimilation of two other taxes, and the presumptive taxation of small traders. In July 1992, the adoption of self-assessment for all returns-based taxes, the revamping of the system of appeals and penalties, and the introduction of a national taxpayer register also improved the legal framework for tax administration procedures.

The IMF team had stated in its 1989 report that these tax measures, although important, would not make it less necessary to introduce a general sales tax, which still does not exist in Angola. In response to a request from the Angolan authorities, another IMF team visited Luanda in 1991 to design a sales tax to replace the consumption tax. It recommended that a single-rate value-added tax (VAT) be introduced initially at the manufacturing level and on imports and that the consumption tax be continued as an excise on a few goods.

Under the IMF-UNDP project, progress has been made in several areas of tax administration, notably in the development of tax administration skills through formal training. The Tax Department, which was structured according to type of tax, has been reorganized along functional lines. The Department was recognized as a spending unit, and now has its own budget and hence better control over the resources allocated to tax work.

Angola has sought a higher level of taxpayer compliance. The field audit service has been organized and its officers trained, and field audits are now performed as a matter of routine. Penalties, which had been eroded by inflation, have been substantially raised. An effort has been made to identify and recover tax arrears. A system for closer monitoring of the largest taxpayers has been designed and implemented.

In the Customs Department, the project's assistance did not progress much beyond the diagnostic stage. Here the needs are enormous, as over the years the Customs suffered not only from the deterioration that plagued other areas of the administration, but also a lack of discipline in the port area, where the war brought the overlapping presence of various armed forces and militia. Notwithstanding these difficulties, the Customs has been able to update and implement in 1990 a commodities classification based on the Brussels Nomenclature and, more recently, to simplify considerably the import tariff structure.

Although significant progress has been made in modernizing the tax administration, the results are less striking than in the areas of the budget and the Treasury. Contributing to this slower pace of change were (1) the greater need for skilled personnel in the tax service than in other areas of the Ministry of Finance; (2) the perception by qualified candidates that tax services are not attractive (in terms of salary and prestige); and (3) the incremental character of tax administration reforms and the inertia personnel face in offices used to working in traditional ways.

The Steps Ahead

From its inception, the IMF-UNDP project had assumed that several years of sustained effort would be needed to strengthen the weak financial management and especially to transfer skills. Two years later, the project, which has achieved most of its intermediate goals, should be seen as a work still in progress. The picture emerging from a more recent review of the project shows that important progress has been made in a relatively short time in developing institutional capacity for the design, implementation, and monitoring of fiscal policies.

The Angolan authorities, who have fully participated in the design of the project and who bear primary responsibility for its implementation, shielded the project, to the extent possible, from administrative discontinuity. Indeed, over the past two years Angola has had three Ministers of Finance, all of whom have strongly supported the project.

The following characteristics of the project's design and implementation were essential for its success. First, a global framework for reform was laid out and agreed on by the three parties involved (the Government, the IMF, and the financing agency). Second, the reform was comprehensive in the Ministry of Finance, with work progressing in parallel in the closely related departments of budget, taxes, accounting, and the Treasury. Third, it was possible to elicit a good degree of cooperation from the National Bank, which was carrying out its own reform. Fourth, the experts assigned to the project were carefully selected, and their work plans incorporated a sequence of actions and clear objectives agreed to by the authorities. In addition, the experts were supervised and provided with guidance before and during their assignment. Fifth, each new stage of assistance was preceded by a detailed assessment of performance in the previous stage.

There is need for further work in the various fiscal areas, which could benefit from continued external technical assistance.

With the basic instruments in place for adequate budget preparation and execution, the tasks ahead include using the budget to improve macroeconomic management and increasing the effectiveness and efficiency of the government sector.[9] Projections drawn for the economy under the programming period, including forecasts for production, labor market, and exports and imports, will allow the authorities to set targets for credit expansion and inflation. Taking into account anticipated foreign financing, the central bank can gauge the amount of credit that it can grant to the Government without crowding out the private sector or imperiling the goals set for curbing inflation and building international reserves.

This limit on bank financing to the Government should be the starting point for the budgetary exercise. Other essential factors are a realistic revenue forecast, based on the same production and price paths assumed by the initial macroeconomic exercise, and a set of priorities established by the Government for public expenditure. With these elements in hand, the various ministries can be provided with global limits within which to frame their budget proposals. This will prevent the presentation of unrealistic requests and will make it unnecessary to cut severely appropriation requests during budget preparation. If macroeconomic conditions and government revenues diverge from budget forecasts, by making use of the instruments already available the budget can be revised, say, by midyear.

Measures to improve the quality (that is, the effectiveness and the efficiency) of public expenditure have been indicated above, notably better articulation of the state budget with the plan and the foreign exchange budget, improved revenue forecasts, and setting up of mechanisms for screening (including the application of project appraisal techniques), monitoring the execution of, and evaluating public investment projects. To this list one should add the establishment of controls on personnel expenditure, which has increased substantially for some years, placing a

---

[9]Although this terminology is somewhat pedantic, it is useful to distinguish between *effectiveness*, which relates to the choice of instruments to achieve a specified objective (for example, the choice among competing expenditure projects), and *efficiency*, which pertains to the more economical way of implementing a given project, that is, reaching the specified result with the minimum cost or, alternatively, maximizing the results (measured, for example, in terms of output) for a given level of costs.

heavy burden on the budget. More generally, there is a need to improve the ability to manage public expenditures and to analyze their macroeconomic and distributive effects. Progress in this area could be achieved, for example, by strengthening the human resources and the analytical capability of the Economic Studies Bureau of the Ministry of Finance.

The political and economic reorientation of Angola tends toward decentralization of government decisions through assignment of greater fiscal responsibilities to the provincial and local governments. As this will clearly influence how the budget is prepared and executed, the next steps in the promotion of improved financial management must include disseminating the technical knowledge already absorbed at the central level to the various regions and assigning to the provinces various tasks currently performed in the various departments of the Ministry of Finance. The Treasury might also need to establish offices in the main provinces.

The system for managing the public debt is still being developed in the Treasury, and, although some results are apparent, much more work needs to be done. Design of the system for financial monitoring of state-owned enterprises is at an early stage. This system should be fully developed even before privatization is carried out.

The Accounting Department is operating on a pilot basis, and substantial work has yet to be done to consolidate it while integrating its procedures with those of the Budget Department and the Treasury to take full advantage of the progress in computerization by those departments. As this is achieved, the Accounting Department should be strengthened in its control function, especially its capability to perform audits and enforce accountability. The Accounting Department has also to address the reconciliation of revenue statistics provided by the tax and Customs administration against the amounts recorded in the Treasury account.

The Accounting Department, as well as the other departments in the Ministry of Finance that are directly benefiting from technical assistance, have been structured or restructured on the basis of executive orders. In order to provide them with a stable legal basis, the organizational reform of the Ministry must be completed and the corresponding legal instruments must be enacted.

The achievements in tax policy and administration should not lead to complacency, as new efforts are needed to continue modernizing the tax structure and the tax administration. This is especially important for the VAT, which the authorities plan to introduce. An adequate administration of the VAT will require fast and automated processing, supplemented by agile desk and field audits. Revamping of tax administration procedures, already advanced at the central offices of the Tax Department, needs to be disseminated to the regional and local offices. Finally, a decisive effort is needed in the Customs area to improve procedures, especially in handling the collection of the VAT on imported goods. Computerization of the Customs will also provide reliable information on imports and exports.

Technical assistance of the type undertaken by the IMF-UNDP project for Angola is intended to create institutions to make the adoption of well-informed economic policies possible. If these are not used effectively, the effort will be wasted. Angola is going through a difficult transition, both economic and political, full of risks and possibilities. The new government emerging from democratic elections will have over previous governments the advantage of institutions for financial management. The newly developed instruments and institutions are expected to support sustainable economic policies.

CHAPTER 19

From Controls to Sustainable Liberalization: Ghanaian Lessons

Sheetal K. Chand

By most accounts, the adjustment strategy pursued in Ghana since 1983 has been generally successful.[1] Ghana has managed the transition from one of the most controlled economies in Africa to one of the most liberal. This was not achieved overnight, but over a span of years and in the face of major adversity, that included notably a persistent deterioration in the external terms of trade. The starting point was one of widespread economic devastation, compounded by drought, the forced repatriation of large numbers of Ghanaians from Nigeria, and exclusion from external financial markets owing to past arrears.

The initial political situation was characterized by uncertainty and deep dissension, with much controversy over objectives and means. At first the Government embarked on a strategy emphasizing disciplined self-reliance but still within a central planning framework. This was soon abandoned in favor of reintegration with the world economy. The first year of adjustment under the latter strategy, which began in 1983, was traumatic. However, the adjustment path thereafter led to a positive rate of growth. Most observers believe that living conditions have improved; this has helped to resolve earlier political and social conflicts, in turn permitting the evolution of a more liberal political system.

There are important lessons to be drawn from this experience, which very few of the countries in transition can match. This paper examines major reasons for the observed success. It describes the starting point, indicating the underlying nature of structural dysfunctions and macroimbalances and their origins in the policies of previous years. The reform strategy that was pursued and, in particular, the critical role played by fiscal policies are examined next, distinguishing between the initial emphasis on stabilization and the subsequent more structurally oriented adjustment. Some outcomes of reform are set out. Drawing on hindsight, answers are provided to the question of how the observed outcomes

Sheetal K. Chand is Chief of the Fiscal Analysis Division of the Fiscal Affairs Department.
[1] For a recent account, see Kapur and others (1991) and for an earlier assessment, Chand and van Til (1988). For a perspective from the chief economist on the Ghanaian side, see Abbey (1989).

353

could have been improved. While technical economic analysis may point to certain preferred solutions, the adjustment path that emerged reflected political and social compromises and a cautious trial and error approach. Although the adjustment demanded sacrifices, their relatively rapid containment and more equitable distribution than in some economies in transition appear to have kept temptations to revert to controls at bay, resulting thereby in a sustainable liberalization. The final section draws lessons of relevance to countries in transition from central planning to a market economy.

Initial Conditions

Although Ghana had acquired the basic institutions of a market economy, pervasive controls and widespread government interference and regulation in the years following independence hampered their operation. This section reviews the structural distortions prevalent in 1983 when the economy embarked on the economic recovery program, their interaction with the macroeconomy, and the underlying poor dynamic of the economy.

Structural Dysfunction

The years following independence in 1957 saw the emergence of a command economy. The scope for private initiative was greatly reduced and replaced by state initiatives exercised through different instruments, including state enterprises. Controls were widely applied to key aspects of economic life and were introduced for a variety of reasons, often in response to perceived macroeconomic imbalance but sometimes as instruments in the extension and exercise of state control. These attempts to override or suppress market forces had the predictable adverse consequences.

In the external sector, the exchange rate had for several years before 1983 been pegged at ₡ 2.75 = US$1.00. Domestic inflation rates that were much higher than in partner countries resulted in a progressive overvaluation of the exchange rate. Initially, this stimulated imports, which were rendered cheaper, resulting in some displacement of domestic production; but at the same time, an ever more burdensome implicit tax was levied on exports as real domestic currency proceeds accruing to the exporter declined. The disincentive to exports was compounded by the high tax applied to them, especially to cocoa. The progressive overvaluation of the exchange rate favored the urban sector population (a major net importer) at the expense of the rural sector (the major supplier of exports). A deteriorating balance of payments resulting from the overvaluation of the exchange rate led to the exhaustion of international reserves, the accumulation of external debt arrears, and the intensification of controls on international transactions. The freedom to import or export was constrained by comprehensive licensing, and strict controls operated on the allocation of foreign exchange. These controls conferred rents on beneficiaries of licenses and stimulated attempts at evasion, while widespread corruption was generated as transactors sought to bribe officials for favors.

The combined effect of a highly overvalued exchange rate and pervasive exchange controls was to shift an increasing proportion of external transactions from the official economy to the underground or parallel market economy. One indication of the incentive to avoid controls was the vast spread between the official and parallel market exchange rates, which by 1983 amounted to some 2,000 percent of the official exchange rate. It paid the exporter to smuggle exports out and convert the proceeds into local currency at the parallel market exchange rate, or alternatively to buy imported goods and sell them domestically, so as to reap the scarcity premium conferred by controls on imports. Export performance deteriorated as Table 1 indicates. Even allowing for some diversion of exports through the more risky parallel markets, overall exports declined, and Ghana, which had been the leading producer of cocoa, lost ground sharply in world markets. Declining incentives to export were reflected in sharply reduced investment and maintenance outlays in the export sector; cocoa trees, in particular, were not being adequately renewed. A vicious circle was generated with a growing shortage of foreign exchange constraining the flow of imports, while domestic production dependant on such imports, especially of critical spare parts, was increasingly disrupted, and export earnings were further reduced.

Just as the economic and institutional structures adopted for controlling external transactions were counterproductive, diverting much-needed entrepreneurial effort into the evasion of controls (rather than in expanding production) that eroded the gains from international market-based specialization, arrangements governing the domestic economy were dysfunctional. By 1983, the prices of thousands of goods were controlled, ostensibly to alleviate the burden of high prices, particularly on the vocal urban sector. However, as production costs rose relative to controlled prices, supplies were reduced and increasingly diverted to parallel markets. Goods disappeared from public display, but could be readily obtained at discreet outlets if the customer paid the parallel market price. This became the case even with essential foodstuffs and critical transport inputs, especially fuel, which were heavily subsidized under conditions of scarcity and largely subject to rationing. Because of their access to rationed goods, pressure from the vocal urban sector was alleviated.

Other parts of the economy were also controlled. Nominal interest rates were regulated (partly to contain the cost of servicing burgeoning public debt) and became heavily negative as a consequence of the high underlying rate of inflation, biasing the intertemporal terms of trade in

Table 1. Ghana: Selected Economic Indicators

	1971	1984	1986	1988	1990	1991
			(Annual percentage change)			
Real GDP	1.9	8.6	5.2	5.6	3.3	5.0
Consumer price index	9.6	39.7	24.6	31.4	37.2	18.0
Terms of trade	−22.6	30.2	12.5	−9.0	−9.5	−4.2
Net domestic assets	71.1	84.3	49.8	8.5	−19.6	−4.2
Credit to the Government	−3.2	15.2	4.4	−7.4	−8.8	−17.7
Broad money	36.0	72.1	53.7	43.0	18.0	15.0
Velocity (GDP/average broad money)	5.3	9.7	7.6	7.0	7.7	8.2
			(In percent of GDP)			
Gross investment	14.1	6.9	9.7	14.2	16.0	16.5
Gross national savings	8.1	5.9	8.2	12.5	11.6	13.1
Budget surplus/deficit (−)	−4.3	−1.8	0.1	0.4	0.2	1.6
Current account balance	−6.0	−1.0	−1.5	−1.7	−4.4	−3.4
Exports (goods and services)	17.8	7.5	16.0	18.4	16.8	17.1
Memorandum item:						
Cedis per U.S. dollar	1.0	36.0	89.2	202.3	326.3	368.4

Source: Statistical Service Accra.

favor of current consumption. This reduced at least that part of savings channeled through the banking system. The allocation of credit through the banking system was controlled and virtually all of it was assigned to the public sector. Stringent controls were applied to the repatriation of profits abroad, which discouraged foreign investment. Domestic investments were heavily regulated and industrial investments were subjected to cumbersome and comprehensive licensing requirements. Organized labor markets were under government control, which extended over pay scales in the private sector as these became closely linked to those in the public sector. The public sector frequently acted as the employer of last resort, for example, in the case of university graduates. This led to overmanning in the public sector, while comprehensive controls on private sector pay scales eroded incentives for those with greater skills to seek more productive careers in the private sector. The result was an exodus of highly qualified technical staff to other countries, which was the only outlet available.

The scope of government operations was greatly extended through nationalization and other policies of extensive state ownership of critical industries and institutions. To the extent that production and distribution were increasingly governed by administrative directives, the role of the market in allocating goods was reduced.

To finance the comprehensive state machine, the Government relied on various forms of taxation. The explicit forms of taxation included a large array of excise duties, export taxes, import duties, and a complex system of taxes on incomes and profits. Tax rates were generally high and constituted a disincentive. This was especially true for the income taxes, which became effective at very low real levels of income—the brackets having been eroded by persistent inflation—and exhibited steep progression. The Government also relied heavily on implicit forms of taxation, particularly of exports and financial transactions. Overvaluation of the exchange rate conferred a major benefit on the Government, which insisted on full surrender of foreign exchange and was able to meet its own foreign exchange requirements cheaply. Arrangements governing financial intermediation ensured that public debt could be placed at very low cost, while credit to other preferred borrowers would be available at highly subsidized rates, the subsidy in effect being paid by depositors. Had it not been for these implicit taxes, the Government's outlays on imports and debt service would have been much higher. The tax structure, taking account of both its explicit and implicit features, was punitive and added further impetus to the effect of controls in shifting transactions to the parallel economy.

The state thus preyed on the private sector through a mix of controls, regulations, and taxes. To secure political support, a system of patronage emerged which tended to favor the more vocal urban sector. Such policies stimulated corruption and counterproductive rent-seeking behavior, thereby destroying the inherent dynamic of the economy, curtailing investment, and adversely affecting the supply side. This is reflected in the progressive lowering of the growth rate of the economy (see Table 1).

Macroeconomic Instability

A highly distorted economy can trigger macroeconomic disturbances through the behavior that it encourages from transactors. It can also amplify the effects of outside shocks. The conceptual distinction between structural factors that influence the terms of private decision making and conjunctural factors that affect macroeconomic stability is useful in understanding the contributions of each to the persistent macroeconomic imbalances that characterized the Ghanaian economy. Most economists are agreed that macroeconomic equilibrium prevails when aggregate demand is aligned with aggregate supply such that the economy is operating close to its potential, with both a low rate of inflation and a viable balance of payments. It is not necessary that all sectors individually exhibit this balance, provided that imbalances in, say, the fiscal sector are offset by imbalances in the opposite direction in, say, the household or private sector.

While in principle it is possible that macroeconomic equilibrium could obtain in a highly distorted economic system, in practice it is difficult to ensure because the primary instrument for ensuring equilibrium in such a system, other than keeping the budget in reasonable balance, is to intensify controls. But this provokes a counterreaction, which destabilizes the economy. The pre-1983 economy of Ghana shows many examples of this phenomenon. At this period in Ghana's economic history, the typical policy response to a shock, whether an external terms of trade shock or a domestic drought, was to intensify controls. As noted earlier, the spread of controls on the prices of goods lowered production and shifted part of the reduced supply to the underground economy. This eroded an important tax base and contributed to the fiscal imbalance. The frequent response of raising tax rates on items of domestic production to restore revenue merely aggravated the underlying problem of disincentive. This was repeated with other taxes, notably the taxes on incomes and profits and the trade-related taxes. Unless the resulting widespread and persistent erosion of tax bases could be financed in a noninflationary manner by the private sector, the budget would aggravate inflationary pressures on the economy. But regulation of interest rates and the controls exercised on the financial sector depressed the flow of private savings. It was inevitable that recourse was had to the printing press. Interestingly, the private sector itself was not a source of inflationary pressure because it lacked access to financing.

Periodic attempts were made to stabilize the economy by reducing the fiscal deficit. Faced with a persistent decline in revenue, which is shown in Table 2 to have dropped from 18.1 percent of GDP in 1971 to 4.6 percent of GDP in 1983, the response was to curtail expenditures, which declined from 22.6 percent of GDP to 8.2 percent over the same period. Outlays on a variety of important social goods were constrained, especially on health and education. Even more critical for the shorter-run growth prospects, outlays on infrastructure investment and maintenance were drastically reduced. Ports, telecommunications, the road network, and the railway system more or less broke down, greatly adding to the costs of doing business. Key state-owned enterprises, such as shipping, the national airlines, and utilities, were badly starved of funds and ceased to function effectively, further contributing to the breakdown of the economy.

Ironically, the attempt by the Government to control and regulate the economy had unleashed forces that led to the steady impoverishment of government itself. Periodic attempts at restoring state control of the economy failed, often because it was difficult to ensure a disciplined response by public employees. Fiscal constraints and the government policy of acting as employer of last resort led to a massive erosion in the real wages of civil servants, which by 1983 had declined to about 13 percent of the level some 20 years earlier. Such a steep loss in real wages that was well below subsistence levels contributed to the corruption of the bureaucracy, which acquired a growing vested interest in the operation of controls. In effect, a parallel wage system of bribes supplemented the eroding official pay scales. Private transactors were prepared to pay bribes to officials to expedite their business. Corruption corroded the government machine and impaired its ability to control the economy and discharge public functions.

The Choice of Alternative Reform Strategies

Disillusionment over the collapse of the economy and with the corrupt political system led to the regime established by Jerry Rawlings at the end of 1981. Vigorous attempts were made at the outset to combat corruption, and a mechanism was devised, relying on so-called committees for the defence of the revolution (CDRs), to identify and root out corruption. Some corrupt officials and politicians were arrested and punished. For a short time, this appeared to have a salutary effect, but corruption resurfaced because the underlying causes were not eliminated. In particular, the system of controls was not at first dismantled. Given the extreme ideology of the new regime, its approach to governance emphasized central planning and state control. The initial perception was that it was the corrupt use of the system rather than the system itself that needed to be removed. The new regime espoused the objectives of disciplined national

Table 2. Ghana: Selected Fiscal Indicators

(In percent of GDP)

	1971	1980	1983	1984	1986	1988	1990	1991
Total revenue and grants	18.1	8.1	4.6	8.4	14.4	14.6	14.1	16.3
Tax revenue	...	7.4	3.5	6.6	12.2	12.3	11.6	13.8
Direct taxes	...	2.1	1.0	1.5	2.8	3.9	2.9	2.8
Taxes on domestic goods and services	...	3.8	0.9	2.1	3.8	3.7	3.8	6.0
Taxes on international trade	...	1.4	2.7	3.0	5.6	4.8	4.9	5.0
Total expenditure and net lending	22.6	20.0	8.2	10.2	14.3	14.3	14.0	14.5
Current expenditure	17.2	16.3	7.4	8.6	11.9	10.6	10.5	10.8
Capital expenditure	6.4	2.9	0.8	1.2	1.9	2.8	2.5	2.8
Overall deficit	-4.3	-11.0	-2.7	-1.8	0.1	0.4	0.2	1.9
Excluding grants	-4.3	-11.1	-2.7	-2.1	-0.7	-0.7	-1.3	0.4
Financing	4.3	11.0	2.7	1.8	-0.1	-0.4	-0.2	-1.9
Foreign (net)	0.9	0.9	0.4	0.7	-1.1	0.2	1.3	0.9
Banking system	3.4	3.8	2.3	1.1	0.5	-0.9	-1.1	-2.1
Memorandum item:								
Government savings (excluding grants)	0.9	-8.3	-3.6	-0.6	1.7	2.7	1.8	3.6

Source: Statistical Service Accra.

self-reliance to promote recovery and growth of the badly blighted economy. It was believed that promoting an egalitarian distribution of income would reinforce social cohesion, and that the nation as a whole would put its shoulder behind the immense task of regenerating the economy. Several steps were taken to redistribute income including notably adjusting pay scales. These became much more compressed with the ratio being less than three between the pay earned by the top echelons and that of the lowest paid workers.

However, the economy did not recover while such policies were being tried. Agricultural production was devastated by the widespread and persistent drought that also badly affected the power supply. Some one million Ghanaians expelled from Nigeria had to be accommodated. Export earnings plummeted. The shortage of foreign exchange was so acute that the country defaulted on short-term supplier's credits and could only procure imports on a cash basis. A critical shortage of imports necessitated further intensification of rationing. By now the economy had ground to a halt. Despite, or as some would contend, because of the egalitarian policies, there was little social cohesion and several attempts were made to overthrow the regime.

Faced with a virtually complete breakdown, the Government modified its policy of self-reliance and turned to the international community for assistance. In particular, negotiations were initiated with the International Monetary Fund, which became the primary donor during the first few years of the recovery process, followed by the World Bank and later by bilateral aid sources.

The Reform

The programs negotiated with the IMF and the World Bank led to the adoption of a strategy that involved a profound change in direction toward both reintegration with the international economy and restoration of market forces. This section reviews key elements of the reform strategy for restoring a positive dynamic to the economy.

Initial Calibration and Stabilization

In 1983, it was obvious that the system of controls had to be dismantled and the macroeconomic imbalances eliminated if the economy was to be put on a path of sustained recovery. How was this to be done? One approach would have been to decree at the outset the removal of all controls—the big bang approach—so as to allow for the spontaneous regeneration of markets. This approach was regarded as problematic for a number of key markets and goods. There was a danger that new market opportunities for speculative and other behavior would be created in very thin markets; this could lead to destabilizing movements in prices, which for such items as fuel or the exchange rate could have undesirable economy-wide repercussions. For example, exchange rate depreciations could overshoot and set in motion an inflation-devaluation spiral. This could cause a loss of control over the budget because it would become more difficult to project and manage fiscal operations with prices gyrating wildly. Furthermore, losses and gains would be generated for different classes of transactors and segments of the population. This could have undesirable political repercussions and unravel the consensus for reform. In principle, such problems can be dealt with if a government is equipped with appropriate instruments to influence undesirable market outcomes. For example, potential instability in the foreign exchange market might be addressed through swap arrangements with foreign central banks and by the flexible use of interest rate policies, provided there is a measure of confidence in the reforms. However, during Ghana's reliance on controls and state ownership, the institutions and procedures for operating a flexible market-oriented monetary and exchange rate policy had fallen into disuse, while the Government lacked credibility.

Even the fiscal instrument, which relies more directly on market interventions through the taxation of incomes and the purchase and provision of goods and services, was badly damaged. The dramatic erosion in revenue bases and the associated pressures on the fiscal deficit meant that the fiscal instrument had itself become part of the problem of disincentive. Before the budget could contribute to solving the country's problems, it would have to be rehabilitated. There was an immediate need for the revenue system to be revamped to mobilize the substantial resources needed for regenerating the economy. Although budgeting practices and procedures to ensure more effective expenditures also needed to be drastically improved, the revenue situation took precedence because of the need to finance critical outlays to overcome crippling bottlenecks.

Even if appropriate instruments were not immediately available, provided sufficient foreign assistance was available, the Government could offset possible destabilizing effects. But such assistance was not forthcoming in the amounts needed, and given the recognition that developing the appropriate domestic instruments would take time, a cautious and selective approach to removing controls was adopted. Initially, the strategy was to remove the most glaring distortions in cost-price relationships, and to reorient controls in a market-supportive direction, while attacking the problem of macroeconomic instability.

The highly overvalued exchange rate was adjusted, first, by adopting a complex system of tariffs and export subsidies to achieve a sizable implicit devaluation that recognized what had already taken place in the informal markets, and subsequently, by replacing this system and rationalizing the implicit devaluation by a unified official exchange rate pegged at ₵ 30 = US$1. It was not expected that the foreign exchange market would clear at this exchange rate (even though it appeared realistic on the basis of international cost comparisons) because of a thin market, a large pent-up excess demand for imports, and persistent capital outflows, owing to a lack of confidence. Physical control of imports was retained, but in a more liberalized manner involving the progressive placement of imports on an open general license, reduction in the negative list of imports, easier licensing procedures, and eventual replacement of physical controls by tariffs. To encourage exports, the administered price paid to the cocoa farmer was substantially adjusted upward.

Nominal interest rates were also adjusted upward, although by much less than needed to offset the underlying rate of inflation, and real rates remained negative. The subsidy on fuel prices was eliminated and an array of goods was freed from price controls. However, to prevent the abuse of prices by monopolies, official oversight of the price adjustments was retained and CDRs were encouraged to report any incidents of price gouging. Following an adjustment in the level of nominal wages, a firm and comprehensive incomes policy was applied that initially covered both the public and the private sectors.

Although the various price adjustments eliminated the most glaring distortions and provided incentives in the right direction, the overall supply response was initially limited. This was because of the effect of the drought and the need at the microeconomic level to restructure investments and to undertake necessary maintenance and repairs. It was also necessary for the devastated infrastructure to be rehabilitated. For the most part what occurred at first was that transactions shifted from the parallel markets to the official market. While less than the response desired, this itself was of considerable benefit because it reduced costs to transactors, which are usually higher in parallel markets, restored some of the bases of taxation, and generally helped promote market-based specialization.

The 1983 rate of inflation of some 160 percent had to be reduced sharply to ensure that relative price adjustments would hold, while containing the deterioration in the balance of payments. Given that a positive overall supply response could not be relied upon initially, the emphasis for restoring macroeconomic equilibrium was placed on demand management. This required a sharp reduction in the rate of bank credit expansion and the fiscal deficit that it financed. Consistent with the stabilization aims of the financial program, and taking account of the limited amount of foreign concessional financing forthcoming, a significant reduction in the fiscal deficit was projected. While the recovery of tax bases, particularly those related to international trade, would increase revenue, the scope for discretionary actions was limited and the tax ratio was not expected to rise by much at first. The burden of the initial adjustment was largely on expenditure, involving substantial sacrifices. The wage bill was frozen, subsidies were drastically reduced, and social outlays and government investment were curtailed.

Reducing the fiscal deficit sharply was the key to successful stabilization, and this condition was met. The broad objective of stabilization of reducing inflationary pressures was achieved, but the economy remained stagnant. While the economic situation of the farmers improved, incomes of public sector and other salaried employees suffered in consequence of the price adjustments. Although many of these adjustments reflected those prevailing in the parallel markets, prices of sensitive and key items, such as fuel (subject to rationing but generally available to public employees) rose sharply and adversely affected real incomes. Instead of passing on the benefit from an overvalued exchange rate on the import side to consumers, the Government, which continued to control foreign exchange allocations, retained some and passed on the rest to the exporter. Although civil servants may have become more disaffected, by adhering to the strict conditions of the financial program the Government began to establish credibility, especially in the eyes of foreign creditors.

Restructuring the Economy

Quickly following the initial successful attempts at stabilizing inflation, attention was directed to overcoming the supply obstacles, in particular, those constraining exports. The foreign exchange bottleneck had to be eased to provide resources for the procurement of essential spare parts and inputs to stimulate domestic production, especially of critically required foodstuffs. While devaluing the exchange rate provided the right export incentives, this needed to be complemented by appropriate infrastructural investments to overcome physical impediments. Foreign assistance was sought, particularly from the World Bank, for the rehabilitation of the ports and the communications network to ensure that exports could be both delivered to the ports and cleared through them. However, domestic outlays were also needed and noninflationary financing had to be mobilized so as not to compromise the hard-fought stabilization achievements. The immediate role of the private sector, which had been ravaged, was limited, both in undertaking the necessary infrastructural investments and in providing financing. Instruments for mobilizing and allocating funds such as capital markets were nonexistent and the financial system was rudimentary, while private savings were very low and showed little prospect for early improvement.

Consequently, government actions and the budget became the principal levers for restructuring the economy, while at the same time preserving macroeconomic stability. For all this to be possible, the fiscal instrument had to be rehabilitated and the corruption that had critically eroded the efficiency with which that instrument could be used had to be removed. Unless the latter was addressed, particularly in the critical area of tax administration, changes in the design of taxation to mobilize more resources were unlikely to be effective, nor would attempts by the government machine at implementing other reforms be successful. The approach pursued at each stage was thus to address simultaneously issues of policy design and implementation capabilities.

Restoring the efficiency of the government machine involved reducing overmanning, improving conditions of service, and combating corruption. A phased strategy for reducing overmanning was developed and implemented notably in cocoa marketing and in the civil service, while salaries were raised, contingent upon the availability of resources. These steps to improve morale were combined with reassignment of some senior managers and the institution of a more effective surveillance mechanism to combat corruption. Because improving the conditions for the civil service as a whole would require additional resources, it was decided to focus on the tax administration initially. The strategy was to use the limited resources available, first, to improve the conditions of service of the tax officers so as to provide them with the incentive to accelerate collections, and more generally to make the tax administration more effective. As revenue performance improved, it would be possible to raise salaries for the rest of the civil service. The tax administration was reorganized into the National Revenue Service headed by a minister, but responsibility for tax policy remained with the Ministry of Finance so as to prevent the possibility of tax collectors defining tax policy in a self-serving manner. A bonus scheme was instituted because salaries of tax officers could not be raised independently of the rest of the civil service and salaries of the latter could not be raised because of the shortage of revenue. To ensure the appropriate incentive effects, the bonus was determined as a percent of the increase in collections over a norm and paid to each of the two revenue departments (Inland Revenue and Customs). With the subsequent improvements in revenue performance it became possible to raise pay for the civil service as a whole and real wages and salaries began to regain ground lost in the previous two decades.

Improving only the efficiency of the tax administration but not reforming the punitive system of taxation could wreak havoc on the private sector, which in collusion with the tax administration had largely managed to escape the tax burden. During the period of protracted decline the tax system had become one of more or less voluntary payments of tax, where the amount to be paid bore little relation to the true tax liability, but was the outcome of a self-serving bargain between the taxpayer and the tax collector. The plan to reform the tax system was to do it in stages to remove distortive and penal characteristics and to facilitate tax compliance. Income tax schedules were adjusted to take account of past inflation: the initial exemption levels were raised; brackets were widened and their number reduced; and the top marginal rate was reduced in stages over several years from 55 percent to 25 percent. To facilitate tax administration, while reducing disincentive effects, the base of the income tax was broadened. The profit tax was reduced to stimulate business activity, and more generally to encourage capital accumulation. A wealth tax was kept in abeyance. The proliferation of excise duties was reduced, and the structure was rationalized in the context of a revamped manufacturers sales tax. Export duties on virtually all products except cocoa were rescinded, while the duty on cocoa was substantially reduced. The import tariff structure was simplified into three bands and the spread between them was compressed.

Although the aim of the tax reforms was to promote economic efficiency and mobilization of revenue, issues of equity were not ignored. A feature of the reforms was to reduce the burden of taxation on the easy-to-tax groups primarily composed of wage earners and cocoa farmers. The burden of taxation was increasingly shifted from these sources to the consumption of luxury goods by the better off, whether domestically produced (which would be captured by the excises) or imported, especially those brought in under so-called special import licenses that freely permitted imports financed through remittances or other private sources of foreign exchange, which could include the proceeds of smuggling. The tax design was periodically adapted to the changing structure. For example, when imports were further liberalized and all importers had free access to foreign exchange, the special import licenses were eliminated, as was the revenue from this source. Alternative revenue sources were found, a prominent one being energy taxation—introduced both for environmental reasons and for the promotion of a more rational transportation policy that conserved foreign exchange needed to cover oil imports.

Government expenditure outlays reflected the goal of creating a more effective government machine. The share of the public wage bill grew initially relative to other expenditures and a new category of expenditure was created—the so-called special efficiency fund—to finance aspects of the redeployment of public servants. The improvement in the revenue position of the budget following the first year of stabilization, together with more foreign aid, allowed an increase in government investment outlays. The composition of investment outlays was changed initially to favor economic sectors and areas such as ports, power, and the railway line. However, the limited resource improvement did not permit an early increase in social outlays, which remained constrained at low levels in comparison to needs and to earlier attainments.

Government expenditure policy was generally directed to achieving levels of outlays consistent with macroeconomic stability, while addressing the most critical requirements. The management of such expenditures initially rested on the application of both cash limits and a stringent system of audits to ensure compliance with allotted expenditures. This technique could on occasion prove disruptive. For example, faced with a sudden revenue shortfall and the need to comply with a forthcoming credit ceiling test of the financial program with the IMF, across-the-board expenditure cuts were made. These, however, could prove damaging, and more rational budgeting and cash management techniques had to be developed to prevent such problems. Emphasizing compliance with expenditure allotments was clearly insufficient if the allotments concealed waste, or worse, fraud. The system of budgeting had to be changed to provide a more program and activity orientation where the emphasis would be on delivering needed public goods at minimum cost. Hence, several important steps have been initiated involving the streamlining of audit and control procedures, more in-depth reviews of expenditure proposals, and the acceptance of greater cost consciousness on the part of spending agencies.

A major use of the budget was to make it the principal instrument for mobilizing foreign resources. Initially, access to foreign financing was extremely limited as the credibility of the reform process had to be established for donors. At first, nonofficial foreign financing was largely limited to short-term borrowings in connection with oil procurement. As these were paid off and as credibility improved, the maturity of the debt lengthened, while over time there were substantial progressive increases in official concessional foreign financing. Some took the form of project loans and grants linked to investment projects undertaken by different government agencies. These flows were kept separate from the so-called program or general budget support flows which featured in the budget. While not in the best tradition of comprehensive budgeting, this feature was useful in budget control under weak institutional conditions because it insulated the traditional narrowly defined budget from disruptions whenever project flows fell behind project outlays. Had the latter been a part of the regular budget, revenues would have had to be diverted to meet any shortfalls in project financing, rendering it more difficult to comply with credit ceilings and fiscal targets applied to the budget.

The sharp improvement in revenue in the early years together with a successful policy of expenditure restraint resulted in a fiscal turnaround. In contrast to the high deficits of earlier years, the central government deficit was greatly reduced in the immediate years of adjustment and by 1986 had managed a small surplus, which was subsequently retained and increased.

The budget surplus and the net positive inflows of foreign financing enabled the budget to provide funds to the banking system. The domestic public debt was sharply reduced and the Government became a net creditor to the domestic economy, so reversing the depredations that had involved using the assets of the economy and passing high debt-service costs on to future generations. A favorable effect of this policy was that interest payments on the domestic debt were sharply reduced, giving room under the overall expenditure ceilings for additional outlays that were increasingly devoted to social purposes. As a net supplier of funds, the budget played a critical role in mobilizing and transmitting savings to the rest of the economy, given the limited capacity of private saving.

Throughout this period, monetary policy was subject to tight credit ceilings, which became progressively tighter in an attempt to reduce the rate of inflation. The budget provided additional resources that could be redirected under the credit ceilings to other sectors of the economy. This was a vital contribution because, after the initial period of net borrowings from the IMF, the fact that repayments were becoming due, together with the need to continue to accumulate additional international reserves, meant that the rate of expansion of credit would have to be lower than that of the money supply. While this is certainly true for the operations of the central bank, the credit ceilings were applied to the banking system as a whole. If the budget had not functioned as a major net supplier of funds, credit flows to the rest of the economy would have sharply declined, aggravating the consequences for the economy.

Some Lessons

What has been the outcome so far of the adjustment policies pursued, and, drawing on hindsight, what should have been done differently?

The Outcome

As Table 1 shows, the outcome in major macroeconomic variables has generally been satisfactory. Real GDP has expanded despite the persistent and severe decline in the terms of trade from 1987 to the present. The inflation rate, as measured by the consumer price index, has come down substantially although the average annual rate over the adjustment period is still high. The overall balance of payments moved into surplus in 1987 and has generated sizable surpluses since. These achievements have been underpinned by a partial recovery in levels of investment and national savings and by growing flows of concessional foreign financing, which have permitted larger current account deficits. Other instruments that have played a major role include the substantial real depreciation of the exchange rate, which has stimulated exports and induced greater backward linkages in domestic production, and the widespread elimination of controls on external and domestic trade. The systematic attempts at rehabilitating the physical infrastructure and the greater outlays on health and education have helped in the improvement.

Despite these achievements more could have been done: the growth rate should have been higher, the inflation rate could have been lower, and the benefits of adjustment could have been more visible and been more widely spread. Even though many fiscal inducements were presented to the private sector, the generally weak response, especially of private investments, is puzzling. The three principal active agents in economic improvements appear to have been the Government and its beneficial fiscal policies, the favorable effects of the real exchange rate depreciation on cocoa production, timber harvesting, and gold mining, and the curtailment of parallel markets by liberalizing policies. The fiscal policies are primarily responsible for improvements in national saving and investment and in the infrastructure. The budget has also helped intermediate financial resources to the private sector through its fiscal surpluses and financing policies. Yet, despite large reductions in marginal rates of taxation and the provision of generous tax incentives, private investment has so far been disappointing, especially in manufacturing, agrobusiness, and fishing.

Hindsight

The main engine of economic growth has to be the private sector. While important steps were taken to encourage the participation of this sector, these have clearly been insufficient. The experience of Ghana demonstrates that decontrolling the economy and having relative prices approximate to international ones, while necessary, are insufficient. Even improving the infrastructure and providing generous tax incentives are insufficient if the potential private investor lacks both confidence and the capital and other resources needed. But should these resources be available, the investment will still not be undertaken if the investor perceives demand conditions as depressed and that it will be difficult to turn a profit. Furthermore, if investors think that government will not sustain its policies, few will risk an investment with a long payback period.

It is difficult to disentangle the separate factors hampering private initiatives in Ghana. One of the most critical appears to have been the failure of the financial sector to mobilize and allocate to private agents the capital required to finance burgeoning investments. That failure is a reflection of the deep-rooted structural problems of the financial sector, which has been beset by nonperforming assets arising from past lending. Decontrol, in combination with relative price adjustments, generated severe losses for many traditional clients of the banks, primarily state enterprises which were, early in the adjustment period, subjected to hard budget constraints, with drastic curtailments of their subsidies. Despite growing losses, which they covered through a variety of techniques, these enterprises have for the most part remained in existence. As a consequence, their failure to service their debts, while continuing in business, forced the banks to capitalize the interest owing on these debts. Given the initial large stock of such debts, even a relatively low rate of interest would tie up a large amount of the fresh funds that banks had to lend. Much of the credit expansion of the banking system in Ghana merely reflected this capitalization of interest.

Resolving the problem of nonperforming loans for the banks requires that enterprises be restructured so that they can service their debts or that they be declared bankrupt and that the banks make adequate provision for the losses. An early and aggressive start on the privatization and restructuring of state enterprises would have been helpful, together with the recapitalization of the banks for any losses incurred in excess of their loan-loss provisions. Elements of this strategy began to be pursued relatively late in the adjustment period. Many bad loans were finally taken off the books of the banks in 1990 and replaced with government bonds that confer an income on the banks (at a fiscal cost to budget). This was intended to enable them to lend more loanable funds for fresh purposes. However, from the perspective of the banks, a critical problem is to find creditworthy private borrowers. This is a serious handicap in a context where, if left to the market, private agents would take a long time to establish their credentials to the satisfaction of bankers who have been badly burned by their past lending. With hindsight a quick way of resolving this problem would have been for a government rating and credit guarantee institution to be set up. In general, this problem is one of market failures that occur during transition, the correction of which requires government interventions.

At the same time, private investors have to be sufficiently assured that conditions are propitious for borrowing. Early privatization and the return of abandoned and confiscated properties to their rightful owners would have provided a much-needed boost in confidence and increased the demand for loans. This demand would have been further stimulated by the targeting of specific sectors for the provisioning of adequate infrastructure, which could have taken the form of setting up well-supplied industrial parks. The early removal of cumbersome licensing and other regulatory requirements would have been helpful as would the establishment of appropriate training facilities.

It is important that the macroeconomic environment be supportive, especially in ensuring that overall demand conditions are adequate. The stringent policy of monetary restraint, applied particularly in the latter years of adjustment for reducing inflation and for reaching the balance of payments target, together with growing fiscal consolidation, will have constrained demand. The question is whether demand was excessively constrained—some constraint is necessary to facilitate the reallocation of resources. Under normal conditions a clear indicator of excessive restraint would have been interest rate levels that are highly positive in real terms. However, throughout the period of adjustment until 1991, real deposit and lending rates have been negative, the rate of inflation has been relatively high, and the banks have persistently held significant amounts of excess reserves. Such indicators point to a loose monetary policy and the need for further tightening.

On the other hand, there are also indications that credit policy may have been too tight, especially during 1988–91. First, the parallel market foreign exchange rates, which are reflected in the rates quoted by the foreign exchange bureaus, remained remarkably stable during that period, indicating that in real terms there was an appreciation. The official market exchange rate nevertheless depreciated, as the foreign exchange market was widened in stages and payments restrictions on current transactions were virtually fully removed and gradually converged to the bureaus' rates (see Table 1). Second, the balance of payments outcomes typically overshot the targeted surplus, indicating that the demand for money was higher than domestically supplied money so that more money had to be generated through the balance of payments. Third, the rate of growth of the economy remained relatively low and below target, despite inflation outcomes exceeding targeted levels, suggesting that inflation was not pushed by excessive demand but rather was a reflection of adjustments to cost increases as a consequence of periodic droughts and the progressive convergence of the official exchange rate to the parallel market rate.

Such confusing signals of the tightness or looseness of monetary conditions are typical of distorted markets. A major problem with the financial sector has been the very long period taken to develop and introduce indirect instruments of monetary control. As a consequence, monetary control has relied heavily on the application of credit ceilings to the entire banking sector. This is a quantitative intervention in the money market that overrides money market equilibration mechanisms, but is needed when mechanisms for regulating the market do not exist or do not function and credit expansion threatens to get out of control. Such quantitative overrides, however, when pursued for a long time can lead to distorted developments, as exhibited by any other market subjected to quantitative restrictions. This can be especially pronounced when combined with monopolistic conditions in the market and other distortions.

In a situation where on the supply of credit side banks are monopolistic, and the demand for credit is heavily dominated by state enterprises having difficulty in servicing their existing stock of debt, but wielding considerable influence, lending rates could easily remain negative in real terms. This could be associated with a high spread between these rates and deposit rates and the holding of excess reserves by the banks. Because the demand for credit is constrained to the amount supplied, which is regulated by the ceiling, there is, at the negative real rate of interest an excess demand for credit. However, this is not allowed by the prevailing market conditions to bid the interest rate up owing to various insider considerations. Banks also are not interested in adding to deposits if the credit ceiling restrains them from lending. Hence, if there is an excess supply of deposits, banks would turn some away (as is reputed to have occurred in Ghana) while forcing down the deposit rate of interest. Since depositors could obtain a higher rate of return on converting their deposits to foreign currency holdings, the distorted money market conditions would have contributed to a sustained capital outflow. In sum, the quantitative credit ceiling overrides hamper domestic financial intermediation if pursued too long.

Lessons

Even though Ghana was fortunate to have basic market institutions, including the legal infrastructure to define, protect, and enforce property rights and contracts, turning the economy around and generating a reasonable supply response took considerable time. This is because converting a negative dynamic into a positive dynamic is more than a matter of simply decontrolling markets and letting prices adjust freely so as to attain internationally compatible relative prices. While all these are necessary, the art is in determining how swiftly these should be undertaken and what other ingredients should be provided to ensure that supply responds fully to these important new incentives. Many factors, not least the political ones, have to be taken into account in developing the optimum time path for sustainable adjustment.

Too fast a process of decontrol could lead to major distributional shifts that, in the absence of large foreign exchange reserves and quick-acting remedial measures, could erode the consensus in favor of reforms. Initially, lacking international reserves and being poorly equipped to promote rapid countervailing supply responses and other adjustments, the Ghanaian approach was to proceed step by step, adjusting by significant amounts relative prices and market restrictions in a manner in which the distributional shifts could be more readily projected and accommodated. Rather than attempt to leap in one jump across the abyss that separates a controlled economy from a free market-oriented economy with a high risk of falling, the Ghanaian solution took the slower but more certain route of building a bridge across. As the credibility of the reform process was established, considerable and growing amounts of foreign assistance became available, and this facilitated the further liberalization, in stages, of the external sector.[2]

The Ghanaian experience shows the importance of the reforming government establishing credibility at the outset. Adopting an austere fiscal and monetary stance to create a stable macroeconomy to support the structural reforms appears to be an essential first step, although once credibility has been established, some relaxation to promote growth appears warranted. The structural reforms themselves and their sequencing need to be carefully defined so that they do not overwhelm the au-

---

[2]A key aspect of the relationship between the pace of liberalization and the flow of foreign financing is discussed in Chand (1989).

thorities, especially in their fiscal planning. Much attention needs to be paid early to revamping the government's instruments, particularly fiscal ones. It is especially important to create an effective, adequately motivated, administrative machine that would support the reforms. Improving the conditions of service of civil servants and reforming and streamlining the administrative machine are essential steps.

In the initial stages government intervention of various forms is needed to remove bottlenecks and to provide support. Thus, national savings are more likely to be increased initially by government through fiscal policies that emphasize a surplus than through private efforts. The physical infrastructure needed to support private initiatives is more readily supplied by government. Reform will place many new demands on government, forcing it to mobilize sufficient resources. This places precedence in the reform process on improving the tax administration and on the design of taxes. Initially, expenditure can be controlled through cash limits and other traditional means, but revamped budget procedures and expenditure management techniques will be essential subsequently to economize efficiently on expenditures.

As the Ghanaian experience demonstrates, improving the public finances and fiscal policies may not be sufficient in themselves to stimulate an adequate private sector response. Measures are needed to restore confidence and to provide working capital and other resources to get private investment off the ground. For a private sector that has long been dormant, access to adequate finance is critical, both to begin the process of taking over state-owned enterprises and to generally rehabilitate manufacturing and other activities. If the financial sector cannot allocate such resources, especially to new private entrepreneurs, the Government will have to step in with appropriate measures.

References

Abbey, J.L.S. "On Promoting Successful Adjustment: Some Lessons From Ghana," The 1989 Per Jacobsson Lecture (Washington: Per Jacobsson Foundation, 1989).

Chand, Sheetal K. "Toward a Growth-Oriented Model of Financial Programming," *World Development*, Vol. 17, No. 4 (1989), pp. 473-90.

―――, and Reinold van Til, "Ghana: Toward Successful Stabilization and Recovery," *Finance & Development*, Vol. 25 (March 1988), pp. 32-35.

Kapur, Ishan, and others, "Ghana: Adjustment and Growth, 1983-91," IMF Occasional Paper No. 86 (Washington: International Monetary Fund, 1991).

PART V

Index

Index